Consul of God

By the same author

Visions of Yesterday
Swordsmen of the Screen
The Popes and the Papacy in the Early Middle Ages 476–752

Consul of God

The Life and Times of Gregory the Great

Jeffrey Richards

Department of History
University of Lancaster

Routledge & Kegan Paul
London, Boston and Henley

First published in 1980
by Routledge & Kegan Paul Ltd,
39 Store Street, London WC1E 7DD,
9 Park Street, Boston, Mass. 02108, USA, and
Broadway House, Newtown Road,
Henley-on-Thames, Oxon RG9 1EN
Set in 10 on 13 pt Palatino
by Input Typesetting Ltd, London
and printed in Great Britain by
Redwood Burn Ltd,
Trowbridge & Esher
© Jeffrey Richards 1980

British Library Cataloguing in Publication Data

Richards, Jeffrey
Consul of God.
1. Gregory I, Pope
2. Popes — Biography
I. Title
262'.13'0924   BX1076   79-42757

ISBN 0 7100 0346 3

For Colin Tyson, Mike Harris, Joe Bettey,
who taught me my first history

Abide with me; fast falls the eventide;
The Darkness deepens; Lord, with me abide;
When other helpers fail, and comforts flee,
Help of the helpless, O abide with me

Swift to its close ebbs out life's little day;
Earth's joys grow dim, its glories pass away;
Change and decay in all around I see,
O Thou, who changest not, abide with me

Henry Francis Lyte

Contents

Illustrations

the Trustees of the British Museum).

Acknowledgments

I am indebted to the following friends and colleagues for advice, assistance and suggestions: the late Professor A. H. M. Jones, Professor R. A. Markus, Dr E. R. Hardy, Dr G. J. P. O'Daly, Dr P. D. King, Mr S. A. C. Lamley, Miss L. Parkinson, Miss S. Hall, Mr L. Cheles, Mr J. Thompson, Dr J. A. Moorhead, Dr D. C. A. Shotter, Miss W. Kenyon, Mr G. A. Inkster and Mrs M. Jackson. I would also like to thank the staffs of the Cambridge University Library, the Lancaster University Library, the Birmingham Reference Library, the London Library, the Institute of Historical Research, and the British Museum Reading Room for their unfailing courtesy and helpfulness. All opinions and errors are of course my own.

The quotation on page 266 is from 'Recessional' by Rudyard Kipling and is reprinted by permission of the National Trust of Great Britain.

Introduction

Gregory the Great was one of the most remarkable figures of the early medieval world. Aristocrat, administrator, teacher and scholar, he ascended the throne of St Peter as Pope Gregory I at a time of acute crisis for the Roman church and for Italian society. The invasion of the Lombards had fragmented the imperial province of Italy and posed a very real threat to the existence of the Roman church. Despite ill-health and overwork, Gregory took on the burdens of the papacy with all the fortitude and energy of the old Roman senators whose last representative he was, a fact recognized by his epitaph, which called him "The Consul of God".

In a very real sense his reign (590–604) marks a watershed in the shadowy period during which the ancient world became the medieval world. Gregory himself fascinatingly embodied all the contradictions and implications of that watershed. A devoted adherent of the Eastern Roman Empire and a tireless supporter of imperial efforts to maintain and extend their frontiers, he nevertheless considerably advanced the power and prestige of the papacy both in Rome itself and in the West in general, thus anticipating the time when the papacy came to inherit the mantle of the old Roman Empire.

His achievements were prodigious. He reorganized and paid minute attention to both the central administration and the estate administration of the papacy. He drew up a detailed code of practice for and supervised the elections of Italian bishops. He sent out the missions which converted the English, and waged unremitting war on heresy and schism. He popularized a new Western pastoral tradition in learning to replace the complex theological tradition of the East. His writings were immensely influential in both East and West. The first monk to attain the papal throne, he devoted his life and much of his writing to forwarding the cause of monasticism. In a very real sense, then, Gregory was both Roman and Christian, both conservative and pioneer, and just as he looked forward to a medi-

1

eval world of monastiĉ orders, emergent Western European states, and a monarchical papacy, he also looked back to the vanishing world of imperial order, discipline and unity, in which Roman church and Roman Empire were one and undivided.

There has not been a biography of Gregory the Great in English since 1912, and F. H. Dudden's magisterial two-volume biography, published in 1905, still remains the standard work on his pontificate. The breadth of Dudden's scholarship and the clarity of his vision remain undimmed by the passage of time, and there are substantial parts of his work which it is still impossible to improve on. But there has been a considerable amount of research on various aspects of Gregory's reign since 1905, and it is now perhaps time for a fresh appraisal, which can take account of the new insights.

The basic sources remain the same. There are Gregory's own writings: his letters, his exegetical works, his *Homilies* and *Dialogues*, and his handbook for bishops, the *Regula Pastoralis*. The early Middle Ages produced four biographies of him: the brief account in the *Liber Pontificalis*, dating from the mid-seventh century; the eighth-century lives by the Anonymous Monk of Whitby and the Lombard Paul the Deacon; and the ninth-century life by John the Deacon. There are chronicles, saints' lives, letters and laws and, on the particular subjects of the Lombards and the English, two medieval masterpieces, Paul the Deacon's *History of the Lombards* and Bede's *Ecclesiastical History of the English People*. Apart from Gregory's own writings, however, all these works are post-contemporary and all therefore have to be handled with care. Gregory of Tours' *History of the Franks*, written by an exact contemporary of Gregory the Great's and embodying some eye-witness reports from Gregory's Rome, provides an invaluable source against which the later accounts of Gregory's early life can be tested.

This book grew out of my work for a previous book, *The Popes and the Papacy in the Early Middle Ages 476–752* (Routledge & Kegan Paul, 1979) and is in a very real sense a companion piece to it. *The Popes and the Papacy* was essentially a study of what went on and why in the 'smoke-filled back rooms' of the Lateran in the Dark Ages, an account of the changing and developing nature of the institution and of the men and events which shaped its destiny. This book concentrates squarely on one of the most important and best-documented of those men. There is, therefore, inevitably some degree of overlap between the books but I have tried to make it constructive and illuminating rather than repetitious.

In *The Popes and the Papacy* I rendered all but a handful of place names (Rome, Naples, Milan, Genoa) in Latin. I have extended the use of Italian place names slightly in this book – for instance, Spoleto, Palermo, and Rimini – to enable readers to get their geographical bearings, but most of the place names remain in Latin, for the very important reason that they help to convey something of the feel of a world still rooted in its Roman past. Rhegium was not yet Reggio di Calabria, nor had Urbs Vetus become Orvieto. By the time the names had changed, that old world of the imperial Roman past to which Gregory clung had passed irretrievably away.

Chapter One

The World of Gregory the Great

In the year of Our Lord 554 a man saw a dream fulfilled, and a nation witnessed the beginning of a nightmare. The man was the emperor Justinian I, who cherished the bright vision of restoring the lost Western provinces to the Empire's bosom. His armies had crushed the Vandal kingdom of Africa, had annexed part of the Visigothic kingdom of Spain, and had finally extinguished the life to which the Ostrogothic kingdom of Italy had clung with such unexpected and costly tenacity. In his capital city of Constantinople from his palace on the shores of the Bosporus, Justinian issued the *Pragmatic Sanction*, which officially re-established direct Imperial rule over Italy, ending seventy-eight years of barbarian dominion. It was a moment of supreme triumph, to be fleetingly savoured before harsh reality supplanted the rose-tinted dreams of imperial revival, for 554 was not so much a new beginning as an agonized delaying of the inevitable triumph of the barbarians in the West. Justinian was himself the last Latin-speaking ruler of a Roman Empire whose powerhouse was Constantinople, whose heartland was Asia Minor, whose culture and sensibility was Greek, and whose interests and preoccupations would shortly turn decisively eastwards. He never visited the ancient capital which had given the Empire its laws, its system of government and its very name – a magical name still, though it barely concealed the reality of a run-down, depopulated and decaying city, fever-ridden and famine-prone. The restoration of imperial rule in the West never extended to Frankish Gaul, Anglo-Saxon England or the bulk of Visigothic Spain, and, with wars in the Balkans and with Persia dominating the councils of the Empire, Italy became little more than a backwater – historic certainly, but removed from the mainstream of imperial policy and strategy.

Before many years had passed, the people of newly 'liberated' Italy were to find themselves living in a nightmare, as plague, famine, war and death, the veritable four horsemen of the Apocalypse, stalked that unhappy land, stilling the rejoicing and inducing the belief that the world's end was at hand. It must all have seemed a dramatic and ironic contrast to the enlightened rule of the Arian and barbarian Ostrogothic kings, under whom the old Western Roman Empire had enjoyed something of an 'Indian summer'. The Ostrogoths had preserved the old Roman administrative system intact, practised religious toleration, enforced law and order, encouraged peace and prosperity, stimulated a cultural revival, and worked for harmony between Goths and Romans. Despite this, there was still for many Italians an overwhelming affinity with the Roman Empire in the East, which now alone embodied their Roman heritage, their Imperial traditions, in some cases even their kith and kin. Strong religious, intellectual, cultural and family ties bound the Roman aristocracy to the East. A doctrinal schism with the East had created an illusory sense of unity between the Ostrogoths and their Roman subjects. But the ending of the schism by the emperor Justin I and his nephew and eventual successor Justinian removed even this.

So the Gothic kingdom fell, largely unlamented. But there was to be a rude awakening for those who had not thought through the implications of the imperial reconquest. The old days of Roman hegemony in the secular sphere were gone forever. The senatorial aristocracy collapsed, undermined by massacre, bankruptcy and migration to the East. The old administration was dismantled and a new provincial government created, based on Ravenna, staffed by Greek civil servants and headed by an Eastern military governor, soon to be called the exarch. The Arian church was suppressed and its property handed over to its Catholic counterpart. But the Roman church lost the freedom of action it had previously enjoyed, and was now expected to toe the imperial line in matters of the faith. The twenty years of war accompanying the imperial reconquest had taken a heavy toll on the life of Italy. Rome was besieged three times, and in 546 was actually captured by the Gothic king Totila, who restrained his men from wholesale slaughter but evacuated the entire Roman population for forty days to permit unimpeded plundering. Other great cities suffered similarly. Naples, taken by the imperial forces, was given over to pillage and massacre. Milan, taken by the Goths, saw its walls razed, its male population slaughtered and its female population enslaved and handed over to the Burgundians.

The country areas were no better off. The provinces of central Italy were ravaged, plundered and fought over from end to end, and in the ensuing famine some 50,000 people died in Picenum alone. The provinces were not only subject to attack by Goths and imperialists, but were also invaded and devastated by the Franks. The extensive rural estates of the Roman church were so badly ravaged that in 560–1 Pope Pelagius I reported: 'After the continuous devastations of war which have been inflicted on the regions of Italy for twenty-five years and more and have scarcely yet ceased, it is only from the islands and the places overseas that the Roman church receives some little revenue, however insufficient, for the clergy and the poor.'[1] The population was reduced to eating acorns, and in some cases even to cannibalism.

The wretched Italians suffered as much at the hands of their Byzantine 'liberators' as they did at the hands of the Goths. The logothete Alexander, a man with a fearsome reputation for raising revenue for the state, was sent to Italy to screw out of the Italians all debts owed to the Gothic treasury. Imperial army commanders plundered and profiteered to enhance their own private fortunes. Indeed, one of them, Conon, disposed of so much of the Roman grain supply for his own profit, that he was murdered by his starving soldiers.[2]

This was the world into which Gregory the Great was born. He first saw the light of day at the height of the war. He was in his teens when the war ended, and he grew to manhood in its bitter aftermath. He was born and apparently brought up in Rome during some of its darkest hours. He never knew it in the days of its glory. As recently as 500 the African monk Fulgentius of Ruspe, visiting Rome, had declared: 'How wonderful must be the heavenly Jerusalem, if this earthly city can shine so greatly.' In the Ostrogothic period, under the patronage and favour of the barbarian kings, life in Rome had continued much as under the emperors. The Senate met regularly, and the great aristocratic families, like Gregory's, maintained their handsome villas and large establishments. Games were held in the circus. Free grain was distributed to the people. Schools flourished. There was a glittering social and cultural life. The war ended all that. The three sieges of Rome had been accompanied by famine, disease and considerable suffering. Large areas of the city were destroyed by fire. Many citizens were ruined. Pope Vigilius appealed to God to preserve 'the integrity of the faith and the security of the Roman name', and the prayers he composed at this time paint a gloomy picture of the city, living under the constant threat of attack, fearful of treachery, oppressed by sickness and want.[3] With the end of the war, a deadly melancholy settled on Rome. The aristocratic households had been largely broken up, and many of the aristocrats emigrated to Constantinople to find fortune and favour at the imperial court. The games ceased; the organized education system collapsed; the grain dole became irregular and was ultimately terminated; the Senate gradually ceased to function. Many of the most famous buildings in Rome were deserted, damaged or decaying, and the city, bearing all the scars of its years of maltreatment, became a prey to fever, flooding, famine and plague. When he became pope, Gregory observed sadly: 'I have taken charge of an old and grievously shattered ship.'[4] Rome had become a city of ghosts and memories, a crumbling relic of lost imperial splendour. St Benedict of Nursia prophesied its gradual and inevitable dissolution: 'Rome will not be depopulated by the barbarians but will be worn out by tempests, lightning, storms and earthquakes.' Gregory accepted the truth of this, writing in 593: 'The secret meaning of his prophecy has become clearer than light to us who observe the walls broken to bits, houses overturned and churches destroyed by whirlwinds. More often all the time we see Roman buildings, wearied by old age, collapsing into ruins.'[5] This is not mere rhetoric, for Gregory records one such occurrence in 590: 'Two days ago by a sudden whirlwind ancient trees were uprooted, houses destroyed and churches overthrown to the foundations.'[6]

But as the imperial standards were being firmly planted in the city he loved, Gregory can have had no inkling of the calamities that were about to burst upon her. Almost simultaneously Italy was subjected to the twin horrors of barbarian invasion and the return of the plague.

Barely fifteen years after the official reinstatement of imperial rule in Italy, as the province still counted the cost of the decades of exhausting and destructive warfare, the Lombards struck. They were a ferocious barbarian race of Germanic origin, living in Pannonia, organized in clans, ruled by an elected king, and for the most part adherents of Arian Christianity. Paul the Deacon gave the following description of them, as they were depicted in a late-sixth-century mural in the royal palace at Modicia:[7]

They shaved the neck and left it bare up to the back of the head, having their hair parted from the forehead and hanging down from the face as far as the mouth. Their garments were loose and mostly linen, such as the Anglo-Saxons are accustomed to wear, decorated with broad borders woven in various colours. Their boots were open almost to the tip of the big toe and were kept together by crossed laces. But later they began to wear trousers, over which they put waterproof woollen leggings when they rode.

Legend had it that the unpopular Byzantine governor-general, Narses, faced with disgrace and dismissal, had called on the Lombards to leave their inhospitable Pannonian homeland and take over the rich and fecund land of Italy, backing up his suggestion with samples of fruit and other alluring Italian produce. This seems inherently unlikely; it is not recorded until at least twenty years later and is not mentioned at all by the most reliable contemporary authorities (Marius of Aventicum and Gregory of Tours).[8] But it rapidly gained currency and entered the mythology. The likelihood is that it was shifts in the balance of power in the Balkans, and in particular the arrival of the Avars, constituting a new and dangerous threat to the Lombards, which prompted them to seek safer, softer and richer pastures.

Their shrewd, ruthless war-leader, King Alboin, led the Lombards into Italy in 568, and they carried all before them, sweeping through the largely undefended north unopposed. In September 569 the old imperial capital of Milan opened its gates to them and Alboin assumed the title 'Lord of Italy'. By 571, they had completed the conquest of the Po Valley and were sweeping southwards into Umbria and Tuscany. Then suddenly in 572, at the height of his triumphal career and soon after he had taken the surrender of Pavia, which had held out for three years, Alboin was murdered by his wife, Rosamunda, who, having failed to secure the throne for her nominee, fled with the royal treasures to the imperialists at Ravenna. Alboin's successor, King Cleph, was himself murdered within two years and the Lombard chieftains decided against electing a new king. Instead the Lombard horde divided itself up into thirty-six separate duchies, based on the already conquered cities. Of this period Gregory of Tours, a contemporary, writes: 'Once they had occupied the country, they wandered all over it for seven years, robbing the churches, killing the bishops and subjecting everything to their dominion.'[9] Their advent was certainly marked by atrocities. Gregory the Great records several in his *Dialogues*: 400 captives slaughtered in one massacre, 40 peasants in another and a group of Valerian monks in a third.[10] Paul the Deacon says: 'In these days many of the noble Romans were killed from love of gain, and the remainder were divided among their "guests" and made tributaries, paying a third part of their produce to the Lombards.'[11] In fact, comparatively little is known of the condition of the Roman population in Lombard Italy. But the most likely conclusion is that the great landowners either fled, were killed or were reduced to economic subjection, the peasants carrying on much as before, tilling the soil and serving new masters. For the principal interests of the Lombards were hunting and warfare, and they retained their clan organization, geared for war and supplied with food and labour by the native population.[12]

By the time the kingship was suspended in 574, the initial impetus of the Lombards had spent itself. But they had effectively gained control of half of Italy. They ruled most of the old northern province Italia Annonaria, with the exception of the coastal areas of Liguria (centred on Genoa), Istria-Venetia (centred on Grado), and Aemilia (centred on Ravenna and the Pentapolis). In Suburbicaria, they established control over the central spine via two powerful and important duchies based on Spoleto and Benevento from which they effectively dominated the Italian interior. Imperial rule was maintained in the duchy of Rome and in the coastal areas around Naples, Rhegium, Hortona, Sipontum and Tarentum. In effect the imperial province of Italy had been reduced to a series of coastal enclaves, linked by sea. The islands of Sicily, Sardinia and Corsica remained untouched, but they were organized separately and not part of the exarchate of Ravenna.

How could this happen? There are perhaps three reasons. First and most important, the imperial government was wholly unprepared for the invasion. Italy seems to have been very weakly garrisoned, and the governor, unwilling or unable to act, simply dug himself in at Ravenna and sat tight. Decisive countermeasures were not immediately forthcoming. Justinian had died, and the throne was now occupied by his eccentric and unstable nephew Justin II, who finally went mad in 574. Only then, with the emergence as regent of the capable general Tiberius Constantine, did the government act. An army of mercenaries led by Justin's son-in-law, Count Baduarius, was dispatched to Italy in 575, only to be annihilated by the Lombards. This disaster effectively prevented the government from taking any further direct military action in the West and allowed the Lombards to secure their acquisitions.

The second reason for the speed of the province's collapse was the plague. Having already devastated the East, the plague arrived in Italy in 543, returning in the mid-560s and the early 570s. It was accompanied by severe famine, and the *Liber Pontificalis* recorded that many cities surrendered to the invaders because of starvation.[13] Famine, plague and war had undermined the Italians' strength to resist. Their will to resist was perhaps further reduced by the ill feeling resulting, particularly in the north, from the condemnation of the 'Three Chapters'. The emperor Justinian, in a bid to conciliate the Monophysite heretics, had arranged for the condemnation of certain writers and writings, which were collectively known as the 'Three Chapters'. Many Catholics felt that this condemnation impugned the validity of the Council of Chalcedon, which had defined the basic tenets of the faith. The West was solidly opposed to condemnation, and yet Justinian persuaded successive popes, Vigilius and Pelagius I, to endorse the condemnation. The archbishops of Milan and Aquileia, the two senior churchmen of the north, had gone into immediate schism from Rome, and Pelagius I, arriving in Rome from Constantinople, had been hard put to it to find anyone willing to consecrate him. Eventually, with the aid of the imperial authorities in Italy, the pope had persuaded the centre and the south of Italy of the condemnation's validity. The north, however, remained unreconciled. This purely theological controversy was overtaken by the political catastrophe of the Lombard invasion. For many Catholics in the north the rule of an Arian ruler may have seemed preferable to that of a heretical pope and emperor. Certainly many bishops hastened to come to an accommodation with the Lombards, with the result that regular episcopal succession and continuity was maintained in many north Italian sees.

Justin II's successors, Tiberius Constantine (578–82) and Maurice (582–602), preoccupied with crises in the East and the Balkans, were unable to spare any additional troops for the Italian front. Even when the Italians themselves raised money, some 216,000 *solidi*, to pay for troops, and sent it to Constantinople in 577 with a high-powered embassy, headed by the senior surviving member of the Senate, the former praetorian prefect Pamphronius, the emperor could only give

him the advice to use the money to buy the services of dissident
Lombard dukes or to purchase help from the Franks. These expedi-
ents became the twin pillars of imperial policy in Italy, and they
sometimes achieved success. The Lombard duke Droctulf came over
to the imperial cause *circa* 585 and recaptured for the Empire the
important port of Classis. The emperor Maurice paid the Frankish
king Childebert 50,000 *solidi* to invade Lombard Italy, which he did
on four occasions (584, 587, 588, 590). The Romans, however, signally
failed to take advantage either of the fact that the Lombard thrust
had been weakened by the suspension of the kingship, or of the
Frankish invasions, until 590, thereby reinforcing the impression,
given by the evidence, that they were militarily incapable of doing
so. Indeed, the main result of the Frankish threat was the revival of
the kingship. The Lombards saw the need for undivided command
again and elected as their king in 584 the young warrior Autharis,
son of their last king, the murdered Cleph, and he repaid their
confidence by crushingly defeating the 588 invasion.

While the kingship was suspended the great Lombard dukes Farwald of Spoleto and Zotto of Benevento maintained the aggressive
advance in the centre and the south of Italy. In 579 Farwald besieged
Rome. Pope Benedict I died during the siege, and Pelagius II was
elected and installed as his successor immediately, without waiting
for the arrival of imperial confirmation as was the custom. The city
held out and Farwald turned north, capturing the port of Classis.[14]
Zotto of Benevento besieged Naples in 581,[15] and although he did
not take it he did destroy Aquinum and capture Venafrum, whose
clergy fled to Naples.[16] He also destroyed the monastery of Monte
Cassino, whose monks fled to Rome, carrying with them St Benedict's original copy of his Rule. The date of this event is uncertain.
The years 570, 577, 580, 581 and 589 have been variously proposed,
but all that can be said with certainty is that it occurred between 570
and 590.[17]

The threat to Rome in these years was very real. Although the
Lombards withdrew without taking the city in 579, they remained
an ever-present menace. Despairing of imperial help, Pelagius wrote
in 580, urging the Frankish Bishop Aunacharius of Auxerre to prevail
on the Frankish kings to come to the aid of the beleaguered city of
Rome.[18] Although they eventually came in 584, the Lombards bribed
them to go away again.[19] The threat to Rome remained, and Pelagius

graphically described the state of affairs there, in a letter to Gregory, then his envoy in the imperial capital, in October 584:[20]

> So great are the calamities and tribulations we suffer from
> the perfidy of the Lombards in spite of their solemn promises
> that no one could adequately describe them. . . . The Empire is
> in so critical a situation that unless God prevails on the heart of
> our most pious prince to show his servants the pity he feels and
> to grant them a commander or a general, then we are lost. For
> the territory around Rome is completely undefended and the
> exarch writes that he can do nothing for us being unable himself
> to defend the region around Ravenna. May God bid the emperor
> to come to our aid with all speed before the army of that
> impious nation the Lombards shall have seized the lands that
> still form part of the Empire.

Pelagius' letter contains the first known reference to the exarch of Ravenna. The emperor Maurice took steps which in effect recognized the fact of Lombard conquest when he organized the provincial government of Italy into the exarchate, a militarized frontier province, consolidating what remained of Italy into a defensive unit. The governor of Italy had previously been a prefect, but he was now superseded by the exarch, who wielded supreme civil and military power within the province. In 584 or 585 the fiery Smaragdus, a capable general and organizer, was appointed exarch, perhaps the first,[21] and almost immediately concluded a three-year truce with the Lombards in order to consolidate his position.[22] The expiration of the truce was followed by the recapture of Classis by imperial forces, but in 589 Smaragdus went insane and was replaced as exarch by Romanus. The arrival of Romanus was the signal for the long-awaited imperial counteroffensive. The emperor had at last been able to provide troops. He sent back to Italy the Lombard mercenary general Nordulf and his men, who had been serving in the East, and they placed themselves under the orders of the exarch. A plan was concerted with the Franks for a joint attack. Three Frankish columns entered Italy, taking and destroying many fortresses, and Romanus wrote to Childebert thanking him for sending his armies to 'liberate' Italy.[23] Romanus immediately launched his own attack in the Po Valley, capturing Modena, Altinum and Mantua. Parma, Rhegium and Placentia were surrendered by their Lombard dukes, and Gisulf, son of Duke Grasulf of Friuli, 'a young man anxious to prove himself better than his father' (as Romanus put it), came over to the Empire with his army. Several other frontier cities were captured by Nordulf and another general, Osso, for the Empire.[24] Unfortunately, however, the imperial and Frankish forces did not effect the expected junction. The Franks found themselves unable to engage the Lombards in pitched battle, for they retreated into their fortified cities and refused to come out, Autharis himself sitting tight in Pavia. After three months, the Frankish army found itself seriously weakened by famine and dysentery, and the Frankish commander Duke Chedin, encamped near Verona, concluded a ten-month truce with Autharis and withdrew from Italy.

Each side blamed the other for the failure of Franks and imperialists to join forces, and Romanus wrote bitterly to Childebert, complaining that he had been on the point of joining Chedin.[25] With the support of his cutters on the river, they could then have besieged Pavia and taken Autharis, 'whose capture would have been the greatest prize of victory'. He went on: 'If they had only had a little patience, today Italy would be free from the hateful race and all the wealth of the unspeakable Autharis would have been brought into your treasury; for the campaign had reached such a point that the Lombards did not consider themselves safe from the Franks even behind the walls of their cities.' He urged that Childebert should send another army under generals more worthy of his trust. He suggested that they attack at harvest time, so that the enemies' crops could be destroyed, that they concert their routes and dates with the imperial troops, and that they refrain from plundering and pillaging the Romans. But Childebert had had enough of Italy and concluded instead a treaty with the Lombards. Autharis, having thus survived the greatest test of his rule, albeit with territorial losses, died in Pavia on 5 September 590. Poison was suspected, but it is more likely that he succumbed to the plague, which was again ravaging Italy.[26]

The plague had become as much a fact of Italian life as the Lombards; indeed, the Lombard invasions coincided with the first great plague pandemic. As far as can be computed from the scattered references, it subsisted from the 540s to the 760s. It seems to have originated in Ethiopia, whence, carried down the Nile, it struck in Egypt in 541. It spread through the East like wildfire, carrying off some 300,000 of the population of Constantinople in 542–4, according to the chronicler Evagrius.

The historian Procopius, an eye-witness of the outbreak in the Eastern capital, penned a graphic description of its effects.[27]

The fever was of such a languid sort from its commencement and up till evening that neither to the sick themselves nor to a physician who touched them would it afford any suspicion of danger. . . . But on the same day in some cases, on the following day in others, and in the rest not many days later a bubonic swelling developed. . . . Up to this point everything went in about the same way with all who had taken the disease. But from then on very marked differences developed. . . . There ensued with some a deep coma, with others a violent delirium, and in either case they suffered the characteristic symptoms of the disease. For those who were under the spell of the coma forgot all those who were familiar to them and seemed constantly asleep. And if any one cared for them, they would eat without waking, but some also were neglected and these would die directly through lack of sustenance. But those who were seized with delirium suffered from insomnia and were victims of a distorted imagination; for they suspected that men were coming upon them to destroy them, and they would become excited and rush off in flight, crying out at the top of their voices. And those who were attending them were in a state of constant exhaustion and had a most difficult time. . . . And in those cases where neither coma nor delirium came on, the bubonic swelling became mortified and the sufferer, no longer able to endure the pain, died. . . . Death in some cases came immediately, in others after many days; and with some the body broke out with black pustules about as large as a lentil, and these did not survive even one day, but all succumbed immediately. With many also a vomiting of blood ensued without visible cause and straightway brought death.

The plague attack lasted four months on this occasion. People died in droves. Heaps of corpses lay unburied in the streets and the stench of death pervaded the city. In the wake of pestilence came famine, and still more citizens were carried off. The imperial capital literally came to a standstill.

The same disease with the same symptoms and the same catastrophic effects reached the West in 543 and thereafter ravaged Italy and France in some ten successive waves, generally with a respite of several years in between outbreaks. Gregory records details of some of the delirious. visions experienced by plague victims. One small boy, who had been wicked in life, saw the emissaries of the Devil, in the form of blackamoors, coming to carry him off. A young monk in Gregory's own monastery felt himself being devoured by a dragon. A soldier, at the height of his fever, had a remarkable vision of a bridge of the dead, spanning a river black, smoking and noisome, but leading to mansions of gold amid green and pleasant fields. Those who had been good in life passed safely across, those who had been evil were plunged into the murky waters.[28] The ravages of the disease were crippling. In the 590s, for instance, its effects were so serious in Rome that there were scarcely enough men to guard the walls and scarcely anyone, lay or cleric, who was strong enough to carry out his ordinary duties.[29] There can be little doubt that the plague constitutes one reason why the Lombards found conquest so easy. The Lombard historian Paul the Deacon discerned this: 'The Romans then had no courage to resist because the pestilence which occurred at the time of Narses had destroyed very many in Liguria and Venetia.'[30] Gregory too, discussing the destruction of Aquinum by the Lombards, explicitly linked it with the plague.[31]

The 545 outbreak chiefly affected southern France. There was, however, a much more serious attack on Italy in the mid-560s during the governorship of Narses, when Ravenna, Istria, Liguria and Rome were stricken.[32] Coming immediately after the end of the Gothic war and on the eve of the Lombard invasion, it was doubly serious. It returned in the early 570s, accompanied this time by a serious famine, which so affected Italy that, according to the *Liber Pontificalis*, many cities surrendered to the invading Lombards to avoid the rigours of want.[33]

The plague was back again in the 590s, this time in the aftermath of unprecedented floods which swept Italy in the period 589–91. They washed away part of the walls of Verona and inundated large parts of Rome.[34] Contemporary eye-witness reports spoke of sea-beasts being stranded on the coast near Rome.[35] The inevitable corollary of this was a revival of plague at Rome and at Portus. By September 591 it had reached Narnia, and by 592–3 it had arrived on the east coast, to devastate Ravenna and Istria in an outbreak as severe as that in the time of Narses.[36] On top of all this came an exceptional drought which gripped Italy for much of 591, suggesting high temperatures which can only have quickened the spread of the pestilence.[37] There was barely a respite before it returned again, sweeping through Ravenna and the east coast in 598 and assaulting Rome in the summer of 599.[38]

The cumulative effect of this pandemic must have been staggering. Specific figures of mortalities are rarely given, but it has been estimated that something like a third of the population was carried off.[39] The initial onset of the plague fastened on a population weakened by years of war, and in its turn it led to famine and depopulation, the precursors of the next round of plague. It seemed an unending cycle of decay.

The psychological effect of the apparently unending onslaught of plague and war was immense. For many religious people, including Gregory himself, they were the scriptural precursors of the Apocalypse. There was a strong stimulus to monasticism, as men and women abandoned the world and took to the cloister in large numbers to prepare their souls for the next life. For many others, the constant plagues and wars provided a powerful stimulus to primitive superstition.

The characteristic state of the ordinary man in the Middle Ages, as of his late antique counterpart, was one of fear – fear of the plague, fear of invasion, fear of the tax-collector, fear of witchcraft and magic, fear above all of the unknown. In the West, although for two centuries worship of the one God had officially replaced worship of the many, the old gods retained their hold on the minds of the rural population at least. In the country areas of Western Europe, paganism was pervasive and deep-rooted. Christianity was the religion of the cities and the Establishment, ironically perhaps, in view of the fact that it had started as a subversive, lower-class faith. The hierarchy, the upper classes, the educated, were in general Christian. In large measure, paganism had been driven from the cities, where the grip of the ecclesiastical and secular authorities was strong, and where the reach of the law was immediate.

The sentimental attachment of part of the Roman population, including the aristocracy, to the last surviving pagan festival, the Lupercalia, in which half-naked youths, decked in goatskins, ran through the streets striking the women to confer fecundity on them, brought down the wrath of Pope Gelasius in 495. He blamed the decline of Rome on such survivals, and the Lupercalia soon disappeared, to be replaced by a Christian festival, the Purification of the Virgin, on the same date.[40] Nevertheless, a nest of magicians, led by a senator Basilius, was discovered in Rome early in the sixth century. Its leader escaped from prison and cheekily took refuge in a Valerian monastery until he was unmasked, returned to Rome and there burned alive.[41] There is a marked decline in the evidence of paganism in the cities after this, though it did crop up from time to time, as in 599 when a priest in Rhegium was found to have an idol in his house.[42]

Central to a consideration of the popular mind at this time is the role of 'the holy' in society.[43] The ordinary man attributed his troubles, whether disease or harvest failure or war, to the exercise of evil spirits. He sought to propitiate them and he venerated whatever he thought possessed the power to combat them, be it trees, stones or holy men. The church took the view that evils were either a judgment from God, which had to be patiently borne, or the work of the Devil, 'the old enemy', who with his legions was constantly abroad, setting snares for unwary mankind, stirring up strife and tempting and taunting the righteous. For good Christians, these demons were none other than the old gods worshipped by man in the days of his error and now revealed as the acolytes of Antichrist. This is why in one of Gregory's stories they meet in one of their old haunts, a ruined temple of Apollo.[44] The Devil was everywhere and could take any shape he wished in order to work his wicked ways. Gregory records him appearing as a serpent, a black bird, a black boy and a foul monster. One had to be terribly careful or suffer the consequences. An unhappy nun, taking a quick snack, swallowed a little devil sitting on a lettuce leaf and had to be exorcised.[45]

For many people, the best defence against misfortune, whether it was caused by the Devil, the forces of Nature, or the unknown, lay in the hallowed practices of paganism. The age-old sacred places of the pagan cults – the groves and pools and mountain tops – retained their mystical potency. The magicians and soothsayers who prophesied and healed and exorcised according to arcane lore and unchristian ritual flourished. Church councils legislated regularly against pagan practices throughout the Dark Ages, and the surviving sermons of crusading bishops in Italy, Spain and Gaul from the fifth to the eighth century, Maximus of Turin, Caesarius of Arles, Martin of Braga and Eligius of Noyon, all record the details of these practices in similar, sometimes identical, terms.[46] They reveal how every aspect of country life was permeated by the old ways, what the sources of supernatural power were, and the full extent of the problem the

Christian church faced. The old gods of forest, fountain, river, mountain and sea were still venerated. Lighted candles were placed at sacred springs, trees, and crossroads. Bread was cast into fountains; charms were hung on trees. Laurel was placed over doors, and libations poured into the hearth. Offerings were made to mice and moths to keep them away from the crops. Horoscopes were cast; divination was employed to tell the future. Magicians and wise women were consulted in cases of illness. Charms were worn, and magic herbal potions were mixed to ritual incantations. The names of the old gods were invoked in daily speech, and the days of the week were still named after them. Certain days were regarded as unlucky; eclipses were feared; special significance was attributed to chance meetings, false steps, the sudden flight of birds, and a person's sneezes.

From the profound to the trivial, paganism dominated everything. The preachers were particularly incensed by the celebration of the start of the year on the kalends of January, when there was immoderate feasting and drinking, lubricious singing and dancing, the exchange of gifts, and fertility rituals in which men dressed as women or as animals, in skins and beast-heads. The preachers were even more outraged when in some areas the peasants transferred these trappings to church services, converting them into drunken bacchanals. In some cases even the local priest found it prudent to join in rather than oppose the traditions of his flock, and the Galician hermit St Valerius in the second half of the seventh century recorded coming across a secret pagan ceremony at dead of night in the depths of the forest, with chanting, gyrations, horned beasts, and the local priest presiding.[47] The peasants for their part participated in both Christian and pagan ceremonies. As Gregory himself protested to the Frankish queen Brunhild in 597: 'We exhort you to restrain the rest of your subjects under the control of discipline from sacrificing to the heads of animals, seeing that it has come to our ears that many of the Christians both resort to the churches and also – horrible to relate – do not give up their worshipping of demons.'[48] The canny peasants were simply taking advantage of two different sources of supernatural power in a sensible form of double insurance.

Although there is rather less detailed evidence for Italy in the sixth and seventh centuries than for Gaul and Spain, the situation was clearly the same. Not all peasants were pagans. Forty of them died during the Lombard invasions for refusing to worship the pagan idols of the invaders.[49] But Cassiodorus assumed as a matter of course that the peasants would be pagans, and urged his monks, as one of their duties, to convert the peasants from worshipping the sacred groves.[50] St Benedict of Nursia found on top of Monte Cassino a shrine to Apollo where sacred groves grew and sacrifices were made. He cut down the groves, destroyed the idol and turned the temple into a chapel to St Martin.[51] The nearby villagers were converted from idol-worship by a sustained campaign of evangelization.[52] Yet fifty years later the peasants of Campania were still worshipping trees, causing Gregory to take action to stop them,[53] and the peasants of Lombardy were still at it in 727 when King Liutprand legislated against the worship of trees and fountains and the consulting of soothsayers.[54]

The countryman remained close to the fundamentals of life, and his faith reflected this. The worship of those conventionalized divinities, the pallid, civilized adulterers of Mount Olympus, had only masked the deeper primeval rites of Man the Farmer. Ever since the first plough broke the first furrow and the first seed grew up into the light, his religion had been dictated by the rhythms of the seasons, by the unending cycle of planting, germinating and reaping, by the eternal verities of birth, death and renewal, by the warding off of dark forces and the propitiation of the beneficent powers of fertility and harvest. Not all the disapproving decrees of church councils or the puritanical sermons of a gaggle of sainted preachers could reshape the spiritual and psychological profile of agrarian society.

Opinions on how to deal with the recalcitrant peasants varied. St Caesarius of Arles wanted to beat it out of them: 'Chastise them most severely . . . so that they who are not concerned about the salvation of their soul, might fear the wounds of the body.' St Martin of Braga believed in the use of persuasion and reasoned argument to win them over. Judging by the evidence, neither worked. But many a saint 'won his spurs' by trying one or other of the methods. In the sixth century Bishop Gallus of Clermont-Ferrand, uncle of Gregory of Tours, discovered a heathen temple near Cologne still in use for miracle cures and pagan feasts. He burned it down and barely escaped with his life from the wrath of the peasants.[55] St Radegund, the Frankish queen, coming across a similar temple on her way to a dinner party, ordered her retainers to burn it down, but they had to fight off the enraged locals before they could do so.[56] The Lombard stylite St Wulfilach found peasants near Trier still worshipping a statue of Diana with alcoholic celebration and persuaded them by exhortation to demolish it.[57] Even when they were converted peasants might backslide. At the turn of the sixth century, St Columban found at Bregenz in Switzerland a ruined Christian chapel once dedicated to St Aurelia which had been turned into a pagan shrine by the peasants. Columban smashed the bronze images which were worshipped there and converted the peasants afresh.[58]

But there was another, subtler way of dealing with the problem. Christianity had over the centuries become adroit at absorbing many of the most obvious pagan festivals, symbols, holy places and deities. It was official church policy to turn pagan temples into Christian shrines and convert their festivals into Christian celebrations.[59] This was encouraged both by St Augustine of Hippo and by Gregory himself in his famous instructions to Augustine of Canterbury. Pagan wells were renamed for Christian saints. Many of the old pagan temples were converted and reconsecrated as churches, the most famous conversion perhaps being that of the Pantheon in Rome into the church of St Maria ad Martyres by Pope Boniface IV.[60] Yet while persecution could be utilized to weaken the forces of unreconstructed paganism, where the obvious external symbols could be absorbed into the fabric of Christianity and those pagan practices not immediately absorbable could be castigated as the work of the Devil, Christianity could not hope to eradicate so easily a total psychological orientation. So in a world of fear where sorcerers' spells, magic, auguries, oracles and lucky charms had such potency, the Christian church developed an alternative source of magic power, in the Christian holy man and the holy relic.

The role of the holy man as mediator between God and man, as the source of supernatural protection, and as the exemplar of the true Christian life of suffering and sacrifice becomes central. Holy men were popularized in hagiography, the characteristic popular literature of the Middle Ages, whose great age lasted from the sixth to the tenth century. It was a literature of miracles and portents, signs and wonders, the exaltation of a Christian source of supernatural power, making a direct and comprehensible appeal to the mentality of the ordinary man. Greek hagiographies of the lives of the ascetic saints of the Egyptian desert had been translated by Dionysius Exiguus at the request of abbots and pious laymen in the early years of the sixth century, and in the middle of the century the future popes Pelagius I and John III had translated the Greek collection *Lives of the Fathers*, reflecting the growing demand for such reading.

But the holy men of the West found their celebrants in Gregory of Tours and Gregory the Great, contemporaries who wrote of the saints of Gaul and Italy respectively, gathering together stories which had been told and retold by their local populations. Gregory of Tours wrote 'The Miracles of the Blessed Martyrs' (*Liber in Gloria Martyrum Beatorum*), 'The Glories of the Blessed Confessors' (*Liber in Gloria Confessorum*), and 'Life of St Martin of Tours' (*De Virtutibus Beati Martini Episcopi*), and Gregory the Great the so-called *Dialogi*, sub-titled: 'The Lives and Miracles of the Italian Fathers'. The pope's book is a veritable survey of the wonders wrought by the holy men and women of sixth-century Italy, in their struggles against evil, paganism and the unknown. The heroes of the *Dialogues* raise the dead, cure the blind, the sick, and the leprous, heal the injured, exorcise demons, put an end to hauntings, stop fires and floods, save threatened buildings, fill empty jars with wine and oil, have prophetic dreams and visions and visitations. The holy man, be he monk, bishop or cleric, replaced the pagan oracle and sorcerer as a source of supernatural power, his sanctity deriving from God as a result of his spiritual and ascetic way of life. Gregory of Tours in 'Miracles of the Blessed Martyrs' specifically contrasted their miracles with the so-called miracles of Greek and Latin mythology, the meta-morphoses of Jupiter, the rape of Proserpine, the flight of Saturn, which he pooh-poohed.[61] The superiority of the Christian holy men's power to that of the pagan is clearly illustrated by a story in the *Dialogues*.[62] A noblewoman is possessed by a devil and taken to the local magicians, who cast out the devil. But God sends a legion of devils, causing her to shriek and writhe in agony, until she is taken to the noted exorcist Bishop Fortunatus of Tuder, who casts them all out. It is a cautionary tale, but it illustrates incidentally that the first recourse of the afflicted was to the magicians and not to the priest. The magicians are clearly shown to have power, but not as much as the priest, whose power comes from God. According to the *Whitby Life*, magical arts were even used against Gregory.[63] He excommun-icated a rich man in Rome for divorcing his wife contrary to the law, and the man hired two magicians to dispose of the pope. They went up to a high place and there summoned up devils who entered Gregory's horse as he was riding to mass. But Gregory made the sign of the cross, cast out the devils, and blinded the magicians. The

magicians revealed the truth of the plot and were subsequently converted to Christianity. The magicians had power, but Gregory, filled
with the Holy Spirit, had greater power. Gregory the Great's involvement in this literary movement was crucial, not because it created
the mood but because it reflected it, and more important because it
gave it the official imprimatur of approval, from the highest level.

The relics of the saints were another source of considerable magical
power, the equivalents of the lyre of Orpheus, the anvils of Vulcan
and the ship of Aeneas, the cult objects of the old faith. Possessing
the body or part of the body of a saint or martyr, or even his clothes,
belongings, or objects associated with his torment, conferred considerable éclat on the towns or villages which housed them – so
much so that Gregory indignantly refused Empress Constantina's
request that he send the head of St Paul, one of Rome's most prized
relics, to Constantinople for a church she was building.[64] The possession of relics came to be regarded as essential for the consecration
of new chapels, churches, monasteries, even episcopal palaces, to
make them power sources, and the papal chancery prepared formula
letters to deal with requests for them.[65] Relics also performed miracles. The cloak of St Eutychius halted a drought, the sandal of St
Honoratus raised a dead boy, and the tunic of St Vincent saved the
city of Saragossa from a besieging Frankish army.[66]

Rome, of course, surpassed everywhere else in the relics league.
The Roman church held the bodies of St Peter and St Paul, and
catacombs overflowing with martyrs' remains, as well as such
treasures as the gridiron of St Lawrence, a piece of the True Cross,
and the chains of St Peter and St Paul. They were regularly added
to. Gregory himself wrote to at least ten different bishops asking for
relics of saints from their dioceses.[67] This made Rome a living, throb-
bing, central source of supernatural power and encouraged a stream
of pilgrims from all over the Christian world. Hostels were built to
accommodate the faithful, and when a group of Irishmen checked
into one in 633, they found also resident there a Greek, an Egyptian,
a Scythian and a Hebrew.[68] There were regular guided tours of the
catacombs and cemeteries of the martyrs.[69]

Visiting the tombs of the holy was one thing, however, and possessing a relic was another. There was a generally accepted prohibition in the West on the movement of the actual bodies of the saints,
except to preserve them from invading pagans or heretics.[70] But there
was a way of getting round this ban, and that was the practice of

placing pieces of cloth next to the bodies of saints to soak up some of their sanctity and then preserving these as relics.[71] Their potency was accepted and was indeed demonstrated by Pope Leo the Great, according to a story related by Gregory to the empress. When a group of sceptical Greeks questioned the potency of such cloths, Pope Leo took a pair of scissors and cut the cloth, which started to bleed.[72] More portable personal charms were provided by the popes in the rather attractive form of either a cross or a key (a pertinent reminder of Peter's role as the keeper of the keys of the Kingdom), to be worn round the neck and containing filings from the chains of St Peter. Gregory sent at least fourteen of these to specially favoured people.[73]

These relics were clearly expected to perform miracles. Gregory promised King Childebert when sending him one that it would protect him from 'all evils'.[74] He sent Patriarch Eulogius of Alexandria a cross containing chains of St Peter and St Paul, as a sort of double-strength talisman, when he learned that the patriarch's sight was failing, and told him, 'Let this be continually applied to your eyes for many miracles have been performed by this same gift.'[75]

There is no question but that all the supernatural power available was needed in the dark days of the later sixth century. Gregory has left us his own picture of what was happening, preached in a sermon in 590 soon after his accession:[76]

> What happiness is there left in the world? Everywhere we see war. Everywhere we hear groans. Our cities are destroyed; our fortresses are overthrown; our fields laid waste; the land is become a desert. No inhabitants remain in the countryside, scarcely any in the towns. The small remnant of humanity surviving is daily and without cease borne down. Yet the scourge of divine justice has no end. . . . Some we have seen led into captivity, others mutilated, others killed. So what happiness is there left in the world? See to what straits Rome, once mistress of the world, is reduced. Worn down by her great and ceaseless sorrows, by the loss of her citizens, by the assault of the enemy, by the frequency of ruin – thus we see brought to pass the sentence long ago pronounced on the city of Samaria by the prophet Ezekiel.

Here then is a world in which the darkness deepens, earth's glories pass away, change and decay is seen all around. It is a world in which only a holding operation can be performed against the imminence of the Apocalypse. It is a world in which all the qualities of the Roman administrator, magistrate, and estate owner are required. But it is also a world where the saving of souls, the performing of good works, and self-mortification can provide a passport to eternal bliss in the Kingdom of the saints. It is a fitting stage for the entrance of the consul of God.

Chapter Two

Gregory's Early Life

Little is known of Gregory's life before he became pope. The precise date of his birth is uncertain, but he is generally agreed to have been born *circa* 540 in Rome.[1] He was christened Gregory, which is in itself interesting in that it is a Greek name, meaning 'watchful', its Latin equivalent being Vigilius. It stands out sharply from the other names from his family that we know (Felix, Gordianus, Palatinus), which are solidly Latin. Probably it reflects the extreme piety of his family and derives from one of the Greek saints, Gregory of Nyssa perhaps.

Gregory was the scion of a wealthy, propertied and aristocratic family,[2] and although there is no evidence to link him with the oldest and most glorious patrician families, such as the Anicii and the Decii, it is likely that his family was one of the most distinguished left in Rome after the Gothic wars. They owned a palatial home on the Caelian hill and extensive estates in Sicily, as well as farms in the neighbourhood of Rome itself.[3] The family was not only socially eminent, it was also ecclesiastically very distinguished. Gregory was descended from Pope Felix III, whom he calls his *atavus*, great-great-grandfather, and was a kinsman of Pope Agapitus, himself perhaps the nephew of Felix III and a former resident on the Caelian hill. Gregory's election to the throne of St Peter makes this perhaps the single most distinguished clerical dynasty of the period. Gregory's father, Gordianus, was, according to John the Deacon, a *regionarius*.[4] John described a picture of Gregory's parents in the monastery of St Andrew, commissioned by Gregory, in which Gordianus is depicted holding the hand of St Peter. What John meant by *regionarius* is not entirely clear and various suggestions have been made. The most likely explanation is that John retrospectively applied to Gordianus the title his office would have carried in John's own time, the ninth century, and that what is actually meant is *defensor*. It was Gregory himself who first organized the *defensores* into a college, thereby creating regionary *defensores*. Such an office involving minor orders

25

would be feasible for Gordianus, and several examples of wealthy property owners who were *defensores* are known.[5] Gregory's mother, Silvia, was equally devout, and on her husband's death she retired into religious seclusion at Cella Nova near the basilica of St Paul's, where several members of the family were buried.[6]

Other members of Gregory's family are known. His three paternal aunts, Tarsilla, Aemiliana and Gordiana, lived in their own house as nuns under a strict self-imposed religious discipline. The first two, renowned for their sanctity, died after seeing a vision of their ancestor Pope Felix. The youngest, Gordiana, who had always chafed at the religious life, caused a family scandal by immediately abandoning it and marrying the steward (*conductor*) of her estates. Gregory remarked sadly of this event: 'Many are called but few are chosen.'[7] Gregory's maternal aunt, Pateria, lived in Campania; she fell on hard times, and in 591 found herself in receipt of a papal subsidy from her nephew.[8]

Gregory also had a younger brother, Palatinus, who attained the titles of *patricius* and *vir gloriosus*. He was prefect of Rome at the time of Gregory's elevation to the papal throne, and after relinquishing that office was several times consulted by Gregory on matters of high public concern, such as the signing of the peace treaty with the Lombards and the imperial investigation into the affairs of the former praetor of Sicily.[9]

The only direct evidence we have about Gregory's education is Gregory of Tours' statement, taken up and fancifully elaborated by subsequent biographers, that Gregory 'was so skilled in grammar, dialectic and rhetoric that he was second to none in the entire city'.[10] Whether he was the best or not, Gregory certainly received the formal classical education of the ancient world in one of the Roman schools, and was probably among the last in Rome to do so, since the schools broke up soon after the Byzantine reconquest.[11] Philosophical and scientific training had ceased long ago, so the idea, advanced by John the Deacon, that he was trained in philosophy is clearly absurd.[12] But Rome was still the centre for legal studies, and on the evidence of Gregory's legalistic outlook and fluency with imperial law it seems likely that he studied law too as preparation for a career in public life.

While there is ample evidence that Gregory knew the Latin patristic writers, such as Augustine and Jerome, and those of the Greek Fathers who had been translated into Latin, scholars have spent many painstaking hours sifting through his works to find out what secular culture he acquired. They have reached the conclusion that he must have been acquainted with Cicero, Virgil, Seneca and Juvenal.[13] He was also keenly interested in natural science and had knowledge of history, arithmology and music.[14]

Gregory's Latin was clear and correct, conforming to late antique practice.[15] But he did not know Greek. He said so several times,[16] and when a Greek monk, Andreas, forged and circulated sermons in Greek purportedly by Gregory, the pope ordered Archbishop Eusebius of Thessalonica to track down and destroy them, saying that he could neither read nor write Greek.[17] This ignorance is all the more remarkable in view of the fact that he spent several years in Constantinople as the official papal representative – but then so did popes Vigilius and Martin, and they never learned Greek either. Indeed, there was a marked decline in the knowledge of Greek in Rome in the second half of the sixth century. Gregory complained several times of the lack of interpreters and translators.[18] Some indication of the theological disadvantage at which his ignorance of Greek placed Gregory, and eloquent evidence of the paucity of Greek works available in Rome, is provided by a single episode. The synodical letter of the newly installed patriarch Cyriacus of Constantinople contained an anathematization of the heretic Eudoxius. Gregory had never heard of him and could find no information on him at all in Rome; so in 597 he wrote to his friend Eulogius of Alexandria seeking information on Eudoxius, and Eulogius sent him extracts referring to the heretic from the works of Basil, Gregory Nazianzen and Epiphanius.[19] It is a far cry from the pre-conquest days, which produced the cultured bi-lingual circle of Boethius, and the popes Pelagius I and John III, who before their elections made excellent translations of the *Lives of the Fathers* from Greek to Latin.[20]

When Gregory abandoned the secular life and embraced a religious life, he also put his classical education behind him. Until recently the received opinion was that Gregory was an implacable enemy of classical culture – a view with an impressive pedigree dating back at least to the twelfth century, when the baseless story was current that Gregory had burned the Palatine and Capitoline libraries.[21] The evidence for this view rests on two texts. Writing to his friend Leander of Seville, he justified the style of his *Magna Moralia* with a rejection of secular rhetoric:[22]

I have disdained to observe the rules of composition which the teachers of secular learning recommend. As this very letter shows, I do not attempt to avoid the collision of words called 'metacism' or the obscurity of barbarisms. I do not care to observe the position, force or government of prepositions, for I think it absolutely intolerable to fetter the words of the Divine Oracle by the rules of Donatus.

Even more decisive is his letter to Bishop Desiderius of Vienne, written in 601:[23]

A report has reached us, which we cannot mention without shame, that you are lecturing on profane literature to certain friends. This fills me with such grief and vehement disgust that my former opinion of you has been turned to mourning and sorrow. For the same mouth cannot sing the praises of Jupiter and the praises of Christ. Consider yourself how offensive, how abominable a thing it is for a bishop to recite verses which are unfit even to be recited by a religious layman. . . . If hereafter it is clearly established that the information I received was false, and that you are not applying yourself to the idle vanities of secular literature, I shall render thanks to God, who has not allowed your heart to be polluted by the blasphemous praises of unspeakable men.

This is on the face of it an out-and-out condemnation of secular learning, but it has been put into perspective by recent scholars, and as a result Gregory's position now appears far less implacable.[24]

Gregory's own words can, in fact, be used to set the above extracts in their true context. In his *Commentary on the First Book of Kings*, now known conclusively to be by him, he writes:[25]

Although the learning to be obtained from secular books is not directly beneficial to the saints in their spiritual conflict, yet, when it is united to the study of Holy Scripture, men attain to a profounder knowledge of Scripture itself. The liberal arts ought, therefore, to be cultivated, in order that we may gain through them a more accurate knowledge of God's Word. But the evil spirits expel the desire for learning from the hearts of some, to the intent that, being destitute of secular knowledge, they may be unable to reach the loftier heights of spiritual knowledge. For the devils know well that by aquaintance with secular literature we are helped in sacred knowledge. . . . If we are ignorant of profane science, we are unable to penetrate the depth of the Sacred Word.

It is clear from this that Gregory was not against secular learning when it was put to the service of spiritual education. He simply regarded it as lower in the hierarchy of knowledge than the wisdom of the just (*sapientia justorum*), which was the search for God. Desiderius had offended against this rubric by studying profane learning for its own sake and was therefore condemned. Gregory himself was perfectly ready to use secular learning, as when he utilized his knowledge of natural science, of animals and plants, to give an allegorical exposition of the Book of Job.

Nor was Gregory alone in rejecting strict rhetorical rules, as represented by Donatus, the fourth-century grammarian, who epitomizes for Gregory the high culture of a secular world. Although Jerome, the translator of the Vulgate, had admired Donatus, other Church Fathers, such as Augustine, Ambrose and Cassiodorus, had declared a preference for Christian truth over the rules of grammar.[26] Gregory firmly placed himself in this tradition, saying in his letter to Leander: 'Nor have those rules been observed by the translators of any authorized version of the Holy Scripture.' But Gregory's attitude was not simply a negative one, a dislike of the preciosity, obscurantism and surface showiness of the old rhetoric, a preference for content over form; he also had a positive motive. He sought to popularize in his own sermons and popular writings a much more approachable, colloquial, informal style, to get his religious message over to a far wider audience than the educated elite of the now defunct high society salons. Certainly his simple and straightforward homiletic style has none of the orotund pretentiousness or strangulated rhetoric of Bishop Ennodius of Pavia, perhaps the sixth century's arch-exponent of the old forms, and Gregory's own works are singularly lacking in quotations from classical authors. Gregory made no bones about his abandonment of formalized cultural elitism, roundly denouncing worldly wisdom and style in his *Magna Moralia.*[27]

It is likely that Gregory gained some experience of estate administration after he came of age. The family estates were extensive, and Gregory's expert knowledge of the minutiae of landlordship when administering the papal patrimony suggests a previous apprenticeship in the field. But the next secure date we know in Gregory's career is 573, and that brings us into the realms of controversy. It is almost always said that in 573 Gregory was prefect of Rome. But the evidence for this depends on a single reference in one of Gregory's letters,[28] when he tells Archbishop Constantius of Milan that he was one of a number of *nobilissimi viri* who countersigned a security delivered to the pope by his predecessor, Archbishop Laurentius of Milan, rejecting the 'Three Chapters'. The most reliable manuscript tradition accepts the reading *gerens urbanam praeturam*, though there is a variant reading *praefecturam*.[29] If the best reading is preferred, it would make Gregory urban praetor, a much less significant figure than city prefect. There is good evidence to support this view. John the Deacon believed that Gregory had been praetor.[30] One of the monasteries Gregory founded in Sicily was called the Praetorian monastery.[31] The urban praetorship, one of the old city magistracies, was usually held by a man in his early thirties, as Gregory would have been. The opponents of Gregory's praetorship say that the office had ceased to exist, because there is no evidence for it after the reconquest. But Justinian had re-established the Senate and the city magistracies, and the argument from silence at a date so soon after the reconquest is not wholly convincing. The Gregorian letter itself is not much help. Either the prefect or the praetor might have countersigned the Milanese security.

The evidence for the prefecture really relies on Gregory's subsequent career. If the praetorship still existed, it can only have been a nominal position. Boethius wrote of it during the Ostrogothic period: 'There was a time when the praetorship was an office of great power, but now it is no more than an empty name, and a heavy burden on the pockets of the senatorial class.'[32] During those days the praetor gave games for the populace; after the reconquest, even that task no longer remained. It is difficult to harmonize tenure of this office with Gregory's obvious eminence in Rome. The rapidity with which he was withdrawn from his monastery to become deacon, the unanimity of his election and his popularity over the archdeacon, the appointment as *apocrisiarios*, the authoritative tone of his dealings with secular officials, the picture Gregory of Tours paints of him in his secular career, 'processing through the city in silken robes sewn with glittering gems', all suggest a prefect rather than a praetor. The prefect, as chief secular administrator of Rome, controlled law and order, supply and public works, was president of the Senate and judge. It is this sort of background that speaks to us through Gregory's Papal Register, in the detailed oversight of a wide variety of matters secular and ecclesiastical, the concern for administrative efficiency, the passion for keeping proper records, the constant requests for lists and inventories, all suggesting a training in practical administration rather than mere magistracy.

The sort of standards by which Gregory operated can be seen in the little homily on the exercise of power he sent to the imperial inspector-general Leontius:[33]

> There is this difference between the kings of the barbarian
> nations and the Roman emperor, that the former have slaves for
> their subjects, the latter free men. And therefore, in all your
> acts, your first object should be to maintain justice, your second
> to preserve a perfect liberty. You ought to value the liberty of
> those whom you are appointed to judge as jealously as though it
> were your own; and if you would not be wronged yourself by
> your superiors, you should guard with respect the liberty of
> your inferiors.

Here are sentiments that would have warmed the hearts of the conscript fathers in the heyday of the Republic, spoken in the voice, stern and just, of a true Roman. In these words the tradition of disinterested and even-handed public service stretching back to the earliest days of Rome's greatness lives on.

When Gregory took up and when he laid down the urban prefecture is not known. It was not usually held for more than a couple of years, and Gregory was comparatively young for the prefecture, so it is likely that he did not hold the office much outside the period 572-4. It was soon after laying down his office that he became a monk. Gregory spoke frankly about his conversion in the preface to the *Magna Moralia*:

> For late and long I declined the grace of conversion, and after I
> had been inspired with a heavenly affection, I thought it better
> to be still shrouded in the secular habits. For although I had
> now disclosed to me what I should seek of the love of things
> eternal, yet long established custom had so cast its chains upon
> me, that I could not change my outward habit; and while my
> purpose still compelled me to engage in the service of this
> world, as it were in semblance only, but what is more serious, in

my own mind. At length being anxious to avoid all those inconveniences I sought the haven of the monastery.

Gregory's long period of tension between the secular and the monastic life, and his later recall to public life, were to have a profound influence on his thinking and would prompt him to seek to rationalize the position of the man divided between the *vita activa* and the *vita contemplativa*.[34]

His decision was probably prompted immediately by the death of his father and his inheritance of the family estates. It is also likely that his mother's retirement to Cella Nova coincided with his decision to take the cloth. Gregory founded seven monasteries – six on the family estates in Sicily, and the seventh in the family home on the Caelian hill, which became the monastery of St Andrew and which he himself entered as a monk. Gregory of Tours says 'he endowed them with sufficient land to provide the monks with their daily sustenance, then he sold the rest of his possessions, including all his household goods, and gave the proceeds to the poor.'[35] This is not strictly true, for Gregory retained sufficient property to make a further endowment to St Andrew's in 587.[36] As Caspar observes, this is not to be taken literally, but as a formal statement of his adoption of the monastic life.[37] The date usually accepted for this is around 574–5, and that would fit the known chronology of Gregory's career.

The most controversial question about Gregory's adoption of monastic life is whether or not he became abbot of St Andrew's. Gregory nowhere says that he did. The first person to claim it is John the Deacon, who alleged that Gregory served as a monk under Hilario and Maximian and was himself subsequently elected abbot.[38] Hilario is otherwise unattested, and John probably means Valentio, whom Gregory refers to as 'my most reverent abbot' in the *Dialogues*.[39] Most subsequent authorities have followed John the Deacon in this and stated that Gregory became abbot on his return from Constantinople. However, a look at the contemporary evidence indicates that this is impossible, and John was probably assuming Gregory's abbacy from the stories in the *Dialogues* where he can be seen acting in an authoritative manner, on one occasion for instance summoning and giving orders to the prior.[40] But this assumption of authority would be compatible with his special position as the monastery's founder, and Gregory certainly took a proprietorial attitude to St Andrew's, frequently referring to it as 'my monastery'.[41] Cassiodorus seems to have held an analogous position at Vivarium – a member of the community, though not abbot, but having a special position as founder. John's testimony on the subject also becomes suspect when we find him deliberately falsifying the evidence. In a letter to Rusticiana, Gregory relates several miracles involving monks of St Andrew's which the current abbot had told him. In retelling them, John makes Gregory the abbot in question.[42]

It seems fairly clear that when Gregory set up his monastery he appointed as its first abbot Valentio, who had been abbot of a Valerian monastery until he fled at the invasion of the Lombards. Valentio would have had the necessary experience and gravity for the office.[43] When Gregory left for Constantinople, he took several of the monks with him and one of them, Maximian, was recalled by Pelagius II in 584 to become abbot, presumably on the death of Valentio, whose rule will thus have lasted about ten years.[44] Maximian was still abbot when Gregory made his donation of property in 587, and in 590 when Gregory became pope; and in the *Dialogues*, written in 593, Gregory says Maximian was abbot 'for a long time'.[45] We know Maximian became bishop of Syracuse in 591, and it seems fairly certain that he was abbot continuously from 584 until that date. There is therefore no room in the abbatial succession for Gregory, and his tenure of the abbacy must be dismissed as a later though entirely understandable fabrication.[46]

Little is known for certain of the form of monastic life practised at St Andrew's. It used to be thought that the Rule of St Benedict operated there; but that view stemmed from the belief that Benedict's Rule was immediately and widely adopted in Western monasteries, a belief largely dispelled by recent research.[47] It is now accepted that rules were drawn up for specific monasteries and not for general use, though some – for instance the Rule of St Basil – became so famous that they were imitated, adapted or copied with variations for several monasteries.

Certain principles, however, were accepted by almost all monasteries, and these undoubtedly prevailed at St Andrew's. The monastery was envisaged as a self-contained community, removed from the world, where the monks lived their lives in common, owning no private property and following rules of poverty, chastity, simplicity of life, obedience to the abbot and constancy of vocation. They were encouraged to spend time in reading of the scriptures and contemplation of the word of God. All these principles were sanctioned by the imperial law code, which had been promulgated by Justinian, and would obviously have been well known to Gregory.[48]

The rules for Gregory's monastery were probably drawn up by Gregory himself and the first abbot, Valentio. Valentio was a product of the Valerian group of monasteries, founded by Equitius in the early sixth century, and the rules probably reflected something of practice there, though we do not know exactly what that was. It seems likely that Gregory knew of St Basil's Rule, which was practised in the Greek monasteries in Rome, and it has been suggested that he also knew the 'Rule of the Master', the now famous precursor of St Benedict's Rule.[49]

It is difficult to believe that elements of Benedict's Rule were not in use at St Andrew's. Gregory knew and greatly approved of Benedict's Rule. He admired Benedict to the extent of devoting an entire book of the *Dialogues* to his miracles. He had met and talked with four disciples of Benedict who had themselves become abbots: Constantine and Simplicius successively abbots of Monte Cassino; Valentinian, abbot of the Lateran monastery in Rome; and Honoratus, abbot of Subiaco. It is not impossible that he had even visited Monte Cassino.[50]

Benedict's Rule envisaged a life dedicated to the service of God.[51] This service took three forms: self-discipline, worship and work. 'Idleness is the enemy of the soul' was Benedict's prime dictum, and he mapped out how the monk's day was to be spent. Pre-eminent was the *Opus Dei*, the strictly scheduled order of service, prayers and psalmody, which punctuated the day at specified intervals. Work consisted of two kinds – manual and meditational. Manual work involved tending the fields and gardens, cleaning the monastery, looking after the sick, manufacturing necessary articles. Meditational work meant reading the Bible and the Church Fathers, and contemplation.

The monk was expected to remain in his monastery for life, and his life-style, under Benedict's Rule, was austere but not unduly harsh. There was a vegetarian diet, early rising and no baths, but there were no hair shirts, no scourgings, no starvation and no rule of total silence. The monks were allowed adequate bedding and warm clothes, shoes and stockings, eight hours' unbroken sleep, and a moderate amount of wine. They were expected to behave with gravity and decorum and to refrain from idle chatter (*taciturnitas et parcitas*). Humility was exalted above all other virtues. This was further emphasized by the necessity of absolute obedience to the abbot as head of the monastery. The abbot's power was absolute. 'Everything is to be done by the abbot's will,' wrote Benedict. He 'holds the place of Christ', controlling all aspects of life in the monastery, and directing the work of the monks. He was to be chosen for 'merit of life and doctrine of wisdom', to be chaste, sober, considerate and merciful, and was encouraged to exercise power and responsibility. For instance, he was advised to vary his disciplinary methods to suit individual cases, using coaxing and persuasion with some and corporal punishment with others. He was a veritable blend of biblical patriarch and Roman paterfamilias.

The primacy of humility, the concept of the abbot, the importance of reading and contemplation, the necessity for self-discipline, the lifelong commitment, are all aspects of the Rule that would have appealed to Gregory.[52] But there are certain differences. Gregory's own rigorous regimen of fasting went far beyond anything prescribed by Benedict and recalled the ultra-ascetic practices of the Egyptian monks. Furthermore, Monte Cassino was a rural monastery and St Andrew's an urban monastery, and this would have meant differences of practice and emphasis. Given Gregory's own predilections, it is likely that biblical exegesis and contemplation took first place at St Andrew's. It was probably during these years that Gregory gave his lectures to the monks on Proverbs, Kings, the Prophets, the Song of Songs and the Heptateuch, which were taken down at the time by the monk Claudius, subsequently abbot of Classis.[53]

The qualities Gregory sought in the monks of his monastery can perhaps be deduced from the comments he made on the monkish heroes from St Andrew's who figure in the *Dialogues*.[54] Antonius is described as 'a conscientious and sedulous observer of monastic discipline, a student of the scriptures seeking not cunning and knowledge so much as tears and contrition'. Merulus was 'wonderfully given to tears and bestowing alms, and always singing psalms, save only when eating and sleeping'. John 'led his life with humility, sweetness and gravity'. These, then, were the practices and characteristics most prized at St Andrew's.

Another story from the *Dialogues*, however, reveals a more savage side to Gregory in the stern application of the monastic rule of poverty.[55] One of the monks at St Andrew's was a doctor, Justus, who tended Gregory during his increasingly frequent bouts of ill-health. When Justus fell ill and knew himself near death, he told his brother, another doctor, Copiosus, that he had hidden three gold coins in his medicine chest. Copiosus duly retrieved them, but when Gregory found out he ordered that Justus should be 'sent to Coventry'. No one in the monastery was to go near him or help him; and when he died his body was to be cast out on a dunghill with the three coins, and the assembled monks were to cry: 'To Hell with you and your money.' When Copiosus told him of the treatment Gregory had ordered, Justus died of grief. Gregory's harshness on this occasion comes rather badly from one who still owned several farms at least thirteen years after becoming a monk.

Gregory always felt that the years he spent as a monk in St Andrew's were his happiest and when he was removed from there and taken back into the world again, he looked back on them with considerable regret. He said later:[56]

> I remember with sorrow what I once was in the monastery, how I rose in contemplation above all changeable and decaying things, and thought of nothing but the things of heaven; how my soul though pent within my body, soared beyond its fleshly prison, and looked with longing upon death itself as the means of entering into life. But now, by reason of my pastoral care, I have to bear with secular business, and, after so fair a vision of rest, am fouled with worldly dust. I ponder on what I now endure. I ponder on what I have lost. For lo, now am I shaken by the waves of the great sea, and the ship of the soul is dashed by the storms of a mighty tempest. And when I recall the condition of my former life, I sigh as one who looks back and gazes on the shore he has left behind.

His monastic sojourn was rudely cut short, however. He was summoned by the pope to leave St Andrew's and be ordained as a deacon, thus becoming one of the senior administrators of the Roman church. He was unwilling to leave the monastic life, but it was made clear to him that it was his duty and that the church needed him.[57] Put this way, he was unable to refuse. We do not know for certain which pope it was who summoned him or in which year. The only one of the early authorities to mention it is John the Deacon, who said Benedict I, and in the absence of any evidence to the contrary most later commentators have accepted this, assuming that the year was 578.[58] But Gregory himself in the preface to his *Magna Moralia*[59] implies that he was specifically withdrawn from St Andrew's to become *apocrisiarios* which would mean that the ordaining pope was Pelagius II. Such a dramatic appointment would certainly fit the crisis situation Pelagius found on his election, and, on balance, I prefer the Pelagian hypothesis to the Benedictine.

Pope Benedict died on 30 July 579, while the Lombards were actually besieging Rome. His successor was elected and installed at once without waiting for the customary imperial confirmation to arrive. The new pope, Pelagius II, although born in Rome, was the son of a Goth, Winigild. Although Pelagius II has been eclipsed by his illustrious successor, he seems to have been a vigorous and active man, who was just the sort of ruler the times demanded. He was a fearless upholder of Roman primacy, making a firm statement of it both to the Gallic bishop Aunacharius of Auxerre and to Patriarch John the Faster of Constantinople. He resumed attempts to end the Istrian schism, which Rome had ignored since the Lombard invasion.[60] He devised a plan to alter the method of choosing the primate of Numidia, in the interests of the faith.[61] He began to institute reforms in the lax Sicilian church, on the basis of reports submitted by his rector there, the deacon Servusdei.[62] In particular, he ordered the strict enforcement of subdiaconal celibacy.[63] He undertook a modest building programme, turning his family house into an old people's home, building a church at the cemetery of St Hermes on the via Salaria, re-covering the tomb of St Peter with silver plates, and undertaking extensive repairs and renovations to the basilica of St Laurentius.[64] This last was a great morale-booster, as a contemporary inscription from the basilica recalls, testifying to the 'wondrous faith' which inspired Pelagius to do all this amid the swords of the barbarians.[65] Not least amongst his achievements was the decision to send Gregory as his ambassador (*apocrisiarios*) to Constantinople. It is likely that Gregory left Rome for the imperial capital late in 579, accompanying yet another senatorial embassy aimed at bringing the parlous state of Rome to the attention of the emperor.[66] It was an excellent choice, for as an ex-administrator Gregory was, of course, used to talking to the imperial government in its own language, and he had friends among the circle of émigré Roman aristocrats in Constantinople, who could provide an entrée into important circles. To get help for Rome was one of Pelagius' principal preoccupations, and he sought help from the exarch of Ravenna and the Frankish king as well as from the emperor. If anyone could activate the imperial government, Pelagius reasoned, Gregory could.

Gregory took with him to Constantinople a group of monks from St Andrew's, with whom he lived in common in the Placidia palace, the official residence of the papal *apocrisiarios*. He found their company a great consolation and believed that their decision to go with him had been divinely inspired:[67]

> so that by their example, as by an anchored cable, I might ever be held fast to the tranquil shore of prayer whenever I should be tossed by the ceaseless waves of secular affairs. For to their society I fled as to the haven of the safest port from the rolling swell, and from the waves of earthly occupation; and though that office which withdrew me from the monastery had with the point of its employments extinguished my former tranquillity of life, yet in their society, by means of the appeals of diligent reading, I was animated by feelings of daily renewed regret [*compunctio*].

Gregory established a close circle of clerical friends, who included the Milanese nuncio Constantius, the former patriarch Anastasius of Antioch, and the Spanish bishop Leander of Seville. Leander in particular became a bosom friend. He and Gregory were about the same age, both monks, both from pious aristocratic families, both theologians and exegetes. They shared the same world-view and the same life-style. Although they were never to meet again after Gregory returned to Rome, Gregory cherished the warmest feelings for him always, writing to him in 591: 'the image of your face is impressed forever on my innermost heart.'[68] It was partly at the instigation of Leander and partly at the insistence of his monks that Gregory embarked on his exposition on the Book of Job, a massive work of biblical exegesis, eventually published in thirty-five books as the *Magna Moralia* and dedicated to Leander. While at Constantinople, Gregory delivered the first part of the exposition in the form of lectures, but he had not completed it at the time of his recall and he subsequently wrote the second half back in Rome.[69]

Probably the best-known episode of his stay is his quarrel in 582 with Patriarch Eutychius of Constantinople.[70] The patriarch wrote a treatise on the resurrection in which he stated that at the Last Judgment and the subsequent resurrection our bodies would become insubstantial. Gregory took issue with this, claiming that the resurrection of Christ demonstrated that the body would still be palpable. The quarrel between the two men became so bitter that, as Gregory recorded in the *Magna Moralia*: 'We began to recoil from one another with the greatest animosity.' The situation finally grew so serious that the emperor Tiberius intervened, and in private the three of them set about thrashing out the basic argument. When, eventually, the emperor came down on Gregory's side and decided Eutychius' book should be burned, the strain of the quarrel had taken such a toll on them that on leaving the meeting with the emperor both Gregory and Eutychius collapsed. Gregory was seized by a fever and was seriously ill, but he recovered. Eutychius, however, died, and his ideas died with him, finding no support after his death. Eutychius was succeeded as patriarch by John IV the Faster, a Cappadocian, whose ascetic life-style appealed to Gregory and with whom he became friendly.

But the main purpose of Gregory's residence in the East was neither to study the Bible nor to engage in theological controversy. It was to get help for Rome, and he received urgent promptings from Pelagius to do so.[71] We must surmise that he sought constantly to bring this matter to the emperor's attention. But however sympathetic he might be, Tiberius Constantine simply did not have the troops to spare for Italian adventures. No more did Tiberius' son-in-law, the prudent and conscientious Maurice, who succeeded him on the throne in 582. The best that Maurice could do was to send General Smaragdus west as exarch in the hope that he could organize what scanty defences there were, and to pay large sums of money to the Franks to induce them to attack the Lombards and thus relieve the pressure on the imperial province. Nevertheless Gregory assiduously established friendly relations with many of the greatest people at the imperial court, and these were to stand him in good stead later. He got on particularly well with Maurice's wife, the empress Constantina, his sister Princess Theoctista, and his cousin Bishop Domitian of Melitene. He also established useful contacts with Maurice's brother-in-law, Count Philippicus, the court physician Theodore, and with the generals Narses and Priscus. This all culminated in his standing godfather to Maurice's eldest son, Theodosius, who was born in 584.[72]

It was around 586 that Gregory was recalled to Rome, probably being replaced as *apocrisiarios* by the deacon Honoratus. He resumed his diaconal duties at the Lateran palace, while continuing to reside in St Andrew's. He was now given by Pelagius II the delicate job of negotiating with the Istrian schismatics for the end of the schism.

Pelagius had made his first approach to them *circa* 585, sending Bishop Redemptus, probably of Ferentis, and Abbot Quodvultdeus, with a conciliatory letter to the Istrian bishops, apologizing for not having written before, blaming the political situation.[73] This had been somewhat alleviated by the truce obtained by the exarch Smaragdus, which had permitted Pelagius to establish contact in the hope of extinguishing the schism. He proclaimed his adherence to the four general Councils, tactfully omitting mention of the controversial fifth, and he urged the Istrian bishops to send a deputation to Rome to thrash out the differences between them. The Istrians did send a delegation to Rome, but with a hostile reply which made no concessions and simply rehearsed all the arguments in favour of the 'Three Chapters'. Pelagius replied to them with 'a more in sorrow than in anger' letter, saying that he did not understand what they were talking about.[74] He had shown their envoys the so-called offending passages in the transcript of the Fifth Council and had talked them through them, explaining away any difficulties. He now quoted from Cyprian, Augustine and Leo the Great to convince the Istrians to abandon their position, and he urged them most earnestly to send envoys either to Rome or to Ravenna, where they could discuss their problems with papal representatives. But the Istrian bishops refused even to discuss the matter further and sent an imperious and uncompromising statement of their beliefs to Rome, implying that the pope could take it or leave it. At this point Pelagius handed the matter over to Gregory,[75] who on the pope's behalf wrote a stern reply: 'I have hitherto written to you words full of sweetness and rather by prayer than by admonition have sought to guide you into the right way. . . . But I now see with grieving wonder the lengths to which you dare to proceed, confiding in your own wisdom and I have to confess to myself that my example has been wasted upon you.' This was followed by a detailed point-by-point allegorical and exegetical refutation of their position. But it did no more good than Pelagius' initiative had. Nevertheless Gregory remained convinced of the efficacy of this document and sent copies of it to each of the Istrian bishops individually six years later, inviting them to study it and suggesting they would be so convinced by it that they would return to the faith.[76] The failure of the third letter to move them was probably reported by the pope to the exarch Smaragdus, for he now took action himself, to the horror of the Istrians.

In 588 Smaragdus sailed to the island of Grado and arrested Archbishop Severus, three of his bishops and an elderly *defensor* and transported them under guard to Ravenna. They were held for a year and were eventually forced to hold communion with Archbishop John of Ravenna, who acknowledged the Fifth Council and was in communion with the pope. After this they were permitted to return to Grado, but once there they were boycotted by the people and many of the Istrian bishops. The position was resolved at a synod held at Marano at which Severus and his companions recanted their recantation and were received back into communion by the bishops. Shortly afterwards Smaragdus went mad and was removed to Constantinople, to be replaced as exarch by Romanus.[77] So the schism went on.

The year 589 was one of natural disaster. Phenomenal and disastrous floods devastated north Italy and in the autumn they hit Rome. The Tiber burst its banks, flooding part of the city, destroying the papal granaries and demolishing several ancient churches.[78] In the wake of the floods came the plague, and among its first victims was Pope Pelagius II, who died on 8 February 590. As with the election of Pelagius himself, the papal throne had fallen vacant at a time of crisis and disaster. In the election which followed, the electors (clergy, nobles and people) turned unanimously to Gregory. Although he was the junior deacon by years of service, his reputation was clearly very great. He represented a combination of personal saintliness, as epitomized by his monastic life-style and addiction to fasting, and experience of public business, both as city prefect and *apocrisiarios*. He was the man for the hour. But just as he had fought against being removed from St Andrew's to become deacon, he also fought against elevation to the papal throne, which would end even the possibility of residence at St Andrew's. He wrote to the emperor, asking him to refuse his consent to the election. But the letter was intercepted and destroyed by Gregory's brother, the city prefect Palatinus, who substituted a letter announcing Gregory's unanimous election as Pope Gregory I. The emperor duly confirmed it.[79]

In the meantime, as custom decreed, the archpriest, the archdeacon, the *primicerius notariorum*, and the pope-elect ran the city. Gregory took immediate action to counter the effects of the plague. He preached a sermon in the basilica of St John Lateran declaring the plague to be a punishment from God and calling upon the people to do penance and repent of their sins. He ordered them to pray and sing psalms for three days, and at the end of that time arranged for a massive city-wide litany, in which seven processions set off from seven different churches to meet at the basilica of St Maria Maggiore. Tradition has it that it was 25 April when these processions set out on the spectacular march. The air of the city was filled with the chanting of the *Kyrie Eleison*, the pope continued to preach throughout the march and the people prayed aloud as they went. No less than eighty people dropped dead of the plague during the procession. It was a moving and spectacular demonstration of faith in the face of the horrific depredations of the pestilence: a fitting note on which to open Gregory's reign.[80]

Confirmation of Gregory's election arrived and preparations were made for his consecration. Gregory of Tours, whose deacon Agiulf had been in Rome at the time and had reported on what he had seen, says that Gregory planned to flee, but 'just as Gregory was preparing to go into hiding, he was seized, carried along, brought to the basilica of St Peter, consecrated for his pontifical duties and then given to the city as pope.'[81] This occurred on 3 September 590. From Gregory's reluctance the hagiographers developed a subsequent but unhistorical story in which he persuaded some merchants to smuggle him out of the city in a water jar. He hid for three days in a cave, but on the third night a column of light revealed his hiding place and he was seized by the people and consecrated.[82] But as Gregory of Tours clearly records that Gregory the Great was seized while preparing to escape, this story must be rejected.

There can, however, be no doubting the genuineness of Gregory's reluctance to assume office. His earliest letters are filled with anguished complaints about the harsh necessity which has catapulted him into the throne of St Peter.[83] His mood is best expressed in his letter to Princess Theoctista:

> Under the pretence of being made a bishop, I am brought back into the world; for I am now more in bondage than ever I was as a layman. I have lost the deep joy of my quiet, and while I seem outwardly to have risen, I am inwardly falling down. Wherefore I grieve that I am driven far from the face of my maker. It used to be my daily aim to put myself beyond the world, beyond the flesh; to expel all corporeal forms from the eyes of the soul and to behold in the spirit the blessedness of heaven. . . . For he is lifted up upon the high places of the earth who in his mind despises and tramples down even the things which in the

present world seem high and glorious. But from this height I have been suddenly cast down by the whirlwind of this trial. I have fallen into fear and trembling, for, though I dread nothing for myself, I am greatly afraid for those who are committed to my charge. I am tossed to and fro with the waves of business, I am overwhelmed with its storms. . . . When my business is done, I try to return to my inner thoughts but cannot, for I am driven away by vain tumultuous thoughts. I loved the beauty of the contemplative life . . . but by some judgment, I know not what, I have been wedded . . . to the active life. Behold my most serene lord the Emperor has ordered an ape to become a lion. And a lion indeed, it may be called at his command, but a lion it cannot become. Wherefore he must lay the blame of all my faults and negligences, not on me, but on the kind feeling which led him to commit the ministry of power to so weak an agent.

It took him the winter to recover, but by January 591 he was reconciled to his duty and wrote to Archbishop Natalis of Salona: 'I undertook the burden of this dignity with a sick heart. But seeing that I could not resist the divine decrees, I have recovered a more cheerful frame of mind.'[84] It was in this cheerful frame of mind that he set to work.

Chapter Three

Character and Outlook

What of the man who thus embarked on what would later be regarded as one of the most eminent medieval pontificates? Unusually for this period, we have some idea of what Gregory looked like, for after his death the monks of St Andrew's commissioned a picture of him, which still survived in the ninth century and was described by John the Deacon.[1]

> His figure was of ordinary height, and was well made; his face was a happy medium between the length of his father's and the roundness of his mother's face, so that with a certain roundness it seemed to be of a very comely length, his beard being like his father's, of a rather tawny colour, and of moderate length. He was rather bald, so that in the middle of his forehead he had two small neat curls, twisted towards the right; the crown of his head was round and large, his darkish hair being nicely curled and hanging down as far as the middle of his ear; his forehead was high, his eyebrows long and elevated; his eyes had dark pupils, and though not large were open, under full eyelids; his nose from the starting-point of his curving eyebrows being thin and straight, broader about the middle, slightly aquiline, and expanded at the nostrils; his mouth was red, lips thick and sub-divided; his cheeks were well-shaped, and his chin of a comely prominence from the confines of the jaws; his colour was swarthy and ruddy, not, as it afterwards became, unhealthy looking; his expression was kindly; he had beautiful hands, with tapering fingers, well adapted for writing.

Of Gregory's character and temperament we have the testimony of his contemporaries and his biographers, and his own writings. The first thing that strikes one is his fortitude. For Gregory, pain was an inescapable fact of life. Throughout his pontificate he was almost continuously ill, his suffering increasing as his reign wore on. His

asceticism?
exegetical?

severe asceticism had completely undermined his constitution, ruining his digestive system and leaving him a prey to the summer fevers which infested Rome. His contemporary Gregory of Tours testified to that: 'His abstinence from taking food, his vigils and his prayers, the severity of his fasting, were such that his weakened stomach could scarcely support his frame.'[2]

This asceticism seems to have begun with his adoption of the religious life. By the time he was in Constantinople, the damage had been done and his health was irreparably damaged. Of his time there and of the circumstances of the composition of the *Magna Moralia*, Gregory wrote:[3]

it was recited in a state of sickness; for when the body is worn down by sickness, the mind being also afflicted, our exertions to express ourselves likewise become faint. For many a long year has passed since I have been afflicted by frequent pains in the bowels. The powers of my stomach having broken down, I am continually weak; and I gasp under the weight of successive slow fevers.

It is perhaps small wonder that he chose for his greatest exegetical work to expound the tribulations and patience of Job.

Despite his clear realization of his state of health, Gregory made no attempt to reduce his fasting on his return to Rome, relating that on one occasion in his monastery, he was so sick that he kept fainting and felt himself at death's door, but insisted on fasting at Easter.[4] At another time he was suffering so badly from stomach cramps that the monks forcibly fed him to save his life.[5] John the Deacon tells the charming story of Gregory's mother, Silvia, who became so concerned about her son's state of health that from her religious seclusion she sent him a supply of fresh vegetables on a silver salver.[6] He was unable to write down any of his exegetical lectures during his monastic career because of his state of health.[7]

Despite his weakened state he, perhaps surprisingly, did not contract the plague. But in 591 he was too ill to deliver in person his homilies on the Gospels. They had to be read for him by the papal notaries.[8] He was ill again in July 591 and in August 593, probably with summer fevers.[9] The summer was a particularly bad time for him, as he himself admitted: 'The summer which is not at all good for my body, has for a long time prevented me from speaking to you about the Gospel.'[10] But as his collapse with fever after the Eutychius debate reveals, he was also prone to nervous stress. It may well be that the strain of assuming the pontifical office had something to do with his poor health at this time. Gregory was himself aware of the link between his psychological state and his physical health. Writing to John of Ravenna in July 592, he said: 'at the very moment when Ariulf was killing and beheading at the gates of Rome, I was seized by such melancholy that I fell into a bilious fever.'

But there seems to have been a respite in his decline over the next few years, until in addition to his other complaints he contracted gout, which was to plague him until his death. He wrote to his fellow-sufferer Leander of Seville in August 599: 'I am myself exceedingly worn down by perpetual pain.'[11] In 598 Gregory took to his bed, and he rarely left it thereafter for the rest of his reign. From 598 to 604 his letters are full of the harrowing details of his ailments.[12] In August 599 he told the patricians Italica and Venantius that he daily expected death.[13] In June 600 he wrote to the patriarch Eulogius of Alexandria:[14]

> In the past year I received the letters of your most sweet holiness, but on account of the extreme severity of my sickness I have been unable to reply until now. For, it is now almost two full years that I have been confined to my bed, afflicted by such severe pains of gout that I have been hardly able to rise on feast days for as much as three hours to celebrate mass. And I am soon compelled by severe pain to lie down, that I may be able to bear my torment with intervening groans. The pain I suffer is sometimes modest, and sometimes excessive: but neither so modest as to depart nor so excessive as to kill me.

His condition had seriously deteriorated by February 601, when he wrote to Marinianus of Ravenna:[15]

> It is now a long time since I have been able to rise from bed. For at one time the pain of gout torments me, at another a fire, I know not of what kind, spreads itself with pain through my whole body; and it is generally the case that at one and the same time burning pain racks me, and body and mind fail me. The other great distresses of sickness afflicting me besides what I mentioned, I am unable to recount. This however I may briefly say, that the infection of a noxious humour so drinks me up that

it is pain to me to live, and I anxiously look for death which alone can hope to relieve my groans.

By February 603 he was asking his correspondents to pray that death would release him from his pains and burdens.[16] In December 603 he informed Queen Theodelinda that he was *in extremis*: 'So great an infirmity of gout has held us fast as to render us hardly able to rise, not only for dictating but even for speaking, as your ambassadors are aware.'[17] By March 604 he was dead.

Revealingly, Gregory had, like all permanent invalids, a fascination with medical ailments and their treatment. An entire chapter of the *Regula Pastoralis* is devoted to an allegorical interpretation of them.[18] Medical terms and allusions are scattered through his writings, no doubt culled from the Alexandrian physician who was in permanent attendance on him.[19] He also displayed a touching and deeply felt concern for the ill-health of his friends and colleagues. When Marinianus of Ravenna fell ill and began vomiting blood, Gregory consulted all the available Roman physicians and sent their opinions to Ravenna.[20] When he heard that Eulogius of Alexandria was going blind, he sent him a miracle-working charm.[21] Learning that Bishop Ecclesius of Clusium was ill and suffering from the cold, he sent him a warm cloak.[22] It is also this background which makes entirely plausible the story that Gregory influenced a Lombard ruler in Rome's favour by successfully prescribing a milk diet for him, which cured a stomach ailment.[23]

Gregory's medical record gives extra force to the instructions he included in *Regula Pastoralis* about the admonition of the sick: 'The sick are to be admonished that they feel themselves to be the sons of God in that the scourge of discipline chastises them' and 'The sick are to be admonished to keep the virtue of patience.'[24] Here is the kernel of his views on his own suffering. It is a punishment sent by God for sin and it is to be borne with uncomplaining patience. Here again, the image of Job.

Despite this crippling burden of illness, Gregory worked on tirelessly in every field of activity, from administration to diplomacy, from exegetical to liturgical work, from preaching to ecclesiastical organization. As Paul the Deacon put it: 'He never rested but was always engaged in providing for the interests of the people or writing down some composition worthy of the church or in searching out the secrets of heaven by the grace of contemplation.'[25] Yet there were times when even his unflagging devotion to duty could not sustain him in the face of his debilitation and bodily agony. From November 599 to February 600 no papal letters were dictated, and in the summer of 600 he wrote to both Eulogius of Alexandria and Maximus of Salona apologizing for the long delay in replying to their letters and blaming his ill-health.[26] It took him two years to answer the detailed questions sent to him by Augustine of Canterbury, and that can also certainly be attributed to his health. Despite this, up until the end, he worked on ceaselessly, striving for peace with the Lombards and salvation for Christian souls to ensure that at the last he entered his house justified.

Beyond his fortitude and his industry, we should certainly give pride of place to his humility. One of the keys to his entire world-view is the primacy accorded to humility. He called it 'the mother and guardian of virtues' and 'the root of goodness',[27] and both the *Regula Pastoralis* and *Magna Moralia* are steeped in it. Page after page exhorts the reader to humility. Gregory was to attack the adoption of the title 'Oecumenical Patriarch' by John the Faster on the grounds that it offended against the necessary humility of the episcopal office. He attacked heresy on the grounds that it was based on pride, that the heretics thought they knew better than the Church Fathers about the tenets of the faith.[28] Gregory himself emphasized his commitment to humility by adopting in emulation of Augustine of Hippo the style 'servant of the servants of God' while still only a deacon and retaining it as pope.[29] After his death, it was rapidly incorporated into the official papal titulature.[30]

In line with the general principle of humility is his modesty about his own works. It is clear that they were enthusiastically propagated by disciples like Marinianus of Ravenna and Claudius of Classis. Gregory was opposed to this, partly because it might lead to his being accused of vainglory and partly because he feared that his views might be distorted by the use of faulty texts. Thus when he heard that John of Syracuse was having his writings read out at table in the presence of strangers, he forbade it, suggesting instead the use of ancient church writers.[31] He rejoiced in the prefect Innocent of Africa's request for a copy of the *Magna Moralia* but suggested that he would be better off reading Augustine.[32] He made a similar suggestion to Marinianus of Ravenna when he requested a copy of the *Homilies on Ezekiel*.[33] He also objected to Marinianus having the *Magna Moralia* read out at vigils, because it was controversial, and suggested the non-controversial *Commentary on the Psalms* instead. He objected to the *apocrisiarios* Anatolius giving the emperor a copy of the *Regula Pastoralis* translated into Greek by Anastasius of Antioch.[34] 'I do not wish while I am alive that what I have said should be readily known to men,' he said. He also called in, after Claudius of Classis' death, his transcription of Gregory's exegetical lectures on the Old Testament so that it might be corrected.[35]

Despite this much-vaunted humility, Gregory could still be waspishly bad-tempered, no doubt as a result of his illness. His harsh words caused much unhappiness to Oportunus, later proposed as bishop of Aprutium, and caused Pretiosus, prior of St Andrew's, to flee from Rome and seek refuge with his former abbot Maximian, now bishop of Syracuse.[36] The exultation with which he greeted the news of the death of the emperor Maurice and his harsh treatment of the dying monk Justus have similarly caused his apologists considerable embarrassment.

Although the memorable pun allegedly uttered by Gregory at the sight of the flaxen-haired Saxon slave boys, *'Non Angli sed Angeli'*, is almost certainly apocryphal, Gregory did have a sense of humour. But it was a bitter, sarcastic sense of humour, which runs scathingly through his correspondence. No one was safe from it. To the emperor he wrote: 'My lords have called me a fool. I must be a fool to stay here and endure what I do amid the swords of the Lombards.'[37] To the patriarch John of Constantinople he wrote: 'Has all your fasting gone to your head, so that you are no longer able to tell the truth?'[38] Writing to criticize the excessive feasting of Natalis of Salona, he said: 'In defence of your feasts, you mention the feast of Abraham in which by the testimony of the Holy Scripture he is said to have entertained three angels. In view of this, we will not criticize you for feasting, so long as you entertain angels.'[39]

He also endearingly admitted to a weakness for gossip:[40]

Because of my position I am often brought into contact with secular persons, and must needs relax a little the guard I hold over my tongue. For if I maintain a position of assiduous aloofness, I know that the weaker ones will shun me, and then I will never be able to draw them on to the end I wish them to reach. And so it happens that often I listen patiently to their small-talk. But because I too am a weak creature, being slowly drawn into this talk, I soon find myself enjoying the gossip to which at first I lent an unwilling ear – and so I end by wallowing where I had first dreaded to fall.

By temperament Gregory was a conservative, an authoritarian and a legalist, an old-fashioned Roman of the best kind, public servant and paterfamilias. This image is stamped on everything he did, but more subtly it reveals the deep intertwining of *Christianitas* and *Romanitas*. There is his strict insistence on justice for all, even the Jews. Of the Jews he wrote: 'Just as permission should not be given to the Jews to do anything in the synagogues beyond what is permitted by the law, so they should not sustain any prejudice in the exercise of what is conceded to them by the law.'[41] The Christian foundation of his thinking is indicated by his command to the Sicilian rector Peter: 'Restore everything that has been unjustly taken away, knowing that you will earn great profit for me, if you heap up for me a reward in heaven rather than earthly riches.'[42] His conservatism, with its root in both an ingrained Romanism and a healthy Western Catholic suspicion of the Greeks, can be seen in his indignant rejection of the rumour that Rome had adopted Byzantine liturgical practices.[43]

Both Christian and Roman roots can also be seen in his belief in the maintenance of discipline. 'Since it is proper to restrain men from illicit deeds by discipline and salubriously to check excesses, the punishment system must studiously be preserved. For if it is neglected, everything will fall into confusion, with one man destroying what another has built up by observing it.'[44] This view extended from the church and society in general to the family, as indicated by the cautionary tale in the *Dialogues* which castigates the permissive parent. The five-year-old son of a notable Roman, who had been spoiled rotten by his father and was given to swearing like a trooper, contracted the plague in 590. After blaspheming God in his final agonies, he died crying out, 'Blackamoors are coming to take me away.' The blackamoors were, of course, the imps of Hell, dragging his soul away to eternal torment.[45] So perish all naughty children. But Gregory's *Romanitas* and *Christianitas* were far more than merely a matter of personal temperament and outlook; they constituted an entire philosophy of life governing his views on church, state, and Christian society. It is to this that we turn next.

Chapter Four

Gregory's World-View

It is clear that Gregory's commitment to his faith, his *Christianitas*, was total and coloured everything he did and said. But second only to this *Christianitas*, and closely linked to it, was his *Romanitas*. His *Romanitas* was both of the city and of the Empire. It was not just a sentimental local patriotism, it was also devotion to an ideal. Gregory loved the crumbling, depopulated, fever-ridden city, where all about him were the reminders of both the Christian and the imperial past. Rome was the city of the Caesars and of the Apostles, whose world-views intertwined to form the *Sancta Respublica*, the Holy Empire whose twin characteristics were its *Romanitas* and its *Christianitas*. Rome, although it had long ceased to be the capital, symbolized this mystical fusion. It was the city of churches and basilicas, renowned throughout the Christian world, of the Lateran and the Vatican, of the wonder-working tombs and relics of countless saints and martyrs, whose blood had cemented the Christian faith into the fabric of the pagan Empire. But it was also the city of the Forum, the Colosseum and the half-empty Palatine palace, where as pope Gregory presided over the installation of the sacred images of the emperor and the empress in the chapel of St Caesarius, the symbol of their invisible presence in the city which had given the Empire its name.[1]

To Rome, then, as city and as Empire, Gregory felt a fundamental devotion. He was aware of Rome's decline, poetically comparing the city to an old eagle that had lost its plumage and declaring sadly: 'See to what straits Rome, once mistress of the world, is reduced.'[2] Yet he wrote impatiently to his old friend the patrician Rusticiana, who had emigrated to Constantinople and could on no account be persuaded to return to Italy: 'How anyone can be so entranced by Constantinople and so forgetful of Rome I cannot understand.'[3] Despite his own sojourn in the imperial capital, Gregory clearly had no understanding of the sort of mentality which could prefer its splendour and comforts and power to the dubious privilege of living in the historic if rundown city of Caesar and St Peter.

His love of Rome and the Roman Empire was, however, coloured by an essentially Latin patriotism, and this may have had something to do with his refusal to learn Greek. For he wrote on one occasion to a correspondent in Constantinople: 'Please give my regards to Dominica. I have not answered her because she wrote to me in Greek, even though she is Latin.'[4] This suggests that he regarded Greek as an inferior language – a view that was an outgrowth of a more general standpoint by which, as Caspar has said, Gregory regarded Greek culture as 'foreign, even objectionable'.[5] From time to time a deep mistrust of the slipperiness, trickery and unreliability of the Greeks, almost amounting to racial prejudice, creeps into Gregory's writings. This was particularly the case in matters relating to the faith. He informed Count Narses that Greek copies of the acts of the Council of Ephesus were untrustworthy because of interpolation, whereas the Latin versions were naturally correct.[6] He denounced John the Faster's assumption of the 'Oecumenical Patriarch' title as being in a reprehensible tradition of Byzantine heresies: 'We know for a fact that many bishops of Constantinople have fallen into the whirlpool of heresy and have become not only heretics but heresiarchs.'[7] The same controversy caused his resentment at the Italian situation to boil over too: 'Since we can in no way be defended by [the Greeks] from the swords of our enemies, since for our love of the Empire we have lost silver and gold, slaves and raiment, it is too disgraceful that through them we should lose the Faith also. But to assent to that wicked word is nothing more or less than to lose the Faith.'[8]

But this mistrust of the Greeks as a race did not diminish Gregory's devotion to the Empire and the emperor as concepts, as we shall see. Unquestionably, however, the single factor which dominated and shaped every aspect of his thought on matters social, political, theological and ecclesiastical was the imminence of the end of the world. This was not a theoretical belief but a practical belief, conditioned by his personal experience. Everything he saw about him convinced him. The plague, the Lombard invasions, the physical decay of Rome, these were the signs that the Bible had foretold. 'The world grows old and hoary and hastens to approaching death,' he declared.[9] His writings abound in references to this belief.[10] For instance, he wrote to King Aethelbert of Kent:[11]

We find in the Holy Scriptures from the words of the Almighty
Lord that the end of this present world is at hand and the
kingdom of the saints, which is everlasting, is about to come.
But as the end of the world approaches, many things occur
which were not seen before, namely changes in the air and
terrors from heaven, and tempests out of the order of the
seasons, wars, famines, plagues, earthquakes in several places
. . . these signs of the end of the world are sent before, for this
reason, that we may be solicitous of our souls, look to the hour
of death and may be found prepared with good works to meet
our judge.

To the Milanese clergy, he wrote:[12]

Behold all the things of this world, which we used to hear from
the Bible were doomed to perish, we see now destroyed. Cities
are overthrown, fortresses are razed, churches are destroyed;
and no tiller of the ground inhabits our land any more. Among
the few of us who are left the sword of man rages without cease
along with the calamities which smite us from above. Thus we
see before our very eyes the evils which we long ago heard
should come upon the world. . . . In the passing away of all
things we ought to take thought how all that we have loved was
nothing. View therefore with anxious heart the approaching day
of the eternal judge, and by repenting anticipate its terrors.
Wash away with tears the stains of all your transgressions. Allay
by temporal lamentations the wrath that hangs over you
eternally. For our loving creator when he shall come to
judgment will comfort us with all the greater favour as He sees
now that we are punishing ourselves for our own
transgressions.[13]

The consequences for his thought of this magnificently apocalyptic
vision were profound. The imminent end of the world dominated
Gregory's thinking, and his writings are informed by the urgent
necessity to prepare for this. As Claude Dagens has observed: 'It is
not necessary to search his work for a philosophy of history, a
theology of the last days or a methodical reflection on his eschatol-
ogy, but simply the expression of his convictions with regard to the
end of the world and the responsibilities of the church attendant
upon the return of Christ and the arrival of His kingdom.'[14]

The central core of Gregory's thought is the *cúra animarum*, the preparation of souls for the Second Coming. This preparation involved the creation of a pastoral episcopate, trained in preaching and teaching: hence the composition of the *Regula Pastoralis*. It involved a programme of missionary activity to win over heathens and heretics to the faith in time for the end: hence the missions to England and Sardinia. It involved the articulation of the best way a Christian could live to reach the perfect state: hence the writing of the *Dialogues*, the *Magna Moralia*, and the *Homilies*.

By setting the missionary activity of Gregory in the context of his thought, we can give it a new dimension and settle once and for all the controversy about its aim and purpose. Some have argued that in propagating the English mission in particular Gregory was seeking to escape from the 'caesaropapism' of the Byzantine Empire and to create an alternative power base in the barbarian West, united in Christian faith under papal Rome. This view is wholly at odds with Gregory's fundamental eschatological position. His aim was purely and simply to win as many souls as possible for Christ before the end of the world and had no jurisdictional ulterior motive.

'With the end of the present world approaching', Gregory wrote, 'The Lord consoles the grief of Holy Church by a great gathering in of souls.'[15] The *Homilies on Ezekiel* constitute an extended lamentation over the destruction of Rome and the way it should be responded to. It is clear that for him Rome equalled civilization, and its decline was a paradigm of the approaching end of civilization. Thus his missionary activity was a logical extension of his concept of a pastoral episcopate. He had a picture of an *ordo praedicatorum*, a school of evangelists as it were: 'It is certain that evangelists and teachers existed in the past but they survive still today, with God's help, because we know that daily unbelieving people are brought to the faith and the faithful are educated in right behaviour by the teachers.'[16]

Although he was steeped in the Church Fathers, at least those available in Latin and Latin translation, his views stemmed principally from his personal experience: as monk and mystic, who had meditated on the best way to reach God; as preacher and moralist, who aimed to convert as many as possible to the best sort of Christian life; and as patriotic Roman, who had lived through and drawn conclusions from the decline of Rome. Gregory believed sincerely in the dictum 'Practise what you preach.' He wrote approvingly of St

Benedict: 'That saint was incapable of teaching a way of life that he did not practise', and that statement can confidently be applied to Gregory himself.[17]

The true Christian life, then, meant the search for God. It began with 'the grace of conversion'. This does not mean conversion to Christianity from paganism so much as the conversion from a secular life to a truly spiritual existence. Gregory had experienced the painful process himself and was surely speaking from that experience when he wrote: 'There are in truth three states of the converted: the beginning, the middle and the perfection. But in this beginning, they experience the charms of sweetness, the mid-time the contests of temptation but in the close the plenitude of perfection.'[18]

Once true conversion had been achieved, one adopted a life-style of humility, personal and intellectual, as the next step on the way of God. Gregory said: 'They that in Holy Church are truly humble and truly instructed are taught about the heavenly mysteries, both some things when viewed to understand, and some things not understood to reverence, so that what they understand they may hold in reverence, and what they do not as yet understand, they may look forward to with humility.'[19]

The search is constant and involves the setting aside of acquired worldly knowledge. 'It is perfect wisdom to know all things and yet in a certain way to be ignorant of one's knowledge; by which, though we already know the precepts of God, though we are now weighing with anxious attention the power of His words, though we are doing those things which we believe we have understood; yet we still know not with what strictness of examination these deeds will hereafter be inquired into, nor do we as yet behold the face of God nor see His hidden causes.' More succinctly, he encapsulated this state of mind in his description of St Benedict as 'knowingly ignorant and wisely unlearned'.[20] This again put into perspective Gregory's attitude to secular learning. It is inferior to the Bible and the Church Fathers, but not without value if put to the service of the search.

The sort of spiritual life a good Christian should lead involved good works, the mortification of the flesh (self-denial, self-discipline, asceticism), but at the top of the tree of knowledge comes contemplation. Gregory was one of the great Western mystics, a fervent believer in contemplation as the best and purest way of reaching the eternal truth. He devoted the whole of one of his sermons to its importance, saying: 'The sweetness of contemplation is worthy of love exceedingly, for it carries away the soul above itself, it opens out things heavenly, and shows that things earthly are to be despised: it reveals things spiritual to the eyes of the mind, and hides things bodily.'[21]

Dom Cuthbert Butler has summed up Gregory's view of mysticism as expounded in his writings: 'It is a struggle wherein the mind disengages itself from the things of this world and fixes its attention wholly on spiritual things and thereby raises itself above itself, and by dint of a great effort mounts up to a momentary perception of "unencompassed light", as through a chink; and then, it sinks back wearied to its normal state, to recuperate its spiritual strength by exercising the works of the active life, till in due time it can again brace itself for the effort of another act of contemplation.'[22]

This form of mysticism involved neither visions nor revelations, but simply a bid to liberate the mind from the flesh. Its results were self-knowledge, humility and the conquest of the flesh. Its rationale was 'the more that holy men advance in contemplation, the more they despise what they are and know themselves to be nothing or next to nothing.'[23] Those who had mastered the true Christian life by these methods achieved spiritual power. The outward sign of this spiritual power was miracles, the power of God manifested through holy men in order to encourage conversion. To publicize these Gregory compiled his *Dialogues* and, significantly, sent a copy to the Lombard queen Theodelinda, who, although Catholic, was a supporter of the 'Three Chapters' schismatics.[24] It is also the reason why Gregory rejoiced in the performance of miracles by Augustine of Canterbury in England, as an important boost to the evangelizing mission.[25]

Obviously the best way of achieving the conditions in which this truly spiritual life could be attained was to withdraw from the world, preferably to a monastery. Gregory declared after becoming pope that while in his monastery, he was able to keep his mind continually stretched by prayer.[26] He expanded on this in the preface to the *Dialogues*: 'My sad mind, labouring under the soreness of its engagements, remembers how it went with me formerly in the monastery, how all perishable things were beneath it, how it rose above all that was transitory and though still in the body, went out in contemplation beyond the bars of the flesh.'[27]

Yet for all this devotion to the monastic life, Gregory was withdrawn from it and plunged into a public life of enormous complexity as pope. This created a deep tension within him, reviving the similar pull of contrary emotions he had experienced when first contemplating leaving the world. It is absolutely characteristic of him that he should have sought to articulate and resolve this tension through his writings.

He defined the two lives as the *vita activa* and the *vita contemplativa* describing them in detail:[28]

There are two lives in which Almighty God by his holy word instructs: the active and contemplative. The active life is: to give bread to the hungry, to teach the ignorant the word of wisdom, to correct the erring, to recall to the path of humility our neighbour when he wakes proud, to tend the sick, to dispense to all what they need and to provide those entrusted to us with the means of subsistence. But the contemplative life is to retain indeed with all one's mind the love of God and neighbour, but to rest from exterior action and cleave only to the desire of the maker, that the mind may now take no pleasure in doing anything, but having spurned all cares, may be aglow to see the face of the Creator: so that it already knows how to bear with sorrow the burden of the corruptible flesh, and with all its desires to seek to join the hymn-singing choir of angels, to mingle with the heavenly citizens, and to rejoice in its everlasting corruption in the sight of God.

The *Regula Pastoralis* was in large part devoted to describing how to reconcile the two types of life. He came to the conclusion eventually that while the contemplative life was the better and more desirable of the two, the active life was unavoidable, and indeed necessary in order to serve one's fellow man. Christ had embodied both, and engagement in the active life against one's innate desire for the ideal and perfect contemplative life was, in fact, a necessary subjugation of self, a demonstration of that all-important humility. There could be no better exemplar of the two lives than Gregory himself, but he would have been less than human had he not from time to time mourned the fact that so much of his time must be given over to the active at the expense of the contemplative.

In spiritual terms, the end of the world was a powerful stimulus to the teaching, preaching and practising of the true Christian life, whether it was the pure contemplative ideal or the sometimes necessary mixture of the active and contemplative. But the end of the world also influenced his social thought.

Not surprisingly, Gregory's social thought involved no concepts of egalitarianism or democracy. It was firmly rooted in Pauline precepts about the acceptance of secular social structure and the authority of lay rulers. Here again *Romanitas* and *Christianitas* reinforced each other. This is exemplified in Gregory's instructions to bishops about the teaching of slaves and masters:[29]

> Slaves must be admonished in one way; masters in another: the slaves, so that they may regard at all times the lowliness of their condition, but masters in such a manner that they be not unmindful of their own natures, in which, equally with slaves, they have been created. Slaves are to be admonished that they despise not their masters, lest they offend God if by behaving themselves proudly they gainsay his ordinance. Masters too are to be admonished that they are proud against God with respect to His gift, if they do not acknowledge those whom they hold in subjection by reason of their condition to be their equals by reason of their community of nature. The former are to be admonished to know themselves to be the servants of the masters: the latter to be admonished to acknowledge themselves to be the fellow-servants of servants.

This says it all. Everyone in society should observe a proper humility, servants remembering that they are servants of their masters, masters remembering that they are servants of God. All men were equal by nature, but in society they had differences of status which should be observed, since they were approved by God. 'Nature begets all men equal but by reason of their varying merits, a mysterious dispensation sets some beneath others. This diversity in condition, which is due to sin, is rightly ordained by the judgment of God; that whereas every man does not walk through life in like manner, one should be governed by another.'[30] In lay life, then, as in the church, there was a hierarchy, but over both was God.

Gregory was perfectly happy to free slaves, particularly if they wished to enter the church. Indeed, his letter of manumission contains the high-sounding statement: 'It is a salutary deed if men whom nature originally produced free and whom the law of nations has subjected to the yoke of slavery, be restored by the benefit of manumission to the liberty in which they were born.'[31] This was not a general principle, however. Freedom may have been a fact of nature, but slavery was a fact of life. Both canon and civil law forbade slaves to be ordained as clerics or to enter monasteries without permission of their masters. The Roman church and the monasteries maintained large staffs of slaves. The Roman church purchased slaves, and the pope regularly made gifts of slaves to his friends.[32] The pope also regularly ordered runaway slaves returned to their masters.[33] At a time of social turmoil, it was essential that the prevailing social structure be maintained, lest its collapse lead to chaos. But its maintenance, Gregory thought, should be seasoned with humility and Christian charity.

Just as the class system was the will of God, so too was kingship. Lay rulers were to be obeyed, even if evil. 'For indeed the deeds of superiors are not to be criticized, even if they are rightly judged to be worthy of blame. . . . For when we offend against those who are set over us, we offend against the ordinance of Him who set them over us.'[34] There were strong moral reasons for this: 'Let no one who suffers such a ruler, blame him whom he suffers: because his being subject to the power of the wicked ruler is doubtless of his own deserving. Let him therefore rather blame the fault of his own evil-doing than the injustice of the ruler.'[35] Indeed, Gregory went on to say that good rulers might become evil, in order to punish their subjects for their sins on behalf of God. 'But even if the conduct of rulers is justly blamed, yet it is the duty of subjects to pay them respect even when they displease them.'[36]

There was a practical as well as a theoretical justification for Gregory's endorsement of secular hierarchy. He placed great reliance on good relations with government officials, aristocrats and military commanders in the carrying out of his duties. He made a point of commending his rectors to the local powers, be they Byzantine governors in Africa and Dalmatia or Frankish kings and queens in Gaul. He gave Peter, the rector of Sicily, specific instructions on how to behave towards the Sicilian praetor, and these probably represent Gregory's general view of relations between ecclesiastical and secular functionaries: 'Let noble laymen and the glorious praetor love you for your humility, not dread you for your pride. And yet, turn your humility at once into exaltation, so as to be always submissive to them when they do well and opposed to them when they do evil.'[37] In its subtle blend of personal humility, hierarchic respectfulness and churchly duty, this is a characteristically Gregorian precept. But Gregory was far from being blind to the ways of the world, and also instructed his rector to make small financial gifts to the imperial recruiting officers (*scribones*) and the officials of the praetor to render them well disposed towards papal estates and personnel.[38]

Just as he supported the maintenance of secular hierarchy, Gregory believed in the preservation of ecclesiastical hierarchy for the same reasons and by the same methods. When Julian the *Scribo* interceded with him for the excommunicate archbishop Maximus of Salona, he replied:[39]

> If in secular offices order and discipline handed down by our ancestors is observed, who may bear to see ecclesiastical order confounded by bold presumption or disregard such reports and postpone their emendation by improperly condoning them?. . .
> For if, which God forbid, we neglect ecclesiastical solicitude and vigour, indolence destroys discipline and harm will be done to the souls of the faithful when they see such examples set them by their pastors.

This brings us to the much-discussed question of the papal primacy, and while Gregory's implementation of it will be examined in detail later, it is necessary to place it in the context of his thought here. The highest ecclesiastical rank was that of patriarch, and there were in the Christian church five patriarchates – Constantinople, Antioch, Alexandria, Jerusalem and Rome. Of these Rome had early on been accorded seniority or primacy. Papal primacy derived initially from the fact that the papacy was sited in the capital of the Roman Empire, on the basic principle of Christian church organization that secular status determined ecclesiastical. But this justification for papal primacy was undermined when the imperial capital in the West shifted first to Milan and then to Ravenna, and, finally and more serious still, when the Western Empire ceased to exist and Constantinople became the sole and indisputable imperial capital. To provide a justification for the continuance of Roman primacy the papacy was forced to develop an alternative basis for it. This new basis, articulated in the fourth and fifth centuries, stressed its Petrine and apostolic foundation, the eminence of St Peter as the Prince of Apostles, the granting to him of the 'keys of the Kingdom', and the gospel texts in which Christ committed the care of the church to him.[40]

From that time on the cult of St Peter was sedulously advanced *allay?*

until by the time of Gregory people actually talked of 'visiting Peter' when they meant 'going to Rome'. Peter's pre-eminence, and with it of course that of the papacy he had founded, was stressed in the liturgy, by pilgrimages to his tomb, which was beautified by successive popes, in the reverent celebration of his feast day, in the invocation by popes of his protection for Rome from Goths and Lombards, in the special efficacy of his relics. The evidence for it can be found in such diverse sources as the prayers in the 'Leonine' sacramentary, in the Vatican inscriptions, and in Arator's epic poem *De Actibus Apostolorum*, of which Peter is the undoubted hero and which was formally recited to the faithful in the church of St Peter ad Vincula.[41]

This inevitably brought Rome into conflict with Constantinople, which under the old dispensation would have had the primacy. Indeed, the Council of Chalcedon decreed that Constantinople, the new Rome, should enjoy equality of status with old Rome, a canon rejected by Pope Leo the Great. However, Justinian settled the dispute when he decreed that Constantinople had second place in the hierarchy after Rome. In fact, Constantinople never sought a position superior to Rome. Petrinity and apostolicity as the basis of Rome's primacy were rapidly accepted by the Eastern church and by the emperor. But the accepting of Rome's primacy as a matter of respect is one thing, its practical implementation quite another.

What did the primacy mean in practical terms? Firstly, Rome saw the primacy as the means of defending the faith, as defined by the Council of Chalcedon on the basis of Pope Leo's *Tome*. The papacy fervently resisted any attempts to tamper with the Chalcedonian settlement, at one stage suspending relations with the church of Constantinople for thirty-five years (the Acacian schism) when the settlement came under threat. This view of the primacy was one Gregory shared. His justification of the need for an apostolic vicar to head the Gallic hierarchy can equally well be applied to himself as the head of the Catholic hierarchy: 'so that the integrity of the Catholic Faith, that is, of the four synods, may be preserved under the protection of God with attentive devotion, and that, if any contention should by chance arise among our brethren and fellow priests, he may always allay it by the vigour of his authority with discreet moderation.'[42]

Secondly, Rome tried to get acceptance of the principle of ultimate papal jurisdiction in ecclesiastical cases. The Council of Sardica decreed in 343 that Rome should enjoy such appellate jurisdiction, and in the imperial West there was a good chance of gaining acceptance for the principle. For Rome was the only Western patriarchate, and its claims gained the backing of successive Western emperors, culminating in the edict of the emperor Valentinian III (445) which stated that 'nothing should be done against or without the authority of the Roman church.'

The popes stressed their jurisdictional rights constantly in the West. Pope Innocent I (401–17) declared that Roman authority must prevail since 'clearly in all Italy, the Gauls, the Spains, Africa and Sicily, and the islands between, no one has instituted churches except those whom the venerable apostle Peter or his successors constituted bishops'.[43] To make this authority effective the papacy established vicariates in the metropolitan sees of Gaul, Spain and Illyricum. Historically, then, with Rome's primacy acknowledged in the Western Empire and with no other see able to challenge her patriarchal status, her position seemed secure. But the Roman Empire in the West collapsed, and the barbarian kingdoms which replaced it were Arian and unconcerned with the rights of the Catholic hierarchy. Some of these regimes even persecuted the Catholics. In due course Justinian restored imperial rule to Africa, Italy and part of Spain; and in Gaul and later in Spain the barbarian kings renounced their Arianism and converted to Catholicism. Where did all this leave papal primacy? The evidence suggests that the barbarian rulers and the Catholic hierarchies of the barbarian states accorded Rome a cautious respect, but that it was little more than lip-service. For there must sometimes have been the suspicion that the Roman church, situated as it was in the imperial province of Italy, was not always politically disinterested in its dealings with the barbarian states.

There is only one known case of an appeal from Merovingian Gaul to Rome in the sixth century, and that came in the reign of Pope John III. Its outcome can hardly have given anyone in Gaul confidence in the efficacy of the system. Two brothers, Salonius and Sagittarius, were made bishops of Embrun and Gap, respectively. As Gregory of Tours records: 'They were no sooner raised to the episcopate than their new power went to their heads: with a sort of insane fury they began to disgrace themselves in peculation, physical assaults, murders, adultery and every crime in the calendar.' As a result a council of bishops deposed them, but they petitioned King Guntram of Burgundy for leave to appeal to Rome. Guntram, who had a soft spot

Simony

for them, agreed. They appeared before Pope John claiming wrongful deposition, and John ordered them restored to their sees, an order which Guntram promptly carried out.[44]

Pelagius II stressed the primacy when seeking help for beleaguered Rome from Bishop Aunacharius of Auxerre: 'it would have been more seemly if you other limbs of the Catholic church, bound together in one body under the direction of one head, had hurried with all your strength to aid our peace and our contentment in the unity of the Holy Spirit.'[45] But it was to no avail. Realistically Gregory set himself very limited objectives, and ones entirely within the bounds of tradition: the conversion of heathen and heretic, the elimination of ecclesiastical abuses, particularly simony, and the maintenance within the imperial provinces of Rome's appellate jurisdiction. But it is interesting to note that when Gregory sent a copy of the imperial law restricting entry into monasteries to the metropolitans who were 'within his writ', it went only to bishops in Italy, Sicily, Sardinia, Greece and the Balkans, conspicuously omitting Africa, and suggesting that even there within the Empire his authority was minimal.[46]

Gregory's attitude to other churches both Eastern and Western is probably best summed up in his letter to Archbishop Dominicus of Carthage:[47]

> Just as we defend our own rights, so we preserve those of the several churches. I do not through partiality grant to any church more than it deserves, nor do I through ambition derogate from any what belongs to it by right. Rather I desire to honour my brethren in every way, and study that each may be advanced in dignity, so long as there be no just opposition to it on the part of another.

The jurisdictional authority of Rome was frequently stressed by the popes in their dealings with the Eastern church – partly, I suspect, to remind it not to aspire to superiority. Pope Gelasius, for instance, declared firmly: 'the voice of Christ, the traditions of the elders and the authority of the canons confirms that [Rome] may always judge the whole church.'[48] Whether or not this jurisdictional right was implemented, however, seems to have depended on personality and circumstance. Its implementation was certainly rare, and generally occurred only when disgruntled clerical defendants turned to Rome as a desperate last resort.[49]

primary ?

humility
exactly .

As to Gregory's view of the papacy, there can be no doubt that he claimed the primacy in the same terms and to the same extent as his predecessors. He expounded it with absolute clarity and fidelity to doctrine when writing to the emperor Maurice in 595:[50]

> It is clear to all those who know the Gospels that by the Holy Voice of the Lord the care of the whole church has been committed to the blessed Peter, Prince of Apostles. Behold he received the keys of the kingdom of heaven; to him was given the power of binding and loosing; to him the care and principate [*cura et principatus*] of the whole church was committed.

Throughout his correspondence, the apostolic foundation and Petrine commission of the papacy are stressed, and the primacy is spelled out again and again: 'it is certain that by God's will the apostolic see is set over all the churches'; 'who can doubt that the church of Constantinople is subject to the apostolic see'; and so forth.[51]

Gregory's words and actions have given rise to two diametrically opposed interpretations of his world-view, both of which must be examined. The first is that Gregory promoted the idea of papal monarchy, particularly in his dealings with the West.[52] But this would have been at odds with everything in which he believed. Gregory's use of the term *principatus* to describe the primacy did not arise from his arrogation of a princely role for the pope. It derived from his stress on St Peter's role as the chief apostle. Gregory regularly referred to Peter as '*Princeps Apostolorum*' and was the first to do so consistently since Leo the Great. It was Peter's 'principate' which provided the basis for papal primacy. For Gregory, the words were interchangeable.[53] But he was at pains to stress the humility of both Peter and his successors, the popes. 'He who was first in the power of the apostolate was also first in humility,' said Gregory.[54] This principle of humility governed his dealings with kings and bishops in East and West just as it governed his personal philosophy of life. 'Unless the jurisdiction of every single bishop is preserved, what else will result but that ecclesiastical order will be confounded by those who ought to preserve it'; 'I seek no honour which shall detract from the honour belonging to my brethren'; 'as to his saying that he is subject to the Apostolic see, I know of no bishop who is not subject to it when any fault has been committed, but when no fault exacts this submission, all are equal by the law of humility'; 'far be it from me to infringe what the elders have established for my fellow bishops in any church, for I do myself an injury if I confound the rights of my brethren.'[55] It was through humility rather than monarchy, Gregory believed, that the unity of the universal church was preserved.[56]

The other view is that Gregory's failure to gain acceptance of primacy in either East or West (itself a questionable assertion) led him to plan to substitute humility for hierarchy as the basic principle of ecclesiastical organization.[57] The evidence advanced for this view is the constant stress on humility and the argument for a tripartite primacy which Gregory seemed to be advancing in his correspondence with the patriarchs of Antioch and Alexandria.

During the 'Oecumenical Patriarch' controversy, Gregory wrote to Anastasius of Antioch and Eulogius of Alexandria arguing that since Antioch had been founded by St Peter, and Alexandria by a disciple of St Peter, both sees shared in the Petrinity and apostolicity that was Rome's: 'Since then it is the see of one, and one see over which by divine authority three bishops now preside.'[58] This is not a radical new principle, for having made the statement about tripartite Petrinity Gregory subtly qualifies it by creating a hierarchy within it. He says that Peter honoured (*decoravit*) Alexandria by sending his disciple Mark to be bishop there; he strengthened (*firmavit*) Antioch by occupying the see himself there for seven years; but he exalted (*sublimavit*) Rome where he spent his later days and died.[59] The clear implication is that Rome remains pre-eminent even in Petrinity.

There is no reference anywhere else in the vast corpus of Gregory's writings to this idea, and it is more than counterbalanced by his frequent assertions of Roman primacy. Against it also is the vehemence of Gregory's attack on the 'Oecumenical Patriarch' title which he clearly saw as an attack on Roman primacy, and also his successful withdrawal to Rome of the appeal of the Eastern priests John and Athanasius, a concrete manifestation of Rome's appellate jurisdiction. The idea of tripartite Petrinity can therefore be regarded as nothing more than a tactical manoeuvre in the 'Oecumenical Patriarch' controversy to enlist the support of the other Eastern patriarchs by suggesting that like Rome they are in reality superior to Constantinople and that John's title is an insult to them as well as to Rome.

There is also clear evidence in Gregory's writing to contradict the idea that humility was to replace hierarchy. In 595 Gregory conferred the vicariate on Vergilius, archbishop of Arles, and wrote to him justifying the hierarchic pre-eminence he was conferring:[60]

To this end has the provision of divine dispensation appointed that there should be different grades and distinct ranks so that while the inferiors show reverence to the more powerful and the more powerful bestow love on the inferiors, one fabric of concord may ensue from the diversity, and the administration of each office may be properly carried out. Nor indeed could the whole otherwise subsist; unless that is, a great hierarchy of differences kept it together. Indeed, we are taught by the example of the heavenly host that creation cannot be governed or live in a state of absolute equality, since, there being angels and archangels, it is obvious that they are not equal; but in power and rank, as you know, one differs from another. If then among those who are without sin there is evidently this distinction, who of men can refuse to submit himself willingly to this order of things which he knows that even angels obey.

It is clear from this that in the field of hierarchy and jurisdiction Gregory did not so much believe in humility *per se* as humility in the exercise of powers conferred by the Bible, the canons or ecclesiastical tradition. He was also ready to abandon humility if these fundamental traditions or beliefs were challenged.

Although the popes were the primates of the Catholic church, they were also subjects of the Roman Empire, and this involved them in a continuing dilemma which was only resolved with the fall of the exarchate of Ravenna in 751 – how to reconcile the elements of *Christianitas* and *Romanitas* in their position. For the prevailing view of society was of two co-terminous bodies, the Roman Empire and the Christian church, both divinely ordained but with essentially different if complementary spheres of influence. The Christian Roman Empire – the *Sancta Respublica* – represented a fusion of two elements which when in harmony strengthened and unified, and when in disharmony provoked in the papacy a crisis of identity.

It was under Constantine that the role of the emperor in the church was defined. According to the Christian Roman kingship theory, the emperor was responsible to God for the well-being of his subjects, and this included their spiritual well-being. For it was his duty to maintain the unity of the true faith. It was not the emperor's duty to define doctrine, as Constantine himself admitted when he told the Council of Nicaea (313): 'You are bishops for all which is internal to the church, I am bishop for all the external affairs of the church.' The

church, whose ministers also received their power from God, decided
doctrine, and the emperor enforced it. The concrete expression of
this arrangement was the oecumenical councils of the church, convoked and presided over by the emperor but deciding doctrine for
themselves. The emperor's role was to enforce these doctrinal decisions, root out heresy and maintain ecclesiastical discipline. It has
already been indicated that the emperor accepted the pre-eminence
of Rome within the ecclesiastical hierarchy, but it was also the case
that in every other matter aside from doctrine the church, its popes
and patriarchs were subjects of the Roman Empire. But harmony and
working together were the keynotes of the ideal relationship envisaged between the Christian church and the Christian emperor.[61] As
long as pope and emperor were content to maintain the division of
labour, then the relationship worked. But during the fifth and sixth
centuries successive emperors sought to make permanent a radical
departure from it – the alteration of doctrine by imperial edict without
recourse to church councils. It was a policy which was to provoke a
severe crisis in papal–imperial relations. Pope Gelasius summed up
the papal dilemma perfectly when he said: 'As a Roman born, I love,
honour and revere the Roman Emperor, and as a Christian, I desire
that he who has a zeal for God shall have with it an accompanying
knowledge of the truth.'[62] It is a definition Gregory would have
endorsed. There were times when the papacy found it impossible to
reconcile the two elements. But this was none of its own choosing.
It was never the pope, always the emperor who rocked the boat
when he started tampering with the Chalcedonian settlement.
Rome's answer each time was not to attempt to redefine the relationship between church and Empire, but to urge a return to the
previously agreed position, stress the fundamentals of the Constantinian settlement.[63] In Gregory's reign there was no attempt by the
emperor to alter the traditional relationship, and there was no major
heresy to combat in the East. Nevertheless there were times when
Gregory found his *Romanitas* and his *Christianitas* in conflict. But as
a good Roman and a good Christian, he always did his best to
reconcile them.

His basic view of earthly rulers is the oft-quoted passage in the
Regula Pastoralis in which he made it clear that a lay ruler, however
wicked, had to be obeyed.[64] Failure to obey was an insult to God and
would result in the upsetting of the divinely ordained earthly structure. It was a view directly in line with both Pauline and Augustinian

thinking and it was of a piece with Gregory's own belief in hierarchy. That Gregory clearly saw himself as a subject is evidenced by his statement of faith to the emperor:[65]

> He is guilty before Almighty God who is not sincere to his most serene sovereigns in all he says and does. I, the unworthy servant of your piety, in the suggestion which I now offer speak not as a bishop nor as your servant by the law of the state but as your servant in a personal sense, since, my most serene lord, you were my lord before you became the lord of all men. . . . I who thus address my sovereign, what am I but dust and a worm?

In detail Gregory stood by the Constantinian settlement and conceded that the duty of the secular ruler was to protect the church and preserve the unity of the faith. He summarized the emperor's role with perfect clarity in a letter to Maurice:[66]

> My most Religious Lord, who has received his sovereignty from God, besides the other weighty cares of Empire, watches with true spiritual zeal over the preservation of Christian charity among bishops. For he justly and truly considers that no man can exercise his earthly rule aright unless he knows how to deal with things divine and that the peace of the state depends upon the peace of the universal church. And indeed what power of man, what might of fleshly arm, would dare raise a sacrilegious hand against the height of your most Christian Empire, if all the priests strove with one accord, as they should, to win the favour of the Redeemer for you both by their prayers and the goodness of their lives?. . . [God] has inspired my most religious lord to repress external wars by first establishing peace within the church and by deigning to recall the bishops' hearts to concord. This indeed is what I wish and for myself give glad obedience to your most serene commands.

This and the similar statements in Gregory's writings are not empty rhetoric masking a papal desire for emancipation from the Empire or monarchy for Rome; they are clear and positive statements of a deeply held belief. This belief can be seen underpinning both Gregory's words and his actions: the free and whole-hearted acceptance of the duality of the papal identity as primate of the Catholic church and subject of the Roman emperor. It makes nonsense of the idea of a 'Byzantine captivity' of the papacy. For Gregory and the other popes of the imperial period were willing subjects and not unwilling captives of the Roman Empire.

Despite Gregory's clear articulation of his world-view, he was, like all great men, pulled in contrary directions. Through his words and his actions, through the pattern of his life, can be seen running the threads of rival ideals. On a personal level, he was torn between the *vita activa* and the *vita contemplativa*. On the public level, he sometimes found his *Romanitas* and his *Christianitas* in conflict. The unending search for a reconciliation of these differing concepts constitutes the restless core of his being.

Chapter Five

The Gregorian Court Circle

Gregory's personal ethos and style were, as has been demonstrated, profoundly monastic, and on the evidence of John the Deacon he was determined to maintain the same life-style even as pope. He wore simple monastic garb, eschewing pontifical finery.[1] He ate frugally, allowing himself only the luxury of a favourite wine, *cognidium*, a retzina which he had specially imported from Alexandria.[2] John also says that Gregory lived a monastic life in common with his favoured *familia* of monks and clerics in the Lateran palace. Indeed, John goes so far as to say: 'The Roman church in Gregory's time resembled the church as it was under the rule of the Apostles or the church of Alexandria during the episcopate of St Mark.'[3] Later authorities have questioned this on the grounds that it is not explicitly mentioned in contemporary sources, but in fact the circumstantial evidence for John's view is very strong.

We know from Gregory's own testimony that he lived in common with some of the brethren from St Andrew's while he was *apocrisiarios* in Constantinople.[4] He valued their company as 'an anchored cable' by which he was 'kept forever fast to the tranquil shore of prayer, whenever I should be tossed by the ceaseless waves of secular affairs'. Then in 595 Gregory decreed the exclusion of lay attendants from the Lateran palace.[5] 'As a result of neglect a shameful custom has become established, namely that lay servants wait upon the pontiffs of this see, even in the privacy of their chambers. And whereas the life of a bishop ought always to serve as an example to his disciples, the clergy generally know nothing of his private life, which, however, is known to his lay servants.' It was therefore ordered that 'certain persons shall be selected from among the clergy or the monks to attend on the pontiff in his bedchamber, so that the life of the ruler may be witnessed in all its privacy by men who can take example and profit from what they see.' Gregory advised Augustine of Canterbury to live in common with his clergy and in apostolic simplicity.[6] Lest this be dismissed as a piece of special advice to a missionary bishop, we can finally quote a letter Gregory wrote to Bishop Maximian of Syracuse asking for a story for his *Dialogues*.[7] He did so, he said, at the urging of his 'brothers who live familiarly with me' (*'fratres mei qui mecum familiariter vivunt'*). All the indications are, then, that Gregory lived in common with some of his monks in the Lateran palace.

But the implications of this style go beyond personal behaviour and into the wider field of papal administration. From fragments of evidence relating to the reigns of Gregory and his successors, it is clear that Gregory carried his monastic preferences into the field of personnel policy, and that as a result of his activities a rival ecclesiastical power base was created in the Roman church, which constituted a serious challenge to the hitherto unquestioned predominance of the clerical establishment.

First of all we need to establish the membership of the Gregorian court circle, the closely knit group of confidants who shared his ideals and can properly be called Gregorians. The starting point is John the Deacon's statement that Gregory removed from his counsels all laymen and chose only the most prudent clerics as his familiars.[8] John lists eight familiars: four clerics (Peter the Deacon; Aemilianus and Paterius the notaries; and John the *defensor*) and four monks (Maximian, abbot of St Andrew's and later bishop of Syracuse; Marinianus, monk of St Andrew's and later archbishop of Ravenna; Claudius, monk of St Andrew's and later abbot of SS. John and Stephen in Classis; Probus, abbot of SS. Andreas and Lucia in Rome). This list can be checked against the evidence of the Register.

The senior clerical administrative grade was that of deacon, and John tells us that the diaconate 'overflowed with nineteen members' at the time of Gregory's election and that he himself only ordained three new deacons: Boniface, Epiphanius and Florentius.[9] This tallies more or less with the information in the *Liber Pontificalis*, which reveals that twenty-four deacons were created between 561 and 590. The death rate must have been remarkably low for nineteen of them to be surviving in 590. But the fact that according to the *Liber Pontificalis* Gregory only created five deacons as opposed to John III's thirteen in a reign of comparable length, and that Gregory's two immediate successors created none, tends to confirm it.[10] Furthermore, many of the deacons were old men, as Gregory himself revealed when telling the emperor Phocas that he had created a new deacon to fill the vacant office of *apocrisiarios* because all the others were either too old or too busy with other duties.[11]

The *Liber Pontificalis'* record of Gregory's diaconal ordinations is to be preferred to John's, because we know of at least four deacons ordained by Gregory. The one closest to him was undoubtedly Peter, whom he described as 'my most beloved son'. Gregory says of him that he had been a close friend since the earliest days of his youth and a companion in the study of the scriptures.[12] This strongly suggests that Peter had begun his ecclesiastical career as a monk in St Andrew's in the period 574–8 when Gregory was there. It looks as if he left the monastery at the same time as Gregory and entered the clerical administration, for during the reign of Pelagius II he held the rank of *defensor* and undertook a special mission to Ravenna.[13] By the time of Gregory's election to the throne he was a subdeacon and was chosen by the pope to combine the positions of rector and vicar of Sicily, a clear indication of his eminence in the inner circle.

Peter was recalled from Sicily in July 592, but not in disgrace as some commentators have suggested.[14] The conclusion, based on the pope's letters to him and the constant exhortations to do more, that Peter was a weak and unsatisfactory rector, is untenable. The frequency of rebukes is a measure of the scale of the tasks Peter had to perform, and Gregory was able to chide so much because he knew Peter so well. Peter's recall is far from being an admission of failure. His appointment had been something of an emergency measure in the first instance, and after his recall, the patrimony was split into two, indicating that it was by now too big for one man to handle. And far from being disgraced, Peter was commended by the pope for his efforts, allowed to choose the next Syracusan rector, and promoted to the diaconate.[15]

After his return to Rome little more is heard of Peter, but occasional references in the Register suggest that he remained high in papal favour. He is represented by Gregory as his interlocutor in the *Dialogues*, composed in 593–4.[16] He was consulted about the Ravenna *pallium* dispute.[17] In 598 he and the *consiliarius* Theodore were put in charge of a special bureau to deal with the flood of complaints coming in from Sardinia.[18] The last reference to Peter comes in July 599 when Gregory sent a dalmatic to Bishop Aregius of Gap, explaining that he had forgotten the bishop's request until reminded of it by Peter, once again clearly acting as a confidant.[19]

A story preserved by John the Deacon suggests that Peter survived

Gregory.[20] According to John, when the great famine occurred in the year of Gregory's death, a hostile party blamed the lavish generosity of the late pope for the general distress. The fury of the people was roused and they set out to burn Gregory's books. But the deacon Peter, Gregory's *familiarissimus*, intervened to dissuade them, telling the people that these works were directly inspired by God. As proof he asked God to take his life and promptly dropped dead.

How much truth there is in this story it is difficult to say. There certainly was a famine at the time of Gregory's death, and it is plausible enough that there should have been riots, perhaps culminating in an attempt to burn Gregory's books and calmed by the intervention of Peter. If Peter died soon afterwards, then all these events could have been run together to provide an effectively theatrical set piece. However he died, Peter's career can be traced in some detail and provides a fascinating insight into the sort of person Gregory most valued in the inner circle.

Exclusively entrusted to the diaconate under Gregory was the office of *apocrisiarios*, a crucial position whose holders must have enjoyed a high measure of papal confidence. The incumbent *apocrisiarios* on Gregory's election was the deacon Honoratus. He is first addressed in October 590, and the absence of any commendatory letters or any other indication of recent appointment suggests that he was the Pelagian envoy retained.[21] He is probably to be identified with the notary Honoratus, who was sent by Pelagius II to Constantinople in 584 with letters for the then *apocrisiarios*, Gregory.[22] A letter from the Frankish king Childebert, dated the same year, asks Honoratus to use his influence to help the Frankish ambassadors to secure a lasting peace between the Empire and the Franks.[23] This would suggest that Honoratus was not just a messenger, but a figure of some standing. It is not unlikely that on Gregory's recall around 586, Honoratus stayed on or was sent back with the rank of deacon to take over as *apocrisiarios*.

In September 591, the archdeacon Laurentius was deposed and replaced by Honoratus.[24] Some have said that the new archdeacon cannot have been the *apocrisiarios*, because at the time of the deposition he was still in Constantinople. But a letter from Gregory to John the Faster, dated June 595, throws some light on this.[25] Gregory, referring to his predecessor's attitude to the use of the 'Oecumenical Patriarch' title, wrote:

And indeed weighty letters were addressed to your holiness by my predecessor Pelagius of holy memory, in which he annulled the acts of the synod which had been assembled among you in the case of our former brother and fellow bishop Gregory because of that execrable, prideful title and he forbade the archdeacon, whom he had sent according to custom to the threshold of our lords [the emperors], to celebrate the solemnities of the mass with you.

The reference to the trial of Gregory of Antioch dates the events under discussion to 588, and some commentators have assumed that the reference is to the then archdeacon, Laurentius. But given the nature of his duties, which required his presence in Rome, it is manifestly unlikely that Laurentius was *apocrisiarios*. Furthermore if he was referring to Laurentius, Gregory would have called him '*quondam archidiaconus*'. The lack of any such qualification suggests that Gregory was referring to the man who was currently archdeacon but had previously been *apocrisiarios*. If this is so, we must accept that Honoratus was appointed archdeacon *in absentia*. Nothing more is heard of him after his recall to Rome.

Honoratus' successor as *apocrisiarios* was the Tuscan deacon Sabinian, a career cleric who had made his way slowly and steadily up the promotion ladder to reach the diaconate. He was appointed *apocrisiarios* in July 593, received the full blast of the 'Oecumenical Patriarch' controversy, and was recalled in the summer of 597.[26] Nothing more is heard of him until he was elected pope in 604. In 593 he was probably selected for his age and experience. He was not a Gregorian diaconal creation and seems not to have been part of the inner circle.

Sabinian's successor, however, was part of the inner circle. In July 597 Gregory appointed as *apocrisiarios* the deacon Anatolius.[27] He was clearly one of Gregory's most trusted advisers, for it was to him that the newly created post of permanent steward of the papal palace (*vicedominus*) was given in 590, and thereafter he had been consistently at the pope's side.[28] The last letter to Anatolius is dated February 601.[29] By January 602 he was dead, having died at his post in Constantinople.[30]

For the rest of Maurice's reign there was no papal representative in Constantinople, undoubtedly as a result of the bitterness engendered by the 'Oecumenical Patriarch' controversy, in which the emperor had sided with his patriarch. In July 603 Gregory wrote to the new emperor, Phocas, apologizing for the vacancy in the apocrisiariate and explaining that while Maurice lived, everyone had been afraid to go to Constantinople. But now that Maurice was gone, Gregory had promoted to the diaconate the *primicerius defensorum* Boniface and was sending him east as *apocrisiarios*.[31]

Gregory had a high opinion of Boniface, 'well known to me from his longstanding devotion to duty; approved in life, faith and morals'. Something is known of Boniface's earlier career. He first appears in February 591 as a *defensor* sent by Gregory to bear his *synodica* to the patriarch of Constantinople.[32] In March 598 he was appointed *primicerius defensorum*, an office he held until his promotion to the diaconate.[33] How long he remained in Constantinople is not known, but in 607 he was back in Rome and elected to succeed Sabinian as Pope Boniface III.

Besides the *apocrisiarii*, three other deacons appear in the sources, at least two of them personally created by Gregory. The first is Epiphanius, who first appears in May 595 when Gregory writes to the Isaurian abbot Elias to inform him that, as requested, he has admitted his 'son' (i.e. a favourite monk) to holy orders and made him a deacon;[34] but he cannot send him back to Isauria, because a man must remain in the church in which he is ordained. It seems likely that it was Epiphanius' monastic vocation that encouraged Gregory to add the Isaurian visitor to his diaconate. Thereafter he appears in the Register only twice – once, interestingly, writing on Gregory's behalf to Eulogius of Alexandria, presumably because, unlike Gregory, he could write Greek.[35]

The second deacon is Florentius, to whom there is one reference. In 598 the deacon Florentius is running a hostel in Rome, the *xenodochium Aniciorum*.[36] The evidence points to this Florentius being the same as the subdeacon Florentius who fled from Naples in 592 to avoid ordination as bishop, after having been sent there as Gregorian patronage nominee.[37] That he returned to Rome is implied in a story, told in the *Dialogues*, of the Valerian priest Florentius, who tried to poison St Benedict of Nursia and is described as '*avus nostri subdiaconi Florentii*'.[38] Since the *Dialogues* were written in 593–4, this implies that Florentius was alive and well and living in Rome. So there is a subdeacon Florentius in Rome in 593 and a deacon Florentius in Rome in 598. John the Deacon's statement that Gregory ordained a Florentius as deacon ties the two together perfectly. His flight from

Naples cannot have been held against him, for conditions there were particularly fraught. He was clearly a trusted man or he would not have been selected for the bishopric of Naples in the first place.

While the deacon Peter was Gregory's principal confidant, the pope's executive lieutenant was unquestionably the deacon Boniface, not to be confused with the *apocrisiarios* of the same name. In the *Dialogues*, Gregory described the Valerian priest Stephen as *'huius nostri Bonifacii diaconi et dispensatoris ecclesiae agnatione proximus'*.[39] *Dispensator*, literally 'paymaster', probably means that Boniface was the papal treasurer, and he can be seen acting in this capacity in November 598 when Gregory orders Bishop John of Syracuse to pay Bishop Basilius of Capua, then in Sicily, ten pounds of gold, an equivalent sum having been handed in to Boniface in Rome for this purpose by the patricians Flora and Cethegus.[40] But the three other references to Boniface in the Register show him to have acted also as a kind of 'secretary of state', combining the duties with those of treasurer – a combination which made him both highly experienced and highly influential, as reflected in his election as pope in 608 to succeed Boniface III. In June 591 Gregory replies to a letter from the Corsican rector Symmachus, the details of which had been communicated to him by Boniface.[41] In September 593, Gregory writes to Archbishop Constantius of Milan about the schism of the Ligurian bishops, also brought to his attention by Boniface.[42] In April 596 Gregory writes to the Papal *apocrisiarios* in Ravenna, Castorius, ordering him to attend to what Boniface had written to him on the matter of the *pallium* dispute.[43] These three references, taken together, suggest that Boniface was deeply involved in the day-to-day running of the papacy.

The only other deacons in the Gregorian Register are Cyprian, who succeeded Peter as rector of Syracuse, and Servusdei, Peter's predecessor, who was dead by 598.[44] It seems reasonable to assume that of all the deacons active during Gregory's reign, it is the group listed above who were the diaconal core of the inner circle.

Turning to the notaries, two, Aemilianus and Paterius, are listed by John. They must have owed their prominence in papal councils to their constant attendance on the pope in the course of their duties. It was to Aemilianus that Gregory dictated his *Homilies on the Gospels*, and to whom Abbot Probus, another papal intimate, dictated his petition for permission to make a will.[45] He clearly occupied the position of a favoured private secretary. Even more favoured was Paterius. To him the pope dictated letters of appointment and manumission.[46] He made a volume of collected extracts from the pope's works.[47] Some time between 597 and 599, he was appointed to the position of *secundicerius notariorum*, the immediate deputy to the *primicerius* in the hierarchy of the secretariat.[48]

Paterius' predecessor in the position of *secundicerius* was Exhilaratus. He is twice mentioned in the Register. In September 594 Gregory informed the *apocrisiarios* Sabinian that he had considered sending Exhilaratus to Constantinople on the matter of Bishop Malchus, whom Gregory was accused of having murdered, but since the matter was now closed he had decided against it.[49] However, later Exhilaratus did go to Constantinople, perhaps to inform Sabinian of his recall.[50]

The *Dialogues* give us a clue to Exhilaratus' origins. Gregory there tells the story of a slave boy sent by his master to take two barrels of wine to St Benedict of Nursia.[51] The boy hides one of them for himself, and St Benedict, divining this, warns him not to drink it but to open it first. He does and a snake jumps out. The boy is described as *'noster Exhilaratus puer'* ('our Exhilaratus as a boy'), and Gregory adds that Peter knew him as a monk. *Noster* is generally used to refer to one of Gregory's clerics, and Exhilaratus is also called *'noster Exhilaratus'* in the letter to Sabinian. It looks as if Exhilaratus was another of those monks turned administrators who surrounded Gregory. If Exhilaratus encountered St Benedict while in his teens, in the 540s, then he would have been in his seventies by 598, a not unreasonable age at which to be filling the post of *secundicerius notariorum*. On this construction he became a monk after his encounter with St Benedict and later left the cloister for the Roman church administration, rising through the notariate to a position of seniority. It is impossible to say whether Paterius' promotion to *secundicerius* meant that Exhilaratus had been elevated to *primicerius* or whether he had died. There is only one reference during the reign to a *primicerius notariorum*, and that is to Gaudiosus, who was one of the experts consulted about the Ravenna *pallium* in 593.[52]

One other notary stands out in the Register – Pantaleo, who is perhaps best described as the papal 'troubleshooter'. He is sent to Sipontum in 593 to investigate the seduction of a deacon's daughter by the bishop's nephew.[53] In 598 he is sent to Sicily to gather up church plate taken there by refugee clerics and illegally sold.[54] In 600 he is in Genoa to supervise the election of a new archbishop of Milan.[55] Finally, in 603, we find him back in Sicily, this time investigating the financial abuses in the Syracusan patrimony.[56]

From the *defensores* only one man stands out, apart from *primicerius* Boniface, and that is John, entrusted in 603 with the highly sensitive task of hearing the appeals of two deposed Spanish bishops.[57] He may also be the *defensor* John, sent to oversee the ransom operations of Bishop Fortunatus of Fanum, though the name is too common to draw any firm conclusion.[58] But the Spanish mission was too important for Gregory to have entrusted it to any but the most reliable of his agents.

Lastly among the papal officials close to Gregory, there is one layman – the *consiliarius* Theodore, *vir magnificus et eloquentissimus*. He was the pope's legal adviser, but he was neither rich nor powerful, for in 593 Gregory sent him a Sicilian slave boy because he had no servants and Gregory wanted to reward him for his loyal service.[59] His comparatively humble status contrasts markedly with that of Pope Vigilius' *consiliarius* Saturninus, a man of high senatorial rank. It harmonizes with Gregory's known desire not to have in church administration powerful laymen with outside interests likely to conflict with their duty to the church.

The four monks listed among Gregory's familiars by John the Deacon are all known from the Register to have occupied places high in his confidence. Three of them were from St Andrew's. Two were appointed to key bishoprics: Maximian to Syracuse in 591, and Marinianus to Ravenna in 595. Claudius became abbot of SS. John and Stephen in Classis at some date before 595.[60] In other words, by 595 three of his four monkish confidants had left Rome for good. Their place was taken in the pope's confidence by Probus, nephew of the late Bishop Probus of Reate and the source of four stories in the *Dialogues*.[61] He had been living in religious seclusion for several years when Gregory appointed him abbot of SS. Andreas and Lucia ad Renati *subito spiritu revelante*, in other words in an act of patronage.[62] Subsequently Probus was dispatched to build a hostel in Jerusalem, and in 598 was chosen for the delicate job of negotiating the peace treaty with King Agilulf.[63] To these known confidants Caesarius, abbot of St Peter ad Baias in Sicily, may be added. He was another of those clerical figures described as '*noster*' by the pope and commended by him to Bishop John of Syracuse.[64] It is likely that he was another alumnus of St Andrew's.

By the nature of their work, the bishops remained for much of the time in their sees. But there were two who seem to have enjoyed

Gregory's special confidence, aside from those whose elections he himself had secured. There was Bishop Secundinus of Tauromenium, to whom Gregory sent two books of his *Homilies* for correction and comment, and to whom he entrusted many important investigations and arbitrations during his reign, an indication of the faith Gregory placed in his judgment.[65] It is likely that he is the bishop Secundinus (see unspecified), sent in 595 to investigate charges against Archbishop Anastasius of Corinth. Gregory declared himself well pleased with Secundinus' conduct of the matter and wrote of him to the new archbishop John of Corinth: 'The equity and solicitude of our brother and fellow-bishop Secundinus, which has long been well known to us, is shown again by the tenor of your letters.'[66] Interestingly, Secundinus is the only Sicilian bishop to attend the 595 synod.[67]

The other influential bishop was Felix of Portus, described by Gregory as *'vir vitae venerabilis'*. He supplied Gregory with three stories for the *Dialogues*, and in 599 Gregory made him a present of a slave.[68] He is probably to be identified with the bishop Felix of unknown see, who was sent in 594 on the special mission to Sardinia to stamp out paganism.[69] It is not known whether either bishop was a monk, although two of the three stories Felix supplied to Gregory concern monks and it was usually Gregory's policy to send men with monkish training on missionary expeditions.

There is one final source of information which provides insight into Gregory's circle. The *Dialogues* consisted of stories Gregory gathered over the years from friends and associates. It is possible to break these sources down into several distinct groups. Three of these groups are irrelevant to a discussion of his circle. The first is those who were dead before his elevation to the papal throne.[70] The second is the old men whom Gregory specifically sought out for their memories of saints and martyrs.[71] The third is a handful of prominent laymen.[72] Apart from these men, the sources of information are exclusively ecclesiastical and divide almost equally: twenty monks, and sixteen priests, bishops, and assorted clerics. Among these are to be found the names of already established confidants: Maximian of Syracuse, the deacon and *dispensator* Boniface, Abbot Probus and Felix of Portus.[73] To these may be added the deacon Epiphanius, who supplied a story for the *Homilies*.[74] One interesting fact is that Gregory received regular visits from various clerics. The Nursian priest Sanctulus visited him every year; Bishop Venantius of Luna was staying with him while he was composing the *Dialogues*; and

Abbot Fortunatus of Balneum Ciceronis visited him regularly.[75] But most interesting of all is the fact that of the clerics who supplied him with information only five are from the Roman clergy, reinforcing the impression of the pope gathering around him a small and fairly close-knit group, the inner circle.

Taking the evidence as a whole, then, it is possible to suggest a group of some twelve whose composition changed during the reign. Of the four monks listed by John the Deacon, only Probus was in Rome after 595. The *defensor* John and notary Pantaleo would have spent much time away from Rome by the nature of their duties. The trusted bishops can only have been in Rome from time to time. The heart of the papal circle was that team of administrators which Gregory built up and in whom he demonstrated his confidence by promotion. It is a group which evidently shared his outlook and sympathies and may reasonably be called Gregorian. They are the deacons Anatolius and Boniface, appointed to the newly created posts of *vicedominus* and *primicerius defensorum*, and the other deacon Boniface, *dispensator* and 'secretary of state'; Gregory's known diaconal appointments, Peter, Epiphanius, and Florentius; and the three notaries, Exhilaratus, Aemilianus, and Paterius.

Two characteristics of this group lend force to the already suggested direction of Gregorian personnel policy. There is an absence of laymen. Apart from his brother Palatinus, the only layman known to have exercised influence in the papal circle was the *consiliarius* Theodore. On the other hand, there is the marked preference for men of monkish background or sympathies. As far as can be ascertained, the deacons Peter and Epiphanius and the *secundicerius* Exhilaratus at least had been monks before beginning their administrative careers, and the *dispensator* Boniface subsequently showed strong monastic sympathies. Thus the inner circle reflects the man at its centre, combining monastic simplicity and administrative experience, the perfect blend of *vita activa* and *vita contemplativa*. Its significance, however, is more than simply a matter of personal preference; it marks a decisive bid to reshape the papal power structure along monastic lines and to use the familial papal household rather than the burgeoning clerical administration as its centre.

The converse of Gregory's monastic bias is the serious snub delivered to the clerical establishment at the outset of his reign. In September 591, in a full-dress ceremony at the Lateran in the presence of the entire clergy, the archdeacon Laurentius was deposed for 'pride and other crimes'.[76] Coming so soon after Laurentius had been passed over for the succession in favour of the more junior Gregory and had seen his power curtailed by the creation of a permanent *vicedominus*, his 'pride' almost certainly consisted of a manifestation of disgruntlement at the turn of events. When this is added to the exclusion of laymen from the Lateran and the institution of monastic communality there, it is apparent that a gulf between the papal circle and the clerical establishment was emerging. One would expect a clerical backlash after Gregory's death, and the *Liber Pontificalis* allows us to trace a fascinating see-saw struggle between the clerical establishment and a group who may reasonably be called 'Gregorians' and who secured the papal throne for Boniface III, Boniface IV and Honorius I. These popes sought to implement a 'Gregorian' programme, which involved the advancement of monasticism and the creation of a familial administration on the monastic model; a commitment to support for the English mission; a policy of close cooperation with the imperial authorities in the preservation of the province; and commitment to the new form of learning epitomized by the *Dialogues* and the *Homilies*, simple straightforward and accessible to ordinary people, a clean break with the old high culture of an intellectual and theological elite.

On Gregory's death, however, the deacon Sabinian, candidate of the clerical faction, was elected pope. His epitaph stressed his credentials: 'He did not receive the Papal crown as a result of instant fame but this holy man earned it by working his way up the clerical ladder.'[77] There is here perhaps an implicit rebuke for Gregory, swept straight from his monastery to the diaconate and thence to the papal throne.

It is recorded of Sabinian that 'he filled the church with clergy'.[78] This does not mean the creation of extra priests: Sabinian created none. It enshrines the reversal of Gregory's policy of filling the papal court with monks. The recall of the clergy was only part of a more general anti-Gregorian reaction. Gregory was blamed for the famine gripping the city at his death, and there was a bid by the enraged mob to burn his writings; small wonder, then, that the election for a successor threw up a candidate of the rival faction.[79]

But Sabinian was soon to learn the fickleness of the mob for himself. His short reign was marked by unrelieved disaster: a renewal of the war with the Lombards and the intensification of the famine. Sabinian was accused of profiteering in grain because he sold rather than give away the contents of the papal granaries.[80] The people turned back to Gregory, and legend has it that Sabinian died because the ghost of Gregory kicked him in the head for not distributing the grain free.[81] At the height of his unpopularity, Sabinian died, in February 606, and his funeral procession had to detour outside the city walls to avoid hostile demonstrations.

The advantage was once again with the Gregorians, and the former *primicerius defensorum* and *apocrisiarios* Boniface was elected as Boniface III. However, after a reign of only eight months (February–November 607) he died. The new pope, Boniface IV, was another Gregorian, the former deacon and *dispensator*. His epitaph speaks of his imitating 'the merits and examples of his master Gregory', he made dispositions for the English church, and a monastic bias is indicated by his turning his house into a monastery and his holding a major synod in Rome to regulate the life and peace of the monks.[82] But like Sabinian's reign, Boniface IV's was a period of unmitigated disaster in the form of famine, flood and plague, and the inevitable consequence was electoral disaster. When Boniface died in May 615, Deusdedit was elected as his successor. The remarkable fact about Deusdedit is that he was a priest and had been for forty years. He is the first priest known to have been elected to the papal throne since John II in 533. This breach with the tradition of diaconal monopoly on the papal throne which had grown up in the sixth century is not so surprising if we realize that the diaconate was in 615 largely Gregorian in outlook. It was the exclusive creation of Gregory I and Boniface IV: no intervening pope had created any deacons. If the anti-Gregorian party were looking for a candidate, they would have to turn to the priesthood. The candidate they chose fulfilled the same criteria as Sabinian had. Deusdedit's epitaph stresses the fact that he had been raised in and had served the church since childhood. Of Deusdedit's pro-clerical sympathies there can be no doubt. The *Liber Pontificalis* records of him: 'He greatly loved the clergy and recalled the priests and the clergy to their former position.'[83] This confirms the fact implicit in the sympathies of his predecessors but nowhere explicitly stated, that Boniface IV had in fact restored the familial, monastic administration of Gregory and had truly 'imitated the examples of his master Gregory'. Deusdedit was reversing the action. He also ordained fourteen priests, the first to be created since Gregory's death, and instituted the tradition of making lavish funeral bequests to the clergy.

Deusdedit died in November 618, and his successor, Boniface V, carried on the pro-clerical reaction. The *Liber Pontificalis* says 'he loved the clergy', he made similarly generous funerary dispositions, and his legislative decrees stressed the maintenance of clerical prerogatives.[84] But after Boniface's death in October 625, the pendulum swung back to the Gregorians again, the reigns of Deusdedit and Boniface having been marked by disease, rebellion and revival of war with the Lombards. The new pope, Honorius I, an aristocrat and administrator in the true Gregorian manner, is said by his epitaph to have followed in the footsteps of Gregory, and in almost every area of his reign echoes of the Gregorian programme are to be found. He turned his Roman home near the Lateran into a monastery, dedicated like Gregory's to St Andrew. He chose as his 'secretary of state' a Greek monk, Abbot John Symponus, and he made the first recorded grant of monastic exemption from episcopal control when he made Bobbio directly dependent on Rome. He undertook a major programme of educating the clergy, whose standards of learning had declined disastrously. He sought to revitalize the flagging English mission by dispatching Birinus to convert the West Saxons and making organizational arrangements for the see of York. In his letters to England he constantly stressed the Gregorian origin of the English church, encouraging King Edwin of Northumbria to read Gregory's works – in marked contrast to the English correspondence of the pro-clerical Boniface V, in which there is no mention of Gregory. He carried the Gregorian dislike of abstruse theological philosophizing to its height in his celebrated denunciation of its practitioners as 'croaking frogs' who were misleading ordinary people.[85]

Honorius was perhaps the greatest of the Gregorian popes. But he was also the last. He died in October 638, making no funerary bequest to the clergy, and his eventual condemnation as a heretic at the Oecumenical Council of 680 set the seal on the repulse of the Gregorian initiative. The clerical establishment secured its hold on the papacy after Honorius' death as a result of the turn of events. The rise of the Monothelete heresy in the East inaugurated a new wave of theological speculation and created a need for Honorius' 'croaking frogs' in order to debate the essential matters of the faith. As Rome and Constantinople once again joined battle, the monastic bid for control of the administration faded, and by the eighth century, far from providing an alternative power centre, the monasteries had been absorbed into the orbit of the clerical administration. Monks staffed the great basilicas and dispensed charity under the aegis of a clerically dominated papal administration. So secure did clerical control become, indeed, that the clergy could permit in 672 the election as pope of Adeodatus, the first monk since Gregory to hold the office. But he was a far cry from Gregory, spending his reign doling out gifts, raising all clerical salaries and seeking no return to the Gregorian programme.[86]

Chapter Six

Central Administration: (1) War, Finance and Supply

Gregory's reign illustrates perfectly the process whereby the popes, without any settled intention of doing so, gradually became the undisputed masters of Rome. There was, of course, a secular government in Rome. The city prefect continued to control the civil administration much as he had when Gregory himself exercised the office. The vicar represented the authority of the praetorian prefect. There was a staff of civil servants with offices in the Palatine palace. A military governor, usually a duke (*dux*) or a *magister militum*, was responsible for defence. But the principal interests and concerns of the provincial government were centred on Ravenna. More often than not in the crucial fields of defence and supply, for instance, Rome was left to fend for itself. Increasingly, secular officials turned to the pope, who had at his disposal all the economic and spiritual resources of the Roman church, to give them help, support, even leadership. The increasing involvement of the papacy in strictly secular matters placed an enormous additional burden on the pope, and already the war and its attendant problems (refugees, ransoms, enforced ecclesiastical reorganization) had considerably extended the responsibilities and duties of the pope and the papal administration. Well might Gregory observe soon after his election: 'With what a bustle of earthly activity I am distracted in this place I cannot express in words; yet you can gather it from the shortness of this letter.'[1] Here, in the bustling, complex, infinitely varied work of the central administration, we see the twin qualities of Gregory triumphantly at work: his majestic *Romanitas* at the service of his humble *Christianitas*; the law bowing the knee to humanity, bureaucratic efficiency expediting the bestowal of charity, Rome preserved for Caesar by St Peter.

The fundamental divergence of view between the pope and the exarch on the question of the defence of Rome was further embittered by Romanus' obvious resentment at what he regarded as Gregory's unwarranted interference in exarchal matters. The gulf between papal Rome and imperial Ravenna during Romanus' tenure of office was one of the most serious problems facing Gregory in the first half of his reign. When he wrote of the burdens under which he laboured, Gregory almost invariably linked the Lombards and the provincial government. He wrote to the exiled Dalmatian bishop Sebastian of Rhisinum in the East:[2]

> We can by no means describe, most holy brother, what we suffer in this land at the hands of your friend, the lord Romanus. Yet I may briefly say that his malice towards us has surpassed the swords of the Lombards; so that the enemies who kill us seem kindlier than the imperial governors who by their malice, rapines and deceits wear us out with anxiety. And to bear at the same time the charge of monasteries and people, and to watch anxiously against the plots of the enemy, and to be ever suspicious of the deceitfulness and malice of the governors; what labours and what sorrows all this involves, your fraternity may the more truly estimate as you more purely love me who suffer these things.

Gregory's involvement in secular activities began at the outset of his reign and increased as the years went by, increasing with it the resentment and hostility of Romanus. The most immediate and pressing problem was the defence of Rome, which was depopulated by plague and war and garrisoned by a seriously under-strength force. The absence of a strong Byzantine military presence or an active governor in the city, and the concentration of the bulk of the imperial forces around Ravenna and along the Rome–Ravenna land corridor, thrust the pope perforce to the centre of the stage, compelling him to deploy both the wealth and the prestige of the church in the interests of the Empire. Although his activities in this area are examined in detail elsewhere, it should be noted here that Gregory consistently took a leading role in negotiating treaties and truces, paying the troops, directing the actions of imperial generals, even appointing temporary commanders to threatened outposts. The church played its full part, even the monasteries being obliged to contribute men to guard city walls, though Gregory drew the line at the billeting of soldiers on nunneries.[3] His concern for the safety of the imperial territories soon extended from Rome itself to other areas of Italy, and he interested himself in defence dispositions for Corsica, Sardinia and Campania.[4] Gregory very properly attributed his success in preserving Rome from capture to the protection of St Peter, writing to Rusticiana in Constantinople: 'You should attentively observe how great is the protection of Peter, the Prince of Apostles, in this city wherein without a large population and without military aid, we have been preserved unharmed among swords by the help of God for so many years.'[5] But his exertions were to earn him not gratitude from the imperial authorities but obloquy, even from the emperor himself, to the extent that his celebrated patience was tried to the uttermost. It is, however, important to stress that Gregory undertook none of this in order to increase papal power. He did not even do it willingly. He did it with reluctance, because it distracted him from his primary pastoral and spiritual role. He was quite simply driven to it by sheer desperate necessity. This is clear from his comments in the *Homilies:*[6]

> How can I think what my brethren need and see that the city is guarded against the swords of the enemy and take precautions lest the people be destroyed by a sudden attack, and yet at the same time deliver the word of exhortation fully and effectively for the salvation of souls. To speak of God we need a mind thoroughly at peace and free from care.

And again:

> Since assuming the burden of the pastoral office my soul can no longer recollect itself with ease, because it finds itself dispersed among a multitude of cares. I am forced now to busy myself with the affairs of the various churches, now with the needs of monasteries, now to investigate the conduct of this or that individual; there are times when I must concern myself with worldly matters, repair the ruin brought on by the barbarian invasions, try to prevent wolves from destroying the flock committed to my care . . . at times I must bear with some whom I know to be plunderers, and even go out of my way to meet them, so that charity may be maintained.

But he was not just concerned with the distraction from spiritual matters that this constituted; he was also worried about the cost to the papal treasury. As he informed Empress Constantina: 'At the same time the Church has to support its clergy, its monasteries, its poor, the people, and in addition to all that, has to pay off the Lombards.'[7] The cost-conscious voice of the trained administrator reinforces the heart-felt laments of the spiritual preacher, enmeshed in the toils of the world.

Just as important as military force in the struggle to preserve Rome was supply. More often than not during the Lombard invasion cities had been starved into surrender rather than successfully stormed. Grain supply in particular was crucial, and in 595 Gregory gave as his excuse to the emperor for having made peace with Agilulf the fact that the grain had run out.[8] So Gregory took a continuing active interest in food supply in general, and particularly the government's free grain dole – the *annona*. Justinian's *Pragmatic Sanction* had ordered the continuation of the grain dole made by Theodoric, and it was continued until the early seventh century. Government grain was a vital weapon in the defence armoury, and one of Gregory's first acts on becoming pope was to write to the praetor Justin of Sicily (the main source of grain), urging him to see that sufficient supplies came to Rome for the public granaries. There had been a quarrel between Justin and *vir magnificus* Citonatus, probably the *praefectus Annonae*, with the praetor alleging that more than the quota had been previously sent. As a result he was holding up grain shipments, at a time when, with the papal granaries flooded and their contents destroyed, the threat of famine hung over the city. Gregory therefore intervened to urge Justin to take swift action for otherwise 'it will mean the death not just of one person but of the entire population.'[9] In February 599 Gregory was urging the rector Romanus of Syracuse to aid the imperial agents sent to Sicily to buy grain for the public granaries.[10] In April 599 there came another major contretemps. For some reason part of the state grain was being stored in the church granaries and handed out on behalf of the government by ecclesiastical *defensores*. But Cyridanus, newly appointed to be head of supply and apparently based in Sicily, declared that there was a suspicion of peculation by the church functionaries and ordered that the grain be removed from their control and their account books requisitioned. It looks like an elaborate cover for the removal of the grain from the city for use by the state elsewhere, and indeed, the following year Gregory had occasion to complain to the praetorian prefect John of Italy that he had improperly removed grain from the *diaconia*, the ecclesiastical grain distribution centres, in Naples.[11] It seems to have been the practice for state officials, when short of grain, to lay illegal hands on the church's grain. Gregory protested bitterly to Cyridanus, warning of the consequences for Rome of the removal of the grain and saying that the church could not be held responsible for the consequences.[12]

In view of the problems connected with the state grain supply, which was in any case to cease altogether shortly after Gregory's death, it is not surprising that the church came to be increasingly involved in the feeding of the people. It had its own granaries beside the Tiber, which were supplied each autumn from the church estates in Sicily. The church indeed already ran its own food distribution service, as part of its charitable programme. On occasions in the past the Roman church had supplied the entire city from its own granaries as an emergency measure – as for instance under Gelasius I when wintry seas prevented the arrival of grain shipments, and under Vigilius, when the city was blockaded by Goths. But increasingly the church rather than the state came to be seen as the source of food supplies. In August 591 Gregory ordered the Sicilian rector Peter to spend fifty pounds of gold to purchase additional grain supplies and then to store them in Sicily until the following February, when the grain was to be dispatched to Rome, because there had been a poor harvest around Rome and famine was almost inevitable.[13] In 604 there was a serious famine. The vines failed owing to an unusually cold winter; and the grain crop failed, partly destroyed by mice and partly by the blight. As we have seen, in the crisis that followed, Gregory's successor, Sabinian, sold instead of giving away church grain and was so unpopular that when he died the clergy were afraid to carry his body through the city for fear of riots.[14] This indicates the extent to which the people now looked to the church for their grain dole. During the seventh century, indeed, a series of diaconal monasteries, specifically devoted to food supply, grew up in the city, many of them built on the very sites of the old imperial grain distribution centres, signalling the takeover of their function.[15]

Gregory was also concerned about water supply. Although the *Pragmatic Sanction* had ordered the appointment of a count of the conduits (*comes formarum*) to oversee the city's aqueducts, they had been scandalously neglected. In 602 Gregory wrote: 'They are so overlooked and neglected that unless more care is taken they will shortly fall into complete ruin.' So he pressed for the appointment of *vir clarissimus* Augustus, whom he knew to be active and conscientious, as *comes formarum*, to undertake their repair.[16]

Gregory did not seek a state of hostilities with secular officialdom. He constantly sought a reasonable *modus vivendi*. He corresponded with them and involved them in the protection of clerics.[17] He gave them *douceurs*.[18] His ideal was to differentiate strictly between clerical and secular spheres of competence; but he stressed the need for clerical administrators to intervene in secular matters whenever they saw evidence of injustice or oppression.[19] He did so himself, and this brought him into conflict with the governors of Sicily and Sardinia. At the outset of his reign, Gregory found that the praetor Justin was preventing the Sicilian bishops from leaving the island to attend the annual St Peter's Day synod in Rome, and causing the church various harassments. Gregory wrote at once, seeking to benefit from their previous friendship – presumably in Constantinople – and urging him to work in harmony with the pope for the good of all.[20] But the problem with Justin remained. He continued to refuse to allow the bishops to leave Sicily. So instead of causing a fuss, Gregory quietly made alternative arrangements. In 591 the Sicilian vicar was ordered to hold annual synods in Sicily and the bishops to come to Rome every three years. In 597 he instructed the bishops to come in future every five years, though they were to come this year without letting the praetor know, in case he tried to stop them.[21]

The situation in Sardinia was much more serious – so serious, in fact, that in the summer fo 591 Archbishop Januarius of Caralis travelled to Rome to enlist the aid of the pope. Theodore, duke of Sardinia, had instituted a reign of terror, screwing money out of the poor in illicit exactions, and beating up and imprisoning any who resisted. Gregory wrote immediately to his representative in Constantinople, the deacon Honoratus, ordering him to present the complaints of the provincials to the emperor and to remind him that in 589 he had ordered the previous duke of Sardinia, Edantius, to desist from similar practices. Gregory also wrote to Theodore's immediate superior, Exarch Gennadius of Africa, to try to get him to restrain his subordinate.[22]

The pope's unique ecclesiastical position and the prestige and moral authority it carried with it made him the obvious person for oppressed provincials to turn to. So inevitably the pope began to emerge as the champion of Italian interests against the corrupt malpractices of imperial officials. It was a role the pope was to fulfil until the fall of the exarchate, but it can in no way be equated with the idea of a revolt against the *status quo* or a desire for a split with the Empire.

In June 595 Gregory wrote to the empress Constantina about the scandalous state of affairs in the islands. In Sardinia, the governor was allowing paganism to be practised on payment of a bribe, and even continued levying the bribe from pagans who had been converted to Christianity. Tackled about this, the governor had frankly admitted that this was the only way he could make up his *suffragium*, the sum of money he had paid out to get the job. In Corsica, the inhabitants were oppressed with such heavy exactions that people were selling their children into slavery to raise the money, and others were actually fleeing from the Empire to take refuge with the Lombards. In Sicily, the *chartularius* Stephanus was guilty of so many acts of oppression and plunder that they would fill a book. Gregory urged the empress to bring the matters before her husband as soon as possible. He concluded:[23]

> I know that he will say that whatever money is collected from these islands is sent back to us for the expenses of Italy. But I answer that he ought to still the grief of the oppressed within his Empire, even though less money be sent to Italy in consequence. It may be that the reason why the large sums spent in this country do so little good, is that they have been acquired in a sinful manner. Let My Most Serene Sovereigns then give orders that nothing be taken wrongfully. For I am convinced that, even though less be paid, yet the interests of the state will be greatly advanced; and even if we should suffer from a diminution of the revenue, it is certainly better that we should lose this temporal life than that you should be hindered in attaining the life eternal.

But in 603 the Sardinians were again complaining of serious oppression and Gregory gave the rector Vitalis leave to take their complaints to Constantinople.[24]

While he was willing to champion the oppressed in general, and even in particular, as when the soap-boilers of Naples complained of oppression by the *palatinus* John, Gregory was unwilling to take cognizance of cases outside his jurisdiction.[25] For instance, he refused to judge a case brought to him which properly belonged to the commandant of Naples, Maurentius.[26] He instructed the rector Romanus of Sicily to exercise ecclesiastical patronage sparingly, especially in peculation cases, lest some of the taint rub off on the church.[27]

But people not only sought to invoke papal help to fight oppression; there were also those who sought papal support to further their careers. Gregory was chary about endorsing candidates for high office in case they misused it and the result rebounded on the papacy. So when he was asked to recommend Bonitus for the praetorship of Sicily he refused, saying tactfully that he did not want to inflict so great a burden on Bonitus.[28] When the patrician Venantius sent thirty pounds of gold to Constantinople to purchase the ex-consulship without having previously held any of the appropriate ranks or offices, he asked for Gregory's endorsement. Gregory cannily informed his *apocrisiarios* Honoratus to do what he could to expedite the transaction without, however, mentioning Gregory's name.[29] His general policy on letters of commendation, as he told the ex-consul Leontius, was that he never gave them to anyone without expressly stating that favour should be shown to the bearer only in so far as justice allowed.[30] They could certainly be misused, as when the vicar John, going to Genoa with papal letters of commendation, used them to extort money from Archbishop Constantius of Milan. When he learned of this, Gregory declared that this was emphatically not what they were intended for.[31]

Nothing demonstrates the pre-eminence of the papacy *vis-à-vis* the secular authorities in Italy more clearly than the reactions of provincial government officials faced with an investigation of their accounts. In 591 the ex-prefect Maurilio took sanctuary in a church in Ravenna to avoid rendering his accounts to the praetorian prefect George of Italy, and Gregory ordered Archbishop John of Ravenna to protect him from oppression.[32] Even more spectacular panic ensued among the secular officials when an imperial inspector-general, the ex-consul Leontius, arrived in Sicily in 598 and sent for them. The ex-prefect Gregory of Rome and the vicar Criscentius both took sanctuary in a church in Rome. It fell to the pope to act as their intermediary with Leontius. The ex-prefect was eventually persuaded to go to Sicily and present his accounts only after Gregory had personally promised to do all he could to help him and Leontius' representative had given his word that no harm would befall him.[33] Gregory duly wrote to his special friends in Sicily, bishops John of Syracuse, Donus of Messina and Secundinus of Tauromenium, to ensure that Leontius kept his word and Gregory came to no harm.[34]

Criscentius was persuaded to leave sanctuary under similar terms, and Gregory again wrote asking John of Syracuse to protect him.[35]

But beyond this, Gregory actually became involved himself in the process, when he sent *vir clarissimus* Laurentius to present and explain the accounts of the late *numerarius* Boniface, head of bureau to one of the senior secular officials, vicar or prefect. Boniface had left a part of his property to the hostel of St Peter's, and Gregory wanted to ensure that the church kept it.[36] He enlisted the aid of John of Syracuse and the rector Romanus to help Laurentius, and he instructed Romanus to get a security (*cautio*) to the effect that the matter, once decided, could not be renewed.[37]

The fears of all these secular officials were amply justified by the fate of the ex-praetor Libertinus of Sicily. Despite the fact that Gregory wrote strongly defending his record in government, Libertinus was found guilty of embezzling public funds, was fined so heavily that he was ruined, and was also flogged. Leontius forwarded a copy of Libertinus' *cautio* to Gregory, demonstrating that he had promised such a large *suffragium* to gain office that he could only have recouped his outlay by embezzlement. The pope replied that in the light of this he would say no more on the matter of Libertinus, but he greatly deplored the flogging, which was both severe and inappropriate.[38] Here, then, is Gregory acting almost as the patron of senior secular officials, dealing with the top-level imperial functionaries on their behalf, demonstrating the extent of his influence and prestige.

Quite apart from this increasing involvement in secular matters, the normal ecclesiastical business of the papacy had been enormously increased by the war. It was no doubt as a response to the pressures placed on the church administrative structure that Gregory undertook reforms in the central administration. Because central re-organization was obviously done centrally, regrettably little of it has percolated into the Papal Register. But the general outline of his reforms can perhaps be traced.

The Lombard invasion and its consequences had made the work of the *defensores*, the papal agents in the regions, crucial. In addition to their traditional work of protecting church interests and property, they were now becoming deeply involved in refugee problems, ransoming prisoners and coping with breaches of discipline. So Gregory organized them into a college, a *schola*, giving them formal corporate status, like the deacons and the notaries. A *primicerius* was appointed to head the *schola*, and the seven senior *defensores* were accorded the title of *regionarius*, putting them on a par with the other *scholae*.[39]

Similarly with the increased burden of work placed on the shoulders of the patrimonial rectors, Gregory developed a system of checks and balances in the interests of administrative efficiency, banning plurality of offices and shuffling round the rectors periodically to prevent them from becoming too complacent.[40]

Observing that some of his deacons, who had formerly been cantors, were neglecting their administrative and spiritual duties for singing, he forbade this and ordered that in future cantors be chosen not simply for their good voices but also for the tenor of their lives and their clerical vocations.[41]

Gregory also created a permanent *vicedominus* to administer the Lateran palace. In 545 Pope Vigilius, leaving for Constantinople, had appointed as *vicedominus* the priest Ampliatus, to run the Lateran in his absence and in the absence probably also of the archdeacon. But in 590 Gregory made this a permanent post, appointing to it the deacon Anatolius.[42] It had a significance beyond the merely administrative in that it meant a reduction in the powers of the archdeacon and consequently of the clerical establishment.

Gregory's own involvement in the administration was total. Of the 854 letters of his which have survived, covering a bewildering range of activities, many are formidably detailed. Many of these letters will have been dictated by the pope to his notaries. In addition there will have been a flood of formula letters to be signed by the pope: petitions for the exchange and leasing of papal land; petitions for permission to build or repair or consecrate oratories, baptisteries, altars, churches; requests for holy relics; notifications of episcopal vacancies, elections, amalgamations of sees; deeds of grant, sale and exchange of papal slaves; invitations for bishops to attend synods; arrangements for the provision of transport and hospitality for papal couriers; instructions to rectors; and so on. The papal chancery was a hive of activity, and part of the pope's day would inevitably have been monopolized by the notaries with their sheaves of parchment.

One of the papacy's most important sources of strength and power was its wealth, and finance formed an important area of activity for the pope. The church's revenue derived from several sources – principally the patrimony of St Peter, but also from bequests and gifts. Gregory's Register records several examples of gifts from the faithful. The emperor Maurice and his sister Princess Theoctista sent thirty pounds of gold, the *émigré* aristocrat Rusticiana ten pounds, and the imperial physician Theodore an unspecified sum.[43] Often these sums would be specifically earmarked, for ransoming prisoners or subsidizing the poor. But Gregory was not prepared to benefit at the expense of others, and when Bishop John of Syracuse sent him money for the relief of the Roman poor, Gregory reprimanded him, saying the sum was too great considering the number of the Syracusan poor.[44]

According to tradition, the revenues of the Roman church were divided into four parts, an arrangement known as the *quadripartitum*. They were earmarked respectively for paying the pope, for clerical salaries, for the maintenance of church buildings, and for charity.[45] But the Roman church clearly had substantial reserves, for it was able to produce 500 pounds of gold to buy off the Lombards in 593.[46]

It was Gregory's practice to divide the clerical quarter on merit, and John the Deacon describes the ceremony of paying the clergy:[47]

> He turned into money the revenues of all the patrimonies and estates, according to the ledger [*polyptycum*] of Gelasius, of whom he seems to have been a most careful follower, and having collected all the officials of the Church, the palace, the monasteries, the lesser churches, the cemeteries, the deaconries, the guest-houses both within and without the walls, he decided from the ledger (according to which the distribution is still made) how many *solidi* should be given to each, out of the above-mentioned payments in gold and silver. The sums thus decided on were distributed four times a year, namely at Easter, on the festival of the Apostles (29 June), on the festival of St Andrew (30 November) and on the anniversary of his own consecration (3 September). Moreover very early in the morning of Easter Day he was accustomed to sit in the basilica of Pope Vigilius, near which he dwelt, to exchange the kiss of peace with the bishops, priests, deacons, and other notables, and on these occasions he gave to all of them an *aureus* apiece. On the festival of the Apostles and on the anniversary of his own consecration he gave them a sum of money and vestments of foreign material and make.

But the principal *raison d'être* of the papal finances, according to Gregory, was charity. John the Deacon calls him 'the most prudent father of the family of Christ' (*prudentissimus paterfamilias Christi*), and

Gregory called himself 'the steward of the property of the poor'.[48] He believed that the papal estates were, so to speak, held in trust for the poor by the Roman church; so the money and goods of the church were paid out in an unending stream of pensions, rent reductions, subventions and charitable doles. Gregory was the first pope to systematize these charitable operations, and John the Deacon records that in his own time there still existed in the Lateran archives a large volume compiled under Gregory which contained the name, age, sex, address, and occupation of all those in receipt of papal charity, and the amounts they received.[49] He gives no further details 'for fear of wearying the readers', but the Papal Register is full of information on this aspect of Gregory's operations. All sorts and conditions of men and women had cause to be grateful to Gregory for their subsistence. There were, of course, subsidies to nuns, monks and priests,[50] in particular 3,000 refugee nuns in Rome who were given eighty pounds of gold annually and a supply of bedclothes.[51] There were annual supplies of food in the form of grain, beans and wine to various blind men.[52] Decayed gentlefolk also received pensions, among them a former urban *defensor*, a lawyer, and the refugee governor of Samnium who was living in poverty in Sicily.[53] To his aunt Pateria he provided money to pay for her servants' shoes, and to the ex-praetor Libertinus, who had lost his fortune, twenty suits of clothing for his servants.[54] To other noble ladies he gave money and food in varying amounts.[55] He cancelled debts owing to the church by the late rector of Tibur, because to have paid would have bankrupted his sons.[56] He ordered that the sons of the Syrian merchant Cosmas, seized as slaves by the papal rector Cyprian of Sicily in payment of a debt, be freed.[57] He sent 2,000 *modii* of wheat to the starving city of Bishop Zeno, probably in Sicily.[58] Generally these grants were to alleviate genuine hardship, but Gregory was also willing to give pensions to facilitate conversion both from the 'Three Chapters' schism and from Judaism.[59]

Once again John the Deacon gives a detailed description of the pope's charitable activities in Rome, which reveals the existence of a mobile meals service, discreet handouts to the gentry, and the exercise of subtle class distinction in the gradation of charitable doles.[60]

On the first day of every month he distributed to the poor in general that part of the church revenues which was paid in kind.

Thus corn in its season and in their several seasons wine, cheese, vegetables, bacon, meat, fish, and oil were most discreetly doled out by this father of the family of the Lord. But pigments and other more delicate articles of commerce were offered by him as marks of respect to citizens of rank. Thus the church came to be regarded as a source of supply for the whole community. . . . Moreover every day he sent out by couriers appointed to the office cooked provisions to the sick and infirm throughout the streets and lanes of all the city districts. To those of higher rank who were ashamed to beg he would send a dish from his own table to be delivered at their doors as a present from St Peter. And this he did before he sat down himself to dine. Thus not one of the faithful in Rome was without experience of the kindness of this bishop, who most tenderly provided for the wants of all.

Here can be seen the base of operations which the papacy gradually widened over the next century until it was literally responsible for feeding the entire population.

Unlike some of his predecessors, Gregory was not a building pope. Paul the Deacon rightly noted: 'Other pontiffs gave themselves to building churches and adorning them with gold and silver; but Gregory, while not entirely neglecting this duty, was wholly engrossed in gaining souls, and all the money he could lay his hands upon he was anxious to disburse and bestow upon the poor.'[61] Gregory's building operations were mainly limited to St Peter's tomb. He had the tomb covered with 100 pounds of gold and had a silver canopy (*ciborium*) erected over the altar of St Peter's.[62] He had timber sent from the papal estates in Bruttium to repair the roofs of St Peter's and St Paul's.[63] He added to the number of Rome's churches painlessly by reconsecrating two Arian churches to Catholic use: one in Suburra dedicated to the Sicilian saint Agatha of Catania, and one next to the Merulan palace dedicated to the popular St Severinus of Noricum.[64] But that seems to be the modest limit of his building policy.

The considerable social and economic dislocation caused by the Lombard invasions created a whole new set of problems for the pope to tackle. Lay people and clerics fled in all directions from the invading hordes, and the papal administration had to become rapidly expert in dealing with refugee problems of all sorts, the ransoming of prisoners and the complications this entailed, and arrangements for churches and clergy in the war zones. Sicily, furthest and safest haven, received many of the refugees, and Gregory's Register records the presence in Sicily of refugees from places as diverse as Tauriana and Myria in Bruttium, Canusium in Apulia, Formiae and Misenum in Campania, Grumentum in Lucania, Larinum in Samnium, and Valeria province.[65] They ranged from imperial administrators to destitute monks. Large numbers of refugee monks and nuns turned up in Rome from various parts of Italy. Several of the monks of St Andrew's were Valerian refugees.[66] Wherever possible Gregory tried to incorporate the refugees into existing monastic communities, and he installed several entire communities of refugee monks and nuns in empty properties belonging to the church.[67] But after all this, there remained some 3,000 nuns whom Gregory had to subsidize from papal funds, which gives some idea of the size of the problem.[68]

Discipline and order, morale and supply, amongst these refugees became a prime concern of the pope, and this is one reason for the extension of charity operations. There was also the breakdown of discipline to deal with. The Register records, for instance, a nun seduced and made pregnant by the refugee son of a Lucanian bishop, and refugee Formiae clerics illegally enrolling in the clergy of Syracuse when their own city was in desperate need of clergy.[69] So many men and women from different areas fled for safety to the island of Eumorphiana that the community of monks there was disturbed and exposed to temptation, a fact leading Gregory to order that all the women be removed from the island and the other islands under the jurisdiction of the Roman church and taken to alternative places of refuge.[70]

A particular problem was presented by refugee clerics selling church plate and ornaments in order to survive. Gregory was very anxious to prevent this because the dispersal of the sacred vessels would make the re-establishment of derelict sees that much more difficult. When he learned that three refugee clerics from Venafrum had sold robes and chalices from their church to a Jew, he ordered that the property be recovered and the clerics put to penance.[71] He also took steps to recover the plate of the derelict see of Compulteria from the son of the deceased Roman church *defensor* who had originally taken charge of it.[72]

The dispersal of church plate and furnishings was particularly serious in Sicily, where so many clerics sought haven, and in October 593 Gregory ordered the rector Cyprian to gather it all together and deposit it for safekeeping with the Sicilian bishops until peace returned and it could be restored to its original churches. He was to make a careful list of what was collected and where it was stored.[73] In May 598 Gregory was urging the same course of action on the Roman notary Pantaleo, who was in Sicily on a special mission.[74] Bishops in charge of large areas containing derelict sees on the mainland were given similar instructions.[75]

There was, however, one circumstance under which Gregory was prepared to see church plate sold, and that was to raise money to redeem captives from the Lombards. If bishops were short of ready cash and there had been a heavy loss of prisoners during a Lombard attack, Gregory sanctioned the disposal of the plate. Such permission was given to Bishop Fortunatus of Fanum in November 596, though Gregory insisted that the Roman *defensor* John be present at the transaction to ensure absolute propriety.[76] Similarly Faustinus, notary of the Bruttian church of Myria, was given fifteen pounds of silver from the property of the Myrian church, lodged at Messina in Sicily, in order to ransom his daughters.[77]

But Gregory did not just leave ransoming to individual initiative; it was one of his major continuing concerns. He believed very strongly that the ransom of Catholics was a proper use of church money, and he constantly urged bishops not only to ransom their flock but also to repay people who had ransomed themselves.[78] Gifts of money from the imperial family were used in 597 to ransom many captives from Crotona, which had fallen to 'the abominable Lombards' the previous year.[79] Gregory even sent the Roman priest Valerian to North Africa to buy Italian captives who were being sold in the slave markets there.[80]

Characteristically, Gregory tackled the problem with businesslike efficiency. In April 596 he wrote to his Campanian rector Anthemius complaining about his neglect of ransoming captives, and informing him that he was sending the *vir magnificus* Stephanus with a supply of money which Anthemius was to use to ransom captives, both free and slave.[81] Anthemius was to redeem those free men too poor to ransom themselves, the slaves of free men too poor to ransom them, and slaves of the church. He was to list the names, whereabouts, occupations and places of origin of the redeemed captives and to list the amounts of money spent on the operation and send records of it back to Rome. Gregory urged Anthemius to recover the captives for as modest a ransom as possible. His instructions reveal that marvellous combination of pure charity, class consciousness, paternalism, bureaucratic efficiency, and canny business sense, which characterizes so much of his administration.

The same sense of administrative tidiness dictated his policy on the war zones, those troubled areas lying between imperial and Lombard territory. At least forty-two sees are known to have gone out of existence during the Lombard period. This is reflected in episcopal ordinations. In the thirteen and a half years of Gregory's reign, he ordained sixty-two bishops, whereas in reigns of comparable length in more settled times Honorius I (625–38) ordained eighty-one and Sergius I (687–701) ninety-seven. Gregory did, however, take decisive steps to organize what sees remained. In those provinces particularly ravaged by the Lombards, Gregory was compelled to create semi-vicarial posts, grouping several sees under a single bishop. Lucania was clearly very badly damaged by the Lombards, though apparently not permanently occupied. Instead it seems to have remained a buffer zone between the imperial province of Bruttium and the Lombard duchy of Benevento. Of the seven Lucanian sees known to have existed before Gregory's reign, none is recorded as operating during his reign. Only one letter in the entire Register is addressed to a Lucanian bishop. It was sent in July 592 to Bishop Felix of Acropolis.[82] Since no such see is recorded, the most likely explanation is that the bishop of Paestum had removed his seat to the nearby imperial fortress of Acropolis. From there Gregory gave him extended visitation over neighbouring sees, for the letter appointed Felix visitor of Blanda Julia, Velia and Buxentum. Interestingly, it did not invite him to initiate elections. He was given permission to ordain clergy where necessary, and ordered to ensure the maintenance of ecclesiastical discipline and collect the scattered church plate. It is clear that the Lucanian hierarchy had collapsed and that Gregory was mounting a holding operation. The fact that Felix's visitation applied only to the coastal Lucanian sees suggests that the inland sees, Consilinum, Grumentum and Potentia, of which there is no mention in the Register, fell within the Lombard sphere of influence.

A similar picture of dislocation and dereliction is to be found in Apulia, where of fifteen previously attested sees only one is found functioning. That is the important coastal fortress city of Sipontum, seat of the bishop, the papal rector, and an imperial military governor. In 591 Gregory appointed Bishop Felix of Sipontum visitor of Canusium, where no clergy survived.[83] He ordered him to appoint two priests to perform the necessary ecclesiastical services but made no mention of an episcopal election. In July 593 Felix was ordered to co-operate with the papal notaries Boniface and Pantaleo in drawing up an inventory of the property of other churches, known to be in Sipontum.[84] The use of the plural in this letter confirms the picture of Sipontum as the last city of refuge in Apulia, where the plate of many churches abandoned in the face of the enemy had been taken for safekeeping.

Elsewhere smaller groups of derelict sees in vulnerable frontier areas were united to sees which still flourished. In Campania the see of Atella was united with several neighbouring bishoprics, which were derelict and prelate-less.[85] It is not known what sees they were, but the most likely candidates are the coastal sees of Suessa, Forum Popilii and Volturnum, none of them attested in the Register, which formed a line between Minturnae and Cumae, themselves both united to other sees. Following the disgrace and deposition of Bishop Benenatus of Misenum, Cumae was transferred from his see to Atella.[86] Further north Bishop Ecclesius of Clusium was given control of several bishop-less and neighbouring sees.[87]

Bishops in sees under attack were encouraged to move their episcopal seats to places of greater safety, generally within the walls of imperial fortresses. Bishop John of Velitrae was ordered in 592 to remove his seat to Arenata ad St Andream since Velitrae was too exposed, and it is likely that the see of Urbs Vetus, destitute of priests in 596, was transferred to the fortress of Balneum Regis, where a bishop appears for the first time in 600.[88] Sees on the frontier, which had lost population and clerical establishments as a result of enemy action but remained in imperial hands, were often formally united to neighbouring sees, more often than not protected by imperial garrisons. This had the effect of utilizing a single clerical establishment to service two towns, and pooling two sets of probably war-damaged finances. Indeed, it became such a common practice that the papal chancery devised a formula letter to cover it.[89] Thus in 590 Minturnae was united with Formiae; in 592, Cumae was united with Misenum, Fundi with Terracina, and Tres Tabernae with Velitrae; in 593, St Anthimus in Cures was united with Nomentum, and in 598 Interamna was united with Narnia.[90] Significantly, Formiae, Terracina,

Narnia and Misenum all had imperial garrisons. It looks as if most of these arrangements were made in the wake of the hostile advances of the Lombards under Ariulf and Agilulf in the early years of Gregory's reign.

When towns or indeed whole areas were recaptured from the Lombards by the armies of the Empire, Gregory took immediate steps to reconstitute the clerical hierarchy. In January 599, for instance, an imperial general, Aldio *magister militum*, informed Gregory of the recapture of an unnamed town and asked him to ordain priests and deacons for it. Gregory gave the task to Bishop Venantius of Luna, the nearest Catholic bishop, and urged him to help launch a programme of evangelization to revive the Catholic faith there. The town was probably Faesulae, for in May of the same year a priest and deacon from Faesulae visited Venantius seeking money to repair their ruined churches. Gregory authorized payment to them of twenty *solidi*, but said that Venantius should hold on to the plate of the Faesulae church, which had been lodged with him for safekeeping, until peace had been definitely established and there was no danger of the recapture of the town by the enemy.[91]

Even more spectacular was the recapture in 598 of a large part of Picenum Suburbicarium by a massive military push southwards from the imperial frontier city of Ancona. This resulted in the reoccupation by imperial troops of Firmum, Asculum, Interamna Praetuttianorum (Aprutium), and Auximum, and probably extended the imperial sphere of influence as far east as Camerinum and Nursia. Firmum had been in Lombard hands since 580, when it had been captured during the overunning of Picenum. Bishop Fabius of Firmum had fled with the church plate to Ancona and there used some of his treasures to ransom captured members of his clergy, including the cleric Passivus, his wife, and their two sons, Demetrianus and Valerianus. Fabius had, however, died in his exile, and so Gregory now had to begin reconstructing the Picene hierarchy from scratch. In December 598 he appointed Bishop Serenus of Ancona as visitor of Auximum, 'for a long time lacking in pastoral solicitude', and urged the electorate to choose a new bishop.[92] Whether they did so is not known. But a bishop was elected in Firmum, the former cleric Passivus, and he became in effect vicar for the whole area. He sought to reclaim the Firmum plate from Ancona, but the deacon Serenus, who held it, refused to give it up until Passivus travelled to Rome to enlist the help of the pope.[93] The re-establishment of communications with Rome after such a long interval prompted the sons of Passivus, both now clerics of the Firmum church, to clarify their legal position with regard to the ransoms that had been paid on their behalf. The pope informed them that they were not liable to repay the money.[94]

Church-building began again in Picenum. In 598 the bishop's son, Valerianus, built an oratory to St Sabinus at Firmum, and Gregory authorized Bishop Chrysanthus of Spoleto to supply him with relics of the saint. The commander of the imperial garrison at Aprutium, Count Anio, built an oratory to St Peter, and Gregory authorized Passivus to consecrate it and appoint a priest to serve it. In 602 Gregory authorized Passivus to consecrate (again to St Sabinus, a local favourite) a monastery built by the deacon Proculus on his property at Asculum.[95] The fact that Passivus is called upon to deal with these consecrations in Asculum and Aprutium confirms the fact that there was no bishop closer than Firmum, endorsing the picture that emerges from the Register of a long period of Lombard occupation and consequent dereliction of the Catholic hierarchy.

Asculum was still without a bishop in 602, but Aprutium had apparently attracted sufficient population, doubtless reassured by the presence of an imperial garrison, to merit a bishop. But that no clergy survived is evidenced by Gregory's willingness to break his oft-repeated ban on the election of laymen. For in 601 Gregory authorized Passivus to tonsure at once as monk or subdeacon a *religiosus* layman Oportunus and speedily thereafter to ordain him bishop.[96]

The revival of the ecclesiastical hierarchy was vital to correct the indiscipline which had inevitably crept in during the long period of Lombard occupation. Gregory learned by many reports that the priests who had survived in the Nursia area were co-habiting with 'foreign', presumably Lombard, women. So in 603 he dispatched the *defensor* Optatus to investigate and report on the situation there. He asked for help and assistance from the local imperial commanders Romanus, Gattulus and Uvintarit, stationed with their forces on what was now the frontier between the Empire and the reduced duchy of Spoleto.[97] He ordered Optatus to hand over any priests guilty of co-habitation to the nearest Catholic bishop, Chrysanthus of Spoleto, for canon punishment.[98] Since Chrysanthus, who was also asked to eliminate this abuse from among his own clergy, was in the ducal capital and his help as well as that of the imperial generals was sought, it looks as if the former province of Nursia straddled the frontier and Optatus was going to have to move back and forth across it in pursuit of his mission. All the evidence points to the pope taking decisive and comprehensive steps to reactivate the Catholic church in Picenum.

The involvement of Chrysanthus of Spoleto in Optatus' disciplinary mission raises the question of the extent to which the Catholic hierarchy survived in the heart of the Lombard duchy of Spoleto. There is no doubt that many Catholic priests and monks fled from Umbria and Valeria when the Lombards invaded, and that many frontier bishoprics went out of existence. But it is also clear that, depending entirely on personality and circumstance, part of the Catholic hierarchy did hold on. The most striking example of this is the priest Sanctulus of Nursia.[99] His survival was due to the reputation for performing miracles which he won among the superstitious Lombards. The miracles were really only common-sense acts. When Sanctulus asked some Lombards working on an oil press for some oil they became angry because they could not get enough out of it for themselves. So Sanctulus called for water, which he blessed and poured on the press, whereupon oil gushed forth. It is quite clear that the oil press had simply stuck and needed damping down to get it to work again, but the Lombards proclaimed it a miracle. Sanctulus' position was finally put beyond doubt when after he had helped a captured deacon to escape, the Lombards decided to behead him. The executioner, who had heard of Sanctulus' miracles, 'froze' and was unable to bring down the sword. The Lombards were so impressed that Sanctulus was able to persuade them to release all their captives; thereafter he carried on his work unharmed, rebuilding the destroyed church of St Lawrence, and being able to visit Gregory in Rome every year until his death in 593, an interesting comment on the nature of communications between occupied and unoccupied Italy. It was probably individual episodes like this that ensured the survival of some clerics inside occupied territories.

It was a similar miraculous process which ensured that a Catholic bishop survived in Spoleto itself.[100] An Arian bishop arrived there, no doubt soon after the Lombard conquest, and demanded of the Catholic bishop a church in which to hold his services. When the Catholic bishop refused, the Arian declared his intention of entering the church of St Paul, near his lodging. That night the guardian of the church locked the doors, put out the lamps and hid. Next morning the Arian bishop arrived with a large following, planning to break the doors down. Suddenly the doors flew open, the lights went on, and the Arian bishop was struck blind and had to be led back to his lodgings. As a result of this episode, there was no further attempt by the Lombards to violate Catholic churches. All this occurred during the reign of the founding duke Farwald and seems to have resulted in the emergence of a satisfactory *modus vivendi* between Catholics and Arians. But there seems to have been another upheaval with the accession around 590 of Ariulf, who was a pagan. It is probably this event which explains the sudden flight around that time of the monk Boniface, who, after living for years peacefully in Spoleto, precipitately left and fled to Rome, where he entered St Andrew's and related to Gregory the story of the Arian bishop.

It may also be this change-over in rulers and consequent shifts in the balance of power within the duchy that led to the events described in the *Vita S. Cethei*.[101] Judging by the internal evidence, this is an oral tradition written down a couple of generations after the event but telling a story entirely consistent with the known situation of the period. Bishop Cethegus of Amiternum was another of those clerics who had managed to survive the initial invasion and to hold on in their see. In the early years of Gregory, however, two Lombard dukes, brothers called Umbolus and Alahis, took over Amiternum and grievously oppressed it, their arrival presumably coinciding with the transfer of power in the capital. Unable to bear their cruelty, Cethegus eventually fled to Rome, and after a while the citizens went to the duke in Spoleto and asked for permission to get their bishop back from Rome. The duke granted permission, and this could plausibly be associated with the more cordial atmosphere prevailing between Rome and Spoleto after the conclusion in 592 of the treaty between Gregory and Ariulf. After Cethegus' return to Amiternum, however, Umbolus and Alahis fell out, and the latter, desiring complete control of the town, secretly contacted the imperial military commander, Verilianus, at Hortona, the nearest Byzantine outpost. They concerted an attack on the town, following which Alahis would presumably hold it as a vassal of the Empire, as Duke Maurisio had held Perusia. The attack took place at midnight, and the imperial forces were beaten off. Next day, however, the citizens discovered ladders up against the walls near the church of St Thomas, and Alahis, in whose half of the town this was, was seized and threatened with torture for plotting with the Byzantines. When Cethegus intervened to try to save Alahis, Umbolus accused him of being involved in the plot too. The upshot was that both Alahis and Cethegus were executed.

The events in Amiternum probably took place at some time before the general peace treaty of 598, for after that date there is a sudden flurry of correspondence between Gregory and the Catholic Bishop of Spoleto, who before 598 does not figure in the Register at all. It is likely that by this date he was the only Catholic bishop functioning inside the duchy. Gregory communicated with no others, and the geographical range of Chrysanthus' duties indicates an analogous role to that of Passivus in Picenum. Chrysanthus of Spoleto was probably not the same bishop who had the dealings with the Arian bishop, but it was no doubt the effect created by that episode that allowed a regular episcopal succession to be maintained in Spoleto. The signing of the *generalis pax* allowed Gregory to take tentative steps to marshal the remnants of the shattered hierarchy within the duchy, and in this connection, five letters to Chrysanthus survive.[102] In November 598 he was ordered to deposit relics of SS. Hermes, Hyacinth and Maximus in the church of the Blessed Virgin Mary in Reate, at the request of the deacon Paul, presumably the senior surviving cleric there. In June 603 he was ordered to assist the *defensor* Optatus in his mission to reform the Nursian priesthood. These matters indicate the survival of some clergy but no bishops in the southern part of the duchy, hence Chrysanthus' involvement.

In June 599 Gregory, having appointed Chrysanthus visitor of Mevania, asked him to find a suitable person to be bishop or to ordain some priests for the city, since a deputation of clerics had reported to him that there were no priests either in the city or in the surrounding countryside and consequently no one to say mass. In 591 Gregory had appointed Honoratus as priest in charge of Mevania in the absence of a bishop, but he had since died and there were now only a handful of clerics left.[103] The appointment of a priest in charge is a very unusual procedure, and that, coupled with the eventual visitation of Chrysanthus of Spoleto, suggests that Mevania was a Lombard frontier city, to which no Italian bishop from the imperial side could gain access.

In November 598 Chrysanthus was ordered to hand over relics for the oratory of St Sabinus at Firmum, and finally in February 599 Gregory informed Chrysanthus of the complaints of the priest and Abbot Valentine that monks of his monastery, excommunicated for some fault, were fleeing to the see of Spoleto and there receiving communion. Chrysanthus was to see that this stopped. Sadly, we do not know whether the monastery was inside or outside Lombard territory. It could be either, since there are known cases of people fleeing to Lombard territory to escape the consequences of crimes committed in the imperial territory.[104] Either way, however, the monks' flight demonstrates a much-improved ease of communication between Rome and Spoleto.

A further evidence of this ease comes in a letter of January 599 to the Campanian rector Anthemius.[105] Stephanus, abbot of St Mark's at Spoleto, had complained that a property at Minturnae, granted to the monastery by Pope Benedict I, was illegally held by the agents of the Roman church. Gregory ordered Anthemius to investigate and if he found the complaint justified to hand it back again. This is a remarkable about-turn, for Eleutherius, the previous abbot of St Mark's, had fled from Spoleto years before, entered St Andrew's and lived there until his death.[106] Either the whole community had not departed with him or the monastery had been revived. Certainly the difficulty of communication between Spoleto and Rome before this time had meant that the Campanian property had simply been taken over by the Roman church, but now there was again a flourishing community at St Mark's and they were ready to reclaim their rights, even inside the Empire. What this group of letters reveals is the gradual re-establishment of church life within the duchy under the oversight of Bishop Chrysanthus, and the re-establishment of regular communications with Rome. It was to be a process that was to continue with increasing impetus in the seventh century, as the Lombards converted to Catholicism, extinguished sees were resurrected, and increasing numbers of Catholic bishops from the Lombard territory made the trip to Rome for the great synods of 649 and 680. This process seems to have begun under Gregory.

Chapter Seven

Central Administration: (2) Law, Discipline and Liturgy

Gregory's natural conservatism in the matters of law and order, discipline and hierarchy was reinforced by his keen awareness of the imminent end of the world. For the clergy to commit misdeeds was not only a betrayal of their sacred responsibilities, it was also potentially damaging to the urgently necessary business of saving souls in preparation for the Second Coming. It was therefore one of the pope's primary responsibilities to maintain discipline. 'If we neglect to deal with those things illegally usurped,' he wrote, 'we leave the way open for others to commit excesses.'[1]

There was as yet no strict definition of the respective competence of canon and civil law. Indeed, canon law was still in the process of growth. Its basis was the decisions of the church councils, of which various collections existed, notably that of Dionysius Exiguus, which was in regular use by the Roman church. But it also consisted of the papal judicial decisions, which were kept in the archives to form a body of precedent. The emperors legislated freely on matters of ecclesiastical discipline and organization, and the papacy was perfectly happy to use these regulations too. For example, when the *defensor* John set out to hear the appeal of two Spanish bishops, Gregory gave him a dossier of eleven imperial laws.[2] In general, imperial laws were used where canon law was lacking, but sometimes both were used. For instance, imperial law said episcopal elections must be resolved within six months, and canon law within three months. Both rulings are known to have been utilized.

Despite this overlapping, the two law codes remained distinct, so that when the church accepted the dispositions of the civil code it did not lose its own particular characteristics. The relationship between *Romanitas* and *Christianitas* is particularly well illustrated by Gregory's operation of the law. He accepted the letter of the imperial law but often modified its spirit in the interests of Christian charity. When a dying woman, who was a tenant of the church, made certain bequests on her deathbed without making a proper will, Gregory ordered that her wishes be respected although they were not legally binding.[3] Again, the law said that an heir was bound to pay if a father bequeathed property that was not his own. But Gregory urged Bishop Donus of Messina to waive his rights to an amber cup and a slave illegally bequeathed by the late father of Faustus, *vir eloquentissimus*, saying: 'We know your Fraternity lives by the law of God and not of the world.'[4] When the widow Stephania petitioned the pope claiming that she was destitute because her little son Calixenus had not inherited his grandmother's house in Catania, which she had left instead to the Roman church, Gregory ordered the papal rector to hand it back to her, even though this violated the law against the alienation of church property.[5]

Gregory was thoroughly conversant with the imperial law code, as one would expect from a former city prefect. Seventy-four explicit and fifty-four implicit citations from the imperial law code have been traced in his writings, and it has been concluded from this that Gregory had a good working knowledge of it and that his principal contribution to its exercise was to temper it with humanity and goodwill.[6]

In his own judicial activities, Gregory displayed a Roman juridical mentality, a fluency with the law, and a characteristic desire to lay down general principles and define particular rights. He declared that the use of violence nullified an act performed under its influence, that laws could not be retroactive, that evidence should not be extracted under torture, that there should be no delays in passing judgment once a case had been decided, and that monies given for the common use could not be used for private purposes.[7] He defined very precisely the rights of *coloni*. They were not to be married apart, so as to break up the family; the marriage fee exacted was not to exceed one *solidus*; their misdeeds were to be punished by corporal punishment and not confiscation of property; and they could engage on private work for profit away from the church estates if permission was given.[8]

Although he accepted the existence of slavery, he was not willing to see people reduced to slavery against their rights. He did not allow the sons of a freed slave mother to be reduced to slavery, nor did he permit captives redeemed from the enemy by church money to be regarded as church slaves.[9] It is a case of firmness with fairness in all things, in the best Roman tradition.

The same spirit underlies his dislike of anything smacking of bribery. When Bishop Felix of Messina wrote to him asking for permission to reduce his clergy's salary and backed up his request with a costly gift of embroidered robes, Gregory refused the request and sent back the equivalent cash value of the robes.[10] Again, when some prominent Sardinians sent him a gift of grain to back up some unspecified request, he sent it back.[11]

When it came to ecclesiastical discipline, Gregory insisted on the strict maintenance of traditional and canonically sanctioned practices; but his overriding sense of fairness did allow him to make some modifications in recently introduced measures. He set the tone for his administration at the synod held at St Peter's on 5 July 595.[12] He introduced six measures, which epitomize the austerity and humility which he believed should characterize the clerical life. Lay *cubicularii* were excluded from service in the Lateran, and deacons forbidden to engage in singing to the neglect of their other duties. Land was not to be claimed for the church by force but through the courts. Dalmatics were in future not to be laid over the pope's body in his funeral cortege because of the common people's habit of seizing them and venerating them as holy relics. Slaves wishing to enter monasteries should serve a period of probation, and then if their conduct was approved they should be emancipated from slavery and should enter the monastery. No fee should be exacted for ordination or conferring the *pallium* or for preparing charters related to these acts. Gregory was very much against 'perks'. Pope Gelasius had banned the exaction of fees for baptism and confirmation, and Gregory banned the payment of fees for burial in consecrated ground, for the marriage of inferior clergy, and for the veiling of women.[13]

The same moral principles underlying these measures can be seen behind several of his continuing policies. Celibacy had been obligatory for bishops, deacons and priests since the time of Pope Siricius (385–99) and for subdeacons since Leo the Great (440–61), but in the south of Italy the implementation of subdiaconal celibacy was lax. Pelagius II, clearly impatient with this laxity and anxious for absolute conformity, had ordered in 588 that Sicilian subdeacons should either become celibate at once or be suspended from their duties.[14] Gregory thought this unfair and unwise, in that it might lead to unnecessary resentment and resistance, so in 591 he modified it by making it obligatory on all who became subdeacons after that date.[15] More specifically, he ordered that no one in future should become a subdeacon unless he was willing to be celibate, that those who since prohibition had become celibate were to be encouraged to continue, and that those who had not been willing to be celibate could stay in office but could not be promoted. He ordered the same rules to be enforced in Rhegium.[16]

Gregory insisted that a cleric's degradation from holy orders as a punishment for some misdeed should be final and absolute, for he believed that the restoration of such men would be subversive to ecclesiastical discipline and deleterious to the moral well-being of the faithful.[17] This rule applied equally to bishops, priests, deacons and subdeacons.[18] When he learned that a deprived priest had dared to celebrate mass, he ordered him excommunicated until death.[19] But he drew a distinction between lapsed priests and lapsed monks. The lapsed monk could – indeed, should – be restored to his monastery after serving his penance.[20] The distinction was that it was the clergy who celebrated mass, and the sacrament was sullied by criminals dispensing it, whereas the monastic vocation was specifically non-priestly and monks were not permitted to celebrate mass.

On clerical revenues, Gregory enforced the fourfold division decreed by Gelasius I,[21] though it is clear that methods of distribution of the clerical fourth varied. Gregory's own method was distribution by merit. But in Catania, for instance, two-thirds of the clerical fourth traditionally went to the priests and deacons, and the remaining third to the junior clergy. Whenever there were pay disputes and Gregory was called upon to arbitrate, he suggested his own method as the best, as for instance when queries arose about the salaries of the exiled Capuan clergy and the clergy of Palermo, and when the senior Catanian clergy complained that their bishop had reversed the traditional distribution there. Gregory also forbade the practice which had grown up in Sicily of bishops keeping new sources of revenue for themselves and only dividing the traditional revenue by *quadripartitum*.[22]

Because of the disturbed and confused state of Italy, the maintenance of discipline was increasingly important, and under Gregory the papal rectors came more than ever to be 'the eyes and ears of the pope', the executive agents of his policies and principles in the provinces. One of their particular duties was to watch over the behaviour of the bishops. As Gregory said of Adrian, newly appointed rector of Syracuse: 'We have charged him if he hears of any irregularities committed by our reverend brothers the bishops, first of all to reprove them privately and modestly, and then, if the offences are not corrected, to report the matter at once to us.'[23] A circular letter to the rectors, once again concerned with Sicily and the south, ordered them to stop living with women, ostensibly their housekeepers.[24] Gregory also urged the rector Anthemius to call the Campanian bishops together for an official reprimand: 'It has been reported to us that the bishops of Campania are so negligent that, unmindful of the dignity and character of their office, they show the care of paternal vigilance neither towards their churches nor towards their sons; nor do they concern themselves about the monasteries nor bestow their protection on the oppressed and the poor.'[25]

He was particularly concerned that the existing privileges of the church should be preserved, and especially that the distinctive privileges of the Roman church should be preserved, not only on the general principle that all change was bad and hastened the approach of cosmic chaos but also on the specific principle that usurpation of Roman clerical privileges diminished Rome's hierarchical pre-eminence. There was also a personal element here, in his dislike of pride and ambition, so that when the deacon Liberatus of Caralis aspired to be archdeacon contrary to the law of seniority, Gregory not only forbade it but ordered him to rank last among the deacons because of his 'reprehensible spirit of ambition'.[26]

In 598 Gregory wrote asking John of Syracuse to find out why Catanian deacons wore *campagi* sandals, a right exclusively reserved to the deacons of the Roman church.[27] More significantly, Gregory became embroiled in the *pallium* dispute with Ravenna – a dispute which highlights the importance of the fixed hierarchical structure in Gregory's thinking. It is also symptomatic of the increasing dissatisfaction with which Ravenna, long the administrative capital of Italy, viewed its subordinate position in the Italian hierarchy. This discontent had been shrewdly fuelled by Justinian I, seeking to create a counterweight to the papacy in Italy, and it was to bear fruit later, in the seventh century, when Ravenna declared its independence (*autocephaly*) from Rome with the backing of the emperor Constans II. But the *pallium* dispute was a potent hint of things to come.

The *pallium*, a triangular woollen vestment decorated with crosses and worn over the other episcopal garb, was granted by the pope to apostolic vicars and other favoured prelates as a mark of honour and special favour.[28] Its use was restricted to the mass, and wearing it in public processions was forbidden.[29] It is interesting to note that for the award of the *pallium* outside the frontiers of the Empire imperial permission had to be obtained.[30]

The problem with Ravenna arose soon after Gregory's consecration. The incumbent archbishop of Ravenna was John III, a Roman by birth and perhaps a former Roman cleric. Gregory learned that John wore the *pallium* not only at mass but also in solemn procession through the city and at audiences with the laity. Gregory instructed notary Castorius, his *apocrisiarios* in Ravenna, to warn John to desist from this practice. Castorius' remonstrance prompted a letter from John to Gregory defending the practice on the grounds of a privilege granted by Pope John III. Gregory replied in July 593 that he had searched the archives and questioned Roman clerics who had visited Ravenna in the time of his predecessors but he could find no justification for this claim.[31] He therefore absolutely forbade the archbishop to wear the *pallium* other than at mass, unless he could produce written evidence to support his claim, something Gregory clearly believed unlikely. But John had not only upset Rome by his *pallium* wearing, he had also encouraged his clergy to use the white linen saddle cloths (*mappulae*) which were another privilege exclusive to the Roman clergy. Taken together these actions indicate a clear declaration by the archbishop of Ravenna of his see's eminence. Gregory, however, was anxious to avoid a confrontation with Ravenna, and despite the opposition of the Roman clergy and the absence of any evidence that such a right had been previously granted, Gregory did inform John that he was prepared to permit the use of the *mappulae* by the senior Ravennate deacons when in attendance on John.

In his reply John III complained that Gregory's letter was a 'mixture of honey and venom'.[32] He claimed that he had done only what was sanctioned by the privileges of his church, a copy of which he attached, that he would never presume to act contrary to tradition, and that he had always upheld the authority of Rome and had earned great enmity for doing so. John also enlisted the support of leading laymen, such as the exarch Romanus and the praetorian prefect George, who were quite happy to support the rise of Ravenna *vis-à-vis* Rome, and they wrote to Gregory supporting John's stand. Gregory's relations with the exarch were already strained, and he was clearly anxious not to impair them further. So in October 594 he replied that he had consulted the experts in Rome and that, although they had declared there was no precedent for it, to allay John's distress he would permit the use of the *pallium* on three occasions, the litanies of St John the Baptist, St Peter and St Apollinaris, while a more detailed investigation was conducted by the archive staff. This was as far as he was prepared to go.[33]

Then Gregory found out, presumably from Castorius, that, for all his humble letters, John in fact reviled Gregory behind his back, telling all manner of scandalous stories about him. Gregory wrote angrily denouncing his two-faced conduct, urging him to humility, and remarking darkly that were it not for the fact that the Lombards blocked communications between them he would act with the utmost severity. In order to be fair, though, he had sent to Constantinople to ask about the use of the *pallium* in public processions in the East.[34]

On 11 January 595, however, John died, and Gregory with considerable skill fixed the election as his successor of the monk Marinianus from Gregory's own monastery of St Andrew's. He conceded to him the use of the *pallium*, urging him to wear it only at the mass and the solemn litanies permitted to John III.[35] Gregory must have thought that the problem had been solved at a stroke, but not a bit of it. Leading laymen continued to press for the use of the *pallium* in all litanies, and in April 596 Gregory instructed Castorius to inquire of the older members of the Ravennate clergy, under oath, what had been the practice before the time of Archbishop John III.[36] Nothing came of this, for Marinianus fell into line with the established Ravennate position and sent the deacon Florentinus to inform Gregory that the archbishop was accustomed to wear the *pallium* at all litanies. Gregory rejected the claim on the basis of the evidence to hand, and again instructed Castorius to make an inquiry.[37] The outcome of this affair is not known, but the likelihood is that, like the 'Oecumenical Patriarch' controversy, it dragged on until Gregory's death without being resolved and that the archbishop continued to wear the *pallium* as he chose.

Gregory's willingness to compromise perhaps reflects a political situation in which he could not afford to alienate the imperial authorities in Ravenna any further. There was, however, no question of compromise with those who had betrayed their sacred duty. He had to deal with many individual cases of wrongdoing, from bishops down to minor clerics, and his powers in this field were well defined by both canon and civil law. An accused bishop was to be tried before the metropolitan, or a bishop deputed by him, for such crimes as heresy, usury, simony, unchastity, and dereliction of duty. To make sure that ecclesiastical discipline was not neglected the metropolitan was ordered to convoke the clergy at least twice a year to hear cases, review regulations, and so on. For guilty bishops, the punishment could be deposition, or suspension from duty for a period of penance in a monastery.[38]

There are six known cases of episcopal depositions in Gregory's reign: Demetrius of Naples, Agatho of Lipari, Paul of Triocala, Lucillus of Malta, Benenatus of Misenum, and the unnamed bishop of Forum Cornelii.[39] In addition, Bishop Proculus of Nicotera was suspended for a period.[40] The charges against them are not known for certain, but Lucillus was involved in the embezzlement of church property, Benenatus was implicated in embezzlement of state monies entrusted to him, and Demetrius' crimes are said to have been so serious as to have deserved the death penalty. The most significant fact about these depositions is that they were almost all of southern bishops, and this confirms the picture of widespread laxity in the south suggested by the non-observance of subdiaconal celibacy and the negligence of the Campanian bishops reprehended by Gregory. It seems likely that the thoroughgoing bounder Bishop Andreas of Tarentum only missed deposition by dying, for he had ill-treated his clergy, kept concubines, and was alleged to have beaten a woman on the church charity rolls so badly that she died.[41]

Aside from depositions, Gregory had to deliver reproofs to negligent bishops to encourage them to mend their ways. Once again, southern bishops figure strongly, with Paschasius of Naples spending all his time shipbuilding and Basilius of Capua immersed in lawsuits, Pimenius of Amalfi charged with persistent absenteeism and Felix of Sipontum with turning a blind eye to the rape committed by his grandson.[42]

The most serious and long-running example of episcopal incompetence and misbehaviour was silly old Archbishop Januarius of Caralis, under whose woebegone rule Sardinia became a major ecclesiastical disaster area. To maintain ecclesiastical discipline, not only did an archbishop have to be an able metropolitan; he also had to provide an effective check on the excesses of the imperial officials, which in Sardinia were particularly gross. It was in the latter connection that Gregory first encountered Januarius, when he travelled to Rome in June 591 to complain about the misdemeanours of Duke

Theodore of Sardinia.[43] But it was not long before complaints about Januarius' own stewardship were reaching Rome. Indeed, by August 592 the stream of complaints had become a flood ('*tanta moles querimoniarum*').[44] One in particular Gregory regarded as very serious – the excommunication of the *vir excellentissimus* Isidore out of pure malice. Gregory therefore sent a special envoy, the notary John, to examine all the cases, appoint arbitrators and execute their decisions. It was the first of three such missions that Gregory was to send, and the beginning of a long and increasingly exasperated correspondence with Januarius, whom Gregory was later to describe as 'elderly and simple-minded'.

John's arrival in Caralis produced yet more complaints and complications, and Gregory was forced to order his rector Sabinus to send Archbishop Januarius, notary John, and the major complainants to Rome, so that cases could be decided before him.[45] Whether they came is not known, but certainly by September 593 there was another mass of complaints to be dealt with, evoking a long letter from Gregory.[46] Gregory complained that Januarius needed the pope's written authority to supplement his 'faltering disposition'. He had entirely failed to appoint the customary clerical officials to deal with the secular business of the Sardinian nunneries, so that the nuns were 'compelled to go in person to the public functionaries about tributes and other liabilities and are forced to run to and fro through village and farm to make up their taxes, and to mix themselves inappropriately in business which belongs properly to men'. He urged the appointment of such officers at once, specified penalties to be imposed on lapsed nuns, insisted on twice-yearly synods for the correction of the clergy, instructed Januarius to cease returning runaway slaves to Jewish masters and exhorted him to fulfil various testamentary dispositions regarding the foundation of monasteries.

As if this were not enough, reports were coming in that paganism was rampant in Sardinia. Gregory therefore decided on a second mission, sending Bishop Felix and Abbot Cyriacus in 594 to tackle both the paganism and the archbishop. The reports of Felix and Cyriacus revealed even more widespread neglect and confusion.[47] The clergy despised the archbishop; the archdeacon cohabited openly with women; the lay authorities oppressed the church; administration of church hostels was neglected; fees were exacted for ordination, clerical marriage and taking the veil; the clergy were resorting to the patronage of laymen; lapsed clergy were celebrating mass.

Gregory, ever sensitive to hierarchical authority, avoided writing directly to the Sardinian bishops lest he undermine Januarius' authority, such as it was. Instead he ordered Januarius to tackle these abuses at once and make the pope's will in the matter known to his bishops.[48]

In 598 there was another welter of cases and another special mission, the *defensor* Redemptus being dispatched to try to sort it out.[49] By October 598 Gregory was very angry. He wrote furiously denouncing the violent and illegal seizure of property by Januarius, excommunicating his advisers for two months and warning that Januarius himself could be next unless he mended his ways. 'The preacher of Almighty God, the apostle Paul, says "Rebuke not an elder". But when an elder sets an example to the young for their ruin, he is to be smitten with severe rebuke. Such great wickedness of your old age has reached our ears that if we were not as humane as we are, we should smite you with a definitive curse.'[50]

Gregory set up a special bureau in Rome to deal with complaints from Sardinia, under the deacon Peter and the *consiliarius* Theodore.[51] The problem, however, continued: a Jewish synagogue desecrated; the clergy neglecting their duties; laymen plundering church estates; the clergy plundering monastic estates; clerical tenants fleeing from church estates; the paupers being oppressed by the powerful.[52] By September 603 Januarius, sick and senile, was totally incapable of governing, and Gregory took steps to remedy some of the faults by bypassing him. Charge of the church hostels was committed to the archdeacon of Caralis and the *oeconomos*. The papal rector Vitalis was ordered to recover lost church property and to convey the complaints of oppression by the lay authorities to Constantinople.[53] It is unlikely that Januarius survived much longer, though he may just have outlived Gregory. Nowhere in the Suburbicarian province were things as bad as in Sardinia, but the situation there does demonstrate the vital importance of securing a good bishop in a key see and helps to explain Gregory's programme of patronage appointments to key bishoprics, which will be examined later.

Among the lower clergy there were cases of breaches of celibacy, homosexuality, usury, violence, neglect of duties, and self-mutilation in imitation of Origen.[54] There were also major irregularities among the clergy of Luna, which Bishop Venantius was incapable of dealing with, and Constantius of Milan was sent in to help him.[55] The problem of dealing with wicked clerics was made worse by lay interfer-

ence. Great men were sometimes inclined to protect them,[56] particularly in Ravenna. Gregory's plea to the exarch not to interfere in
ecclesiastical cases because such action undermined clerical discipline
indicates how high this interference went.[57]

Like Gelasius before him, Gregory was very keen to delimit ecclesiastical and secular spheres of competence strictly and wherever
possible to prevent uncertainties or clashes of jurisdiction arising. He
urged bishops to avoid getting involved in secular affairs 'except in
so far as the necessity of defending the poor compels them to do
so'.[58] Gregory resolutely defended the right of sanctuary but saw it
not as a shield for the guilty but as a means of obtaining justice for
the innocent.[59] Thus if slaves sought sanctuary they could be handed
back to their masters only upon the giving of a promise of pardon or
the arrangement of trial.[60] If free men sought sanctuary, the church
authorities should again try to arrange a fair trial for them and should
extend protection to them while they awaited it.[61]

The position with regard to clerical trials was complicated. Bishops
could not be brought before secular courts for any case, but although
the rest of the clergy were exempt from the secular courts for ecclesiastical and lesser criminal charges, they could still be called before
lay courts in major criminal cases (e.g. murder) or in civil financial
cases with laymen, if the laymen were unwilling to have recourse to
the bishop's court. Gregory strove consistently to preserve the exclu-
sivity of the clerical caste in judicial matters. Dudden summarizes his
policy succinctly:[62]

> We find Gregory frequently insisting that accusations against
> clerics must be heard only in the bishop's court, when the
> bishop should either deliver judgement himself, or, if suspected
> of bias, should appoint a commissioner to see that the litigants
> chose referees, and that the case was thus properly settled by
> arbitration. While, however, Gregory fought for the right of the
> bishop to preside at the trials of his clergy, he at the same time
> urged the episcopal judges to abstain from provoking the
> litigants by distressing delays and remands, and to arrange that
> judgement when given, should be promptly executed.

From the first, one of the principal interests and responsibilities of
the popes had been for the liturgy, the framework of Christian worship which contained the essence of the sacred magic and constituted
what has been called 'that sense of community which transcends the

limitations of time'. The fundamental elements of the liturgy – the eucharist, the rites of the sacraments, prayer in common, and the sermon – had been established early on, and the basic form of the service was more or less fixed by the end of the fifth century.[63]

Since at least the eighth century, however, Gregory has been credited with a major liturgical innovation – the creation of a new and comprehensive sacramentary (the *Sacramentum Gregorianum*). The most detailed account of this comes in John the Deacon's ninth-century biography.[64] John says that Gregory undertook a major revision of the existing 'Gelasian Sacramentary', rearranging, adding, abbreviating, simplifying and codifying the orders of service. John was not inventing but expanding on a tradition current in the eighth century, when Walafrid Strabo ascribed the creation of a sacramentary to Gregory, when Pope Adrian I sent to Charlemagne a copy of the sacramentary arranged by 'our predecessor, the God-inspired Gregory', and when Egbert of York claimed that Augustine had brought the 'Gregorian Sacramentary' to England.[65]

Because of this testimony, and the existence of the manuscript sacramentaries called the 'Leonine', the 'Gelasian' and the 'Gregorian', it was for centuries believed that the Roman mass went through three formative stages, associated with the reigns of Leo I, Gelasius I and Gregory I. As a result of the work of liturgical historians during the last seventy-five years, this view has now been very largely abandoned.

Liturgical history is pure scholarship: painstakingly detailed, extremely technical, highly esoteric and compulsively fascinating. Its practitioners, like the initiates of an ancient mystery cult, pour the fruits of their researches into learned journals with splendidly arcane titles like *Ephemerides Liturgicae* and *Sacris Erudiri*. It is hard for a mere layman to penetrate these mysteries, but what I want to do is to take their general conclusions and set them in a wider historical context, so that Gregory's role can be made clearer. So far as I understand it, the present state of knowledge is as follows.

There were no formal, authoritative, papally promulgated mass-books until the seventh century. Before that time the arrangement was much more fluid and *ad hoc*. Sheets of parchment (*libelli*) containing liturgical prayers were kept both in the Roman titular churches and in the papal archives and were drawn on when necessary for use in church services, whose form was traditional and accepted but not written down.[66]

The earliest sacramentary, the so-called 'Leonine', which exists in a single seventh-century manuscript, is now known not to be an official, systematically arranged massbook promulgated by Leo the Great. It is a random collection of liturgical prayers, compiled in Rome *circa* 550 and drawn from the various collections in the city. A reasonable hypothesis would be that the compilation was undertaken by the papal archives as part of the general process of setting the papacy in order again after the close of the Gothic wars and the arrival of Pope Pelagius I from the East. He is known to have been active in filling church vacancies, collecting together scattered church plate, and generally tidying up and sorting out the affairs of the church, which were in considerable disarray. A gathering together of prayer texts from various sources would be in line with these other activities.

Until the seventh century it seems that the principal contribution of the popes was in the composition of liturgical prayers, which expressed with 'almost juridical precision' and in polished rhetorical Latin the fundamental and dogmatic truths of the Christian faith. But this process was fluid and continuous, not frozen and fixed. Prayers could be used, abandoned, added to, revised. Special prayers could be composed under the stimulus of external events, such as Pope Vigilius' prayers alluding to the Gothic siege of Rome and Pope Gregory's referring to the Lombard terror. Gelasius is known to have revised some of Leo's prayers. The store grew constantly. The 'Leonine Sacramentary' contains prayers by Leo I, Gelasius and Vigilius. Ninety-seven prayers are common to all three sacramentaries.[67]

When we come to the 'Gelasian' and 'Gregorian' sacramentaries we are on different territory, for unlike the 'Leonine', they are formalized, systematically arranged collections of texts. What is significant, however, is that these two sacramentaries had entirely different purposes, which makes it inherently unlikely that one superseded the other. The *Gelasianum* exists in a single manuscript probably deriving from the monastery of Chelles near Paris and dating from *circa* 750. Although it contains interpolated Gallican elements, the bulk of it is an organized set of prayer formularies for use in the Roman titular churches. In other words it is a presbyteral massbook.[68]

The earliest version of the *Gregorianum* is a ninth-century Aachen manuscript, based on the sacramentary sent to Charlemagne by Adrian I, and it is specifically a papal massbook, for use when the pope himself celebrated mass in the Vatican or the Lateran or when he went to the selected so-called 'stational churches' in the city to celebrate mass on certain Sunday festivals and every day during Lent except Thursday. The likelihood is therefore that during the seventh century the *Gregorianum* and the *Gelasianum* existed side by side for different uses.

But when were these sacramentaries created, and by whom? The context here is important. During the first half of the seventh century there was a dramatic influx into Rome of Eastern monks and clerics, refugees from Arab invasion and Monothelete persecution. For the next hundred years they were to dominate the councils of the papacy and swamp the native element in the Roman clergy. In their wake there came a large-scale introduction of the cults of the Greek saints, Greek ecclesiastical rites and rituals, and even Greek church institutions into Rome. Many of the brooding, shuttered, roofless temples of the pagan gods came to life again, renovated and reconsecrated by the priests of the Christian God. Candles burned, incense smoked, and the 'Alleluia' rang out through the columns and porticoes. A lavish programme of painting, ornamentation and elaboration, much of it undertaken by refugee Eastern artists, bid fair to turn the churches of Rome into Oriental sacred domes. Although Latin remained the language of the official documents, Greek was spoken freely, by bishops at synods and even by priests in church services. *Ordo Romanus I* records the pope asking on Easter morning: 'How many infants were baptized in Latin and how many in Greek?' All this is in stark contrast to the reign of Gregory I, who had indignantly rejected charges that Greek practices were creeping into the Roman liturgy.[69]

Perhaps the most dramatic development was the introduction of a new papal rite, modelled on Byzantine ecclesiastical and court ceremonial. It has been described as 'a rigid etiquette admitting neither change nor improvisation on the part of the assistants, an awe-inspiring solemnity of ceremonies and a unique grandiose *organum* chant [which] became symbols of Papal sovereignty in the West, turning the congregation into spectators and listeners'. The distinguishing feature of the old urban rite, which was symbolic of the Roman community and was here displaced, was participation in the ritual by the congregation as well as the clergy. The new papal rite excluded the congregation and was built around the glorification of the pope.[70]

This was surely the matrix of the formal papal sacramentary. It should be seen alongside other developments, all of which aimed to formalize and regulate precisely every aspect of the liturgy. There was the *capitulare evangeliorum*, the collection of selected gospel readings for each liturgical day, the earliest surviving version of which dates from 645.[71] There are the *Ordines*, the ceremonial handbooks, describing the ever more elaborate ritual procedures involved in the dressing of the pope, the timing of entrances and exits, the order for processions and the kissing of the papal hands and feet. The earliest of these is late-seventh-century.[72] There is the so-called 'Gregorian Antiphonary' to provide the singers with their part in the service, which was probably introduced by the new *schola* set up by Pope Vitalian to train singers in the papal chant. This strong contextual evidence argues for a mid-seventh-century origin for the 'Gregorian Sacramentary' too.

What was Gregory's role in all this? There is clear evidence that the Adrianic version of the *Gregorianum* cannot be Gregorian, because it contains references to festivals and churches which date from after Gregory's death: for instance the festival of the Exaltation of the True Cross and the anniversary of the translation of Leo I's relics, introduced by Sergius I; the station of St Maria ad Martyres introduced by Boniface IV; the stations of St Adrian, St Andrew near the Lateran and St Lucia introduced by Honorius I; and Gregory's own feast day. On the other hand, 82 of the 927 prayers in the sacramentary are demonstrably by Gregory.[73]

On internal evidence an argument has been put forward for Honorius I as the compiler of the sacramentary.[74] This is plausible, because Honorius made a conscious effort to revive Rome by building many new churches and introducing new cults and festivals, but the date is perhaps a little early, given the dating of analogous liturgical developments. All that can be said for certain is that the papal sacramentary existed by 683, from which year a version survives, embedded in a later text. This may be an edition revised by Sergius I, to accommodate his many liturgical innovations. There was almost certainly also a revision by Gregory II, who introduced Thursday stational masses in Lent and thus altered the papal liturgical year.[75] It is probably here that the origin of the attribution to Gregory I lies, from a simple but understandable confusion with Gregory II, who had undertaken a major revision of the papal sacramentary which had appeared towards the middle of the seventh century to accompany the developments in papal chant and rite. It may also be this confusion of Gregories which created a second confusion – the dubbing of the presbyteral massbook as 'Gelasian'. Eighth- and ninth-century liturgists, knowing that the priestly book antedated the papal book and believing the papal book to be by Gregory I, may well have scanned the *Liber Pontificalis*, discovered that the last pope before Gregory to be credited with major liturgical changes was Gelasius I, and leaped to the obvious but, as it happens, erroneous conclusion.

What, then, did Gregory do in the liturgical field? He wrote prayers, as his predecessors had done, and he undertook some minor liturgical changes, in the interests of simplifying and shortening the service. He added some words to the prayer *Hanc igitur*, ordered the Lord's Prayer to be recited before the breaking of bread instead of after, ordered the *Alleluia* chanted at times other than Easter, to which it had previously been confined, forbade the subdeacons to wear chasubles when they processed to the altar, and forbade the deacons to perform any of the musical portions of the service except the chanting of the Gospels. He outlined these changes himself in a letter to John of Syracuse, carefully setting out the precedents for all of them.[76] This would seem to be the limit of his liturgical innovations. The fact that the *Liber Pontificalis* does not say that Gregory introduced a sacramentary is not necessarily conclusive evidence that he did not, since the *Liber Pontificalis* does not say that anyone introduced a sacramentary. But the rest of the evidence is surely conclusive enough to show that Gregory did not compile a papal sacramentary. Pious sentimentalists continue to cling to Gregorian authorship, but the trend of the evidence is irreversibly away from such a theory.

This conclusion, of course, invalidates the idea that Augustine could have brought a Gregorian sacramentary to England, and there is other evidence to confirm that such an idea is untenable. Gregory's letter to Augustine giving permission for the use of the Gallican rite suggests that this had already been introduced to England by Queen Bertha's Frankish chaplain, and, again, it was not until the seventh century, with the strongly pro-Roman activities of St Wilfrid of Hexham, St Benedict Biscop, and the arch-cantor John, and with the arrival of Theodore of Tarsus as archbishop of Canterbury that there was a positive effort to introduce Roman usages, culminating in the declaration of the Synod of Cloveshoe in 747 that henceforth services should be conducted exclusively according to the Roman rite.[77]

Gregory's name has also been attached to the 'Gregorian Anti-phonary' and to 'Gregorian chant'. The evidence for this is similar to that claiming Gregorian authorship for the sacramentary. Egbert of York and Walafrid Strabo both asserted that Gregory composed an antiphonary, and John the Deacon confirmed this claim, saying that an authentic copy of it was still extant in his own day. He also added that Gregory set up a *schola cantorum* for the singing of the Gregorian chant.[78] Again the earliest surviving manuscript is a ninth-century Frankish production.

In fact the situation of the antiphonary is exactly the same as that of the sacramentary. The likelihood is that 'Gregorian chant' was the quasi-Byzantine chant which was developed to accompany the new papal rite in the latter half of the seventh century.[79] The key reign seems to be that of Vitalian (657–72). It was probably Vitalian who set up a *schola cantorum* to teach the new papal chant; certainly its members were known as *vitaliani*. The eighth-century St Gall manu-script of *Ordo XIX* lists the men who are said to have arranged or edited the chant as Damasus, Leo, Gelasius, Symmachus, John I, Boniface II, Gregory I, and Martin I, and then three abbots, Cato-lenus, Maurianus and Virbonus. This refers almost certainly to the chant of the old urban rite, which the papal one superseded, and suggests that it was at least after the reign of Martin I that the popes ceased to rearrange the urban chant. It is even possible that *Ordo XIX* was compiled *circa* 675 by John, arch-cantor of St Peter's and abbot of the adjacent monastery of St Martin. The three previously named abbots were perhaps his predecessors as arch-cantors. This all sug-gests that, as with the liturgical prayers, there were constant re-arrangements being made when the urban rite prevailed, but that after Martin's reign, and probably as a result of Vitalian's creation of the papal chant *schola*, a fixed and final form was arrived at for the new papal chant. The creation of a formal antiphonary embodied this development, and again was almost certainly revised by Gregory II along with the sacramentary. Writing of the antiphonary, Pope Adrian I said it was composed by Pope Gregory but calls him *'iunior'* which firmly suggests Gregory II. It was no doubt an authentic manuscript of this 'Gregorian Antiphonary' which John the Deacon saw, and there was once again confusion over names.

Despite this, it is still possible that Gregory, concerned as he was to prevent deacons spending their time singing, did set up a *schola cantorum*, as John suggested, but for the urban rite.[80] However, his

musical innovations must be limited to one of the periodic rearrange-
ments of the musical texts which the popes customarily made when
the urban rite prevailed. If any Gregory should be credited with
sacramentary and antiphonary it is Gregory II.[81]

Chapter Eight

Patrimonial Administration

One of the most celebrated areas of Gregory's activities is in patrimonial administration. The Register testifies eloquently to the meticulous care with which he administered the estates of the Roman church, suggesting yet again that background in civil administration and estate management which has already been postulated. His execution of these duties provides one of the best demonstrations of the synthesis of *Romanitas* and *Christianitas* that was the hallmark of everything he did. *Romanitas* can be seen in the efficient and painstaking fulfilment of his role as landlord in the best traditions of Rome. The Register shows time and again his scrupulous fairness, attention to detail, and mastery of every myriad aspect of estate management. *Christianitas* can be seen in the application of Christian charity to temper the stern demands of absolute justice, and in the objective of his patrimonial administration. He regarded it as something to be run not for the profit of the church but for the alleviation of hardship and want among the poor.

Gregory's letters give the fullest and most detailed picture of the papal estates and their management in the early Middle Ages. The landed estates of the papacy, collectively known as the patrimony of St Peter, provided one of the principal sources of revenue for the Roman church.[1] These estates had been acquired over the years by endowment and bequest, ever since the legalization of bequests to the church in 321. One of the earliest and most lavish benefactors was the imperial family, whose last great donation was probably the lands of the Arian church in Italy, confiscated after the extinction of the Ostrogothic kingdom and handed over in 554 to the Catholic church. The church of Ravenna received the largest slice, but Rome must also have benefited. There were certainly Arian churches with their own endowments in Rome which passed to the papacy.[2] Apart from this there was a regular stream of benefactions from less prominent but equally well-disposed figures. Gregory's Register reveals that the patrician lady Campana left her Roman home and gardens to the Roman church, the priest Felicianus left a garden in Rome to the Roman church, and the notary Primigenius left a third of his Sicilian property to the Roman church.[3]

How much revenue these estates actually brought in is very difficult to estimate, though there are some hints. According to the chronicler Theophanes, the value of the Sicilian and Calabrian patrimonies confiscated by the emperor Leo III in 729 was 250,000 *solidi*.[4] The annual revenue of the Ravennate patrimony in Sicily in the mid-seventh century was 31,000 *solidi*, 50,000 *modii* of wheat and sundry other goods.[5] That of Rome would have been much more, but we can probably still not improve on Dudden's statement: 'It is at least quite certain that at the beginning of the seventh century the Roman Church owned many hundreds of square miles of land and drew annual revenues amounting to hundreds of thousands of pounds.'[6]

There were certainly fluctuations in the fortunes of her landed estates. The war and disturbance afflicting mainland Italy in the sixth century told heavily on the patrimony. For instance, the Picene patrimony, estimated under Gelasius I (492–6) at an annual value of 2160 *solidi*, had by the reign of Pelagius I (556–61) dropped in value to a mere 500 *solidi per annum*, and by Gregory's reign had vanished altogether, swallowed up by the Lombard invasions.[7] The Gothic wars had a serious effect on the papal estates, the Lombard invasions a disastrous one. No papal patrimony survived inside Lombard-held territory, which meant, apart from the loss of the whole Picene patrimony, the loss of parts of the Samnite, Sabine and Apulian patrimonies. There was also considerable loss of population on some of the estates which remained. Gregory refers, for instance, to the 'few peasants' still left on the Callipolis estates. Typically he took prudent steps to remedy this, ordering that the *coloni* of Callipolis should pay only what they could afford in rent to prevent the diminution of manpower still further.[8] It was a problem not confined to Italy. In Africa there were considerable tracts of papal land unpopulated, and the Exarch Gennadius of Africa earned Gregory's fervent thanks by settling them with prisoners of war.[9]

At Gregory's accession, there were some fifteen separate patrimonies making up the patrimony of St Peter. Four of these were outside Italy proper, none of them apparently extensive. There was a small Gallic patrimony (*patrimoniolum*) in Provence. The 400 *solidi* in rental revenue which Gregory received from Gaul in 593 might at first sight seem large for a so-called *patrimoniolum*, but it almost certainly includes rent arrears.[10] There was a problem with the revenues from these estates in that rents seem to have been paid in locally struck coinage of a different weight and type from the official imperial coinage, and to prevent depreciation the popes encouraged the spending of the money locally. Gregory suggested the purchase of warm clothing for the use of refugees in Rome, and the purchase of teenage English slave boys for service in the Roman monasteries.[11]

The Roman church possessed estates in North Africa, mainly in Numidia, a *patrimoniolum* in Illyricum, and estates in Sardinia and Corsica – islands which, although they came within the patriarchal jurisdiction of the pope, were under the administrative control of the exarch of Africa.[12] The importance for the papacy of all the extra-Italian patrimonies seems to have been primarily political rather than fiscal. In the Sardinian and Corsican correspondence, for instance, there is comparatively little mention of estate business. The papal rectors there were employed in checking the excesses of the bishops, keeping a watchful eye on the lay authorities, and supplying Rome with information on the running of the Catholic church. This seems to have been the pattern of business in all the non-Italian patrimonies. They were useful papal footholds outside Italy proper but Rome did not depend on them overly for revenue.

The principal revenue-producing estates were in Italy itself. The smallest papal patrimony was probably in the Cottian Alps, where Gregory described the estates as *possessiuncula*.[13] The richest and most extensive estates were in Sicily. All the formulae in the *Liber Diurnus* relating to the appointment of rectors refer to Sicily, suggesting its pre-eminence.[14] The most frequent and detailed letters on patrimonial matters in the Gregorian Register are directed to Sicily. By Gregory's reign, in fact, the patrimony had become so large that the pope divided it into two rectorships, centred on Palermo and Syracuse respectively. The Syracusan rector was always the senior of the two, and some idea of the extent of the Sicilian patrimony can be gained from the fact that his bailiwick included properties in Catania, Messina, and Agrigentum as well as Syracuse itself.[15]

The next most important patrimony was probably Campania, where the estates seem to have been large enough to absorb Lombard depredations around the edges. Several other once-important patrimonies were less fortunate, however. The patrimony of Lucania and Bruttium was curtailed by the extensive Lombard activity in Lucania.

The same situation obtained in Apulia and Calabria, where the loss of most of Apulia to the Lombards left the papal rector isolated in Sipontum and unable to exercise close control over the Calabrian estates. Only Hortona and its environs remained under the control of the papal rector of Samnium, and the Sabine patrimony came to be known as the 'Tiburtine' after the rector concentrated his activities on Tibur after the loss of part of the province to the Lombards.

Close to Rome itself were the Appian patrimony – a cluster of estates around the Appian Way yielding oil for the lamps of the Roman churches – and the Tuscan patrimony, which included estates around Blera and was safely within the boundaries of the duchy of Rome, as indicated by its survival and attestation under Pope Zacharias. Finally, there were estates in Ravenna and Istria, administered from Ravenna by a rector who also acted as papal *apocrisiarios* at the court of the exarch. The position was a vital one, since it involved dealing with and keeping an eye on the exarch, the archbishop of Ravenna, the Lombards, and the Istrian schismatics, all of whom could prove difficult and frequently did, sometimes all at once.[16]

Each patrimony was subdivided into individual estates. Some were farmed directly by the church but most were leased out to tenants, on lifetime leases (*emphyteusis*), generally to rich men, or on fixed-term leases to lesser men (*conductores*).[17] There were 400 *conductores* in Sicily in Gregory's time.[18] Gregory was extremely concerned about leasing arrangements. He informed the Sicilian rector Peter in August 591 that many people were coming to Rome seeking *emphyteusis* leases on estates and islands in the Roman church's possession, and that although some were granted many were refused.[19] Great care was to be taken in granting them and the conduct of leases was to be closely watched. The *scribones*, imperial recruiting officers, had such a bad record as tenants that Gregory absolutely forbade the granting of leases to them.[20]

The manager of the patrimony was the rector, appointed by the pope and holding office at his will. Designated in Rome, he would take an oath on the tomb of St Peter to defend the interests of the church and protect the poor. He received letters of appointment, the estate account book, and a detailed set of instructions from the pope pertaining to his area.[21] Letters of commendation were sent to local bishops and important lay officials.[22] Letters would also be sent to the *coloni* and *conductores* of the patrimony, enjoining their obedience to the new rector. A good example is the letter to the Syracusan *coloni* on the appointment of the *defensor* Romanus as rector:[23]

> We would have you know that we have thought fit to place you under the care of our *defensor*. We therefore charge you to yield an ungrudging obedience to such commands as he shall see fit to give you for promoting the interests of the church. If any attempt to be disobedient or contumacious, we have given him the power of punishing them severely. We have also directed him to recover for the property of the church carefully, vigorously and promptly, all runaway slaves and all land which has been unjustly occupied by anyone. We further inform you that he has been charged upon his peril not to venture on any pretext whatsoever to seize unjustly or by force the property of others.

At the end of the financial year (*indiction*) in September, the rector sent his account books to Rome to be checked. Before Gregory, such checks seem to have been irregular, enabling some of Pelagius I's rectors to defraud the papacy by falsifying their accounts.[24] It may be that Gregory was the first pope to institute an annual check.

Obviously, one of the major duties of a rector was the actual management of the patrimonial estates. The rectors collected the rents, awarded leases, and supplied Rome with produce such as grain, timber, horses and oil. But there were other important areas of involvement for them. They were charged with the protection of the oppressed, the relief of the poor, and the upkeep of the church hostels (*xenodochia*). They dealt with much minor litigation. They oversaw episcopal elections, kept an eye on episcopal behaviour, rectified abuses in churches, monasteries, and hospitals, enforced ecclesiastical discipline, and cracked down on heresy. A single letter written in July 592 to Peter, rector of Sicily, gives a good insight into both the rector's spheres of competence and the detailed nature of papal oversight.[25] The pope makes businesslike and equitable dispositions on a wide variety of matters. He instructs Peter on property disputes and lawsuits, the sale of unprofitable herds, the reduction of estate duty paid by converted Jews, hostel management, the selection of his subordinates, the building of a monastery, the payment of poor relief and subsidies to individuals, the using of his influence with the bishop of Syracuse in the case of two individuals, the payment of gifts to imperial officials to ensure their goodwill towards the church, the execution of various provisions in the will of a deceased churchman, and the provision of horses for the papal equipage. A personal note creeps in here when Gregory declares the previous consignment of mounts to be unsatisfactory: 'You have sent me a sorry nag and five good asses. The nag I cannot ride because it is so wretched; the asses I cannot ride because they are asses.' Not for the pope the vehicle of the Saviour, but the noble steed of the Roman consul. There were, after all, limits to humility.

The rector had an extensive staff at his disposal. He was assisted by a corps of *defensores*, senior administrators whose importance and influence can be judged by the appearance of *pseudo-defensores*, claiming the papal commission and committing illegal acts in the name of Rome.[26] Below them were the bailiffs and agents (*actores* or *actionarii*), who were obliged to be tonsured – as a sign of their provenance – and who received diplomas.[27]

Over the activities of the rectors and the patrimonial officials the pope needed to keep a watchful and informed eye. There were many opportunities for misconduct. The position of the Roman church as a landlord was extremely powerful, and its name carried considerable weight. Examples of overstepped authority, of the use of the name as a licence to plunder, abound. The pope dealt with complaints about money, slaves, land, goods, and houses seized by his representatives even from monasteries and other churches.[28] Gregory's answer was consistently that if the complaints were justified, the property should be returned: 'I will not have the church's purse defiled by base gains,' he said.[29] He constantly stressed his view of the agent's role. The seizure of a man's sons as slaves of the Roman church by the Campanian rector Anthemius led Gregory to write angrily to him: 'You should fulfil your duties in our place there not so much for the good of the church as to relieve the necessities of the poor and free them from whatever oppressions they suffer.'[30] His maxim was: 'Just as the church ought not to neglect its own property, so also should it refrain from invading that of others with the ardour of rapacity.'[31]

The conflict between the aims of the rectors (profit) and the objective of Gregory (justice) is graphically illustrated by the career of the *defensor* Romanus, who as manager of a hostel was reprimanded for devoting too much time to making money and not enough to spending it on the poor, but whose obvious efficiency earned him promotion to the rectorship.[32] Then as rector he had again to be reprimanded for exceeding his authority by setting aside episcopal judgments on his own responsibility. This put the fundamental papal principle of hierarchy in jeopardy. As Gregory wrote: 'If you do not respect the rightful jurisdiction of every bishop, you are doing nothing but destroy that ecclesiastical order which it is your special duty to maintain.'[33] There was no question, then, of the pope using his agents to seek to erode the powers and jurisdiction of the bishops. But he always had to be on his guard lest the actions of his agents had that result.

It seems to have been Pope Gelasius I who took the first steps towards organizing the papal patrimony into a coherent administrative unit, for it is from his reign that the *Polyptycum*, the great account book of the patrimony, dates. It was still in use in the ninth century, and Gregory refers to it in his Register.[34] It probably resulted from a full-scale investigation of the papal estates, prompted by the need to check on war damage.[35] There seems, however, to have been no regular rectorial system in operation under Gelasius. By the time of Pelagius I (556–61) there was a fully operational rectorial system, but it was not as yet staffed exclusively by clerics of the Roman church. Both local bishops and laymen exercised rectorial authority in some areas.[36] At some point between the reigns of Pelagius and Gregory it became customary for Roman clerics to administer the Italian patrimonies. They had also expanded their activities from mere estate management to being the 'eyes and ears of the papacy' in the regions. Unfortunately, it is not possible to trace the development of the rectors' powers and responsibilities. The Gregorian Register presents the first real opportunity to assess the nature of the fully formed rectorial system.

It may even be that Gregory himself made the move to complete the romanization of the Italian rectorate, but however this may be, Gregory certainly instituted some important reforms in the system. Foremost among these was Gregory's determination to bring all the patrimonies, not just the Italian ones, under the control of Roman clerics. As John the Deacon noted, Gregory 'appointed industrious men of his own church as *rectores patrimonii*'.[37] This was of particular significance in the extra-Italian patrimonies, where in some cases this was happening for the first time. For there is no doubt that Gregory saw these rectors not primarily as agents of estate management but as the unofficial envoys of the papal see resident abroad.

Traditionally the Gallic patrimony had always been administered by local dignitaries, lay or ecclesiastical.[38] On Gregory's elevation to the throne of St Peter, Dynamius, governor of Provence, was the papal rector. When he retired in 595, Gregory did not appoint the new governor, Arigius, as rector. He simply allowed Arigius to administer the patrimony until the new rector arrived from Rome.[39] To ensure that he did not profit from the vacancy, Arigius was not permitted to collect the rents. The *conductores* were ordered to nominate one of their number to collect and hold the rents until the arrival of the new rector.

The new rector was in fact the Roman priest Candidus, whom Gregory commended to the goodwill of Queen Brunhild. Gregory pointed out that it was a long time since a man of the Roman church had been sent to govern the patrimony. Candidus had now been sent 'so that he may be able both to manage with profit this little patrimony, which is evidently beneficial to the expenses of the poor, and also to recover into the patrimony's possession anything that may have been taken away from it'.[40] Someone whom the pope could trust was certainly needed. Rents collected by the archbishop of Arles, when he had been rector ten years before, had still not been paid over to Rome in 596.[41] But this was not the only or, indeed, arguably, the principal reason why Gregory wanted a Roman cleric to be rector in Gaul. The point of choosing uniquely a priest rather than a representative of one of the administrative orders emphasizes this. The job was to be predominantly a missionary one. The rector was to try to expedite Gregory's long-cherished and ultimately unsuccessful project to instigate a great synod in Gaul to eradicate the abuses with which the church there was rife.

Gregory's African rector was the notary Hilarus, who had held the same office under Pelagius II and was confirmed in it on Gregory's election.[42] The few references to his activities contained in the Register indicate that his role was similar to that of Candidus in Gaul – that is to say, staying on good terms with the civil authorities, overseeing church discipline, and combating heresy and schism.[43]

The incumbent rector of Dalmatia on Gregory's election was the local bishop, Malchus, who can be seen acting in a rectorial capacity in March 591 when he was ordered to persuade the bishop of Scodra to submit his dispute with the *consiliarius* John to arbitration.[44] Malchus was later accused of the sale of church property and other illicit acts and summoned to Rome for trial. He eventually reached Rome, was tried and found guilty late in 593 or early 594, but died the same day the verdict was reached. This unfortunate turn of events gave rise to a rumour which circulated freely in Constantinople that Gregory had had him poisoned, a story Gregory took pains to refute.[45]

Malchus' removal from office did allow Gregory to install as Dalmatian rector the subdeacon Antoninus, one of his own clerics.[46] He took office in March 592, but his rectorship was dominated and eventually terminated by the question of the election to the metropolitan see of Salona. When violence flared up following the installation of the anti-papal candidate, Maximus, in late 593, Antoninus fled back to Rome in fear of his life. Thereafter during the prolonged dispute between Gregory and Maximus, there was no resident papal representative in Salona, as is evidenced by the fact that during this period Gregory always had to write directly to the Dalmatian bishops to make his views known. However, after a reconciliation was effected between Gregory and Maximus in August 599, it was safe – indeed, desirable – to send a papal representative to keep an eye on Maximus. The new rector was the Roman notary John.[47] It is interesting to note that in the three countries Gaul, Africa and Dalmatia, the only incumbent rector to retain his job under Gregory was the sole Roman cleric; the other, non-Roman rectors were replaced by Roman clerics.

What the arrangements had been in Sardinia and Corsica under previous popes is not known; but under Gregory Roman clerics were certainly sent as papal rectors, and their jobs corresponded very much with those of the other overseas rectors. This seems to have been recognized by the islanders themselves, both lay and clerical. In 599, for instance, the clergy of Caralis, deserting their duties and defying their archbishop, resorted to the protection and patronage of the papal rector Vitalis. Gregory ordered this to stop, but he did permit Vitalis to act as an intercessor on their behalf in disputes with the archbishop when he thought that the clergy should be pardoned rather than punished.[48]

Within Italy, Gregory maintained the tradition of appointing Roman clerics as rectors. But in the interests of honesty and efficiency, he did not permit them to remain in the same post throughout his reign, changing them after a few years to prevent complacency or the entrenchment of interest. The known transfers of power seem in the main to have been routine, but two at least were made because of unsatisfactory conduct.[49] The Samnite rector, *defensor* Scholasticus, was the son of Bishop Blandus of Hortona, and when his father died he refused to hand over the episcopal palace to the new bishop, Calumniosus, and held on to vestments and other property belonging by right to the bishop. He also detained in the name of the Roman church lands rightfully belonging to the church of Hortona. In 599 he was ordered by the pope to hand over the property illegally detained, and it is likely that this behaviour led to his replacement by the *defensor* Benenatus.[50] The subdeacon Anthemius, the first Gregorian rector of Campania, who had frequently to be reminded of his duty towards the poor and was neglectful of monastic discipline, was recalled in 592 and replaced by the subdeacon Peter. But upon Peter's elevation to the Sicilian see of Triocala in 594, Anthemius, who had apparently learned his lesson, was reappointed.[51] Only one patrimony is known where there was no change of rector – Appia – but the evidence for the patrimony is so scanty that it would be unwise to draw conclusions from it.[52] In general, then, apart from known cases of removal for unsatisfactory performance, Gregory seems to have pursued a calculated policy of periodic replacement of patrimonial rectors.

Gregory also made various internal adjustments to structure and staffing. The Cottian Alps patrimony was initially administered by an exiled Milanese priest, Magnus. He died at some point before 600, and soon after this Gregory brought the Cottian Alps under direct Roman rule by appointing as rector the *defensor* Hieronymus.[53] An adjustment was necessary in Calabria because of the isolation of the rector in Sipontum. In 599, Gregory, concerned about the danger to the papal estates in Callipolis, threatened by enemy attack, depopulation, and oppression by the local military commandant, detached them from the control of the Apulian rector and placed Bishop Sabinus of Callipolis in charge of them. Although this looks like a breach of Gregory's own rule about not employing bishops as rectors, the bishop in question was one of his own patronage appointments, a former monk of St Andrew's, and so the breach was more one of letter than of spirit.[54]

In Sicily, there was an even more spectacular structural change – the division of the patrimony into two. Gregory's reign opened with the appointment of his friend and disciple, the subdeacon Peter, as rector of the Sicilian patrimony and vicar of the Sicilian church. His tasks were to overhaul the patrimonial administration at all levels and begin the Gregorianization of the episcopate. He held office from September 590 to July 592.[55] On his recall the patrimony was divided into two, one half centred on Syracuse and the other half on Palermo, with the former retaining an overall supervisory responsibility. The deacon Cyprian was appointed to the senior post.[56] The appointment of a deacon to a rectorship, though rare, was not unprecedented. When it did occur, however, it was usually in Sicily, further testimony of the patrimony's importance.[57]

To the junior Sicilian post of Palermo was appointed the notary Benenatus, but by July 594 he had been replaced by one of his subordinates, the *defensor* Fantinus.[58] Cyprian seems to have been recalled in 598, and there was then a hiatus before the appointment of a new rector. In the interim Bishop John of Syracuse was given charge of the papal patrimony, an arrangement resisted by some of the *defensores*, who refused to obey his orders and had to be threatened with punishment by the pope.[59] Like Sabinus at Callipolis, John was an appointee of the pope and could therefore be trusted with the temporary administration of the patrimony. Eventually the *defensor* Romanus was appointed Syracusan rector.[60] Romanus, the former hostel manager whose excessive concern with making a profit worried Gregory, overreached himself in 601 by setting aside the episcopal judgments of Bishop John. He was soon afterwards recalled, and was replaced, probably in 603, by the notary Adrian, who had proved himself as acting rector of Palermo during the absence of the rector Fantinus in 601–3. Fantinus was probably in Rome in connection with the trial of Bishop Exhilaratus.[61] All in all, the surviving details of the rectorial arrangements in Sicily provide a rare and valuable insight into the career structure of the administration, the personnel, and some of the ideas underlying Gregory's policies.

Gregory's reign saw positive advances in the rectorial system. Men from all grades of the administrative service were used as rectors, and they were changed fairly frequently. Gregory kept a close eye on their activities, using them to implement his personnel policies but not allowing them to step outside their limits and infringe the rights of the episcopate. His innovations lay in bringing the outlying patrimonies directly under the control of Rome by the appointment of Roman clerics to administer them and by making various internal adjustments in the interests of greater efficiency. His watchwords throughout were prestige, efficiency and discipline.

The principles and practice of Gregory's estate policy are best illustrated by his Sicilian correspondence. When Gregory became pope, he was extremely disturbed by the state of affairs in the island.

In the time of Pelagius II reports had been reaching Rome of wide-spread injustice and corruption in the patrimonial administration. Relations with the lay authorities were bad, and the Byzantine governor of the island was refusing to allow the bishops to leave the island to attend synod in Rome. The premier Sicilian see, Syracuse, was vacant, and the entire Sicilian episcopal bench needed a radical overhaul.

Gregory acted at once, recalling Pelagius' rector, Deacon Servusdei, and sending in Subdeacon Peter as rector and vicar.[62] Gregory set out the situation as he saw it in a letter to Peter, dated March 591:[63]

It has come to our knowledge that during the last ten years from the time of the *defensor* Antoninus to the present day, many persons have been unjustly treated by the Roman church – so much so that some of them publicly complain that their lands have been forcibly occupied, their slaves taken away and their property removed not in consequence of any judicial decision but by violence.

He laid down general guidelines for dealing with these problems. He ordered that all such claims should be investigated, and whatever property had been removed by force should be at once restored. He forbade absolutely the use of force in any matter involving church property and urged recourse to reasonable argument and due process of law. The principal complaints against the church concerned runaway slaves, who if they claimed to belong to the church were simply taken on to the patrimonial strength by the rectors without any investigation. Gregory ordered that such claims should be investigated and that slaves wrongfully held should be restored to their proper masters.

By May 591, on the basis of reports received from the retiring rector and from Peter, Gregory was tackling specific abuses. His letter, dated to that month, reveals a miasma of corruption and oppression, which he was determined to eradicate.[64] Firstly, the *coloni* on church estates paid an annual corn rent, which could, as was the practice on lay estates, be commuted to a money payment. The amount of the commutation varied, however, and at a time when corn was plentiful they were charged more than the market value in commutation. Gregory ordered that commutation be fixed according to the market price of corn, so that in times of plenty they paid correspondingly less in tax. Another oppressive practice was that if grain was lost during shipment to Rome it was levied again from the tenants. Gregory ordered this stopped. If the loss was no fault of the peasants, they were not to be burdened with it. If special extra grain supplies were needed, they were to be acquired not from the peasants but from independent grain dealers. Yet another problem was that church officials varied the weight of the *modius*, the corn measure. Gregory insisted that the *modius* should consist of 18 *sextarii*, the official weight adopted by the church granaries, and this should not be varied.

He had also learned that various extra financial burdens were being added to the standard rate of taxation on various grounds, sometimes custom, sometimes formalized additional payments, sometimes plain corruption. Gregory ordered that Peter should consolidate and fix the rate of the extra imposts, and that in order that they should not be varied again after his death, the peasants should receive charters of security specifying the fixed amount and signed by the rector. Some of the *conductores* had been using false weights to measure the corn. These were to be seized and destroyed, and replaced by fair measures.

Peasants, who were not allowed to marry without permission, were being charged immoderate fees for this permission. Gregory fixed it at one *solidus*. If a peasant were poor he should be charged even less, but never more. The money was to go to the *conductor* and not to the church.

Besides their rents and dues to the church, the peasants were liable for the imperial land tax (*burdatio*), which was paid three times a year (January, May and September). Gregory learned that the first of these payments was a serious inconvenience to the peasantry, because they did not have the money to pay at that time, before the harvest, and were forced to mortgage their crops at less than their true value or to raise money by borrowing at exorbitant rates of interest (25 per cent was quoted in a similar case in Campania).[65] He therefore ordered the rector to pay the money on their behalf from papal funds and allow the peasants to repay by instalments.

Peasants who committed misdeeds were not to suffer confiscation of property, which would affect the whole family, but instead were to suffer corporal punishment. Anything illegally taken from peasants by a *conductor* was to be taken from him and restored to the peasants. *Conductores* were not to pay the rector fees for their appointment, since this encouraged a too frequent change of *conductores* to profit the rector. When *conductores* died, their relatives were to be allowed to succeed to the land, and if the heirs were minors someone was to be appointed to administer the land for them. This amounts in effect to a Bill of Rights for church tenants, peasants and *conductores*, and Gregory ordered that his instructions be read out to them publicly, and that they be given copies of his rulings so that their rights might be preserved.

Many of the old abuses persisted, however. In 594 the *burdatio* payment regulations had still not been implemented.[66] In 603 the papal 'troubleshooter', the notary Pantaleo, was sent on a commission of inquiry to the Syracusan patrimony and once again found that the *modius* of grain the *coloni* were charged was 25 *sextarii*.[67] When he learned in 603 that a large sum of money had been illegally extorted from peasants in the Syracuse region by *conductores* to buy livestock, Gregory refused to allow the Roman church to retain the animals and ordered them to be distributed among the *coloni* who had been forced to pay for them.[68] More is known about Sicily than elsewhere because it was the biggest and therefore the most troublesome patrimony, but it is likely that similar problems existed on a smaller scale in other patrimonies. Gregory's Sicilian response gives a fair indication of how he would have tackled similar abuses elsewhere. The Sicilian correspondence provides ample evidence to describe Gregory as a liberal, fair-minded, but nevertheless efficient landlord of the best kind. It is clear that he did all in his power to preserve the rights of church tenants and that his guiding aim throughout was truth and justice.

Chapter Nine

Gregory and the Episcopate: (1) Sicily

Following the imperial reconquest, circumstances and the exigencies of war saw an increase in the powers of the papacy and the scope of its activities. The same is true of the episcopate in general. With the aristocracy broken and dispersed and the imperial provincial government weak and preoccupied, it fell more and more to the bishops to undertake such responsibilities as the handling of refugees, the negotiation of treaties, the provisioning of cities, and the making of defence dispositions. The people came to look to the bishops, as they did to the pope, to protect them from the wrath of the barbarians. It was therefore increasingly important that the bishops be well versed in statecraft and administration.

This extension of episcopal involvement in secular matters was reflected in the law code of Justinian. He gave the bishops effective oversight in the whole field of local government, demanding that they report infringements of the law by imperial officials and that they bring the complaints of the people before the emperor. They were expected to oversee the treatment of prisoners, orphans, foundlings and lunatics, civic expenditure, public works, aqueduct maintenance, public order, and supply of foodstuffs to the troops. In the *Pragmatic Sanction* bishops were even associated with the appointment of provincial governors. All in all it involved an awesome responsibility.[1]

The Gregorian Register gives examples of bishops undertaking these duties. The bishop of Terracina was ordered to see that the walls of his town were kept properly manned; the bishop of Misenum was given money to fortify his town; the archbishop of Caralis was ordered to see to the defence and provisioning of his city.[2] Both the political and the psychological significance of the bishop is confirmed by Gregory's order that the bishop of Amalfi should remain in residence in his town and cease his wanderings abroad lest his absence should invite the enemy to attack.[3] *term/office of bishop*

The oversight of the Italian episcopate was one of the pope's principal responsibilities, and the extension of episcopal duties made papal supervision more imperative than ever. It meant that the higher needs of an overall papal personnel policy might have to take precedence over the desires of the inhabitants when it came to elections. In other words, it signalled the operation of a system of papal patronage, the intervention of the pope in episcopal elections either directly or through his agents to secure the appointment of a man known to be fitted for the enhanced responsibilities of the office.

The evidence on episcopal elections in the sixth and seventh centuries is extremely fragmentary, but it looks as if systematic interference in elections did not begin until the late sixth century, coinciding with the extension of episcopal responsibilities after the reconquest, and it may even have been Gregory who initiated the policy.[4]

The key to the selection of satisfactory bishops obviously lay in the election. The procedure following the death of a bishop in the Suburbicarian see is clearly outlined in papal letters. Notice of an episcopal vacancy was sent to Rome, the metropolitan see. The pope then appointed a visitor to administer the see and provide for a speedy election. The letters of Gregory are very precise in the standard instructions to visitors. The pope ordered the visitors to arrange an election so that the clergy and people might get together and with one consent choose a bishop who was worthy of the office and against whom there was no canonical impediment. The bishop-elect was then dispatched to Rome together with the electoral decree testifying to his literacy, countersigned by the visitor, to be consecrated by the pope.

The actual electorate consisted of clergy, nobles (*ordo*) and people, but in general the chief clergy and the local nobles fixed matters between them. Even though the election was officially decided in the local church, the pope as ordainer had considerable legal powers which he could use to influence the choice. He was entitled to veto an election on canonical grounds. If a man had a criminal record, if he was illiterate, if he held government office, if he was a layman, if he had been married twice or had married a divorcee, or if he was under thirty, then he could not become a bishop.[5]

In the event of electoral deadlock, the pope was empowered by the canons to choose and ordain a candidate himself. However, what the pope invariably did, indicating his full awareness of local sensitivity in the matter, was to summon representatives of the clergy and citizens to Rome and there in discussion with them choose a mutually acceptable candidate. More often than not, it would be a case of the pope suggesting and the electorate agreeing.

Gregory's patronage policy assumed a distinct pattern and possessed the sort of coherence one might expect from someone with his background in both secular and ecclesiastical administration. It is important to stress that the policy stemmed not from an ideological desire to dominate the episcopate but from a pressing practical need to ensure good government, something not necessarily guaranteed by free elections.

What constituted for Gregory an ideal bishop? The evidence on this is conflicting, for his practice did not always follow his principles. His standard visitation letter, for instance, ordered 'that no one from another church shall be allowed to be elected unless no one can be found among the clergy of the church under visitation, which we do not believe likely'.[6] This affirms a desire to maintain the local character of the episcopate, but it conflicts directly with the idea of nominating Roman clerics to key bishoprics. Gregory did, in fact, devote an entire book to outlining the character of the ideal bishop, the *Regula Pastoralis*. It was divided into four sections: who should be called, what sort of life he should lead, how he should address his flock, and how he should discipline himself. It clearly emerges from the book that care of souls, teaching and preaching both actively and by example, are the keynotes of the bishop's life. A typical extract defines the qualities needed.[7]

> He ought by all means to be drawn to become an example of
> right living, he who, dead to all fleshly passions, already lives
> spiritually; who disregards worldly prosperity; who fears no
> adversity; who desires only spiritual things; whose intention
> thus well known the body does not oppose by weakness nor the
> spirit by disdain; who is not led to covet the goods of others but
> gives freely of his own; one who through the bowels of
> compassion is moved to grant pardon but is never plucked from
> the citadel of righteousness by pardoning more than is fitting;
> who perpetrates no illicit deeds but deplores those perpetrated
> by others as if they were his own; who out of heartfelt feeling
> sympathizes with another's infirmity, and rejoices in another's

good fortune as if it were his own; who so suggests himself to others as an example of all that he does, that he has nothing to blush for in his own past deeds; who studies so to live that he may be able to water even the dried-up hearts with streams of the faith; who has already learned by the use and practice of prayer that he can obtain what he has requested from the Lord.

Character was clearly crucial, for 'no one does more harm in the church than one who has the name and rank of sanctity while he acts perversely.'[8] But sometimes character was not enough. A shorter and pithier phrase from one of Gregory's letters sums up the more realistic attitude determining his dealings with elections in the provincial capitals: 'You know that at this time such a one ought to be constituted in the citadel of government who knows not only how to be solicitous for the safety of souls but also for the external advantage and security of his subjects.'[9] It is on the basis of this maxim that he rejected as a possible bishop of Syracuse Trajan, a man who amply fulfilled the ideal of the *Regula Pastoralis* but lacked the requisite administrative experience. In electoral terms, then, the ideal would be someone who combined character and experience.

Thanks to John the Deacon, what is in effect a partial patronage list survives.[10] John writes: 'He took care to ordain as bishops the best men wherever he could find them', and adds that from the Roman priesthood he ordained Boniface as bishop of Rhegium, Donus as bishop of Messina, and Habentius as bishop of Perusia; from the Roman subdeacons he ordained Gloriosus as bishop of Ostia, Festus as bishop of Capua, Peter as bishop of Triocala, and Castorius as bishop of Rimini; and from the monks of his own monastery, he ordained Marinianus as bishop of Ravenna, Maximian as bishop of Syracuse, and Sabinus as bishop of Callipolis. What is interesting about this list is not just that it is a unique record of papal patronage, indicating the three sources on which Gregory drew for his bishops, but that, with the exception of Messina and Triocala, for which special circumstances can be adduced, the other sees are all important cities, and in several cases provincial capitals.

Sicily was the largest unit free of Lombard control, and as a self-contained unit provides an ideal starting point for an examination of Gregory's policy in detail.[11] His first recorded letter, dated September 590, is to the bishops of Sicily, suggesting that it was high on his list of matters to deal with. Firstly, he announced to them that the Roman subdeacon Peter had been appointed rector. Secondly, he announced that Peter had been appointed vicar, the only occasion in the entire Register when a man outside the episcopate received this exalted honour. Peter was, of course, not just any subdeacon; he was one of Gregory's closest friends and confidants. But Gregory was fully aware that the appointment was unusual and likely to cause resentment among senior bishops unaccustomed to being presided over by a mere subdeacon. There was, therefore, a stern injunction. 'From this council let hatreds, the nourishment of crimes, be absent and let internal jealousies and discord of spirits, which is most dreadful, melt away.'[12]

It was an unusual measure, then, but one which Gregory felt was merited by the difficult situation in the island. The praetor was refusing to allow the bishops to leave the island to attend the synod in Rome, prompting Gregory to authorize an annual Sicilian synod to be held on the island under the presidency of the vicar. Several Sicilian sees, including the principal see, Syracuse, seem to have been vacant, and the episcopal bench as a whole was in urgent need of an overhaul, as subsequent correspondence reveals. Peter's vicarial appointment gave him responsibility for the episcopal bench, and Gregory gave him an explicit directive about his duties in this regard in January 591.[13] He informed Peter that if any Sicilian cities were without pastoral care because their bishops had been deposed for misconduct, he should seek successors for them from amongst the clergy and the monasteries and send them to Rome for ordination. 'But', he added, 'if you should find any vacant places and there is no one from that church fitted for such an honour, inform us after careful inquiry so that God may provide someone whom he has judged worthy of such ordination.' For 'God' read 'Gregory' and there is a clearly expressed willingness on the part of the pope to intervene in the electoral process in the interests of good government.

Of the thirteen Sicilian sees several seem to have been vacant, as has been mentioned. The circumstances surrounding the Syracusan vacancy are not known, but the see would have been empty for at least seven months, the period between the death of Pelagius II and the consecration of Gregory, and it looks as if even before that there had been electoral deadlock. The election was almost certainly referred to Rome, for in October 591 there is a new bishop in Syracuse, a man hand-picked by the pope, as John the Deacon's list confirms and as circumstantial evidence strongly suggests. The new bishop is Maximian, who had been a monk in St Andrew's with Gregory, had accompanied him to Constantinople, and had been recalled in 594 by Pelagius II to become abbot of St Andrew's, a post he still held in 590. He was also a priest, ordained in order to say mass for the brothers, and so his elevation to the episcopate presented no problems.[14] He was the ideal blend of character and experience, and Gregory demonstrated his trust in him by transferring the Sicilian vicariate to him in October 591.[15] It was conferred with two major limitations: the reservation to the pope of all major cases, and the granting of the office to Maximian personally and not to his see in perpetuity. The reason for the latter provision is obvious. Gregory knows and trusts Maximian and will not necessarily know and trust his successor. What has happened is that one close and trusted friend has been replaced as vicar by another close and trusted friend. Maximian will now be able to manage the Sicilian episcopate for Gregory much more unobtrusively and uncontroversially than the rector could. It is the first successful Gregorian patronage operation.

After Syracuse, the three most important sees were Palermo, Catania, and Agrigentum, whose incumbent bishops were Victor, Leo, and Gregory, respectively. In August 591 all three were summoned to Rome.[16] It seems that reports of widespread misbehaviour by the inhabitants of Palermo had reached the pope, bespeaking dereliction of his pastoral duties by Bishop Victor. Gregory wanted to see him to give him a stern lecture on duty, the result of which was that on his return to Palermo Victor immediately ordered a city-wide clean-up campaign.[17] The other two bishops were wanted for trial. Of the charges against Leo nothing is known except that they were rapidly disproved and Leo took an oath of compurgation on the tomb of St Peter.[18] The case of Gregory of Agrigentum was more prolonged. The pope wrote to Maximian of Syracuse in November 592 ordering him to send at once to Rome the accusers, documents and petitions in the case and complaining that he had written before asking for them, without result.[19]

Though there are no further details about Gregory's trial in the Register, they are yielded by another source, for this Gregory is almost certainly to be identified with the eponymous hero of the *Vita Sancti Gregorii Agrigentini*, composed in Rome in the seventh century by the Greek monk Leontius.[20] This account reveals that Gregory, a distinguished theologian and exegete resident in a Roman monastery after many years in the East, was appointed to the see of Agrigentum after electoral deadlock had caused the matter to be referred to the pope. His election can be dated to 589, making the ordaining pope Pelagius II. However, a disgruntled section of the clergy, headed by men who had sought the episcopate for themselves, fabricated charges of immorality against Gregory, causing him to be taken to Rome for trial. After a long delay he was acquitted and eventually returned to Agrigentum in triumph – an outcome confirmed by the Gregorian Register, which shows him back in his see carrying out his duties in 603.[21]

While Leo and Gregory were acquitted, two other Sicilian bishops were not so fortunate. Bishop Agatho of Lipari and Bishop Paul of Triocala were deposed. Agatho was deposed in 591, perhaps the first victim of the episcopal overhaul begun by Peter and later carried on by Maximian.[22] The deposition of a bishop was a matter of the utmost seriousness, and the pope must have felt that the choice of a successor was too important to be left to the electors. Clearly someone of proved ability and beyond personal reproach was needed to correct the impression left by the ex-bishop, whatever his crimes may have been. Once again Gregory went for a blend of character and experience. In February 592 he appointed Paulinus as bishop of Lipari.[23] Paulinus was bishop of Tauriana in Bruttium, a former monk who like Gregory had lived in common with his monkish brethren after his elevation. But in 590 his city had been sacked by the Lombards and he and his monks had fled to Sicily, where Gregory had installed them in the monastery of St Theodore in Messina with Paulinus as abbot.[24]

Paulinus' appointment to the see of Lipari while still bishop of Tauriana did not contravene the canonical prohibition of the translation of bishops, for technically Tauriana and Lipari were being temporarily united in Paulinus' person and he retained all his rights over Tauriana while being resident in Lipari. Tauriana was almost certainly derelict following the Lombard attack, but since Lipari was separated from it by only a short sea voyage it could be visited whenever necessary. Indeed, Gregory ordered Paulinus to reside in Lipari but to visit Tauriana from time to time. The uniting of the sees was effected by the exercise of the papal prerogative (*'ex nostra auctoritate'*), thus obviating the need for an election at all. But the apostolic vicar Maximian of Syracuse was brought into play, being ordered to see Paulinus safely installed and to ensure that the clergy of Lipari obeyed him.[25] Once more Gregory's rule about the election of local men had gone by the board in the interests of personnel policy.

The other victim of the Gregorian purge was Bishop Paul, deposed probably in 593 and apparently guilty of the embezzlement of church property and dereliction of duty.[26] His see is not explicitly given in the Register; but its visitor was Bishop Theodore of Lilybaeum, and only two of the thirteen Sicilian sees are unaccounted for at this time, one of them being Triocala, which is quite close to Lilybaeum and can with confidence be assigned to Bishop Paul. Once again the situation called for a tried and true man to be installed, and once again Gregory acted. This time he appointed the subdeacon Peter, the former papal rector of Campania, who is listed by John the Deacon among the papal patronage nominees. By November 594 Peter was safely installed in Triocala and had been appointed visitor of nearby Agrigentum, whose bishop was still in Rome for trial.[27] How long this visitation lasted is not known, but as mentioned earlier, Gregory was eventually cleared and was back in his see by 603. The circumstances of Peter's appointment are also unknown. Whether there was a stage-managed election in Triocala, or, more likely, direct suggestion by the pope in Rome after the matter had been referred to him, the fact remains that Gregory got his man installed in Triocala.

The fourth Gregorian patronage appointment occurred in Messina. The incumbent bishop on Gregory's election was Felix, who seems from the evidence to have been a bad lot – at the very least an opportunist and probably worse. In 593 Gregory had to threaten him with canon punishment for not dealing fairly with a case involving a tenant of the Messina church.[28] Felix died in 595, and in September of that year Gregory conceded the *pallium* to his successor, Donus.[29] He was another Gregorian patronage nominee, listed by John the Deacon as a Roman priest. He is probably to be identified with Donus, priest of St Eusebius, who attended the 595 Roman Synod. Gregory's dissatisfaction with Felix and concern about the state of affairs in Messina had prompted yet another intervention.

The bishop of Tauromenium under Gregory was Secundinus. He first appeared in the Gregorian Register in August 591 when Gregory ordered Peter the rector to restore to him the house, lands and goods, seized by officers of the Roman patrimony but rightfully belonging to the church of Tauromenium.[30] He also ordered Peter to meet with Secundinus and discuss how certain monies lost during the time of his predecessor, Bishop Victorinus, could be recovered in the best interests of the church.

This letter strongly suggests a recent vacancy in Tauromenium, exploited by overzealous officers of the patrimony. This impression is reinforced by the subscription list of the 595 Roman Synod, which was signed by the bishops in order of seniority.[31] Secundinus signed after Candidus of Vulsinum, who became a bishop some time between December 590 and October 591, and before Homobonus, who was ordained as bishop of Albanum in 592. The evidence also suggests that Secundinus was a particular friend of Gregory's.[32] Beyond this point we cannot go, however. John the Deacon does not mention him among the list of Gregorian friends and nominees. The Register is silent on the circumstances of his election. He was elected in 591 and was a friend of Gregory: there the evidence stops, but arguing by analogy, there must be a suspicion of a Gregorian intervention.

The remaining Sicilian bishops seem to have been satisfactory for the moment. They were Theodore of Lilybaeum, praised for his energy and vigilance as visitor of Triocala; Eutychius of Tyndaris, encouraged in his efforts to convert the pagans and heretics in his diocese; Zeno of Leontini; and Lucillus of Malta, who was ordered to see that those of his clerics who held possessions of the African church paid their rent, which they had been refusing to do.[33]

The entire carefully built up structure in Sicily was threatened when its pivotal agent, Maximian of Syracuse, died suddenly in November 594.[34] It was a bitter blow to Gregory, both personally and politically. Maximian had implemented Gregorian episcopal policy in Sicily with great efficiency. He had been charged with the installation of Paulinus of Lipari, and it must have fallen to him also to smooth the passage of the other outsiders in their early days.[35] Theodore, the visitor of Agrigentum, was made responsible to him.[36] He undertook investigations and arbitrations and was directly responsible for the maintenance of discipline among the bishops. He must have taken much of the burden off Gregory's shoulders in the matter of Sicilian ecclesiastical affairs, which was, of course, the reason for his appointment. At the time of his death he was engaged in a campaign against clerics who were castrating themselves in imitation of Origen.[37]

Unless Gregory's hold over the ecclesiastical organization of the island was to be lost, it was vital that he secure an acceptable bishop of Syracuse. Fortunately, a revealing series of letters survives on the subject of this election. It may well be letters on this pattern, now lost, which furnished John the Deacon with his episcopal patronage list.

The first was to the rector Cyprian and was dated February 595.[38] Gregory urged him to see that a worthy successor to the late bishop was elected:

> And indeed I believe that the majority would choose the priest Trajan who, as is said, is of good disposition but as I suspect, not fit to rule in that place. Yet if a better cannot be found and if there is no charge against him, compelled by extreme necessity it can be yielded to him. But if my will in this election is sought, I indicate secretly to you what I wish: it seems to me that there is no one in that church so worthy to follow the lord Maximian as John, archdeacon of Catania. If his election can be brought about, I believe that he will be found an extremely suitable person.

So despite his good disposition and popularity with the majority of the electors Gregory did not propose to allow Trajan to become bishop. He lacked the requisite qualities for governing a great see. Gregory did not say what these were, but they surely included being known to and trusted by the pope. Cyprian is asked by Gregory to arrange with Bishop Leo of Catania for John to stand in the election, and to carry out Gregory's wishes regarding him.

The moral of this letter is quite clear and underlies the whole field of patronage operations. Whatever the will of the majority may be, the interests of the church as discerned by Gregory must be served first. There can be little doubt about his involvement in electoral patronage after this.

Unfortunately, the election did not go smoothly, as the next letter on the subject, dated July 595, reveals.[39] Gregory wrote to the nobles of Syracuse, praising their decision to opt out of the electoral process and leave the choice of bishop to him. The letter also reveals that the clergy and people of Syracuse had nominated for bishop a certain Agatho, and certain others another, unnamed nominee. Gregory ordered that both candidates be sent to Rome so that he might decide between them.

Reading between the lines, the story unfolds as follows. On Maximian's death there was a large measure of support for the priest

Trajan. This was undermined, probably as a result of the rector Cyprian's activities in privately communicating the pope's wishes to certain influential people. The nobles agreed to support whoever Gregory should choose. The clergy and people, two-thirds of the voting body, now transferred their support to Agatho, almost certainly another local cleric. They had accepted the disqualification of Trajan but, still preferring a Syracusan to a Catanian, had settled on another local man, Agatho, who they hoped would be more acceptable to the pope.

The pope, however, wanted Archdeacon John of Catania, and he was almost certainly the unnamed candidate supported by the minority of the electorate, a group undoubtedly mobilized by the papal rector. There seems, then, to have been a straight split between the nobles, who understood and supported the papal need to choose the right man for this key position, and the majority of the clergy and people, whose natural sentiment was to favour the local man.

Once the case was withdrawn to Rome for arbitration the result was a foregone conclusion, however, and by October 595 John was installed as bishop of Syracuse.[40] It seems likely that Gregory knew him personally, for to put someone he did not know into this key position was asking for trouble. The most obvious opportunity for a meeting would have been if John had accompanied Bishop Leo to Rome for his trial in 591 and had favourably impressed the pope. The important fact is that Gregory wanted him and got him, despite majority local support for two successive non-Gregorian candidates. In this context it is worth mentioning that it was about this time that the priest Donus was sent from Rome to be bishop of Messina. It might be that, given the amount of support for rival candidates to John in Syracuse, Gregory had seen fit to strengthen his hand on the Sicilian episcopal bench and with it the committed support and backing for John by the introduction of another Gregorian.

The election of John of Syracuse more or less brings to a close the first phase of Gregory's personnel policy in Sicily. The final seal is set on this by the letter dated May 597 in which Gregory conceded that in future the Sicilian bishops needed to come to Rome not every three but every five years on St Peter's Day.[41] This concession could not have been made had Gregory not felt strong enough and confident enough to leave the day-to-day running of affairs in Sicily to his hand-picked bishop of Syracuse, who had now had two years to establish himself.

1 Roma placing her hand on the shoulder of the consul Basilius, from a sixth-century ivory diptych

2 The Pantheon, the pagan temple converted into a Christian church in 608

IMAGINES AD VIVVM EXPRESSAE
EX AEDICVLA SANCTI ANDREAE
PROPE BEATI GREGORII MAGNI ECCLÆSIAM,
NECNON EX VITA EIVSDEM BEATI GREGORII
A IOANNE DIACONO LIB.IV. CAP. LXXXIII. ET LXXXIV.
CONSCRIPTA.

3 Gregory the Great and his parents, based on John the Deacon's description, from a sixteenth-century engraving

4 The throne of Gregory the Great, from the church of S. Gregorio Magno on the
Caelian hill, Rome

5 Ivory diptych on the gospel book presented by Gregory to Queen Theodelinda.
The figure in state dress is thought by some to be Gregory himself

6 The palace of the exarchs, Ravenna

7 Basilica of S. Apollinare in Classe, Ravenna

8 The great gate of Perusia, the key to the Rome–Ravenna land corridor

9 Bishop Euphrasius of Parentium, Archdeacon Claudius and his son, from a sixth-century Istrian mosaic

10 Grado cathedral, built by Archbishop Elias (571–86)

11 King Agilulf and his warriors, from part of a Lombard helmet decoration

12 Hen and seven chicks in silver gilt, thought to have been presented to Queen Theodelinda by Gregory the Great

13 Jewelled gospel book, presented by Gregory to Queen Theodelinda

14 The cross of Agilulf, all that remains of his crown

15 Emperor Justinian I and his court, including Archbishop Maximian of Ravenna, from a sixth-century mosaic in the church of S. Vitale, Ravenna

16 The column of Phocas in the Roman Forum

17 Coin portrait of the emperor Maurice

18 Coin portrait of the emperor Phocas

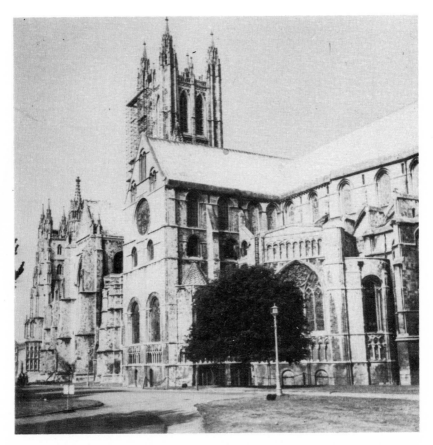

19 Canterbury cathedral, permanent symbol of Augustine's mission

20 Bede, from an engraving in the fifteenth-century Nuremberg Chronicles

21 An eighth-century Northumbrian scribe in his library, from the *Codex Amiatinus*

22 St Benedict performing a miracle, watched over by his sister St Scholastica, from the church of Sacro Speco, Subiaco

23 Gregory the Great by Nicolo Pizzolo, from the church of the Eremitani, Padua

24 Gregory the Great with St Augustine and St Silvester, from a twelfth-century mosaic in Cefalu cathedral

A glance at the Gregorian achievement during the period 591–5 reveals clearly enough why he should have felt this confidence. When he came to the throne the Sicilian episcopate was an entirely unknown quantity. He had no personal representatives on the episcopal bench and few, if any, friends. In this situation, there was nothing for it but an emergency measure, the dispatch of Peter as rector and vicar. Gregory's greatest coup was the appointment of two successive bishops of Syracuse, first Maximian and then John, who were able to take over the vicariate.

From the existing episcopal bench three bishops, Leo of Catania, Gregory of Agrigentum, and Victor of Palermo, were summoned to Rome in 591 and kept there for some time, the first two for trial, the third for a lecture on his duties. Two more, Agatho of Lipari and Paul of Triocala, were deposed, and another two, Felix of Messina and Lucillus of Malta, were threatened with canon punishment unless they kept up to scratch. Of those left, Tyndaris and Leontini were of minor importance, and Lilybaeum apparently satisfactory.

By 595, then, the Sicilian bench had been completely Gregorianized. Gregorian nominees ruled in Syracuse, Messina, Lipari, Triocala (with lengthy visitation in Agrigentum), and just possibly in Tauromenium. Catania and Palermo had been vetted at close quarters, Malta was under observation, and the rest stood. It was a major achievement, and one which had been managed with subtlety, skill and a great measure of success.

Phase Two of the Gregorian policy in Sicily was rather less active than Phase One. The hierarchy had been successfully remoulded and the policy from 595 onwards was one of maintaining the new system and upholding discipline, with changes in the episcopal structure dealt with as they arose.

The key man in the operation of this policy was, of course, John of Syracuse, who almost certainly received the vicariate in view of the extended interval between the visits of the Sicilian bishops to Rome. But in the management of the Sicilian bench John had less to do than his predecessor. The absence of any mention of further bishops of Triocala and Messina suggests that the two Gregorian nominees, Peter and Donus, outlived their patron. Paulinus of Lipari did not survive Gregory, dying in 602, but his successor is not known.[42]

Of the three old stagers, Leo, Gregory and Victor, the first two probably outlived the pope. Leo of Catania had a rather chequered

career. He seems to have been something less than satisfactory, and
the Register is regularly punctuated with letters reprimanding his
remissness.[43] There was, indeed, a second investigation of his conduct, undertaken by the rector Romanus in 598, but he survived this
too.[44] The picture of him that emerges is of an easy-going prelate
who needed periodic promptings to keep him up to the mark. There
can, however, be little doubt that if there had been anything seriously
wrong with his administration, he would have been deposed like the
other miscreants.

But, if Leo and Gregory survived, Victor of Palermo did not. He
died some time in 602, for in the November of that year Bishop
Barbarus of Carina was appointed visitor and ordered to arrange an
immediate election.[45] What follows is revealed in a letter from Gregory to the patrician Venantius, dated 602.[46] Gregory began by saying
that he was delighted that Venantius had nominated for bishop
Urbicus, abbot of St Hermes in Palermo, but he adds: 'Because someone else is proposed by the rest, we cannot disturb his quiet, so that
while he advances externally, he declines internally, lest when we
promote him to higher things, we compel him to a life of turbulence.'

This has been quoted as an example of Gregory's solicitude for
people – an unwillingness to withdraw Urbicus from his monastic
quiet and plunge him into the cares of office.[47] But there is perhaps
more to it than that. Urbicus was a Gregorian *par excellence.* He was
the abbot of one of Gregory's monastic foundations in Sicily and had
in the past been entrusted by the pope with important jobs.[48] He
certainly fulfilled the requirement of being known to and trusted by
the pope.

Venantius seems to have been acting as the head of the pro-papal
faction in the electorate, probably drawn from the *nobiles,* on the
analogy of Syracuse. He emerges as a devout layman and trusted
friend of the papacy.[49] It may well be that Venantius, who knew
Urbicus well and had served on commissions of inquiry with him,
believed him to be the best man for the job. But the involvement of
Gregory in such detail suggests that Venantius may also have been
acting for the pope in the matter.

Finally, the reference to Urbicus being plunged into turbulence if
elected must be looked at in the context of the unhappy outcome of
other Gregorian patronage appointments. Three notable cases, Castorius of Rimini, Festus of Capua, and Boniface of Rhegium, stand
out. All three had experienced the utmost difficulty in gaining accept-

ance from their own clergy, and in the case of Castorius the experiment had ended in dismal failure. It is precisely this that Gregory sought to avoid, and it prompted his suggestion that Urbicus' candidacy be dropped.

The other candidate, clearly a majority choice, was the deacon Crescens. He was certainly a local man and, with the aristocracy favouring Urbicus, the clergy and people are the likely electors. Since he did not know the man, Gregory asked Venantius to investigate the character and qualifications of Crescens, particularly the running of the hostel of which he had charge. If the investigation proved that he was satisfactory, then Venantius was to see that the pro-Urbicus party transferred its support to him. If, however, he proved unsatisfactory, then Venantius was to get the electorate to nominate an alternative to be sent to Rome with Crescens to allow the pope to choose between them. If, on the other hand, there was no viable alternative in Palermo – and for once the pope did not say that he thought this unlikely – then he was to see to the nomination of the alternative from another church. If all else failed and no fit person was to be found in Palermo or elsewhere, then the electors were to choose representatives who were empowered to decide in their name, and send them to Rome to see if they could find some suitable candidate there.

The pope seems genuinely reluctant to involve himself here, for the reasons already suggested. He seems to be laying down a purely disinterested procedure, but this disinterest is belied by the choice of Venantius as investigator of the character of the prospective bishop. In nearly all the other recorded cases, the visiting bishop does this, but of the visitor, Barbarus, there is no mention in these proceedings. Instead of the presumably impartial visiting bishop, Gregory entrusts the evaluation of the rival candidate to the leader of one of the factions in the election.

The pope's involvement in the election is further revealed in the instructions to Venantius that he should ask of the messengers who took his letter to Rome what they had discussed with the pope in detail. From the juxtaposition of sentences in this part of the letter it is possible to reconstruct the discussions that took place in Rome. The messengers apparently presented to the pope the situation as it was: a majority of the electorate favoured the deacon Crescens, a minority favoured Abbot Urbicus. Venantius seems to have asked the pope either to summon the candidates to Rome or to declare in favour of Urbicus or, failing that, to send down from Rome another hand-picked candidate from the Roman clergy. Gregory replied that he did not want to promote Urbicus against the will of the majority if that would cause problems with the flock. He did not have sufficient people for ordination to the vacant sees already existing and could not spare one for Palermo. There were sufficient Gregorians on the Sicilian bench to prevent Palermo being a vital see, and there was no pressing problem such as that presented by a deposition. Therefore Gregory proposed that if Crescens was found suitable, by a layman Gregory knew and trusted, he should be elected. Failing that, another candidate should be chosen from inside or outside Palermo, again by Gregory's agent on the spot. So the Palermo election represents an interesting half-way stage in papal electoral intervention.

The next information is contained in a letter of July 603 conferring the *pallium* on the new bishop of Palermo, John.[50] Crescens had clearly been overruled and another candidate introduced – but who, how, and from where? One possibility is that he was another local cleric, selected as suitable by Venantius. But in the light of the previous letter it seems more likely that the choice was the result of consultations carried out in Rome by the pope and the representatives of the Palermo electorate.

In this context the wording of the *pallium* letter is interesting. Other Gregorian *pallium* letters survive, for instance to John of Syracuse and Donus of Messina.[51] They are completely formulary and consist of an injunction to live up to their high office and a confirmation of the customary privileges of the church. But the letter to John of Palermo contains an order, inserted into the middle of the letter, to see that no one questioned the authority of the pope. The absence of this injunction from the other *pallium* letters can only mean that in Palermo there was some reason why the authority of the pope might be questioned, and the overruling of a favourite son in favour of an outsider would constitute such a reason.

There is another letter which might be adduced to support this hypothesis. Dated July 603, it is a letter to John giving papal confirmation to what is, in effect, a Bill of Rights demanded by the clergy and already confirmed by John.[52] It includes an annual publication of the accounts, drawn up with the participation of the clergy; the distribution of clerical salaries on merit; the right of the clergy to buy wine from the ecclesiastical estates, something hitherto denied them;

and the right for charges against clerics to be fully investigated before the bishop passes sentence.

The presentation of this bill by the clergy again suggests that John is an outsider, imposed on them by Rome. They were seeking to ensure that he made no restrictive innovations, and indeed in some cases to secure a better deal than the one they enjoyed under Victor. Acceptance of this bill by John and Gregory was the price they paid for the peaceful acceptance of the new bishop by the clergy and the evidence of attacks on papal authority. The evidence is admittedly circumstantial, but it does point to a Gregorian intervention and the admittance of an outsider to Palermo. As to who John was, there is no hard evidence.

Of the other important sees, Tauromenium probably remained under Secundinus throughout the reign, but there were changes in Lilybaeum and Malta. By February 595 Theodore of Lilybaeum was dead and his will was being investigated by the rector Cyprian to ensure that the church suffered no less from his bequests.[53] The election did not go smoothly. There was deadlock and the canonical three months was well exceeded. In September 595 Gregory informed Cyprian that a deputation of the Lilybaetan clergy had come to Rome to look for a suitable bishop and Gregory had given them permission to search for one.[54] They had come up with Decius *presbyter forensis*, but whether he was *forensis* just to Rome or to the Suburbicarian see in general is not clear. He was most likely a refugee from the Lombards or the Istrian schism. The deputation requested his ordination, and with some reluctance the pope agreed. This reluctance may be explained by his order to Cyprian to lose no opportunity to help Decius because the regime of Bishop Theodore had left much to be desired and many things which he should have amended he had left untouched. Theodore had been praised for his energetic visitation of Triocala, but since his death his mismanagement at home had become known in Rome. In these circumstances Gregory was reluctant to appoint someone he did not know to the see. However, he did ordain him, and there is no evidence that he tried to force anyone else on them. It is worth remembering that at just this time he was involved in settling the Syracusan election, which was of far greater moment than Lilybaeum. So Lilybaeum got its bishop and Decius apparently proved satisfactory.

The case of Lilybaeum, like that of Palermo, shows the pope concerned and rather unhappy about the outcome, but not prepared to push the issue. He had probably hoped that their search for a bishop in Rome would lead the deputation from Lilybaeum to choose a Roman cleric who was known to him; but it did not and he therefore made the best of it.

Even after the Gregorian purge of the episcopal bench, however, there was still misconduct, and the case of the bishop of Malta is a good reminder that discipline could never be relaxed, even when a bench had been as successfully reconstituted as the Sicilian one had. In September 598, Gregory wrote to John of Syracuse to say that since the guilt of Bishop Lucillus of Malta had been proved, he was to be deposed.[55] There was to be a full investigation of the clergy, and all those found guilty of being his accomplices were to be stripped of their ranks and relegated to monasteries. The worst offenders were to be excommunicated. The clergy and people of Malta were to be admonished to elect a new bishop.

Lucillus remained contumacious, and in the autumn of 599 Gregory ordered the rector Romanus to see that Lucillus and his son Peter restored to the new bishop Trajan property that they had removed from the church.[56] It seems that they had not only removed church property but had also pocketed sums earmarked for church repair, leaving the buildings to decay. The pope ruled that unless they returned what they had taken, they should answer for their behaviour to John of Syracuse.

Even more interesting is the rest of the letter, which fills in the background of the new bishop of Malta. He had requested that four or five monks from the monastery in Syracuse, of which he had been abbot, should be sent to keep him company, since he knew no one on Malta, a request to which Gregory readily assented. Trajan was not, in fact, a Sicilian at all. Born in Valeria, apparently of wealthy parents, he had become a monk in a monastery founded by his father. He had fled from Valeria when the Lombards came, and had taken refuge in Sicily, where he had become abbot of the Syracusan monastery founded by Capitulina. It is likely that he was the same Trajan who stood for election to the see of Syracuse in 595. Trajan is an unusual name, and its only bearers in the entire Register are the would-be bishop of Syracuse and the Syracusan abbot who became bishop of Malta. The fact that the Syracusan candidate was described as 'priest' is no difficulty to this identification because in many monasteries monks were ordained as priests in order to say mass. Presumably Trajan became abbot after his disappointment in the 595 election.

What is significant is that although Gregory found Trajan incapable of governing Syracuse, he made no objection to his governing Malta. It may be, of course, that by 598 he had made such a good job of governing the monastery of Capitulina that his ability was at last recognized. The situation in Malta was one which, on the analogy of Triocala and Lipari, called for intervention. Bishop Lucillus and his son and a ring of ecclesiastical embezzlers had been systematically mulcting the church of its property and income. To restore the prestige of the see, to maintain discipline, and to win back the faithful, a trusted and reliable man was needed, and Trajan seems to have fitted the bill. He had had the administrative experience as abbot; his monkish calling was a recommendation; and his intention to live in community with some of his monks indicated an emulation of Gregory's own practice which would not have harmed him in the pope's eyes. Gregory had, after all, commented on his 'good disposition' at the time of the election in Syracuse.

Given the fact that John of Syracuse had been charged with conducting the Malta investigations and arranging for the election, given also that Trajan came from John's own see and was prominent enough to have been considered as its bishop, the odds here are on another intervention, but by John rather than by Gregory. It is a good indication of how far John, as Gregory's representative in Sicily and knowing Gregory's requirements in personnel policy, had taken over the running of the ecclesiastical set-up in the island. Trajan apparently settled down well enough, and is last heard of alive and well in January 603.[57]

The two least important sees in Sicily were probably Leontini and Tyndaris, and there were routine change-overs during the reign on the deaths of the incumbent bishops.[58] There remain, however, two controversial cases to be considered: those of Bishop Barbarus of Carina and Exhilaratus of see unknown. In the first case, the problem lies in the two letters of Gregory which are specifically devoted to Carina. The first, dated September 595, is a letter to Bishop Boniface of Rhegium.[59] Although Carina was destitute of a bishop, the desertion of the place and the diminution of its population made an election for a new bishop impracticable. Gregory therefore united the see to Rhegium, giving Boniface the usual episcopal powers over Carina. The second letter, dated November 602, appointed Bishop

Barbarus of Carina visitor of Palermo, with orders to see to the arrangement of the election of a new bishop.[60]

Commentators have never been able to reconcile the uniting of the see of Carina, close to Palermo, with a see many miles away in Bruttium. However, what has long been inexplicable in geographical terms, becomes explicable in terms of patronage. Firstly Boniface of Rhegium was a Gregorian patronage appointment, a Roman priest appointed to the see in the early years of the reign and the only such appointee in Lucania and Bruttium. Secondly, there is the timing. Carina and Rhegium were united in September 595, the very time that John was being installed after a hard-fought election in Syracuse. Probably his early passage was difficult, and another trusted ally on the Sicilian bench to back him up would have been welcome. That Boniface counted as a Sicilian bishop in his capacity as bishop of Carina is evidenced by a letter of May 597, ordering to Rome the Sicilian bishops plus the bishops of Lipari and Rhegium.[61] This does not mean that Lipari and Rhegium were two non-Sicilian bishops being added to the group for that occasion: it refers to the fact that both were double sees. The bishop of Tauriana was also bishop of Lipari but resident in the latter; the bishop of Rhegium was also bishop of Carina but resident in the former. This explains the titulature. Gregory mentioned them so that the rector would be sure that he meant all the Sicilian bishops, even those with duties in Bruttium.

There can be no doubt, then, that Boniface counted as bishop of Carina until some time between 597 and 602. By the latter date, the situation had changed, either because John's standing in Sicily had improved or because the size of the population in Carina had increased, perhaps both. An independent election in Carina was permitted and Bishop Barbarus emerged.

Then there was the case of Bishop Exhilaratus, who, as emerges from a letter to the Palermo rector Fantinus in September 603, had been on trial in Rome.[62] He seems to have been charged with excessive cruelty towards his clergy, who had complained to Rome. The pope had summoned Exhilaratus to Rome and kept him there for a long time. Eventually Leo of Catania had come to his aid by declaring that Exhilaratus had imposed punishments after a trial, in which Leo had participated, and he was not pursuing a private grudge or indulging in violent excesses. Gregory therefore acquitted Exhilaratus, but the clergy remained aggrieved and Fantinus was ordered to see that the bishop and the clergy were reconciled.

Exhilaratus' see is not given, but it was clearly in Fantinus' bailiwick; of the six sees therein two are accounted for, and it must therefore have been either Tyndaris (last attested in 599), Lilybaeum (last attested in 599), Triocala (last attested in 598), or Lipari (vacant in 603). The participation of Leo of Catania suggests that Exhilaratus' see was between Palermo and Catania, which makes Tyndaris the most likely possibility.

Finally, there is one more example of patronage to consider – one which did not come off, but which constitutes admirable evidence for Gregory's administration of patronage on the island. There is a letter dated June 595 to Bishop Sebastian of Rhisinum, a Dalmatian prelate in exile in the East.[63] He was an old friend of Gregory's, and hearing that he had been offered and had refused a see in the patriarchate of Antioch Gregory wrote to say that, if ever he wanted another see, there were sees vacant in Sicily, any of which he would be welcome to take and rule. The offer was apparently not taken up, but it indicates the extent to which Gregory was willing to treat the Sicilian sees as a useful patronage reserve, in this case for employing the talents of exiled bishops.

Phase Two of Gregory's personnel policy ended with his death in 604. In retrospect it can be seen to have been much quieter and less active than Phase One. Bishop John of Syracuse remained firmly in control, but Gregory made fewer direct personal interventions in elections than in Phase One. The policy had become one of maintaining the *status quo* as it existed at the time of John's election.

Several conclusions can be drawn about the operation of papal personnel policy under Gregory. First, there was active involvement in elections, whether at grass roots level or by arbitration in Rome. Of the fourteen elections known to have occurred in Sicily under Gregory, six, including Boniface of Rhegium's appointment to Carina, were certainly Gregorian patronage appointments; two were probably and one was possibly so. There were also six trials of bishops, some of them held in Rome. Of these six trials, three bishops were acquitted (Leo, Gregory and Exhilaratus) and three deposed (Lucillus, Agatho and Paul). The pattern of involvement is that there was considerable activity in the early years of the reign when the episcopate was unknown and under review, but this activity declined when key episcopal positions were filled to papal satisfaction.

It is clear that Gregory was above all vitally concerned to secure a suitable appointment to the premier sees, and in two successive Syracusan elections his nominees carried the day. He also became deeply involved in the aftermath of depositions.

Besides involvement in elections and trials, there are two other salient features of papal personnel policy to note. One is the unification of sees, usually for demographic reasons. The other is the redeployment of experienced ecclesiastical personnel who had lost their sees through enemy action (Paulinus of Tauriana to Lipari, the offer of a see to Sebastian of Rhisinum). These elements should be borne in mind when considering the patronage activities on the mainland.

The papal patronage operations in Sicily also throw light on a long-standing controversy about whether Sicily was a Greek or a Latin island. It has been conclusively demonstrated that throughout Roman times the population of Sicily by and large spoke Greek.[64] This invalidates the old theory, heavily dependent on the Gregorian Register, that Sicily had been completely romanized for several centuries.[65] It has nevertheless been maintained that there was a conscious policy of latinization under Gregory, its effects overwhelmed by the results of massive immigration from the East in the seventh century.[66] It is now known that while there was immigration from the East during the seventh century, prompted by the Arab invasions, it was limited quantitatively and qualitatively.[67] There was certainly an influx of refugees, lay and clerical, into Sicily, and there was a movement of Byzantine soldiers and officials into the island during the period that the emperor Constans II made his headquarters in Syracuse (664–8). The important point to make is that there is no need to adduce a mass movement of population to account for the hellenization of Sicily. It was already hellenized and always had been.

The fact that it is possible to talk of 'latinization' under Gregory I implies that something unusual was happening in his reign. However, this phenomenon is what we have been examining as patronage, and if it is accepted that the appearance of Roman ecclesiastical personnel as bishops in Sicily is the result of papal patronage, the latinizing argument loses force. These outsiders were appointed as Sicilian bishops not because they were Latins but because they were known to and trusted by Gregory. He would have had a better chance of knowing Latins, hence the fact that the largest proportion of his patronage appointments were Latins. The fact that he selected a local man, John of Catania, for Syracuse, and that he was reluctant to ordain Decius for Lilybaeum, because although he was Latin he was unknown to Gregory, confirms the theory that any latinization that occurred was a reflection of patronage rather than *vice versa*.

If this is the explanation of 'latinization' under Gregory, then it is likely that any other apparent 'latinizations' in the sixth and seventh centuries might indicate papal patronage programmes. The bishops' names are a guide here. As with the rest of Italy, the episcopal lists for sixth- and seventh-century Sicily are very fragmentary, but a glance at them reveals an overwhelming preponderance of Greek names: Theodore, Agatho, Elpidius, Leo, Elias, Eleutherius and Eusanius.[68] In some cases there is background information which confirms their local origin. In the sixth century Eulalius of Syracuse had a monastery locally to which he occasionally retired;[69] the family of Eleutherius of Syracuse was resident in the island;[70] so too was the family of Eusanius of Agrigentum, whose son was called Euplus;[71] Gregory of Agrigentum was a native of that town and a Greek-speaker.[72] In the seventh century Zosimus of Syracuse was certainly a native Syracusan and Greek-speaker, though the seventh century is complicated by the fact that Rome itself was filled with Greek priests and there were hardly enough Latin priests about to start exporting them to Sicily.[73] The full span of Latin names in the Sicilian episcopate (Decius, Donus, Trajan, Maximian, and so forth) only occurs under Gregory. The embassies of Pope Hormisdas to the East furnish a further clue.[74] He sent three embassies to Constantinople to negotiate the end of the Acacian schism. The first two included Sicilian bishops – Fortunatus of Catania in 515 and Peregrinus of Messina in 517. On the third there was no Sicilian bishop, but there was the refugee Alexandrian deacon Dioscorus, who was to act as spokesman and interpreter. It seems likely that the inclusion of the Sicilian bishops in the earlier missions had been due to the fact that they were Greek-speakers. For the sixth century it looks as if there was only one 'latinization' and hence only one comprehensive patronage programme in Sicily – and that was Gregory's.

Chapter Ten

Gregory and the Episcopate: (2) Italy

On the pattern of Sicily, we should expect to see in mainland Italy a programme of active intervention in the first five years of Gregory's reign and a decline thereafter. We should also expect particular attention to be paid to the provincial capitals. An investigation of Gregory's electoral activities on the mainland reveals both these things.

The principal town of the southernmost province, Bruttium, was Rhegium, of which the Roman priest Boniface was appointed bishop early in Gregory's reign. He is first referred to in a letter dated September 592.[1] Gregory wrote praising him for the good works he had been doing and which he had been assiduously reporting to the pope, but he warned Boniface that he should do them not to win golden opinions from people but for the greater glory of God. The obvious interpretation to put on this letter is that Boniface was simply a vainglorious prelate singing his own praises to impress Gregory. If, however, we take into account the delicate nature of local sensibilities and known local reactions to the intrusion of outsiders, then this letter takes on a subtler meaning. As a new man and an outsider, Boniface was trying to ingratiate himself with his new flock and was reporting on his progress to his patron. Gregory was pleased to hear that things were going smoothly, but felt impelled to point out what should be the real motive for doing good works.

This busy popularity-getting activity reinforces the impression that Boniface had just been elected. Further confirmation comes in two other letters, dated June and September 593. The first ordered Boniface to examine the case of a woman who claimed that certain property of hers had been seized by agents of Boniface's predecessor, Bishop Lucius.[2] This suggests that the recent death of Lucius was prompting the woman to act. The second letter contains a strict admonition to Boniface not to be indulgent towards his clergy to the point of releasing them from their appointed duties, and to enforce the celibacy regulations among the subdeacons.[3] He was ordered to keep a strict watch on their behaviour. This relaxing of discipline looks like another attempt to win popularity, but one which Gregory of all men would not tolerate.

In September 595 Boniface was appointed bishop of Carina, a position he held until some time before 602, by which date the see had its own bishop again.[4] In April 599 there was trouble in Rhegium, when Boniface was in dispute with his clergy over some matter unknown to us.[5] Things were so bad that the Rhegine clergy had asked for leave to plead their case against their bishop in Rome. Gregory did not want this, perhaps because as Boniface's appointer he was an interested party, and he set up a commission of Bruttian bishops to hear the case and decide between the parties. It is possible that Boniface had decided to tighten up on discipline again and the clergy did not like it. The outcome of the quarrel is not known and Boniface does not appear again in the Register, but the absence of any known successor suggests that he survived Gregory.

The picture that emerges is quite clear. When the senior Bruttian see fell vacant, Gregory decided to utilize the situation to install one of his own clergy as bishop. But the appointment caused problems, and they emphasize again how difficult the position of an outsider was.

Gregory also found occasion to place an appointee in Calabria when the see of Callipolis fell vacant. The candidate was the monk Sabinus, also called Sabinian in one of Gregory's letters. In June 593 the bishop of Callipolis was John, who was ordered by Gregory to investigate charges of excessive brutality brought by the Tarentine clergy against Bishop Andreas.[6] By November 595 John was dead and Bishop Peter of Hydruntum was appointed visitor and authorized to arrange an election.[7] Sabinus, the monk from St Andrew's, emerged as bishop, and Gregory demonstrated his trust in him by granting him the job of sub-rector of the papal estates at Callipolis. No other bishop of Callipolis is recorded during Gregory's reign, and no other Calabrian bishop appears in the patronage list.

The principal see in Campania was Naples, the seat of the papal rector and the centre of one of the most important imperial enclaves. During Gregory's reign its ecclesiastical history was so turbulent that the inhabitants seem to have spent more time fighting each other than they did fighting the Lombards. The incumbent bishop on

Gregory's election was Demetrius, who had himself only gained the episcopate in 588.[8] In December 590 Gregory commended to him a certain Stephanus, who had been sent there to reconcile certain lapsed Neapolitans to the faith.[9] By September 591 Demetrius had been deposed and Gregory was writing to urge the Neapolitans to make haste to elect a new bishop.[10] Though the reason for the deposition is not stated, Gregory did say that Demetrius' crimes were such as to deserve the death penalty but that he, Gregory, had tempered justice with mercy. This deposition following so soon on Stephanus' visit and coupled with Gregory's reference to Demetrius as *'perversus doctor'* suggests that he may have been guilty of one of the grosser heresies.

In January 592 Gregory wrote to the clergy, nobles and people to say that he was delighted that they so much approved of their visitor that they had elected him bishop.[11] He reminded them, however, that elections were not to be dealt with so precipitously and asked them to think again, but in the meantime to demonstrate their affection for the visitor by obeying him. To the visitor himself, Bishop Paul of Nepe, Gregory wrote in the same month confirming him in his visitatorial office and conceding to him certain episcopal rights (ordination of clerics, payment of clerical stipends, manumission of slaves) pending the election of a new bishop of Naples.[12]

At some point between September and January, therefore, Gregory had appointed Bishop Paul of Nepe as visitor. This is very curious, for Nepe is north of Rome and it was customary for a neighbouring bishop to be appointed visitor. Paul is the sole glaring exception to this in the whole of Gregory's reign. He was certainly not sent down as a candidate, as Gregory's prohibition on his election shows, nor was he an exiled bishop in need of gainful employment. The answer must be that the fraught and turbulent Neapolitan situation had prompted Gregory to dispatch as visitor a senior and trusted bishop who, not being local, would be less likely to be influenced by powerful local issues and personalities.[13]

However, Gregory's plans went immediately awry when there was a rush to elect Paul himself as bishop. The most likely explanation of this is that one of the rival factions did it, in order to block the candidate of another group. Within a month of Gregory's veto on Paul's election, however, he was asking to be relieved of his visitorship.[14] Gregory refused permission, on the grounds that the election had not yet taken place, but clearly the pressures on Paul had built up so much that he felt his position to be untenable. In March 592 Bishop John of Falerii was appointed visitor of Nepe in order to conduct Easter services, and we get the unparalleled spectacle of a bishop appointed to visit a vacant see miles away from his own and another bishop appointed to visit the visitor's see in his absence.[15]

In Naples Paul's position deteriorated even further, and in September 592 comes the first explicit reference to violence. The violence occurred at Castrum Lucullanum, a fortified island off the coast, where the patrician Clementina resided. Bishop Paul visited the island and was beaten up by her slaves, which strongly suggests that Clementina was among the leaders of one of the electoral factions. The pope acted at once, appointing two special investigators, Scholasticus *iudex Campaniae* and the Roman subdeacon Epiphanius, to look into the matter. They were both instructed to punish the slaves at once if they were proved guilty, and not to lessen the punishment out of respect for Clementina. Indeed, they were to find out whether she had been privy to the attack. Gregory could not believe that this was so and suggested that the slaves had transgressed out of pride at being the servants of a noble lady. Gregory also wrote to Paul consoling him on his injuries and informing him of the impending investigation.[16]

Papal intervention apparently calmed the situation, and once again the inhabitants proceeded to an election, which proved immediately abortive. In December 592 Gregory wrote to the *iudex* Scholasticus saying that he had been greatly relieved when the Roman subdeacon Florentius was elected bishop, but then Florentius fled from Naples to avoid ordination and now Gregory's mind was again burdened with worry about the election. He urged Scholasticus to summon the nobles and people together to agree on a new candidate. If they could find no one, they were to send three men chosen by the electorate to try to find a suitable candidate in Rome.[17]

What seems to have happened is that Gregory, after waiting for over a year for the electorate's decision, had finally sent down to Naples his own nominee, the Roman subdeacon Florentius, who had been elected bishop by the clergy. But it would seem that he was rejected by the nobles and the people, the two sections of the electorate specifically mentioned by Gregory to Scholasticus. The dissident electors had apparently made the city so uncomfortable for Florentius that he had fled from Naples and, according to the pope, 'tearfully' refused ordination. This is the first known case of a candidate actually being sent down from Rome by the pope to stand in an election; but it did not work, and Gregory was forced to give them a free hand once again, though indicating his willingness to withdraw the case to Rome and settle it there once and for all.

In May 593 Gregory ordered the papal rector Peter to get the Neapolitan clergy to choose two or three of their number to come to Rome and join the representatives of the nobles, who were already there.[18] They were to bring with them the episcopal vestments and as much ready money as the bishop would need – instructions which leave no doubt that the pope had settled the contentious matter and had chosen a new bishop in Rome. This is confirmed by a further order to Peter to relieve Paul of Nepe of his visitorship and send him home with 100 *solidi* and a slave boy as a reward for his services.

In August 593 came the first letter from the pope to the new bishop of Naples, Fortunatus, in which Gregory said that he was delighted to hear of the new bishop's favourable reception by the Neapolitans. He told Fortunatus that he must repay them for their affection towards him in his behaviour: restraining the evil, encouraging the good, and letting the Neapolitans rejoice in having found so excellent a father.[19]

The indications are that Fortunatus was a Roman cleric and a patronage nominee. Gregory's determination to end the vacancy, his suggestion to Scholasticus that the electors might find someone suitable in Rome, and his palpable relief at the peaceful acceptance of Fortunatus all point to the same conclusion. Very likely the majority of Neapolitans were tired of the struggles and glad to have a bishop again after a two-year vacancy.

Fortunatus' actions as bishop throw further light on the circumstances of his election, and indeed they led to a revival of factional strife, for in the autumn of 598 the city was once again convulsed by riots.[20] The cause of the dispute was the possession of the city gates and aqueducts, and presumably, and more important, the revenue that accrued therefrom. The gates and aqueducts were originally held by Theodore, the mayor of Naples, and Rusticus, a city councillor, but another group, led by Faustus and Domitius, disputed their possession, took the matter to the episcopal court, and got the bishop to award the gates and aqueducts to them.

Theodore the mayor travelled to Rome to protest that the bishop had decided the case prejudicially, and Gregory wrote in October 598 ordering Fortunatus to return what had been taken from the mayor, to send representatives to Rome to explain his conduct, and to submit the dispute to arbitration. In November 598 Gregory wrote to the *magister militum* Maurentius, the imperial commandant in Naples, saying that he was surprised that with Maurentius in the city Theodore had come to Rome to complain about a case which, though properly belonging to the *patronus*, had been dealt with by the bishop.[21] Characteristically Gregory deplored the idea of priests usurping cases properly belonging to the secular authorities and denied giving Fortunatus permission to do so. Furthermore Gregory commended to Maurentius the case of Theodore, urging him to act in all things according to the law so that the inhabitants might write to Gregory singing the commandant's praises.

In the same month Gregory wrote again to Fortunatus, reprimanding him for failing to return what had been seized and for failing to send representatives to Rome to explain his conduct.[22] Gregory discounted Fortunatus' claim that he had been forced into these actions by his supporters and that the men who had come to Rome to plead his case were the representatives of his supporters rather than himself. The pope insisted that the matter should be settled through the proper legal channels and that either Fortunatus or his supporters should claim the gates and aqueducts through the courts if they wanted them. Nothing more is heard of the case, but it may be supposed that the quarrel was settled in favour of the mayor on the basis of a letter from Domitius to the pope, dated May–June 599, in which Domitius claimed that Maurentius was victimizing him out of personal enmity.[23]

The significance of this quarrel must be seen in the context of the election. There were clearly two factions in Naples – effectively the 'ins', the city council, represented by Theodore and Rusticus, and the 'outs', represented by Faustus and Domitius, and the latter sought to use the arrival of a new bishop to prise some of the fruits of office from the former. The 'outs' had taken the case of the gates and aqueducts to the bishop's court rather than that of the commandant in the clear expectation of receiving a favourable judgment. Their reason for such an expectation must have been that they supported the candidature of Fortunatus in the discussions in Rome and now expected a reward. Fortunatus describes them, indeed, as his '*filii*', which in this context is perhaps to be understood as supporters. We may surmise that the 'ins', who already controlled local politics, would have preferred an internal candidate whom they could control to a papally-nominated outsider. The very existence of the dispute with the bishop pushed by his supporters into opposing the municipal establishment suggests that this interpretation is correct. It also seems to be the case that Fortunatus, like other papal nominees, had trouble with his clergy, since at the time of his death he was withholding part of the clergy's salary which his successor was instructed by the pope to pay.

Naples had not yet seen the end of electoral disputes, for when Fortunatus died in the summer of 600 after reigning only seven years, the trouble started all over again.[24] In June 600 Gregory informed the clergy, nobles and people of Naples that there was nothing new or reprehensible in being divided between two candidates for the bishopric, but that it was serious when the election was decided by partisan feelings rather than by impartial judgment based on merit.[25]

The two candidates upon whom the electors were deadlocked were the deacon John and the deacon Peter. Both factions defamed their rivals in submissions to the pope. One group claimed that John had a daughter, and Gregory declared that this evidence of unchastity was sufficient to rule him out of the contest. But the other faction claimed that Peter was 'simple-minded' and also engaged in usury. Gregory ordered that the charges should be looked into, and that if they proved incorrect Peter should be sent to Rome to be examined by the pope for his episcopal suitability. The pope also suggested that, to be on the safe side, they should select an alternative candidate whom they could send to Rome with Peter and who could be chosen by the pope if Peter proved unsatisfactory.

It is evident that Gregory knew neither of the protagonists personally. But he was involved, vetoing one candidate and insisting on a detailed investigation into the suitability of the other. He did not, however, suggest a candidate himself. His experience of the previous election had surely convinced him of the danger of plunging an outsider into the whirlpool of Neapolitan politics. Moreover his intervention last time had been partly prompted by the need to remedy the effect of a deposition, and that situation did not apply on this occasion. Nevertheless, the pope exercised a negative influence in ruling out both Peter and John, for the new bishop was Paschasius, about whose origins and antecedents nothing is known for certain. He was in office by January 601 and was to reign for fourteen years.[26]

Further light is thrown on this election by a letter of June 601 from Gregory ordering the rector Anthemius to urge the bishop to punish without delay the subdeacon Hilarus, whose perjured testimony had caused the deacon John to be found guilty and to be punished by an ecclesiastical tribunal which had included Anthemius. Hilarus was to be deposed from office, flogged and exiled.[27] This must surely be linked with the unchastity charge which destroyed John's chance of becoming bishop. It looks as if Hilarus had brought the charge against John in the interests of a rival faction but had subsequently been found out.

Two further references to Paschasius hint at both his character and his origins. The second part of the letter to Anthemius contained an order to him to get Paschasius to appoint a *vicedominus* and *maior domus* to assist him in his administrative duties, and if he delayed, to call together his clergy and elect two such officials. This suggests that Paschasius was neglecting his duties, an impression confirmed by another letter to Anthemius, dated March 603.[28] Gregory had heard that Paschasius was ignoring all his duties and responsibilities in favour of shipbuilding, that he went down to the seashore every day with one or two clerics, dressed in such mean attire that he had become a public scandal, and that he had lost 400 *solidi* on these ventures. Anthemius was to summon him before the clergy and exhort him to fulfil his duties, and if this failed, to send him to Rome to be disciplined. Paschasius' record confirms that he was not a Gregorian nominee and suggests that he was, in fact, a local cleric, something of a last resort after the two front-runners had been eliminated. Naples does, however, fulfil the expectations aroused by the Sicilian patronage model. Gregory used an early election to install a nominee and then took a negative rather than a positive role in the later election.

There was another early patronage appointment in the important Campanian frontier city of Capua. John the Deacon lists the Roman subdeacon Festus as Gregorian nominee to Capua. The appointment must have taken place between 591 and 593, for in April 593 Gregory was ordering the Campanian rector Peter to effect a reconciliation between Bishop Festus and his clergy, who he claimed despised and insulted him.[29] It is the same story that we have seen elsewhere – an appointed outsider at loggerheads with the native clergy. But in November 594 Gregory appointed Bishop Gaudentius of Nola as visitor of Capua following the death of Festus in Rome.[30] He was, however, given no orders regarding the holding of an election. At the same time Gregory informed the Capuan clergy 'residing in

Naples' of the appointment of the visitor and urged them to persist in the maintenance of church services and ecclesiastical discipline even though in exile.[31] Further to this, in March 595 Gregory ordered Gaudentius to pay the Capuan clergy resident in Naples their accustomed salaries from the revenues of the Capuan church.[32] He was also to pay the archdeacon Rusticus, who was in dire need, the 10 *solidi* which he claimed the late Bishop Festus owed him.

The story revealed here is a sorry one, for the squabbling between bishop and clergy had been cut short by the capture of Capua by the Lombards. The bishop had fled to Rome and died there soon afterwards; the clergy under the archdeacon fled to Naples. There they were placed under the control of the bishop of Nola, whose see was significantly closer to Naples than to Capua, and who was therefore effectively acting as the ecclesiastical superior of the exiles. The absence of any mention of an election perhaps means that Gregory was hoping for a speedy recapture of the city so that the normal processes could be set in motion.

Intriguingly, a new bishop of Capua does eventually appear, but he must from the outset have been a bishop in exile. He is first attested in Sicily in November 598 when Gregory wrote to Bishop John of Syracuse ordering him to pay Bishop Basilius of Capua ten pounds in gold, such an amount having been handed in by the patricians Flora and Cethegus in Rome for this purpose.[33] In autumn 599 Gregory informed the rector Romanus that it had been reported that Basilius' constant engagement in lawsuits was bringing his office into disrepute and so Romanus was to see to it that Basilius left Sicily within five days and returned to Rome.[34] Basilius duly returned, and attended the November Synod in Rome in 600.[35] He is last attested still in Rome in September 602, vainly trying to prevent the union of two Campanian monasteries, claiming that one of them came under his jurisdiction.[36]

The evidence on Basilius is straightforward. He was in Sicily in 598–8 and in Rome in 600–2; but he was never once in Capua. His entire conduct bespeaks an exiled bishop who has nothing better to do than litigate. The question of Basilius' election is not so straightforward, for he represents the only known case of a bishop elected in exile. The election occurred between 595 and 598, but where and by whom was he elected? There are two alternatives: either he was elected by the exiled clergy in Naples, or he was appointed by the pope in Rome. None of the evidence places him in Naples, but he did spend time in Rome. Another clue lies in the gift of gold from Flora and Cethegus. Basilius and Cethegus are among the favoured names of two of Rome's most distinguished aristocratic families. Furthermore, a Basilius and a Cethegus had fled together to Constantinople during the Gothic wars and had become companions in exile.[37] It is entirely possible that the late-sixth-century Cethegus and Basilius were relatives, perhaps grandchildren of the mid-sixth-century fugitives, and this might help explain the generous gift. This would make Basilius a Roman aristocrat and would tip the balance in favour of his nomination to the bishopric by the pope. Why Gregory should have wanted to make a nomination to a non-existent see is more problematical. If he did, it can only have been because he believed the recapture of the city of Capua to be imminent. But the scheme backfired. Capua was not recaptured, and Gregory was left with a redundant bishop on his hands.

Gregory did not have much more success with his nomination to Rimini, the capital of the Pentapolis. Its bishop died in 591 and Bishop Severus of Ficuclae was appointed visitor. Gregory wrote to him in July 591, curtly announcing that the candidature of Ocleatinus, whose election Severus had reported to him, was unacceptable.[38] The inhabitants were to choose someone else or, failing that, the bearer of the letter would indicate someone Gregory had chosen.

The letter to Severus was accompanied by one to clergy, senate and people, and to Duke Arsicinus, the military commander of the Pentapolis, repeating the pope's instructions.[39] The inclusion of a military commander in an election letter is unparalleled in the Register and suggests that his influence may have been behind the candidature of Ocleatinus, about whom nothing more is known. The next stage occurred in April 592, when Gregory wrote to Archbishop John of Ravenna to thank him for visiting and later receiving in Ravenna Bishop Castorius of Rimini, who was ill.[40] Gregory says that he would have refused to ordain Castorius, because of his *simplicitas*, but the importunity of those seeking his appointment caused him to do so. He adds that if Castorius was up to the journey, he should be sent to Rome.

John the Deacon includes the Roman subdeacon Castorius in his patronage list and, in the light of that, Gregory's excuse sounds like buck-passing. Gregory was not the man to be overborne by *importunitas*, as his conduct in the Naples election showed. The most obvious conclusion to draw from the evidence is that, following the rejection of Ocleatinus, a delegation was sent from Rimini to consult the pope. The pope, asked for a suggestion, must have put forward the name of Castorius, though perhaps suggesting that his *simplicitas* might be a drawback. But even a qualified suggestion from the pope would be good enough. It is difficult to see any other reason why an obscure Roman subdeacon should turn up in a city on the other side of the country – and inside the exarchate, to boot.

Castorius was in office by January 592, but later that year he fell ill and was removed to Ravenna by Archbishop John.[41] Then in March 593 Bishop Leontius of Urbinum was appointed visitor of Rimini during the time Castorius was detained in Rome by his illness,[42] so he had clearly made the recommended journey. The cause of Castorius' illness, which was either a nervous breakdown or a mental disorder, was the hostility of his flock, for Gregory wrote to the citizens of Rimini upbraiding them for their *'inquietudo et tribulatio'* which had brought upon Castorius the illness currently detaining him in Rome.[43] Their attitude resembles that greeting other patronage appointments, though in this case the fact that the letter was addressed to *'universi habitatores'* indicates massive local opposition. So even if Gregory had persuaded the electoral delegation from Rimini to accept Castorius, it seems that the people at large were not prepared to tolerate papal interference.

The people of Rimini were to suffer for their hostility to Castorius. Their visitor, Leontius, proved to be a greedy opportunist who gave over the administration of the church patrimony to his own agents, cheated on the fourfold division of the revenue, and appropriated grain from the public granaries. The situation grew so bad that Gregory had to write admonishing him for his behaviour.[44] In the meantime, the pope was trying to persuade Castorius to return to his duties. The clergy and people added their voice to his, doubtless keen to see the back of Leontius, but Castorius had had his fill of Rimini and in May 599, still in Rome, he abdicated. This was one patronage operation that had been a disaster from start to finish.

Gregory now wrote to the clergy and people of Rimini and to Bishop Sebastian (see unknown), who had replaced Leontius as visitor, ordering an immediate election.[45] He also wrote to Archbishop Marinianus of Ravenna asking for his assessment of character of the man the electors chose.[46] This time Gregory was not prepared to intervene directly, but he did involve Marinianus, himself a nominee of the pope and someone presumably *au fait* with Gregory's requirements in a bishop. John, doubtless a local cleric, was duly elected and installed as bishop of Rimini in July 599, and there was no further trouble there.[47]

Among the Roman priests promoted to bishoprics, John the Deacon lists Habentius, bishop of Perusia. The subscriptions of the 595 Roman Synod include among the priests Aventius, who is clearly the same as Habentius, given the interchangeability of *v* and *b* in the orthography of the period.[48] He survived Gregory and in 607 was to be found at the deathbed of St Floridus of Tifernum Tiberinum along with Bishop Laurentius of Arezzo and Bishop Leontius of Urbinum.[49]

The date of his election is not certain, but it was probably dictated by the political vicissitudes of the city. Perusia was a key imperial fortress on the Via Flaminia. In July 591 Gregory wrote to the clergy, senate and people of the city urging them to elect a bishop at once and marvelling at their long delay in doing so.[50] It is unlikely that this election took place, for in 592 the city was captured by the Lombard duke Ariulf of Spoleto. It was retaken by the exarch Romanus the following year but almost immediately recaptured by the Lombard king Agilulf. How long it remained in Lombard hands is not known for certain, but it was back in imperial hands in 599 and it seems likely that it was returned to the Empire as part of the 598 peace treaty. Given the disruption the city had suffered, it is likely that Gregory felt obliged to intervene to secure a bishop he knew to be capable of restoring the Perusian church, hence the appearance of the priest Aventius as bishop.

Lastly, within the Suburbicarian diocese there was the see of Ostia, important as the see whose bishop traditionally consecrated the pope. John the Deacon lists the Roman subdeacon Gloriosus as Gregory's nominee to this bishopric, and the Register includes a single letter to him, dated 598.[51] Nothing more is known about him.

Gregory's greatest patronage coup did not come in the Suburbicarian diocese at all, but in Ravenna, technically in the diocese of Italia Annonaria and therefore subject ecclesiastically to the archbishopric of Milan. By the time of Gregory, with the Lombards occupying northern Italy and Milanese jurisdiction effectively limited to the coastal enclave of Liguria, the archbishopric of Ravenna had become more and more dependent on Rome, in ecclesiastical terms. This replacement of Milanese influence by Roman had had one immediate, palpable result. In 578 a Roman cleric was installed as Archbishop John III of Ravenna, and it is hard to see this as other than a pre-

Gregorian act of papal patronage.[52] John was still in office when Gregory became pope, and initially they were on excellent terms. Gregory dedicated the *Regula Pastoralis* to John, praised him for his efforts against the Istrian schismatics, and in 592 entrusted to him control of those bishops subject to Rome who could not reach Rome because of the Lombards.[53] But the friendly relations between pope and archbishop were soured by the *pallium* dispute, which was still unresolved when John died in February 595.

Gregory appointed Bishop Severus of Ficuclae as visitor, with orders to arrange an election.[54] It was an election that was of crucial importance to the pope, not only because of the *pallium* dispute but because the archbishop possessed access to the exarch and the potential for interference in government policy for good or ill. At the same time Gregory ordered his Ravennate *apocrisiarios*, Castorius, to oversee the election, to warn the electors not to be influenced by bribes or private interests in their choice, and to ensure that a delegation of five leading priests and five leading citizens with whatever clerics Castorius deemed necessary was sent to Rome to report on the proceedings to the pope.[55] These orders are a clear indication that the pope feared that local interests would pre-empt the decision, and that, whatever local feeling on the matter, he was determined to have a say in the final choice.

The next stage came in June 595, when Gregory wrote to the *scholasticus* Andreas, one of the exarch's senior officials.[56] He regretted that he had been unable to fulfil the wishes of the exarch and ordain as archbishop the archdeacon Donatus, but an investigation had revealed many things which rendered him ineligible, though Gregory did not specify what these were. Nor had he been able to ordain the other candidate, the priest John, because of his ignorance of the psalms.

What Gregory feared had happened. The exarch had put forward a personal nominee, the archdeacon, and so Gregory had exercised his veto. He asked the Ravennate representatives who had come to Rome to choose someone else. According to the version of events Gregory sent to Andreas, they claimed there was no one else suitable in Ravenna and therefore they unanimously chose the priest Marinianus, who they knew had been in St Andrew's with Gregory for many years. Gregory, who knew and approved of the choice, ordained Marinianus at once, despite the latter's reluctance, and then sent him back to Ravenna, inviting Andreas to help him take up his duties.

All this has the look of brilliant stage management. The papal *apocrisiarios* Castorius had selected the Ravennate delegation. Gregory had used his veto to eliminate the official Ravennate candidates. Then he had produced from St Andrew's a monk and priest whom he had known for years and who had the added advantage of being the nephew of the late Archbishop John.[57] Gregory must have been hoping for a greater say in Ravennate affairs than he had previously enjoyed. Why else would he have selected for the second most important see in Italy the sort of inexperienced monastic candidate he had recently rejected for the see of Syracuse? Indeed, the first thing Gregory did once Marinianus was installed – and this reflected what was uppermost in his mind – was to repeat his orders about the wearing of the *pallium*.

But Marinianus' installation did not go as smoothly as had been hoped. Certain malicious people sought to discredit Marinianus by putting it about that he was a supporter of the 'Three Chapters', and Gregory was forced to send to the clergy and people of Ravenna his own testimony to Marinianus' orthodoxy and his lifetime of service in the church.[58]

As archbishop, Marinianus was something of a mixed blessing. His advent did not resolve the *pallium* dispute. His administrative inexperience put him at a great disadvantage, and he was constantly being sent instructions by Gregory about what should have been routine matters. He was susceptible to what Gregory regarded as 'evil counsel', and there remains a suspicion that Marinianus' motto was 'When in doubt, do nothing.' Indeed, Gregory wrote of Marinianus 'He seems to have gone to sleep', and was reduced to writing to the Ravennate deacon Secundinus in order to relay his admonitions.[59] In a letter tinged with a characteristic Gregorian acerbity, the pope declared:

Tell him that with his place he should change his disposition too. Do not let him believe that reading and prayer alone are enough for him, that he should think to sit apart and nowhere do good works. But let him have a generous hand; let him succour those who suffer need; let him believe the wants of others to be his own; for if he does not have these feelings, the name of bishop he bears is an empty one. I did indeed give him some admonitions about his soul in my letters; but he sent me no reply whatever; from which I suppose that he has not even deigned to read them. Because of this there was no necessity for me to admonish him in my letter to him; and so I have written only what I was able to dictate as his adviser in earthly matters. For it is not incumbent upon me to tire myself by dictation for a man who does not even read what is written to him.

Marinianus does seem to have improved his episcopal performance, so that he was eventually entrusted by Gregory with several important cases.[60] Gregory showed genuine concern for his health when in 601 it was reported that Marinianus was vomiting blood.[61] The pope dispatched prescriptions from all the leading doctors available and urged him to come to Rome to recuperate. Marinianus recovered to outlive Gregory by some two years.[62] His performance as archbishop demonstrates the danger of plucking someone from a monastery and setting him on the episcopal throne. Marinianus had all the unworldliness of the cloister and none of the guile and experience called for in an archbishop.

The archbishopric of Milan, once Rome's most powerful ecclesiastical rival in Italy, had been virtually wiped out by the Lombard invasion. Although a handful of the clergy remained in Milan, the bulk of them, together with the archbishop, had taken up residence in the imperial stronghold of Genoa. This put Milan within reach of papal influence. The papacy had no authority over Milanese elections, but as a result of the changed circumstances of the see it began to assume such authority.

This process of papal interference can be seen developing throughout Gregory's reign and must therefore be a Gregorian innovation. The first Milanese archbishop in exile, Laurentius II, had ruled for nineteen years before his death, on 21 August 592, necessitated only the second archiepiscopal election since the flight from Milan.[63] It was reported to Gregory in Rome by two Milanese clerics that the electors had chosen the deacon Constantius, the former Milanese *apocrisiarios* in Constantinople and a man well known to Gregory. Nevertheless the pope wrote to the electors urging them to think carefully before making their final decision, since they could not change their minds once it was completed.[64] He disclaimed any desire to interfere, but he did send the subdeacon John for reassurance that the election had been unanimous (since there had been no electoral decree attached to the letter from the Milanese clergy), and to oversee the consecration of the new archbishop.[65] In effect Gregory was simply reducing Milan to the status of one of the Suburbicarian sees and assuming the right of oversight. In fact he ordered John 'to cause him to be consecrated by his own suffragans as ancient use demanded, with the assent of our authority and the help of the Lord, so that by the preservation of the custom, the Apostolic see may both retain its proper authority and also preserve intact the rights which it has conceded to others'. It is rather stretching the meaning of the term 'ancient use' to apply it to the consecration of the Milanese archbishop by his suffragans, for until the middle of the sixth century it had been traditional for the archbishops of Milan and Aquileia to consecrate each other. This tradition had only lapsed when the archbishop of Aquileia separated himself from Rome on the question of the 'Three Chapters'. In September 593 Gregory wrote congratulating Constantius on his unanimous election, sending him the *pallium* and addressing to him a few well-chosen words on the duties of a bishop.[66]

It is clear that the Milanese archbishops were not entirely happy with the subordinate position to which Rome was consigning them. There was, indeed, a quarrel between Gregory and Constantius when Constantius took the unprecedented step of mentioning John of Ravenna in the mass, something Gregory sought to stop, fearing that it marked the beginning of a clerical alliance against Rome.[67] The nomination of Marinianus to Ravenna seems to have nipped such an alliance in the bud, however, and when Constantius died on 3 September 600, Gregory once again asserted his right to participate in the Milanese election. There was an air of crisis about this election, for the Lombard king Agilulf sought to get the metropolitan see back to Milan by putting up a puppet Lombard candidate in Milan itself. But Gregory wrote to the Milanese clergy in Genoa urging them to ignore Agilulf's approaches to them because he, Gregory, would never recognize an archbishop put up by the Lombards in Milan. The electors took the pope at his word and duly elected the deacon Deusdedit in Genoa.[68] Gregory followed the same procedure as in the previous election, dispatching the notary Pantaleo to oversee the consecration.[69] Deusdedit was installed on 17 September 601, and ruled as archbishop for twenty-eight years.[70] It is clear that the residence of the archbishop of Milan in one of the imperial enclaves made it possible for Rome simply to assume authority over him and that this humiliating situation was likely to endure until the see reverted to Milan.

Certain general conclusions are possible about Gregory's patronage policy. He considered it worthwhile installing his nominees only in the most important cities in imperial Italy, and he did so with a consistency that implies the implementation of a carefully thought out policy. Unlike Sicily, only one of his Italian interventions (Naples) seems to have been occasioned by a deposition. However, the effects of his nominations were far from what he must have hoped. The bishops of Rhegium, Capua and Naples all had problems with their clergy, and the bishop of Rimini was driven out of his mind by the hostility of his flock. It may well be that Gregory learned from his mistakes, for almost all his patronage nominees came in the first five years of his reign and he explicitly refrained from interfering when new elections occurred in Naples and Rimini – with the result that Naples, at least, ended up with a thoroughly unsatisfactory bishop.

Apart from his specific intervention in favour of nominees in the major cities, Gregory's concern with episcopal elections was still comprehensive. He took very seriously the question of examining the suitability of candidates, since too often he found existing bishops wanting. His concern for even small sees is evidenced by the cases of Locri, Surrentum and Balneum Regis. In July 597 Gregory informed the Sicilian rector Cyprian that he deemed as unworthy the priest chosen by the Locrians to be their bishop.[71] He therefore ordered the rector to investigate the character of Marcianus, an exiled priest from Tauriana living near Catania, and if he had no criminal record he was to be sent to Locri, elected and dispatched to Rome for ordination. Here, then, Gregory exercises his veto and recommends an alternative candidate, though not someone personally known to him. It looks as if Rome kept lists of suitable episcopal candidates, and further evidence for this is provided by a letter to Maximian of Syracuse in which Gregory asks him to send to Rome a priest recommended by *chartularius* Felix if he considers him suitable for the episcopate.[72] Locri was not important enough to warrant the dispatch of a Roman cleric to the bishopric, but Gregory was sufficiently concerned to provide the best man for the job from his approved pool of appropriate personnel. The Locrians took the pope's advice and Marcianus was duly elected and installed.

There was a similar case in Surrentum in 600. The pope overruled the Surrentines' first choice and ordered a fresh election.[73] This time the electors chose Amandus, chaplain of the patrician Clementina at Castrum Lucullanum. Clementina objected to losing him, but Gregory ordered the rector Anthemius and Bishop Fortunatus of Naples to investigate Amandus' character and, if it proved suitable, to send him to Rome for consecration. He also wrote to Clementina consoling her on the loss of her chaplain but declining to uphold her opposition. Amandus' tombstone reveals that he was ordained on 23 March 600 and reigned for seventeen years.[74]

Gregory always had to be on his guard against powerful laymen, as when in 600 Duke Ansfrid, commander of Balneum Regis, wrote to him to say that he and the inhabitants of the town had chosen the deacon John to be their bishop. Gregory was not prepared to accept this evidence of John's worthiness alone, and in January 600 he ordered Bishop Ecclesius of Clusium to make a strict examination of John's character and fitness for office and send him to Rome together with his report.[75] If he was unsuitable, Ecclesius was to inform Rome by the letter and arrange for the people to elect someone better qualified.

A perfect example of Gregory's detailed concern with the personnel in episcopal elections comes in the Ancona election. In December 603 Gregory wrote to Bishop John of Rimini ordering him to join with Bishop Armenius, visitor of Ancona, in investigating the characters of the three candidates for election: Florentinus, archdeacon of Ancona; Rusticus, deacon of Ancona; and Florentinus, deacon of Ravenna.[76] Gregory ordered the investigators specifically to find out if it was true that Rusticus, though vigilant, was ignorant of the Psalms, and that Florentinus, the archdeacon, though wise in the Scriptures, was old, stingy and had sworn never to become bishop. Gregory indicated that he knew Florentinus of Ravenna to be an able man, for he had served as Ravennate envoy in both Rome and Constantinople. He admitted, however, that he knew nothing of Florentinus' character, so that he must be investigated for his moral stability as well as permission being obtained from his bishop to consider him for the office. The investigators were to send their reports to Gregory and he would make a decision. Sadly, the outcome is unknown but the episode does demonstrate Gregory's close, continuining interest in elections everywhere.

It is clear from several of the episodes discussed in connection with Gregory's patronage policy that the supply of suitable candidates for the episcopate was limited. It was therefore vital to make the best use of the available manpower resources. We have already seen that Gregory was prepared to offer a Sicilian see to a refugee Dalmatian bishop and actually appointed the refugee bishop of Tauriana to the see of Lipari. This was a policy he followed on the mainland too. In 592 he appointed the refugee Dacian bishop John of Lissus to the see of Scyllacium in Bruttium, informing him that if his own city was freed from the barbarians he must return there but that in the meantime he should govern Scyllacium.[77] John was almost immediately appointed visitor of Crotona, devastated by the Lombards in 596,[78] and apparently he never did return to Lissus. His appointment to Scyllacium did not, of course, infringe the canonical prohibition on the translation of bishops, for technically Lissus and Scyllacium were being united in John's person. The same thing happened in Tarracina. When Bishop Peter of Tarracina died in 592, the people requested as their new bishop Agnellus, bishop of the nearby city of Fundi which had recently been devastated by the Lombards. Gregory complied with their request and united Fundi and Tarracina in Agnellus' person.[79] Similarly, in Corsica, Bishop Martin of Tainas was appointed to the see of Aleria following the destruction of Tainas by the barbarians.[80] It was not just a matter of sensible economy to utilize existing out-of-work personnel. They could become a problem if not gainfully employed. The case of Bishop Basilius of Capua, who immersed himself in lawsuits, has already been mentioned. Another bishop, Mennas of Telesia, took himself off to Gaul, and his behaviour there began to bring his office into such disrepute that Gregory wrote in 599 to Bishop Syagrius of Autun ordering him to send Mennas back to Rome, where he duly appeared in 600.[81] It is clear from the foregoing that a mastery of all aspects of personnel management was not the least of Gregory's accomplishments.

Chapter Eleven

Gregory and the Lombards

The greatest political problem Gregory had to face was that of the Lombards. It was his increasing involvement in all aspects of this problem which did so much to enhance the temporal powers and involvement of the papacy; but the Lombards presented him with a spiritual as well as a political dilemma. For him the Lombards were 'unspeakable' and 'abominable', heretics and savages, despoiling the fair land of Italy, squatting presumptuously in her ancient cities – Milan, Pavia, Spoleto, Benevento – even daring to lay siege to Rome itself. The Lombards' pagan auxiliaries wantonly butchered Catholic peasants and clerics for refusing to adore their outlandish beast-gods, yet Gregory's Christian principles did not permit him to connive at their extermination. As he told the emperor: 'If I had wished to lend myself to the destruction of the Lombards, that nation would today have no longer either a king or dukes or counts and would be given over to irremediable confusion; but because I fear God, I did not wish to participate in the destruction of anyone whomsoever.'[1] He sought to fulfil his obligations both to *Romanitas* and *Christianitas* by seeking a peace treaty between the Empire and the Lombards and, on the other hand, by encouraging the conversion of the Lombards to Catholicism. These twin objectives were to call for all his skill, energy and dedication.

Gregory's consecration as pope coincided with the death of the Lombard king Autharis. Only a year before his death Autharis had married the Catholic Bavarian princess Theodelinda, who was to emerge as the key figure at the Lombard court during Gregory's pontificate. As the living symbol of the blood royal, she played the leading role in selecting Autharis' successor. Having taken counsel with the leading men of the kingdom, she selected and married Duke Agilulf of Turin, a kinsman of her late husband. In May 591 at a solemn gathering of all the Lombard chiefs in Milan he was accepted as their king. So Gregory faced a new Lombard monarch, who was both an able war-leader and a respected chieftain.[2]

By coincidence the two Lombard duchies fell vacant at the same time, with the deaths of their founder dukes. Farwald of Spoleto died *circa* 591, to be replaced by the pagan warrior Ariulf, and Zotto of Benevento died probably in the same year, to be replaced by Arichis. With Agilulf's early days preoccupied with concluding peace with the Franks and suppressing rebellions by those dukes who did not recognize his right to the throne, it was the new dukes of Spoleto and Benevento who posed the immediate threat to Rome.[3] Gregory wrote sadly to the quaestor John in Constantinople soon after his installation: 'For my sins I have been made Bishop not of the Romans but of the Lombards whose compacts are swords and whose favour is a punishment.'[4] He was immediately confronted both by the failure of the exarch of Ravenna to act in response to his urgent promptings and by the inadequacy of Rome's defences. He wrote to the *scholasticus* Paul in Sicily complaining that the city was ringed by hostile swords and threatened within by the sedition of the soldiery.[5] There were several sources of trouble. The exarch's strategy was to concentrate the available troops in the duchy of Rome along the Via Flaminia to protect the single land corridor linking Rome and Ravenna. This inevitably meant the denuding of the city of Rome itself, which the pope wanted strongly garrisoned. This difference in objectives led to increasingly bitter clashes between pope and exarch. Secondly, the troops were not being paid and were becoming restive. Thirdly, the ravages of the plague had taken a serious toll of the imperial defensive strength in the city.

Castus *magister militum*, the military governor of Rome, seems to have had his hands full keeping his near-mutinous garrison under control. He certainly took no decisive action when news reached the city that Ariulf was moving on the duchy. It was Gregory who took over the effective command of the city and sought to supervise the co-ordination of military operations in the duchy. There were three generals with military forces stationed on the frontiers of the duchy: the *magistri militum* Velox and Vitalian, and a commander called in the sources variously Martius, Maurilius, and Mauricius, but who is probably to be identified with Duke Maurisio of Perusia, a Lombard serving with the imperial army. On 27 September 591 Gregory wrote to Velox informing him that he was sending him reinforcements from Rome and urging him to concert plans with Vitalian and Maurisio to thwart Ariulf.[6] If Ariulf moved towards either Rome or Ravenna, they were to attack him in the rear. In the event the expected attack from Ariulf did not materialize, but Gregory was desperately worried about the gaps in the defences of the imperial enclaves. The surviving imperial territories were studded with fortified towns and military bases to which the Romans retired at the approach of the Lombards, and it was essential that these be under proper command.[7] Learning of defects in the command structure, Gregory moved to remedy them. He appointed *vir clarissimus* Leontius commandant of Nepe, and sent the tribune Constantius to take command of Naples because this vital imperial stronghold lacked a commander and the exarch had apparently refused to appoint one.[8] Gregory threw the full weight of his authority behind the appointments, informing the population of Nepe: 'Whoever resists his lawful commands, will be deemed a rebel against us and whoever obeys him will be obeying us.'

Ariulf proceeded no further against the duchy of Rome during 591, but seems to have blocked the Rome–Ravenna land corridor, causing Gregory to entrust to the care of John of Ravenna those Suburbicarian bishops unable to communicate with Rome because of the enemy presence. In the summer of 592 Ariulf was again reported to be advancing into the duchy, and Gregory repeated his previous instruction to Maurisio and Vitalian to attack Ariulf in the rear.[9] But scarcely had these instructions been dispatched than a messenger from Ariulf arrived in Rome bearing a letter intended to demoralize the city. In the letter Ariulf announced that the frontier town of Suana had agreed to surrender to him. Gregory hastily contacted Maurisio and Vitalian, instructing them to investigate this claim.[10] If it was found that the people of Suana were still loyal to the Empire, the generals were to take hostages, administer new oaths of fidelity and win the confidence of the people by discussion. But if Ariulf was correct in his claim, Gregory was in a quandary. His duty as a Roman and his duty as a Christian were in clear conflict. He could not urge the Suanese to break oaths taken to surrender to Ariulf, but equally he could not allow a key town to fall to the enemies of the Empire. So he summarized the problem and left it to the generals: 'If you distinctly ascertain that they have treated with Ariulf about their surrender to him or at any rate have given him hostages . . . then after wholesome deliberation, lest your souls or mine be burdened with respect to our oaths, do whatever you judge to be of advantage to the Empire. But let your glory act in such a way that nothing is done for which we can be blamed by our enemies nor anything omitted which the advantage of the state requires.' He went on to give them the latest information on the whereabouts of Ariulf's army and urged them to plunder the enemy positions as far as possible.

The fate of Suana is not known; but it is almost certain that it did surrender, for Ariulf now mounted his big push, taking Sutrium, Horta, Luceoli, Tuder, Perusia and Polymartium, and advancing on Rome.[11] Simultaneously Arichis of Benevento attacked Campania, devastating several cities and besieging Naples.[12] Ariulf now laid siege to Rome, 'killing some of our people and mutilating others'. Gregory's plight was desperate. He himself was ill, attributing his condition to the strain of the situation. Rome had been virtually stripped of troops in pursuit of the exarch Romanus' frontier strategy, and only the Theodosiac regiment remained, unpaid for so long that they could barely be persuaded to man the walls. Gregory contacted the exarch urgently, pleading for military help or, failing that, permission to negotiate.[13] Romanus refused both courses. Despite this prohibition, Gregory opened negotiations, only to find Ariulf's terms impossible. Ariulf had asked for the back pay for the armies of Autharis and Nordulf. This demand explains the rapid and total success of Ariulf's campaign. Nordulf was a Lombard general in the service of the Empire, as presumably was Autharis. They, like the Roman garrison, had not been paid, and so they and their men had simply gone over to Ariulf. So too had Duke Maurisio, the commander of Perusia, who had surrendered his city to Ariulf and remained in control of it in the name of his new master.[14]

In July 592 Gregory wrote to Archbishop John of Ravenna urging him to prevail on the exarch to agree to the conclusion of a peace with Ariulf, and to send a commander to Naples, threatened with capture by Arichis.[15] It is clear from subsequent events that Romanus had his own plans and was preparing a counter-attack, though he did not feel it necessary to take the pope into his confidence. But Romanus also had his immediate problems, for in 592 Gregory commented on a recent and destructive Lombard attack on the town of Fanum, deep inside the exarchate.[16] The situation in Rome was, however, too desperate for Gregory to await the maturation of Romanus' plans, and he concluded a treaty with Ariulf, paying him an unspecified sum from the papal treasury for his withdrawal from the city.[17] He may have been aided in his negotiations by Ariulf's illness. The *Whitby Life*, the oldest life of Gregory, tells the delightful story of an unnamed Lombard ruler who led his army against Rome, purposing to destroy it.[18] Gregory went out and spoke to him, and won his promise that he would never again lead his army against Rome while Gregory was pope. Then falling ill, the ruler sent to Gregory for advice, and the pope prescribed a milk diet, on which the ruler recovered. The prescribing of the diet has a splendidly authentic ring. Gregory certainly took a keen interest in medical matters, Ariulf did not in fact attack Rome again, and one should not underestimate the superstitious awe that the power of Christianity, as embodied in a milk diet, could inspire in a pagan like Ariulf. He is, for instance, said to have been convinced that an apparition of St Sabinus fought at his side in the battle of Camerinum.[19] A combination of talk, money and a 'miracle cure' might well have persuaded Ariulf to retreat from Rome.

No sooner had Ariulf withdrawn than Romanus launched his counter-attack, marching down the Via Flaminia and recapturing Luceoli, Tuder, Ameria, Sutrium and Polymartium.[20] Maurisio surrendered Perusia and rejoined the service of the Empire, and Nordulf probably came over too.[21] Romanus entered Rome only long enough to withdraw most of its garrison to defend Perusia and Narnia and then returned to Ravenna, leaving Rome even more poorly defended than before. 'Rome was abandoned', lamented Gregory, 'so that Perusia might be garrisoned.'

Ariulf made no response to this reverse; but King Agilulf could not permit such a humiliation for the Lombard cause, and he now moved south to attack the duchy of Rome with his army in 593. He captured Perusia and executed Maurisio, holding the city until the peace of 598, when it seems to have reverted to the Empire.[22] At the same time Arichis renewed his attack on Campania and captured Capua.[23]

Once again Rome was besieged, and Gregory responded by preaching a series of mournful homilies on the Prophet Ezekiel to the unhappy populace. From the walls of the city the spirals of smoke from burning farms were clearly visible. Gregory himself witnessed the pitiable sight of lines of Italian prisoners, tethered and despairing, led beneath the walls, to be sold in the slave markets of Gaul. He wept over the lengthening casualty lists and grieved at the sight of captured soldiers being returned to the city with their hands cut off, to demoralize the citizens.[24] When the grain ran out and negotiation became imperative, Gregory once again took charge.[25] He had the

full backing of the military governor, *magister militum* Castus, and of
Gregory, prefect of the city, both of whom saw that the situation was
hopeless. But it was the pope who took the leading part. According
to the Continuator of the Chronicle of Prosper of Havnium, he met
Agilulf on the steps of St Peter's and agreed to pay a tribute of 500
pounds in gold.[26] Agilulf took his spoil and retired to Milan.

Two sieges in two years were enough for Gregory, and he now set
his sights on a general peace treaty between the Lombards and the
Empire. This became the major diplomatic aim of his pontificate. His
reasons for wanting peace blended all the aspects of his complex
character: a deeply felt Christian desire to put an end to misery and
suffering, a patriotic wish to give the Empire a breathing space for
retrenchment, and an estate owner's clear realization that all this
turmoil and destruction was bad for business. So in September 593
Gregory wrote to Archbishop Constantius of Milan, who kept him
informed on the activities of the Franks and the Lombards in the
north, asking him to act as his intermediary with the king and to
assure Agilulf that the pope was prepared to use his best efforts to
secure peace.[27] An armistice was concluded between Romanus and
Agilulf, and the exarch, now apparently alive to his precarious position, initiated negotiations with the Lombards for a general peace.
But the negotiations were difficult and protracted, and were not
helped by violations of the armistice by imperial troops.

Gregory kept in close touch with both the Lombard and the imperial side during the negotiations, and as they dragged on, his concern
mounted to the extent of writing a strongly worded note to the
exarch's legal adviser, the *scholasticus* Severus:[28]

Agilulf is willing to make a general peace if only the Lord Exarch
will consent to arbitration on the matters in dispute between
them. He complains that during the armistice he was grievously
wronged in various parts of his dominions. And as he demands
satisfaction for himself, if his claims are judged reasonable, so he
promises himself to give every satisfaction if it is shown that any
act of hostility was perpetrated on his side during the peace. As,
then, it is clear that his proposals are reasonable, there ought to
be a judicial investigation of the matter, so that compensation
may be made for any wrongs done on either side, provided that
a general peace may be thus securely established under the
protection of God. How necessary such a peace is for us, you

well know. Act, then, with your usual wisdom, so that his excellency the Exarch may give his consent to the proposal without delay, lest it be thought that the offer of peace is rejected by him, which is not desirable. For if he will not give his consent, Agilulf offers to make a special peace with us. But we know that in that case various islands and other places will be ruined. Let Romanus take this into consideration, and make haste to conclude peace, that at least during this reprieve we may have a short time of rest, and the empire may, by God's help, the better recruit its powers of resistance.

Several things strike one about this letter: its common sense, its balance, its sporting concern for achieving justice for the Lombards, its realistic appreciation of the value of a peace to the Empire, and its threat to deal separately with Agilulf. It emphasizes the distinction that the Lombards drew between the Empire and the papacy, but confirms that Gregory saw the papacy as being an integral part of the Empire and had imperial interests close to his heart.

In the meantime, in the spring of 595, the back pay of the Roman garrison finally arrived, to silence their complaints.[29] Gregory was at this time in touch with Ariulf as well as Agilulf, for he now informed the emperor that Ariulf had expressed a willingness to come over to the Empire. This move by Ariulf is not too surprising, given the tension which existed between the Lombard kingdom and the southern duchies, but the emperor wrote back to Gregory castigating him for interfering in matters of state and accusing him of being simple-minded and of being duped by Ariulf. In June 595 Gregory sent a biting reply, agreeing that he was indeed a fool 'for otherwise I should never have endured what I do here amid the swords of the Lombards'.[30] He warned the emperor against listening to his detractors ('While my statements are disbelieved, the strength of the enemy is terribly increasing'). He recounted all he had suffered and all he had tried to do for the Empire: the peace made with the Lombards 'at no expense to the state', the removal of the garrison from Rome, the siege by Agilulf. But he hastened to defend the diligence and loyalty of the prefect Gregory and *magister militum* Castus, who had fallen under imperial displeasure for working with Gregory to secure a peace.

The negotiations continued, and despite worsening relations between pope and exarch the papal *apocrisiarios* in Ravenna, Castorius, was kept informed of their progress because of the pope's influence with the Lombard court. In April 595 Gregory was writing to Secundus, who had been negotiating with Agilulf and had reported on the progress of the talks to Castorius.[31] But there were opponents to peace with the Lombards, and the pope's involvement in the negotiations led to a placard attack on Gregory and Castorius in Ravenna. Gregory wrote an angry open letter to the clergy, people and rulers of Ravenna denouncing this attack and excommunicating those responsible.[32]

The need for a conclusion of the negotiations, which had now dragged on for three years, was made evident by a revival of military activity by Arichis, who raided Campania causing 'a great calamity involving many captives carried off' and launched an attack on Bruttium, capturing and devastating Crotona.[33] It is possible that these attacks were prompted by the death of Romanus, who expired suddenly in 596 or 597.[34] He was succeeded as exarch by Callinicus, whose relations with Gregory were much more cordial and who appears to have been rather more statesmanlike than Romanus.[35] Callinicus did, however, have in his entourage advisers hostile to the pope, and Gregory was warned of them by the *scholasticus* Andreas. 'Inasmuch as the times are evil, we bear all things with a groan,' replied Gregory resignedly.[36]

Although there is no explicit evidence for it, there is a good deal of circumstantial evidence to suggest that Callinicus was first concerned to establish his negotiating position from strength. Gregory talks darkly in May 597 of the exarch being 'busied in the valley of the Po', and the evidence of ecclesiastical reorganization in Picenum suggests an imperial push into that province to recover long-lost territory. The province of Picenum Suburbicarium had been under the control of the dukes of Spoleto since at least 580, when Firmum was captured and its bishop fled to the imperial refuge of Ancona. In 598 the *magister militum* Bahan headed an imperial offensive into the province, which recovered territory stretching as far south as Asculum and Aprutium.[37] A possible western limit to the conquest is provided by the battle of Camerinum, in which Ariulf defeated the Romans, reputedly with the help of St Sabinus. This battle has never been dated, but Paul the Deacon links it with Ariulf's death in 601, suggesting it came towards the end of his reign rather than the start.[38] Camerinum is on the borders between Umbria and Picenum, and a battle there would fit with the known evidence of the imperial advance, its limits and progress.

Having made his point, Callinicus now renewed the negotiations with Agilulf, associating the pope with them. The envoys were Abbot Probus, one of Gregory's closest confidants, and Theodore, curator of Ravenna.[39] They were given written instructions by the exarch and on the basis of them concluded a treaty. But until it was actually signed there was still a danger of attack, and Gregory wrote in September 598 urging Archbishop Januarius of Caralis to make sure the city walls were guarded in case the enemy sought to take advantage of the inevitable delays in obtaining the signatures of all the parties to the treaty.[40]

There was now a bizarre and intriguing development. Agilulf signed the peace treaty in 598, unconditionally for two years, and the treaty was taken from the king in Pavia to Callinicus in Ravenna, who also signed it. It was then sent to Ariulf in Spoleto, Gregory in Rome, and Arichis in Benevento, who were all expected to sign to inaugurate the *generalis pax*.[41] Ariulf, however, refused to sign unless certain conditions were agreed to: that no act of violence should be committed against him, and that no one should march against his ally, Arichis of Benevento. Warnfrid, Ariulf's chief adviser, refused to swear to the peace at all. But Gregory's attitude was strangest of all. He informed the curator Theodore that he would not sign the treaty but would allow his brother, one of the bishops, or the archdeacon to do so on his behalf. His reason – and it parallels his attitude over the Suana question – was that if anything was privately carried out, Gregory, who had been a mediator between Agilulf and the exarch, would seem to have broken his pledged word. Here again is the conflict between *Romanitas* and *Christianitas*: what was good for the Empire might not necessarily be good for Gregory's soul. The explanation may well lie in the Picene expedition. Ariulf, angry at losing one of his provinces, wanted to ensure freedom from further attack. Warnfrid, having perhaps lost Picene estates, was totally opposed to the treaty, wanting to recover his losses by force of arms. Gregory, after the violations complained of by Agilulf during the armistice, did not trust the imperial forces not to break the treaty. He was also concerned about Ariulf's conditions, fearing that Ariulf was providing himself with an excuse to renew hostilities.

However, it seems that Ariulf and Arichis did sign, albeit reluctantly, and in November–December 598 Gregory wrote to both Agilulf and Theodelinda thanking them for their good work in arranging the peace.[42] He clearly appreciated the importance of the queen in all this, urging on her that she should constantly remind Agilulf of the value of alliance with the Empire. He also asked Agilulf to order his dukes, particularly those in the neighbourhood of Rome, to keep the peace and not to seek opportunities for strife. The Roman landlord's voice can be heard in the phrase 'If it had not been made, which God forbid, what would have happened but that the blood of the wretched peasants, whose labour benefits both of us, would be shed to the shame and ruin of both parties.'

Nevertheless, the peace was an uneasy one. Gregory did not believe it would be renewed, warning Januarius of Caralis to strengthen his city's defences and lay in provisions in preparation for the expiration of the peace. Ariulf continued to be a worry, and in August 599 Gregory wrote to the army paymaster Donellus in Ravenna, urging the payment of the soldiers' back pay because the garrison of Rome, already depleted by plague, was once again disgruntled by its lack of pay and there was a danger from the Lombards because of breaches of the peace.[43] To keep them loyal, Gregory had paid the soldiers himself in the past.[44] What Gregory had feared was occurring. Faesulae was captured by an imperial expedition under Aldio, and Gregory was constantly aware of the need to keep alert.[45] This explains his efforts to heal a quarrel between Count Comitaticius of Misenum and Maurentius, the *magister militum* of Naples.[46] He feared that any sign of disunity in the imperial ranks might bring the Lombards down upon them.

The danger from Ariulf ended with his death in 601. A civil war followed his death, and from it Theudelap, son of Farwald, emerged as duke. Agilulf apparently took no hand in the Spoletine succession, because he was fully occupied with a revolt by dukes Gaidoald of Trent and Gisulf of Friuli. At this point the treaty ran out, and Callinicus seized the opportunity to attack Parma and capture Duke Gottschalk and his wife, who was Agilulf's daughter. Agilulf furiously concluded an alliance with the Avars, ravaged Istria, destroyed Padua and captured Monselice.[47] Gregory wrote to all the bishops of Sicily declaring that an invasion of Sicily was imminent and urging two litanies a week to avert the danger.[48] Reunited with his rebel dukes, Agilulf launched a fresh assault in 603, capturing Mantua, Cremona and Brexillum. Gregory was surely referring to this campaign when he lamented to Eulogius of Alexandria 'the

immense ravages of mortality among the swords of so many barbarians'.[49] Meanwhile the emperor Maurice had fallen and Callinicus
had been recalled. He was replaced as exarch by Smaragdus, now
recovered from his insanity and restored to his former position.[50] He
at once concluded an eighteen-month truce with Agilulf, paying him
12,000 *solidi* and restoring to him his daughter, who immediately
died in childbirth.[51] There was peace until 1 April 605, though as a
result of his military operations Agilulf had extended Lombard control over the Po valley, nullifying the advances made by Romanus in
the 580s. There was, however, one consolation for Gregory, in that
in 603 a son was born to Agilulf and Theodelinda, who was baptized
as a Catholic and named Adaloald.[52] This was an important step
forward in the catholicization of Lombardy, another of Gregory's
long-term aims, for although his relations with the Lombards were
chiefly political, he was also concerned about the spiritual relationship between Rome and Pavia.

With the Lombards, Gregory faced all three major religious problems at once – heresy, paganism and schism. The Lombards were in
the main Arians, though there were still groups of pagans amongst
them. Such Catholics as there were were supporters of the 'Three
Chapters' schism.

The predominant area of paganism seems to have been the duchy
of Benevento, where all the Catholic sees were extinguished and
where Barbatus, the seventh-century missionary bishop who re-
established a Catholic see in the ducal capital, found the inhabitants
worshipping a snake.[53] The principal problem was Arianism, because
it was the faith of the king. Autharis had seen Catholicism as an
instrument of the Empire, sapping the warrior vitality of his people,
and he had forbidden the sons of Lombards to be baptized according
to the Catholic rite.[54] The baptism of Agilulf's son by that very rite
effectively abrogated that rule, and confirms the rightness of Gregory's strategy with regard to the Lombards.

On his election, Gregory had sought to capitalize on the plague
and the death of Autharis by instructing the bishops of Italy to preach
Catholicism to the Arians, pointing out that God had struck down
Autharis for banning Catholic baptism and had sent the plague as a
punishment for heresy.[55] But thereafter his personal exertions to
convert the Lombards declined. He sent no missionary team and
took little initiative, for the obvious reason that in Lombard eyes
Romans would be associated with the Empire and might be suspected

of being fifth-columnists. Gregory's plan was to put his faith in Queen Theodelinda, to leave her and her circle to convert the Lombards from Arianism to Catholicism and to concentrate his efforts on winning the queen over from the 'Three Chapters' schism. Her influence on Agilulf meant that Catholicism was now tolerated, even favoured, though Agilulf himself refrained from abandoning Arianism. Paul the Deacon places the responsibility for this change squarely on Theodelinda:[56]

> By means of this queen, the church of God obtained much that was useful. For the Lombards, when they were still held in the error of heathenism, seized nearly all the property of the churches, but the king, moved by her wholesome supplication, not only held the Catholic faith but also bestowed many possessions on the church of Christ and restored to the honour of their wonted dignity the bishops who were in a reduced and abject condition.'

It is not true that Agilulf became a Catholic, but it was under him that the Catholic church revived. The hierarchy in the north had remained more or less intact, and it is reasonable to suppose that they played a full part in the work of converting the Arians.

The principal problem, then, as far as Rome was concerned was the 'Three Chapters', to which Theodelinda and her circle were devoted. This was a serious embarrassment, and indeed St Columban later informed Pope Boniface IV that it was this problem which alone prevented Agilulf from abandoning Arianism and embracing Catholicism.[57] The problem came to a head over the election of Constantius as archbishop of Milan. The north Italian hierarchy still acknowledged the headship of the archbishop of Milan, despite his residence in imperial Genoa, and the improvement in status and toleration which the Catholic church enjoyed under Agilulf led to a re-establishment of contact between the bishops and their archbishop. But whereas most of the north Italian bishops remained 'Three Chapters' supporters, Archbishop Laurentius II had renounced the schism and become reconciled to Rome. He had even signed a *cautio* testifying to his abandonment of the schism, and it had been countersigned by Gregory as prefect of the city. But in 593, following the death of Laurentius and the election of Constantius to succeed him, three of Constantius' suffragan bishops inside Lombard Italy had informed him they were breaking off communion with him because he had signed a *cautio* denouncing the 'Three Chapters'.[58] To make matters worse, the queen supported them in their action, and this factor certainly influenced the nature of Gregory's response. He did not want to alienate Theodelinda, but he could not sanction a statement recognizing the validity of the 'Three Chapters', so he settled for two ambiguous letters in which he sought to sidestep the issue. He wrote to the bishops via Constantius to say that no such document had been signed, that the 'Three Chapters' had not been discussed between them, and that the papacy kept faith with Chalcedon.[59] To the queen, he expressed his regret that she should endanger the result of all her good works by listening to the talk of 'unskilled and foolish men who do not even know what they are talking about' and separating herself from the communion of the Catholic church.[60] He declared that the Fifth Council at Constantinople, which had condemned the 'Three Chapters', had done nothing to impair the integrity of Chalcedon. Gregory also sent this to Constantius to deliver, but the archbishop feared that the direct allusion to the Fifth Council might cause more trouble and suggested a revised version, which Gregory duly supplied, stressing the church of Rome's adherence to the four General Councils and refraining from mention of the fifth.[61]

The pope's letter did not, however, satisfy the bishop of Brescia, who insisted on a letter from Constantius swearing that he himself did not condemn the 'Three Chapters'.[62] Gregory advised Constantius that he should do no such thing, though it might be politic to write a letter saying he endorsed the four General Councils. But it seems that ill-feeling between Constantius and his suffragans continued, for in November 596 Gregory wrote encouraging him to bear the attacks of his detractors with equanimity.[63] In 599 when a dispute arose between the church of Comum and the church of Rome about a piece of property, Gregory suggested that the property might be conceded to them if they abandoned support for the 'Three Chapters'.[64] But it does not seem that this approach had any more success than the letters of support for the four Councils.

With the queen, whatever she thought of Constantius, Gregory's relations resumed their previous cordiality. He praised her role in securing the *generalis pax*, and in 603 she wrote to inform Gregory of the baptism of her son.[65] But she was still agitated about the 'Three Chapters', and her ambassadors carried a paper from her adviser, Abbot Secundus of Trent, arguing for Rome's acceptance of the 'Chapters'. Gregory replied that ill-health prevented him from replying in detail to the paper, but he sent Secundus the proceedings of the Fifth Council, in the clear hope that it would convince him that the 'Three Chapters' condemnation did not impair Chalcedon. There was, in fact, to be no end to the 'Three Chapters' schism until the end of the seventh century, when it was officially ended by the Synod of Pavia. However uncertain things may have looked to Gregory on his deathbed, the catholicization of the Lombards was under way, and the seventh century was to see the progressive elimination of Arianism and the eventual realization of Gregory's dream of seeing the true faith prevail.

Chapter Twelve

Gregory and the West

It is frequently alleged that the profoundest significance of Gregory's reign lay in his 'opening up the fallow Western Germanic soil to Roman ecclesiastical influence', and that this was undertaken because of Gregory's historic realization that it was futile and dangerous to attempt to push Roman primatial claims against the imperial government. He therefore consciously evolved a policy of 'bifurcation' – speaking humbly to the emperor in the East and seeking to avoid confrontation, while addressing Western rulers in the language of a Roman governor who expected to be obeyed and making concrete the papal primatial claims in the West.[1] There is, in fact, very little evidence to support this view, but in order to scrutinize it effectively it is necessary to look at three aspects of papal activity: relations with the West, relations with the East, and involvement in missionary enterprises.

We begin with those parts of the West still under imperial rule. The provinces of North Africa had a tradition of independent-mindedness in the matter of religion. From the time of Constantine until at least the fifth century, North Africa had been the home of Donatism. A schismatic rather than a heretical church, it maintained its own ecclesiastical hierarchy and conducted its own services but was persecuted by both the Catholic church and the imperial government. From the time of the Vandal conquest of Africa, however, there is virtually no mention of the Donatists until they suddenly crop up in the correspondence of Gregory the Great. His letters are crucial evidence in the controversy about precisely how long Donatism survived.

Both the Catholic and Donatist churches of Africa suffered grievous persecution at the hands of the Arian Vandals. But after imperial rule was re-established, Justinian confirmed in 533 the privileges of the Catholic church and once again proscribed the Donatists. It was not long before the Catholic church itself was at loggerheads with the imperial government. Justinian's condemnation of the 'Three Chapters' had brought him into conflict with the entire Western church, and even when the papacy was won over to the imperial viewpoint, the African bishops continued the struggle long and hard. In common with the Istrian and Milanese churches, the Africans regarded the papacy as having betrayed the Chalcedonian settlement by endorsing Justinian's policy.

It is against this background that Gregory's dealings with the African church must be judged. First of all there is the question of the Donatists. On the evidence of Gregory's letters there was a revival of Donatism in Numidia, the least romanized of the three ecclesiastical provinces of North Africa, with which Gregory had dealings. His letters talk of Catholic priests being turned out of their churches by Donatists, Donatists infiltrating the Catholic episcopate, Donatist clergy being placed in charge of churches by Catholic bishops, Catholic bishops issuing licences for the consecration of Donatist bishops, Catholic persons allowing their children and their slaves to be baptized by Donatists.[2] The established view is to take the evidence at face value and argue that Donatism survived the Vandal occupation, was revived in Numidia, was successfully combated by Gregory, and was finally extinguished by the Arab conquest.[3] But this view has recently been persuasively challenged.[4] It is argued that by Gregory's time Donatism no longer existed in its fifth-century form; that, perhaps as a result of the Arian persecutions jointly suffered by the two churches, the Catholics and Donatists had established a *modus vivendi*; and that what was at issue in the late sixth century was a revival of non-Roman Christianity, associated with the resurgence of the Berber kingdoms of Numidia. 'The distinction between Donatist and Catholic had lost much of its old sharpness and in all probability had by this time ceased to have any meaning to African churchmen. The two communities had learned to live in peaceful coexistence', is the verdict of Robert Markus.

The question of non-Roman Berber Christianity probably needs further research, but there is a good deal of evidence to support the view that the Catholic and Donatist hierarchies were peacefully coexisting. All the instances cited by Gregory suggest this, and it was undoubtedly being connived at by the Catholic episcopate if it is true, as was alleged, that Bishop Argentius of Lamigia was appointing Donatist priests to his churches and that Bishop Maximian of Pudentiana had licensed a Donatist bishop in his own town. This practice of coexistence would also explain the secular authorities' complete failure to do anything about the situation, despite Gregory's pleas to them. Gregory put this failure down to bribery, unable apparently to comprehend the possibility of peaceful coexistence. Further evidence for the widespread practice of Donatism comes in the case of Bishop Paul (see unknown), who complained to the pope that his great unpopularity with many people derived from his zealously Catholic anti-Donatism, or, put another way, to the fact that he was needlessly stirring up trouble and rocking the boat.[5] In this connection it could also be noted that most of Gregory's evidence about the Donatists came from disaffected clerics taking cases to Rome when decisions had gone against them in Africa. In these circumstances, it might be argued that to call one's opponents Donatists would be akin to the practice nowadays of calling someone a 'Red' or a 'Fascist', a term devoid of substantive content.

Whatever Donatism meant in Africa, Gregory unquestionably saw it as a threat to the faith, talking of the Donatists 'wounding many with the sword of their error' and describing it variously as a 'disease', a 'poison' and a 'diabolical fraud'. He tried two lines of attack against it. The first was to invoke the assistance of the secular authorities. In 591 he wrote urging the exarch Gennadius of Africa to 'subdue their proud necks to the yoke of rectitude', and in 594 he urged the same course of action on the praetorian prefect Pantaleo of Africa.[6] His pleas were ignored. Even when the emperor issued orders that Donatism should be suppressed, perhaps at Gregory's instigation, still the officials did nothing. Gregory once again blamed bribery, lamenting to the emperor that in Africa 'the Catholic faith is publicly put up for sale'.[7]

Gregory's second line of attack was to stir up the Catholic episcopate of Numidia. It is clear that he felt they lacked leadership and cohesion, and that this derived in part from the peculiar Numidian system of choosing a primate. The Numidian primacy was not attached to a particular see but rotated according to seniority. Pelagius II had tried to alter the system, and one of the early matters Gregory had to deal with was the Numidian bishops' petition for confirmation of their traditional method of selecting a primate. Gregory suggested, perhaps reiterating Pelagius' plans, that they should fix their metropolitan see in one place and choose their primate for merit and not by age. But the Numidians rejected this idea, and

Gregory duly confirmed their tradition, though appealing to them not to choose a Donatist primate.[8]

Gregory still needed to ensure leadership in the anti-Donatist struggle. He had a rector, Hilarus, on the spot and initially employed him, but he felt he also needed someone on the Numidian episcopal bench on whom he could rely.[9] His choice fell on Bishop Columbus, whose see is not given in the Register but has been identified as Nicivibus.[10] He was chosen for his rectitude and absolute devotion to the papacy and became a sort of unofficial vicar. 'I know that you are devoted to the apostolic see with your whole heart and mind and soul,' wrote Gregory rapturously to him in 593.[11] Columbus and Hilarus were instructed to work together, and in July 594 Gregory began pressing for a church council to stamp out the Donatists.[12]

An anti-Donatist council was, in fact, held in September 594, but in Carthage, the metropolitan see of proconsular Africa, the most romanized of the provinces and one in which there is no evidence of Donatism at this time. The council seems to have been held in response to the *iussiones* issued by the emperor Maurice and was convoked by Archbishop Dominicus of Carthage, a friend and correspondent of Gregory's. It issued stern instructions that any bishop who neglected the task of searching out and punishing heretics should be deposed and his property confiscated. Gregory's response to this is interesting. While applauding Dominicus' zeal, he expressed grave misgivings that the ruling would cause disaffection in the church, and in particular would cause grave offence to other primates. 'It is best, dear brother, that in dealing with matters outside the church that require correction, charity within should be first and foremost preserved.'[13] This is the politician in Gregory coming out. Striving as he was to correct matters in Numidia from within, he clearly felt that dictation from Carthage would be counterproductive.

After this there is no further mention of Donatism in his letters, but there can surely be no justification for arguing that Gregory had therefore been successful in suppressing it. All the evidence points to the opposite conclusion. It is much more likely that he failed and that his attention became diverted elsewhere, particularly in the direction of the English mission. This conclusion is supported by the evidence of Gregory's failure in the wider context of his relations with the African church not involving Donatism.

He was always anxious to eradicate abuses and purify the body of the church, and he hoped to use Columbus to facilitate this too in

Numidia. In July 593 he wrote to him urging that he bring up at a local council measures to stamp out simony and the ordination of boys. Gregory felt that boys were too susceptible to ambition and promotion-seeking instead of performing their duties conscientiously.[14] He backed this up with a letter to the elderly and infirm Numidian primate Adeodatus, urging the same measures and pressing him to listen to the advice of Columbus.[15]

Columbus failed, however, for in September 593 Gregory was writing angrily to the exarch Gennadius of Africa, complaining: 'Many things are being done in the Council of Numidia contrary to the usages of the Fathers and the ordinances of the canons.' He explained that he had appointed Columbus to root out certain abuses and urged Gennadius to support him, but there is no evidence that Gennadius was any more willing to enforce the papal will in this matter than he was in the matter of Donatism.[16]

In the area of the pope's appellate jurisdiction, there were some nine cases of appeals to Rome during his reign. Two of them were *causes célèbres*, and an examination of them indicates the particular difficulties under which the pope laboured in endeavouring to exercise his rights. The first case, which arose in July 594, was that of the Numidian bishop Paul.[17] Paul was excommunicated by the Numidian Council of Bishops for some unspecified offence and appealed against the sentence to the pope. Gregory wrote to the praetorian prefect Pantaleo, the Numidian primate Victor, and Bishop Columbus, urging that Paul be sent to Rome to plead his case. Two years later Paul had still not left Africa, and Gregory complained to Gennadius that he was being prevented from leaving, clearly by the exarch. Eventually Paul reached Rome, with or without exarchal permission. Bishop Columbus sent a deacon to give an account of the Numidian Council's actions, and the exarch sent his chancellor to explain the charges. The chancellor was, however, forbidden to participate in a formal hearing. Gennadius was evidently prepared as a matter of courtesy to fill the pope in on the background but not to see the matter reopened. Paul had alleged that he was hated because of his zeal on behalf of the Catholic church, but, reading between the lines, he seems to have been a meddlesome busybody who was stirring up the two communities and whom both the Numidian Council and the exarch had taken steps to silence. Under the circumstances the pope was powerless to act, and when Paul asked permission to take the case to the emperor he consented. The emperor could make no more headway than Gregory had and referred the case back to Africa. In the end, Gregory had to settle for writing letters to various Numidian bishops, urging them to support Paul in his efforts to clear himself. We do not know how the case ended, but the likeliest bet is that the Numidian Council confirmed its original decision and Paul was duly disciplined. The case amply demonstrates the grudging courtesy the African church and the exarch were prepared to accord to the pope, and also the extent to which they regarded internal church matters as their own affair.

The second case, which arose in October 598, concerned Crementius, primate of the third African province, Byzacena.[18] He was accused of certain crimes by some of his bishops, who travelled to the imperial court in Constantinople to lay evidence against him. The emperor quite properly referred the case to the pope (*iuxta statuta canonum*) since it fell within his patriarchal jurisdiction. But the *magister militum* Theodore, having been bribed, refused to allow the parties to the dispute to leave Africa for Rome, and Gregory, unable to get any information on the case, referred it to Bishop John of Syracuse for resolution, declaring sadly: 'We have not wished to get involved in this case because of the contrariness of the men.' John made no headway either, and in March 602 the pope's attention was drawn to the fact that the case was still unresolved. He wrote to the bishops of Byzacena suggesting that they assemble in council and judge the case. As with the case of Bishop Paul the outcome is not known, but once again the pope had been effectively powerless to take any action at all. The other seven appeals to Rome were almost all by disgruntled clerics at odds with their bishop for one reason or another, and in every case the pope referred the matter back for an investigation on the spot by a panel of bishops or a designated bishop, usually Columbus.[19]

All the evidence suggests that both church and state authorities wished to keep the papacy at arm's length. Despite the fact that Gregory enjoyed a friendly correspondence with Archbishop Dominicus of Carthage, and that Exarch Gennadius earned papal thanks for settling farmers on the papal estates, papal authority in Africa was virtually non-existent. Columbus complained to Gregory that he was unpopular because of his role as Rome's agent.[20] Gregory complained that it was the exarch rather than the Numidian primate who had informed him of Paul's excommunication.[21] Bishops took their cases to the emperor rather than to the pope.[22] Gregory urged the exarch to allow Numidian bishops to visit Rome if they wanted to, but there is clear evidence that the authorities actively prevented people leaving Africa for Rome.[23] Despite the presence of a rector and an informal vicar in Numidia, and despite Gregory's friendship with Dominicus, the pope found to his frustration and despair that it was impossible to get accurate information out of Africa, especially about cases referred to him. The evidence also suggests that Gregory gradually came to realize the extent of his powerlessness. No African bishop is among the addressees of a letter promulgating an imperial decree among the metropolitans of the Western patriarchate in November 597.[24] Gregory discouraged Dominicus from taking too hard a line with the church hierarchy for fear of alienating them. In 602 he also admitted that he was distracted from African affairs by 'the presence of many different tribulations and with the enemy raging all around us'.[25] Perhaps the clearest evidence of his withdrawal from active involvement is the difference in tone between the situation in 591 when, newly come to the throne, he ordered his rector Hilarus to summon a church council in Numidia to try the case against Bishop Argentius of Lamigia, and the situation in March 602 when, older and wiser, he suggested to the Numidian primate Victor that he call a council to try the case of Bishop Paulinus of Tegesis and invited him to call on the assistance of Hilarus 'if the case should require it'.[26] Gregory had bowed to African independence.

The imperial province closest to Italy was Dalmatia, militarily and administratively within the jurisdiction of the exarch of Ravenna and ecclesiastically within the patriarchal jurisdiction of the pope.[27] Its metropolitan see was Salona, and there the pope became involved in a trial of strength with the imperial authorities over the episcopal election. It is important to stress that the pope was not seeking to extend his powers *per se*. He was seeking to secure a fit and proper archbishop of the kind he had described in the *Regula Pastoralis*. His activities here parallel the personnel operations he undertook in Italy, and he found himself up against the same ingrained local prejudice against outside interference.

When Gregory came to the throne, the see of Salona was beset by a serious conflict of personalities. The archbishop was Natalis, a jovial, easy-going *bon viveur* renowned for his lavish banquets where gossip, funny stories and sophisticated backbiting were relished.[28] But Natalis' archdeacon, Honoratus, a stern and uncompromising moralist, intensely disapproved of his superior's life-style and they were constantly at loggerheads. Their disagreements came to a head when Honoratus accused Natalis of distributing church plate amongst his relatives. Natalis decided to rid himself of this vexatious subordinate and planned to ordain Honoratus as a priest – technically a promotion but a not uncommon device for disposing of troublesome deacons. Honoratus promptly petitioned Pope Pelagius II to forbid the promotion, and Pelagius ordered the archbishop to send representatives to Rome to answer the charges Honoratus had brought.[29] The matter was unresolved at Pelagius' death, and in November 590 Gregory wrote to Honoratus encouraging him to patch up his difficulties with Natalis; if they could not be resolved he was to come to Rome and Gregory would hear the case.[30] However, Natalis went ahead and promoted Honoratus to the priesthood, appointing a more amenable archdeacon in his place. Honoratus protested to the pope, and in January 591 Gregory ordered Natalis to restore Honoratus to the archidiaconate and send his representatives to Rome to put his case.[31] Natalis ignored the instruction, so in March 592 Gregory threatened him with withdrawal of the *pallium* and even excommunication if he did not restore Honoratus and send representatives to Rome: 'Do not provoke us any further, dear brother, if you do not want to find us very hard in our severity.'[32] He repeated his instructions in letters to the bishops of Dalmatia and the papal rector Antoninus.[33] He also wrote to the praetorian prefect Jobinus of Illyricum warning him not to take Natalis' side, since the matter must be resolved by canon law.[34] It is clear from this that Natalis had powerful friends among the lay authorities and that Gregory was all too well aware of this.

Natalis, however, gave way and restored Honoratus, but he wrote Gregory a whimsically tongue-in-cheek letter defending his conduct, in particular his feasting, and revealing in the process why the lay authorities found him such an agreeable and urbane host. He said that his dinners were held with the aim of bestowing charity, and defended his feasting with reference to the Old Testament and to St Paul, particularly Romans 14:3: 'Let not him which eateth not judge him that eateth', a sly reference to the pope's renowned abstinence. He defended himself against Gregory's accusations that he was not devoting his time to reading and preaching by saying that the tribulations he suffered prevented study but that he was winning many back to the faith by preaching. He ended with a warning to the pope not to interfere in Salonitan affairs contrary to custom.[35]

Gregory replied in sanctimonious and sarcastic style, rebutting each biblical quotation with another, dismissing Natalis' defence of not reading with an apposite reference from St Paul, congratulating him on his preaching successes, and indignantly repudiating any desire to interfere. But having expressed his belief in tradition, he stressed his primatial rights, reminding Natalis that he had flouted the orders of two popes in the matter of Honoratus: 'If any one of the four Patriarchs had done this, such great contumacy could by no means have been allowed to pass without the gravest scandal.' He ended by exhorting Natalis once again to send representatives to Rome so that the case might be heard and resolved.[36]

The case was never heard, however, for although Honoratus came to Rome, complaining of fresh alienation of church property by Natalis, news arrived in March 593 that the archbishop had died.[37] Gregory immediately absolved Honoratus of all the charges against him and ordered the rector Antoninus to investigate the allegations about the malversation of church property by Natalis. He also ordered the holding of an election and the sending of the election decree to Rome so that papal approval could be given 'according to custom' before consecration by the suffragan bishops. He added that he wanted a list of church plate drawn up, just to make sure it was all still there. The ensuing election graphically illustrates the problems Gregory faced in working his will in such matters.

The electorate split into two factions. One group among the clergy chose Honoratus, and it may well be that Antoninus had been indicating the pope's preference in the matter, for in July 593 Gregory wrote to the Salonitan clergy congratulating them on their choice. He expressed his complete approval of the candidate, but since the election must be unanimous he urged them and Antoninus to win over the dissenting faction to their position.[38]

It is clear that Honoratus was far from being the majority candidate. As was subsequently to emerge, the people, the suffragan bishops, the soldiers, the provincial government officials, and another part of the clergy preferred the candidature of a certain Maximus.[39] Gregory was later to express his astonishment that only two people, Archdeacon Honoratus and a Bishop Paulinus, opposed Maximus' consecration, which suggests that the original pro-Honoratus faction cannot have been very large.[40]

When Gregory learned of the support of the Dalmatian bishops – there were twelve in all – for Maximus, he wrote to them in November 593, roundly castigating them: 'Your characters are so perverted by worldliness that, entirely forgetting the nature of sacerdotal dignity and all considerations of heavenly fear, you endeavour to do not that which will please God but what pleases yourselves.'[41] He declared them excommunicated if they ordained anyone as archbishop without his consent. He said that he was willing to consider another candidate if Honoratus was unacceptable, so long as testimony of his worthiness and evidence of electoral unanimity were forwarded to Rome. But he absolutely forbade the candidature of Maximus, of whom he had heard many bad things.

What followed is somewhat confusing. Maximus claimed to have obtained imperial consent to his consecration. Gregory insisted that the emperor had refused Maximus permission for consecration and that the soldiers of the exarch Romanus of Ravenna had been bribed to secure his consecration by force.[42] The backing of the emperor and the imperial authorities for Maximus in the subsequent struggle does suggest that Maximus' claim was correct. But perhaps what happened was that Maximus reported his election to the emperor, who granted permission for consecration as a matter of course, assuming that papal confirmation had also been granted. This would certainly explain Maurice's subsequent stance, and would reconcile the diametrically opposed interpretations that Rome and Salona put on the imperial will. The widespread support for Maximus in all sections of the population suggests that there was little need for force, and it is likely that the exarch of Ravenna can be added to those influential figures who backed Maximus.

Whatever the truth of the matter, Maximus was consecrated as archbishop by his suffragans in blatant defiance of Gregory's orders, and the papal rector Antoninus fled from Salona, where a violently anti-papal mood prevailed, and returned to Rome. Gregory wrote to Maximus in April 594 accusing him of having used bribery to get elected and force to get installed. He affected not to believe that the emperor had sanctioned the consecration: 'He is not accustomed to interfere in cases concerning the priesthood lest he should in any way be burdened by our sins.' He ordered Maximus and his followers to refrain from all priestly duties under pain of excommunication until he had ascertained from the emperor the truth about his order.[43]

Maximus did not take delivery of the pope's letter in person. Instead he had it publicly pinned up in the middle of Salona, where it was torn to pieces by the mob. He then continued to say mass, despite his excommunication, and started spreading rumours in Constantinople to discredit Gregory, in particular that he had done away with Bishop Malchus, the former Dalmatian rector.[44]

Maximus was strongly supported by the provincial officials, who wrote to Gregory in his favour. Marcellus, the proconsul of Dalmatia, begged the pope in July 594 to recognize Maximus.[45] Gregory replied cordially enough, saying that he could not overlook the unlawful celebration of mass by Maximus, though Gregory was to write to him later accusing him of being Maximus' principal supporter ('All assert that you are the author of all that great mischief in the case of Maximus').[46] Julian the *Scribo* also wrote supporting Maximus and testifying to the 'goodwill of the palace and the love of the people' for the archbishop.[47] But Gregory refused to be deflected from his purpose, even by the emperor. In 595 the emperor took a hand in the dispute, ordering Maximus to go to Rome, but he also wrote asking the pope to receive him with honour and confirm his election. Gregory expressed his shock at this request to Empress Constantina: 'It is a very serious thing that a man of whom so many things of such a nature are reported should be honoured before such things have been inquired into and sifted.' He went on to make his own position quite clear. At the request of the emperor he had forgiven the slights to himself, but he could not overlook the dangers to the church in Maximus' conduct, particularly obtaining the election by bribery, celebrating mass while excommunicated, and breaking the celibacy laws. He lamented the emperor's involvement in the case. 'If the causes of bishops committed to me are settled before my most pious lords under the patronage of others, how am I expected to run this church?' He said he would give Maximus a little longer to comply with his instructions, but that thereafter he would exercise strict canonical discipline.[48]

So Gregory took an absolutely forthright line with the imperial government here and tenaciously defended his rights. As he wrote in September 594 to the *apocrisiarios* Sabinian in Constantinople: 'You know my character well; I am very long-suffering. But once I have decided that something is insupportable, I press on regardless of all danger.'[49] In September 595 Gregory ordered Maximus to answer the charges against him in Rome.[50] He did not come, and in January 596 Gregory repeated the order.[51] Maximus replied that the emperor had ordered the case to be heard in Salona. Gregory rejected this claim, saying that the emperor would not issue such an order and that even if he had, Gregory would ignore it for the good of the emperor's soul because it would certainly have been elicited by fraud. Gregory then wrote to the clergy and people of both Salona and Jadera, urging them for the good of their souls not to have communion with the excommunicate Maximus, asking them to bring pressure to bear on him to present himself in Rome, and assuring them that he would get a fair trial because Gregory did not, as some had alleged, have a personal grudge against him.[52]

The schism between Rome and Salona dragged on, and it became evident that neither side intended to back down. Gregory insisted on trial in Rome; Maximus refused to go to Rome. The rift began to cause alarm to senior dignitaries of both church and state. In 597 Bishop Sabinian of Jadera withdrew from communion with Maximus, did penance for his sin, and was reconciled with Rome.[53] John the Deacon says other bishops followed suit,[54] but Gregory, although he mentions Sabinian in his letters, mentions no other bishops, and it looks as if he valued Sabinian's defection because of its uniqueness. Further evidence of Sabinian's uniqueness can be seen in the fact that Maximus intrigued against him at the imperial court, seeking to discredit him, and Gregory specifically ordered his *apocrisiarios* to defend Sabinian's interests.[55] After the schism was resolved, Gregory specifically ordered Maximus to be reconciled with Sabinian, another indication of his solitary state of opposition.[56] It was to Sabinian also that Gregory entrusted the only known appellate case from Dalmatia during his reign, when the inhabitants of Epidaurus petitioned for the return of their bishop, Florentius, who had been exiled without trial by Archbishop Natalis in 592.[57]

But the imperial government became concerned that the solid front of support for Maximus was in danger of breaking down, with the renewed threat to public order at a time when barbarian tension was a permanent danger. The emperor summoned one of Maximus' chief supporters, the proconsul Marcellus, to Constantinople for talks, and Marcellus, worried that his job was at risk, wrote hastily to Gregory in the summer of 599 seeking a reconciliation with him.[58] Gregory denounced him as one of the chief instigators of the trouble but suggested that he could prove his goodwill by withdrawing support from Maximus.[59] Marcellus now began to put pressure on Maximus to compromise, and in Italy the exarch Callinicus kept up unremitting pressure on Gregory also to compromise.[60] Eventually both sides agreed. There would be a trial, but in Ravenna, presided over by

Archbishop Marinianus, and, if Maximus doubted his impartiality, by Archbishop Constantius of Milan.[61] Gregory ordered Marinianus to summon both Maximus and the archdeacon Honoratus before him and to investigate the case thoroughly. In the end, however, even this was not done. At the suggestion of Marinianus, and presumably as a result of discussions with the exarch and other interested parties, Gregory agreed that, instead of a trial, Maximus should simply do penance and then take an oath of compurgation on the tomb of St Apollinaris.[62] So in July 599 Maximus lay for three hours in a street in Ravenna crying: 'I have sinned against God and the blessed Pope Gregory,' and he was then raised up by the exarch Callinicus, Archbishop Marinianus, and the papal rector Castorius, and led to the tomb of St Apollinaris, where he swore that he was innocent of the charges alleged against him.[63] After that, he was handed a letter from Gregory re-admitting him to communion and inviting him to send for the *pallium*. Once it was done, Gregory wrote to his *apocrisiarios* Anatolius in Constantinople, recommending him to help Marcellus the proconsul and to explain to the emperor that Marcellus had disobeyed the order to go there for a meeting because he was helping to resolve the schism.[64] Thus after seven years relations between Rome and Salona were restored. Gregory had made his stand and had been almost completely defeated, not so much by the emperor, whose role had been a background one, as by the weight of local opinion. But he seemed genuinely relieved when it was over. What the case does show is that Gregory tenaciously defined and defended his primatial rights and spoke with much greater candour to the emperor than ever he did to the barbarian rulers of the West.

The prefecture of Illyricum, comprising Greece and the Balkans, was the easternmost province within Gregory's immediate patriarchal jurisdiction. It was the area closest to Constantinople and a good test, therefore, of the extent to which Gregory's patriarchal supremacy was a real and meaningful concept. The apostolic vicariate in Illyricum had since the time of Pope Damasus resided with the archbishop of Thessalonica, but when Justinian created a new ecclesiastical province in northern Illyricum, with Prima Justiniana, newly named after himself, as the metropolitan see, the pope duly conferred a vicariate on that see too.

Two major cases involving papal jurisdiction are contained in the Gregorian Register.[65] The first is the case of Bishop Adrian of Thebes.[66] In 592 two deposed Theban deacons, John and Cosmas, degraded for unchastity and malversation respectively, wrote to the emperor accusing Adrian of embezzlement, of denying baptism to certain infants who thereby died in sin, and of retaining in office a deacon of known wickedness. The emperor ordered Archbishop John of Larissa, the Thessalian metropolitan, as the presumed ecclesiastical superior, to investigate the embezzlement charge and pronounce sentence, and to report back to the emperor on the other two charges. John found Adrian guilty of embezzlement, whereupon Adrian appealed to the emperor. Maurice ordered the papal *apocrisiarios* Honoratus and the imperial chancellor Sebastian to investigate, and they pronounced Adrian innocent. The emperor upheld the appeal therefore. Meanwhile John of Larissa kept Adrian in prison and tortured him into confessing his guilt and signing a confession. In the light of this, the emperor ordered the whole case tried again and committed it to the papal vicar, John of Prima Justiniana. At the trial no evidence was produced, and the Theban clergy insisted that the charges were groundless, but John still found Adrian guilty and deposed him. Adrian now proceeded to Rome and appealed to the pope. Gregory ordered John of Prima Justiniana to send representn-tatives to Rome to defend his actions before a papal court. When John failed to do so, Gregory had the trial records examined; he discovered that normal rules of procedure had been ignored, that there was no evidence against Adrian, and that the charges had been brought by enemies and detractors. In addition he found that Thebes had been exempted from the jurisdiction of Larissa by Pelagius II. Gregory therefore reversed the judgments of the previous trials and restored Adrian to office. Furthermore he wrote to John of Larissa condemning his conduct and forbidding him on pain of excommun-ication to exercise metropolitan jurisdiction over Thebes again. Invok-ing his Petrine and apostolic *auctoritas*, he excommunicated John of Prima Justiniana for thirty days and severely reprimanded him. He also declared that, in any future case involving Adrian, if the matter was small it was to be dealt with by the papal *apocrisiarios* and if large referred to the pope in Rome. By May 593 Gregory learned that Adrian and his opponents had been reconciled, and the case was officially closed.[67]

It is clear from this case that bishops in Greece and the Balkans looked first and immediately not to Rome but to Constantinople and the emperor. The accusers petitioned the emperor, Adrian appealed to the emperor; three times the emperor arranged trials. Only when all other avenues had been exhausted did Adrian appeal to Rome. On the other hand, the emperor clearly recognized papal rights in the matter by committing the trials to the presumed metropolitan superior, the papal *apocrisiarios*, and the apostolic vicar. It is worth noting too that Gregory's final judgment was accepted.

Gregory's primatial rights, this time to try the case of a metropolitan, were exercised directly in the second case. When in 592 Archbishop Anastasius of Corinth, metropolitan of Achaia, was accused of various unspecified crimes, the pope sent a special judge, Bishop Secundinus (probably of Tauromenium), to hear the case. Penetrating a conspiracy of clerics bribed by the archbishop to subvert the evidence, Secundinus tried, condemned and deposed Anastasius. A successor, John, was immediately elected and Gregory sent him the *pallium*.[68]

Turning from the Empire to the barbarian kingdoms, Gregory's election to the papacy coincided with the conversion of the Visigothic kingdom of Spain from Arianism to Catholicism. This major religious transformation was the work of Reccared, who in 586 had succeeded his father, Leovigild, as king. Leovigild, who has been called 'the most remarkable of the Arian kings of Spain', had bequeathed to his son a state strong, stable and increasingly centralized. He had extended his frontiers by incorporating the Catholic Suevic kingdom of Galicia. He had reformed the coinage, revised the law code and considerably enhanced the authority and power of the crown. Seeing the value of religious unity in cementing his kingdom together, Reccared decided to convert to the majority Catholic faith, and after discussion with both Arians and Catholics he established Catholicism as the official religion of Visigothic Spain at the Third Council of Toledo in 589. Having suppressed the inevitable Arian reaction, Reccared proceeded to stamp out Arianism by burning its holy books, banning Arians from public office and suppressing the Arian church organization. The transformation was completed with remarkable speed and totality, but Rome played no part in the conversion.[69]

Gregory first learned of it from his old friend Archbishop Leander of Seville, who had played a leading role at the Council of Toledo, and in April 591 he wrote to him expressing his delight.[70] Reccared himself later wrote to report the conversion and sent gifts to the pope.[71] Gregory replied in August 599: 'I cannot express in words, most excellent son, how greatly I delight in the work you have done and in the life you lead.' He lamented that his own efforts at converting the heretic paled into insignificance beside the marvellous achievement of the Visigothic king and sent him holy relics as a token of his appreciation.[72]

Yet despite the warmth of the exchanges, the conversion signalled no papal initiative in relations with Spain and no intensification of papal activities in the peninsula. Only ten letters from Gregory to Spain survive, and they indicate the limited areas of contact.

There are essentially two sets of letters. The first are the personal letters. Gregory sent copies of the *Regula Pastoralis* and the *Magna Moralia* to Bishop Licinianus of Cartagena, and Licinianus wrote an appreciative letter of thanks, discussing various of the points raised in the *Regula* and observing rather whimsically that if Gregory's advice that ignorant men should not be ordained were followed in Spain, there would be no bishops. Gregory also sent copies of his works to Leander of Seville, together with a *pallium* for wearing in the mass. This latter was almost certainly sent as a mark of respect and affection rather than as an indication of the conferring of a papal vicariate, for unlike previous popes, Gregory made no vicarial appointment in Spain, a further indication of a lack of detailed interest in the kingdom. The great respect that Gregory's works enjoyed in ecclesiastical circles in the seventh century suggests that his importance for the Spanish bishops was as a writer and theologian.[73]

The second set of letters is official, but apart from the letters to Reccared, they are exclusively concerned with a *cause célèbre* which prompted Gregory's exercise of his appellate powers. Two bishops, Januarius of Malaga and Stephanus, whose see is not known, appealed to the pope against sentences of deposition and exile imposed on them by a council of bishops. They claimed to have fallen foul of the Byzantine governor Comitiolus, now dead, who had instigated the proceedings against them, and that their trials had been improperly conducted. In August 603 therefore Gregory dispatched the *defensor* John to Spain to hear the appeals. He furnished him with a battery of documents, extremely detailed and precise and testifying perhaps to the singularity of the occurrence. These included a schedule of instructions about what John was to look for, what questions he was to ask and how he was to proceed when he had gathered his evidence. There was a dossier of the relevant imperial laws to cover the charges, and a formula of acquittal for use if necessary. The outcome of the case is unknown.[74]

Apart from Gregory's clear and obvious concern that justice should be done, the other fact which emerges is that the appeal was coming from bishops in the Byzantine province of Spain. The Justinianic reconquests of Italy and Africa had been followed by a Byzantine expedition to Spain which had established a Byzantine province in the southeast of the country, centred on Malaga and Cartagena. It survived from 552 to 624 and one of its governors had been Comitiolus. But its existence was resented by the Visigoths, and Reccared's successors gradually whittled down its territory and finally overran it completely.[75] Even more resented was Byzantine interference in Visigothic affairs, for the imperial government in the sixth century had supported rebellions against the crown by Athanagild and Hermenigild.[76] It is perhaps no coincidence that from the time of the Byzantine conquest of southeastern Spain communications with Rome tail off. Letters from popes Hormisdas, Symmachus and Vigilius to the Spanish episcopate survive from the first half of the sixth century. But there seems to have been no regular communication after this, and that was certainly not the result of travel difficulties, for Gregory was able to communicate freely with his friend Leander when he wanted to.

That the Visigoths associated the papacy with the Byzantine Empire can be seen from a letter from Reccared to Gregory in 599 in which the king asked the pope to obtain from the emperor a copy of a treaty between Justinian and the Visigoths defining the frontiers between them. Gregory replied warily that documents from Justinian's reign had been destroyed by a fire at the record office and suggested that the king would not like what he found even if he got hold of a copy: 'You ought to look in your own archives for documents which are unfavourable to you and not ask me to produce them.'[77] It is the canny politician speaking again. He clearly had a good idea what was in the treaty and did not want to be associated in Reccared's eyes with imperial policy towards the Visigoths.

It seems likely that the attitude of the Catholic Visigothic kingdom towards the papacy was polite but distant, an acceptance of its primacy in principle but an ignoring of it in practice. Reccared in his letter to Gregory calls him 'you who are powerful above all other bishops', and if this letter is genuine (and there has been some doubt cast on it), then it is an acknowledgment of the primacy.[78] But there were no appeals from Visigothic Spain to Rome, and after Gregory's death there were during the whole of the seventh century only two known exchanges between the Spanish church and the papacy, both of them acrimonious.[79] There was clearly no intensification of papal activities here.

Frankish Gaul, which had been Catholic since the early sixth century, was divided into three kingdoms, Neustria, Austrasia and Burgundy, ruled by the Merovingian kings, whose long hair was the badge of their blood royal and whose intermarriage was already producing degeneracy and incompetence. The history of Gaul at this time, as recorded by the contemporary historians Gregory of Tours and Fredegar, is a dispiriting chronicle of treachery, bloodshed and confusion. The administration was ramshackle, crime was rampant, trade and agriculture languished and the church was in a sorry state. Gregory of Tours paints a lurid picture of the Gallic bishops, many of whom seem to have been habitually drunk or wantonly cruel, appallingly lecherous or deeply embroiled in politics and intrigue. The lesser clergy seem to have been little better, and dereliction of duty was rife.[80]

In this situation, what was Gregory's response? Was he, as some have suggested, seeking to extend his control over the Gallic church? The answer seems to be in the negative again. He first became interested in the affairs of Gaul in 595, explaining in a letter to King Childebert II that he had intended to get involved earlier but pressure of business prevented it.[81] He now took two steps which some have seen as the first move in his campaign to extend control. He appointed in 595 a rector for the small papal patrimony in Provence, and an apostolic vicar for Austrasia and Burgundy, the kingdoms ruled by Childebert.

The Gallic patrimony had hitherto been administered by Gallic bishops or local lay dignitaries, and Gregory appointed the first Roman rector for years, the priest Candidus. The administrative duties of the patrimony would have been slight, and it is clear that Candidus had other, more important duties. The central theme of Gregory's relations with Gaul lies in the elimination of abuses from the church. But he did not see this as a means of extending his personal control over the church, for he entrusted the job in the main to the men on the spot and sought to employ the traditional method of stimulating reform – a church council. His correspondence with Gaul from 597 onwards was filled with the prospect of a reform council, and it must have been one of Candidus' main jobs to report to Gregory on the state of affairs in Gaul and keep up the pressure for the summoning of a council.

It seems not to have occurred to Gregory to appoint an apostolic vicar for Childebert's kingdom, even though popes Symmachus, Vigilius and Pelagius I had all conferred vicariates on the archbishop of Arles. But in 595 Childebert petitioned Gregory to confer the vicariate and the *pallium* on Archbishop Vergilius of Arles.[82] Gregory duly granted it to Vergilius and used the opportunity presented to fire the opening shot in his campaign against the prevalent abuses in the Gallic church. He wrote to Vergilius: 'I have learned from information given me by certain persons that in parts of Gaul and Germany, no one attains to holy orders except for a consideration given. If this be so, I say it with tears, I declare it with groans that when the priestly order has fallen inwardly, neither will it be able to stand outwardly for long.' He urged him to take action to eliminate these abuses, his clear and avowed concern being with the spiritual health of the church. He also defined the rights and obligations of the vicariate, telling Vergilius to limit the travelling of bishops so that they did not neglect their sees, and, in the event of difficulties arising about the faith, to call a council to resolve them, and only if it did not resolve the difficulties to refer the matter to Rome.[83] The vicariate arose, then, at the suggestion of the king rather than of the pope, involved no extension of papal intervention in Gaul, but did provide Gregory with the opportunity to air his chief concern about the state of Gaul.

As with Lombardy, Gregory saw that the best way of ensuring that action was taken was to enlist the support of the royal family. Austrasia and Burgundy had been ruled since 593 by Childebert II, who was in his early twenties, but the real power in the kingdoms lay with his formidable mother, Brunhild. A Visigothic princess who had married King Sigebert of Austrasia, assassinated in 575, she had secured the proclamation of her infant son Childebert as king and for the next thirty years was to control Austrasia. Even when Childebert came of age and inherited the throne of Burgundy from his uncle, she still firmly retained the reins of power in her hands. A builder of churches and a benefactor of the Catholic establishment, she was also a ferocious political animal, prepared to do anything to retain her power. She ruthlessly suppressed friends and enemies alike and navigated with consummate skill through the treacherous and murky currents of Merovingian politics. Fredegar called her 'a second Jezebel'. This was the woman with whom Gregory established contact in the autumn of 595. He was to write her ten letters, in which he addressed her in caressing courtier-like tones that put one in mind of Disraeli's dealings with Queen Victoria. Gregory's first letter to her began: 'The laudable and God-pleasing goodness of your excellence is manifested both by your government of your kingdoms and by your education of your son.'[84] He reached even greater heights in later letters: 'How many good gifts have been bestowed on you by the bounty of God and how completely the goodness of heavenly grace has filled your heart is clearly shown to all men by your many meritorious deeds and also by the fact that you rule the savage hearts of the barbarians with skill and prudence and – what is still more to your praise – that you add to royal power the ornament of wisdom.'[85] Indeed, it is clear from the correspondence that Gregory used the same honeyed tones towards the Austrasian family as he did towards the imperial family in Constantinople. This was no stern, commanding governor speaking to his inferiors.

Brunhild became even more important when, in 596, Childebert died and his infant sons Theodoric and Theudebert respectively inherited the thrones of Austrasia and Burgundy. She retained her dominance over the kingdoms, and Gregory's lack of freedom of action in the Gallic church is indicated by the events of 597, when Brunhild requested the *pallium* for her favourite bishop and adviser, Syagrius of Autun. Autun was not a metropolitan see, and there was neither tradition nor precedent for such a grant. Nevertheless, having consulted the emperor, Gregory informed the queen in September 597 that he was willing to grant the *pallium* to Syagrius, in recognition of Syagrius' help with the English mission.[86] He added that it was customary for the bishop himself to petition for the *pallium*, and he asked Syagrius to organize such a petition; but so that Brunhild did not think that this was a polite evasion, he would send the *pallium* to the papal rector Candidus, who would hand it over as soon as the formalities were completed.

Not only was the whole *pallium* grant and the way it was handled revealing, so too were Gregory's subsequent actions. Both Syagrius' superior, the metropolitan Aetherius of Lugdunum, and Bishop Desiderius of Vienne requested the *pallium*, and Gregory turned both of them down on the grounds that there was no precedent for it.[87] The absence of precedent had, of course, not stopped Syagrius' grant, and it is not without significance that the *pallium* grants to both Syagrius and Vergilius had been made at the specific request of the crown. Gregory was clearly unwilling to grant honours in Gaul without the consent of the crown. Furthermore, Aetherius was Syagrius' superior, and a grant to him might be seen as negating the singular honour to Syagrius, thus offending Syagrius' patron. Desiderius, on the other hand, was hated by Brunhild, who contrived his deposition and exile in 603, and when he returned from that exile in 607 had him stoned to death.[88] An honour for him would therefore also be politically unwise.

But Gregory did turn the *pallium* grant to his advantage by tying it to the hoped-for council to eradicate abuses. He informed Syagrius in July 599 that the *pallium* was granted to him on condition that he presided at a synod for the elimination of simony.[89] He did not spell this out for Brunhild, but in his letter confirming the *pallium* grant he did urge her to take action against simony, paganism and the ordination of laymen.

The year 599 was the year of the all-out effort. Gregory decided to send a papal envoy to Gaul to attend the council and observe conditions for himself. His choice fell on Abbot Cyriacus, who had already been sent as special papal envoy to Sardinia to root out paganism there. Gregory sent a circular letter to the four senior churchmen in the kingdoms – Vergilius of Arles, Syagrius of Autun, Aetherius of Lyons, and Desiderius of Vienne – urging them to attend a council to stamp out simony, unchastity and lay ordination, and announcing the arrival of Abbot Cyriacus.[90] He sent a gift of dalmatics to Bishop Aregius of Gap, suggesting that he should attend the council and report on its proceedings to the pope.[91] He wrote asking Brunhild to permit the summoning of a reform council to be held in the presence of Abbot Cyriacus but to be presided over by 'your particular favourite' Syagrius.[92] He wrote in similar terms to kings Theodoric and Theudebert.[93] But nothing seems to have come of this flurry of activity, possibly because of the death of Cyriacus soon after his arrival in Gaul.[94]

Nothing daunted, Gregory tried again, and in 601 he renewed his appeal for a reform council in Austrasia, asking permission of Brunhild to send a special envoy to investigate the stories of many wicked priests which he was receiving, and urging on kings and bishops a reform synod.[95] Brunhild wrote back agreeing to the sending of the envoy, but once again nothing came of it, this time probably because political events had supervened.[96] Around 601 Brunhild was expelled from Austrasia by the aristocracy with the connivance of her grandson Theudebert, now fifteen. She took refuge with Theodoric in

Burgundy and from there sought with remorseless single-mindedness to encompass the destruction of Theudebert. Eventually the two brothers waged war on each other, and Theudebert was captured and killed in 612. Theodoric now aimed to unite the whole of Gaul under his rule; he attacked Chlothar II of Neustria, but then died suddenly in 613. Chlothar took a terrible revenge on the scheming queen mother. She was captured, tortured for three days, and finally tied to the tail of an unbroken horse and dragged to her death.[97]

It is clear that in his relations with Gaul, as in his relations with Africa, Gregory was not concerned with extending Rome's power. His objectives were very limited. He initially sought to enlist the aid of bishops and kings for Augustine's mission on its journey across Gaul and for Candidus the rector. But his main aim was to tackle some of the most serious abuses in the Gallic church. To attain this aim, he worked with Queen Brunhild and her nominees. Gregory's letters were full of the usual references to Petrinity and apostolicity, and he praised all and sundry for their devotion to St Peter; but in practice this meant little. As he stressed in his vicarial grant to Vergilius of Arles, he only wanted to be called in as a last resort if the local episcopate could not decide matters between them, and there are no known cases of judicial appeals from Gaul to Rome. There is also one interesting hint that for Gaul, as for Spain, the papacy was closely associated with the Empire. In 601, perhaps in order to strengthen her position for the struggle with Theudebert, Brunhild communicated to Gregory plans for an alliance with the Empire, eliciting this reply from the pope: 'Whatever is possible, whatever is profitable, and whatever tends to the settlement of peace between you and the Empire, we desire under God with the utmost devotion that it should be accomplished.'[98] But nothing came of that plan, and the reform synod remained a chimera to which Gregory clung until the day of his death.

Chapter Thirteen

Gregory and the East

The conflict over the 'Oecumenical Patriarch' title dominated Gregory's relations with the church of Constantinople, and highlights the considerable insecurity that Rome still felt about its position, and the tenacity with which the popes defended their primacy against attack.[1] At the time of Gregory's election in 590, the patriarch of Constantinople was John IV, 'the Faster', who had been appointed patriarch while Gregory was *apocrisiarios.* Gregory knew and approved of him, describing him as 'a most modest man, beloved of all, occupied in alms, deeds, prayers and fastings'.[2] Gregory dispatched to him his *synodica* announcing his election to the papacy and professing his orthodoxy. In a circular letter to the Eastern patriarchs, Gregory listed John first, indicating that he recognized his seniority among the Eastern patriarchs.[3] Soon, however, Gregory and John were at loggerheads, for in 588, at a council held in Constantinople to settle the affairs of the Antioch church, John had been referred to as 'Oecumenical Patriarch'. When Pope Pelagius II received copies of the conciliar proceedings, he immediately annulled that part of them which contained the offending title, ordered his *apocrisiarios* in Constantinople to withdraw from communion with John, and lodged a formal protest. He clearly saw this as an infringement of papal primacy. But John apparently made no response to this protest, and Gregory therefore renewed it, ordering his own *apocrisiarios* to abstain from communion with John unless he abandoned the title.[4]

The dispute between the two churches soon took on a palpable form, giving Rome the opportunity to assert papal primacy in the matter of appellate jurisdiction. Two Eastern priests, John of Chalcedon and Athanasius of Isauria, who had been tried before the patriarch's court in Constantinople and found guilty of heresy, appealed to Rome claiming irregularities in both trial procedures and sentences. Gregory wrote several letters asking for an explanation of the case from John, and John, having ignored the first few inquiries, eventually replied that he knew nothing about it. Incensed by this, Gregory sent in July 593 a strongly worded and extremely sarcastic letter, in which he implied that John was under the influence of evil advisers and that because of this Gregory was not able to follow his natural inclination, waive his canonical rights and refer the case back to John. The pope suggested that if John wished to do what was right he, Gregory, would send back the priests and John should either restore them to their ranks or deal with them properly according to the canons. 'If you adopt neither of these courses, although we do not wish to have a quarrel with you, we shall certainly not shrink from one if you start it.'[5]

There was concern in court circles about the deteriorating relations between the two churches, and Count Narses, who knew both Gregory and John, wrote to the pope to assure him that John wished to maintain the canons. Gregory replied in August 593 that he was determined to carry the matter through with the full force of his strength and authority: 'If I see that the canons of the apostolic see are not preserved, God will show me what to do against those who despise them.'[6] Gregory instructed his *apocrisiarios* Sabinian to press John on the matter, and eventually John gave way, writing in the summer of 595 what the pope described as a 'most sweet and reasonable letter' and sending to Rome the evidence in the case of the two priests.[7] The cases were duly heard, and both John and Athanasius were acquitted of the charges of heresy, restored to their ranks and returned to Constantinople. Gregory sent letters to the patriarch and the emperor explaining his decision and commending the returning priests to their protection.[8]

Compelling John to acknowledge Rome's appellate jurisdiction was a major victory for Gregory, and John was clearly irked by it, for he stressed again his 'Oecumenical Patriarch' title as a way of reminding Gregory of his position. Gregory, who declared angrily that in the records of John's trial the patriarch was called 'Oecumenical' in almost every line, and who clearly regarded it as a calculated snub, protested both to John and to the emperor Maurice. The emperor now wrote to Gregory admonishing him to keep the peace with John, and Gregory upbraided Sabinian in June 595 for not properly informing Maurice what was at stake and allowing John to mislead Maurice. He reiterated his resolve not to give way: 'We will keep to the right way, fearing nothing in this course except Almighty God.'[9] But he conceded that, in accordance with the emperor's wishes, he was writing 'a sweet and reasonable letter' to convince John of the error of his ways. The letter has survived, and if this was one of Gregory's 'reasonable' letters it is hard to imagine what one of his unreasonable letters would be like,[10] for Gregory's letter was bitter, threatening and condemnatory. He lectured John on humility: 'Though your office is to teach humility to others, you have not yet learned yourself the elements of the lesson. My brother, love humility, and do not try to raise yourself by abasing your brethren. Abandon this rash name, this word of pride and folly which is disturbing the peace of the whole world.' Warming to his theme, he adopted an apocalyptic tone, calling John's action the precursor of Antichrist and comparing him to Lucifer. 'And now pestilence and the sword rage throughout the world, nations rise against nations, the globe of the world is shaken, cities with their inhabitants are swallowed up by the gaping earth. For all that was foretold is come to pass. The king of pride is near and, terrible to say, there is an army of priests preparing the way for him; because those who had been appointed to be generals in humility are raising the stiff neck of pride.' All this, of course, followed on from the assumption of the 'Oecumenical Patriarch' title. It is splendid 'hellfire and damnation' rhetoric, but it does emphasize a point Gregory felt passionately: there was a God-appointed hier- archy, and any disturbance in it would lead to chaos and confusion.

The head of the God-appointed hierarchy within the church was, of course, the pope, and the protector of the church and its earthly lord was the emperor. Gregory stressed both these facts when he wrote both to the emperor Maurice and the empress Constantina on the subject.[11] He called upon Maurice to help suppress the wicked title, reminding him of his responsibility in the Constantinian scheme of things: 'He therefore who will not condescend to obey the canons must be coerced by the commands of my most religious lords', and 'since the cause is not mine but God's, since not I alone am disturbed but the whole church with me, since the holy laws, the venerable synods, yes, even the very ordinances of our Lord Jesus Christ himself, are set aside by the invention of a certain proud and pomp- ous title, let my most religious lord cut out this infection and, if the patient resists, bind him with the fetters of imperial authority.' But he also made it clear that he saw the title as a challenge to papal primacy by giving a clear definition of the primacy and then saying that since the pope was never called 'universal' no one else should be. He sought also to get the empress to bring pressure on her husband: 'My most serene lord has distressed me in that he has not rebuked him who is acting proudly but endeavours to bend me from my purpose, who am in this cause defending the truth of the gospels and canons, of humility and rectitude: whereas my aforesaid brother and fellow priest is acting against evangelical principle and also against the blessed apostle Peter and against all the churches and ordinances of the canons.'

Gregory also sought to enlist the support of his friends Eulogius of Alexandria and Anastasius of Antioch in the struggle against John, creating a united front of patriarchal opposition. He wrote to both of them denouncing the offending title and giving his reasons ('In a new act of pride all the bowels of the universal church are disturbed').[12] But neither patriarch understood what he was upset about, and both assumed that Gregory wanted the use of the title exclusively for himself. Anastasius wrote back warning Gregory about the sin of pride and envy and declared the matter to be of no importance. Gregory ruefully described his letter as 'stinging like a bee'.[13] Eulogius wrote to say that he would refrain from addressing the patriarch of Constantinople as 'universal' in obedience to the commands of Gregory, whom he described as 'universal pope'. Gregory wrote back in exasperation, saying that he was not making commands but suggestions, and that he did not want the title for himself but wished to suppress it altogether in the interests of general humility.[14] But neither patriarch got involved in the campaign, and Gregory's attempt to create a united front against John's 'proud presumption' failed miserably.

The conflict was unresolved when John died on 2 September 595, and after some deliberation Maurice appointed Cyriacus, *oeconomos* of the church of Constantinople, to succeed him. Maurice wrote to Gregory instructing him to receive kindly the envoys bearing Cyriacus' synodical letters and to make no further disturbance about a 'frivolous name'.[15] Gregory knew and approved of Cyriacus ('He has kept a tranquil heart in the midst of turbulent throngs and always restrained himself with a gentle bearing').[16] He clearly hoped that some accommodation with Cyriacus would be possible, and in October 596 wrote to the emperor praising his choice of new patriarch, celebrated mass with the envoys, and wrote to Cyriacus welcoming his appointment but urging him to let there be no cause of dissension between them.[17] Cyriacus showed no sign of abandoning the title, however, and in June 597 Gregory informed Eulogius of Alexandria: 'There is a serious difference between us on account of the appellation of a profane name'.[18] He urged Cyriacus to drop the title and told the emperor that he could not regard as a 'frivolity' something which presaged the appearance of Antichrist.[19] The Eastern authorities simply ignored his appeals and Cyriacus continued to use the title.

Undaunted, Gregory continued the struggle. In 599, learning that the bishops of eastern Illyricum had been invited to attend a synod in Constantinople, he warned them to do nothing that would sanction the use of the title 'Oecumenical Patriarch'.[20] In July 603 he was again writing to Cyriacus urging him to give up the title and restore the peace of the church. The dispute was still unresolved when Gregory died.[21]

The irony of it all is that the whole thing was based on a misunderstanding. Gregory saw the title 'Oecumenical Patriarch' as an attack on the primacy of Rome, interpreting it as meaning 'universal' and supreme, as he indicated when he compared John IV to Lucifer: 'he imitates him who, scorning the joys of community with the legions of angels, endeavoured to gain the height of solitary preeminence.' But the title did not mean what Gregory thought. It meant supreme within his patriarchate and not over the other patriarchs. The title had been granted to both popes and patriarchs in the sixth century; and in the seventh century, inviting them to attend the sixth General Council of the church, Emperor Constantine IV called both the pope and the patriarch 'Oecumenical', thus emphasizing the title's non-exclusivity. The response of the patriarchs of Alexandria and Antioch to Gregory's concern confirms that they understood the meaning of 'oecumenical' in this context and could not understand what the fuss was about. But the fact that the East did nothing to allay the papacy's fears suggests that the title was maintained primarily to annoy the papacy. In 607 the emperor Phocas issued a confirmation of papal primacy at the request of Pope Boniface III;[22] but the patriarchs of Constantinople continued to use the title 'Oecumenical Patriarch', and eventually the papacy gave up the struggle and adopted it themselves.[23]

Apart from this controversy, there was comparatively little contact with the Eastern church, though Gregory maintained a regular and friendly correspondence on matters theological and spiritual with the patriarchs Eulogius of Alexandria and Anastasius of Antioch, and with the emperor's cousin Bishop Domitian of Melitene. Anastasius had been a friend while Gregory was *apocrisiarios*. He had been deposed as patriarch of Antioch in 570 and had moved to Constantinople as a private citizen. Gregory valued his company so much that he planned to invite him to Rome after he became pope. But when Patriarch Gregory of Antioch died, Anastasius was restored to the patriarchal throne in 593, to the pope's great delight. It is possible that he had canvassed privately for Anastasius' restoration.[24]

Although Gregory accepted the role of the emperor in the church, there were occasions when he found his *Romanitas* and his *Christianitas* in conflict. His endeavours to reconcile the two and to avoid open conflict with the emperor instructively illustrate the fundamentals of his world-view discussed earlier. Perhaps the most serious problem, and one which admirably demonstrates the nature of his response, is the one which occurred in 593. The emperor Maurice sent Gregory a recently issued edict which declared that no one engaged in public business should undertake any ecclesiastical office or retire to a monastery and no soldier should become a monk until his term of service had expired. It was, from the government's point of view, a sensible measure – to stem the chronic loss of manpower in the civil administration and the army, both of which lost people to the monasteries and churches when the duties became too burdensome and oppressive. Gregory understood the nature of the problem and did not question the right of the emperor to legislate on it. He was also willing to accept that civil servants be barred from the church: 'for the man who is anxious to exchange the secular life for an office in the church wishes not to abandon his worldly life but only to change the form of it'. But the monastic ban was another matter and Gregory could not accept it:[25]

> Inasmuch as I feel that this ordinance is directed against God the creator of all things, I cannot remain silent. Power over all men has been given by God to the piety of my lords for this purpose, that men may be helped in their pursuit of goodness, that the way to heaven may be opened wider, that the kingdom upon earth may minister to the kingdom of heaven. And now, behold, it is distinctly said that a man who has once been enrolled in the earthly soldiery shall not be allowed to become a soldier of our Lord Jesus Christ, until the time of his earthly service is completed or he has been discharged from the army for ill-

health. To this, behold, Christ answers through me, the lowest of his servants, and yours, 'I advanced you from being a notary to be captain of your guards, from captain of the guards to be Caesar, from Caesar to be Emperor, yes, and more than this, I have also made you the father of Emperors. I have committed my priests to your charge, and you now withdraw your soldiers from my service.' Reply, I pray you, my most pious lord; tell your servant what answer you will make to your Lord when he comes and thus addresses you on the judgment day. . . . In obedience to your command, I have caused this law to be transmitted to the various countries. I have also informed my most serene sovereigns by this letter that the law is certainly not in accordance with the will of God. I have thus done my duty on both sides. I have obeyed the Emperor and yet have not kept back what I felt ought to be said on behalf of God.

Significantly, Gregory did not send the letter to his *apocrisiarios* for official delivery to the emperor. He sent it instead to the emperor's physician Theodore to be presented privately, 'because you who are in the familiar service of the emperor can speak to him more freely and openly for the benefit of his soul, since he is very much occupied with business and his mind is rarely free from greater cares. Speak then for Christ, most glorious son; if you are listened to, you will benefit the soul of the emperor and your own; if you are not listened to, you will still benefit your own.'[26]

This classic papal response demonstrates both *Romanitas* (in its acceptance of the emperor's rights and the obedient transmission of a law the pope does not agree with) and *Christianitas* (in seeking to change the law by remonstrance, but with a clear desire to avoid open conflict). It paid off, for after lengthy negotiation the emperor agreed to a modification of the law, to the effect that no *curialis* might be received into a monastery until officially released from his public duties, and no soldier until careful inquiry had been made into his previous life and until he had served a three-year novitiate, in order to ascertain whether he was genuinely motivated and not seeking merely to escape from his military duties. The revised law was issued in 597 and circulated with papal blessing to the metropolitan bishops of the imperial West.[27]

In 591 the emperor decreed that bishops forced to flee before the incursions of the barbarians should be taken in and looked after by bishops in safe areas. Gregory confirmed this order in a circular letter to Illyrican bishops, warning that it did not mean that they should share their episcopal authority with the refugees,[28] for he saw that there was a danger to the established ecclesiastical structure in this. That danger became manifest when the exiled bishop John of Euria took refuge on the island of Corfu and sought the protection of Bishop Alcyson of Corcyra. John petitioned the emperor for episcopal jurisdiction over the refugee Eurian community which had set up home at Castrum Cassiopi. The emperor duly granted the petition, probably not realizing that he was in effect creating a new see and infringing the episcopal rights of Bishop Alcyson. Alcyson objected, and the emperor ordered the metropolitan of Epirus, Bishop Andreas of Nicopolis, to investigate the case and decide it according to the canons. Andreas decided in favour of Alcyson, and Gregory confirmed the decision by the authority of the Holy See. But before the sentence could be put into effect, Andreas died, Maurice was deposed, and Phocas, becoming emperor, reconfirmed the original imperial decision. Gregory therefore wrote to his *apocrisiarios* Boniface in Constantinople, urging him to present to Phocas the facts of Andreas' judgment and to get him to reverse his decision. Gregory added: 'I have thought it right not to publish my decision, lest I should appear to be acting contrary to the commands of my most gracious lord the emperor or in contempt of him, which God forbid.' He clearly felt that he was in the right, but his policy was one of consultation rather than confrontation, and it worked. The affair ended in January 604 when John of Euria agreed to give up his claims, provided that he could bury in Castrum Cassiopi the remains of St Donatus, which he had brought with him. Permission was duly given. Once again, it seems that in the first instance the bishops' recourse was to the emperor, and the pope was a last resort. But there is no attempt here by the emperor deliberately to reduce papal power. It was simply that the cases were swallowed up into the administrative maw of the Empire and fed into the inexorable bureaucratic machine.[29]

While Gregory did seek conscientiously to maintain what was canonically and ecclesiastically right, he was enough of a realist to be aware that considerations of national security and foreign policy might sometimes make this impossible – a view which explains his attitude in the case of John of Prima Justiniana. In February 601 Gregory learned from his *apocrisiarios* Anatolius that Maurice intended to depose and replace Archbishop John of Prima Justiniana, who was not only the metropolitan of Dacia but also the apostolic vicar. John had been elected as archbishop in 594 to replace a previous Archbishop John, reprimanded and excommunicated by Gregory in the case of Adrian of Thebes. Dacia was a frontier province, and clearly the appointment of its metropolitan was of keen interest to the emperor. In confirming the election and conferring the vicariate, Gregory had noted in passing that the electors had taken account of 'the will of the Emperor'. By 601, however, Archbishop John was suffering from *aegritudo capitatis,* which is probably a polite way of saying insanity, and Gregory fully appreciated the emperor's concern in the matter. Maurice feared 'if the city be left without a bishop's authority, it may be destroyed by the enemy, which God forbid', but Gregory wrote to say that it was uncanonical to depose a bishop for ill-health. The proper course was either for a coadjutor to be appointed to do the work until the bishop recovered, or for the bishop to request official permission to resign. However, Gregory conceded at the end of his letter: 'But if he [the bishop] will not ask for permission to resign, our most pious lord has the power to do whatever he pleases. He may make such arrangements as he sees fit; but he must not expect us to take part in the deposition of this man. If he does what is in accordance with the canons, we confirm it; if it is not, we submit to it, as far as we can do without sin.'[30]

When the emperor ordered him not to harass the 'Three Chapters' schismatics, Gregory obeyed even though he thought the church's interests were being sacrificed to political considerations. It is worth noting that all the matters discussed concerned sees within Gregory's patriarchal jurisdiction and yet there was no hard-line attempt by the pope to reject the emperor's decisions out of hand. Gregory did sometimes express his exasperation and stand his ground, as in the affair of Maximus of Salona. He lamented the emperor's intervention: 'If the causes of bishops committed to me are settled before my most pious lords under the patronage of others, how am I expected to run this church?' Even so, he sought to maintain his long-established distinction, saying that at the emperor's command he would forgive Maximus for his disobedience and contempt towards himself but that he could not overlook canonical offences. These examples show that Gregory pursued a consistent policy with regard to imperial intervention in church affairs. It was not so much a double standard as a split-level response, illustrating his desire to keep church and

Empire in harmony and preserve the balance of *Romanitas* and *Christianitas*.

For all Gregory's loyalty to the Empire and his willingness to compromise so far as the faith allowed, it is clear that cumulatively Maurice's actions rankled, for only by this can the unholy glee with which the pope greeted the news of Maurice's death be explained. In 602, following Maurice's order to the Balkan army to winter across the Danube in the interests of economy, the army mutinied and marched on the capital. They chose as their leader a hard, coarse, rough-hewn centurion, Phocas, and planned initially to depose Maurice and replace him with another member of the imperial family. On the approach of the army, however, revolt broke out in the city too and the imperial family fled. The result was that Phocas was hailed as emperor and was crowned by the patriarch on 23 November to initiate one of the most disastrous reigns in the entire history of the Empire. The imperial family, their flight halted by adverse weather and ill-health, took sanctuary in a church, from which they were dragged when Phocas' cohorts located them. Maurice was compelled to watch his four younger sons butchered before his eyes and was then himself beheaded. His eldest son and co-emperor, Theodosius, the pope's godson, was executed shortly afterwards. The empress Constantina and her three daughters were initially immured in a nunnery but were themselves executed in 605 on suspicion of involvement in a conspiracy to overthrow the new emperor. Maurice had been a conscientious, hard-working and dedicated ruler, but his policies of financial stringency and economic retrenchment, necessitated by costly foreign wars, had made him massively unpopular and had eventually proved his downfall. Phocas, by contrast, was a savage and incompetent tyrant, whose cruelty and misgovernment soon caused people to regret the unfortunate Maurice.

When news of Maurice's overthrow and the accession of Phocas reached Rome in the spring of 603, Gregory wrote to the new emperor exultantly:[31]

> Glory to God in the highest! who, as it is written, changes time and transfers kingdoms, who has now made clear to all men what he deigned to speak by his prophet saying: 'The Most High ruleth in the kingdom of men and giveth it to whomsoever He will.' In the incomprehensible providence of Almighty God there is alternation in the government of our mortal state.

Sometimes when the sins of many are to be punished, one man is raised up, by whose severity the necks of the people are bowed beneath the yoke of tribulation; and this we have ourselves experienced in our prolonged afflictions. Sometimes, however, when our merciful God has decreed to revive the sad hearts of the multitude with His own consolation, He raises one man to the supreme power, and by the clemency of that one He pours the grace of a Divine gladness into the hearts of all.

Given that Byzantine diplomatic language was always effusive, and given that Gregory was bound to welcome the accession, the tone of exultation that a troublesome emperor had finally been disposed of is unmistakable. Gregory cannot have been unaware that a bloodbath had accompanied the ending of Maurice's reign, and that one of its victims was his own godson, and under those circumstances, the papal glee can only be described as unworthy and misplaced, a very definite blot on his record.

It is clear from the examination of Gregory's relations with both East and West that there was no policy of bifurcation, no intensification of activities with Gaul or Spain, no abdication of primatial authority. Gregory's aims in East and West were the same: the preservation of the faith, the maintenance of good relations with the state, and the defending of Rome's existing pre-eminence.

Chapter Fourteen

Gregory's Missionary Activities

The preaching of the true Catholic faith and the elimination of all deviations from it was a key element in Gregory's world-view, and it constituted one of the major continuing policies of his pontificate. Heresy, which he evocatively described as 'the hot wind from the south', not only offended against the true faith; it also offended against Gregory's philosophy of humility. He attributed it to the sin of pride, i.e. setting oneself above the wisdom of the Church Fathers. 'For the place of heretics is very pride itself . . . for the place of the wicked is pride just as conversely humility is the place of the good.'[1] He inveighed against the Manichaeans, though there is not much evidence of a threat from them at this date.[2] He encouraged Queen Theodelinda and King Reccared in their campaigns against Arianism, but he did little himself by way of evangelization. His main areas of activity were Judaism, paganism and schism. Each group was subjected to attack from Gregory, using force, preaching or bribery, and sometimes a combination of all three.

Gregory did not regard Judaism as a religion, but as a *superstitio* whose adherents needed rescue. His treatment of them demonstrates both his *Romanitas* and his *Christianitas* in action. Judaism was not proscribed by law, and the law said that Jews were not to be persecuted because of their religion nor were their synagogues to be destroyed or plundered. They were nevertheless subject to serious legal disabilities. They were not allowed to make converts, to marry non-Jews, to own Christian slaves, to hold office of any sort, to make bequests, or to build new synagogues. More seriously for the Jews, they were not permitted to circumcise their slaves, despite the fact that the Talmud insisted on it. The Samaritans, though distinguished as a sect under the law, were subject to the same disabilities.[3]

Characteristically, Gregory was concerned to preserve for the Jews their rights under the law, yet to convert them if possible to the true faith. But he was quite clear on the Jews' rights. 'We will not have the Hebrews oppressed and afflicted unreasonably. According to the liberty of action justly granted to them by the Roman law, let them manage their own affairs as they think best and let no man hinder them.'[4] Again: 'For just as these people ought not to be allowed to do anything in their synagogues but what the law permits, neither should any injury or loss be inflicted on them contrary to justice and equity.'[5] But as always with Gregory, there were, besides his undoubted love of justice, good practical reasons for not stirring up trouble with the Jews, who lived in most of the great cities of Italy. He wrote to Januarius of Caralis on one Jewish case: 'At this time especially when there is danger from the enemy, you must not have a divided population.'[6]

There were several cases in which the pope intervened to protect Jewish interests. In 591, when the Jews of Terracina complained that Bishop Peter had seized their synagogue and ejected them from it because the sound of their singing was audible in a nearby Christian church, Gregory ordered that another building in the town be given them as a synagogue, where they could celebrate their services unimpeded.[7] In 599 a gang led by a converted Jew broke into the synagogue in Caralis on Easter Sunday and placed a cross, a picture of the Virgin and a baptismal robe there, thus preventing the Jews from worshipping. Gregory ordered Archbishop Januarius to remove the items and restore the synagogue for Jewish worship.[8] In 598 Victor of Palermo seized a Jewish synagogue and consecrated it as a Christian church. Though he was unable to deconsecrate it, Gregory ordered that the bishop should pay its full value to the Jews and restore books and ornaments seized from it.[9]

Gregory was just as keen to prevent abuses of the law by Jews, in particular the possession by them of Christian slaves. 'It is altogether unwholesome and accursed for Christians to be in servitude to Jews', he declared, and he consistently opposed the owning and circumcision of Christian slaves by Jewish masters.[10] In 593 Gregory wrote to the praetor Libertinus of Sicily urging him to take immediate and severe action against a Jew who not only owned Christian slaves but had converted Christians to his faith, gaining impunity for his actions by bribing the previous praetor, Justin.[11] The slaves were to be freed immediately. Gregory also opposed judaizing tendencies, as a letter to the people in Rome in September 602 demonstrates. He was alarmed at the growing practice of observing the sabbath on Saturday, Jewish style, and he wholly forbade it.[12]

Gregory had an answer for every situation. When a case of Jews owning slaves arose in Luna, Gregory ordered that the slaves should be freed, and that the tenants working on land owned by the Jews should also be freed.[13] But he encouraged them to continue working the land as free men and paying the customary dues, another practical solution. In the case of pagan or Jewish slaves of Jewish masters who wished to become Christians, they were either to be sold within three months to Christian masters or, when that time limit was up, to be freed.[14] This case arose in connection with the importation of Christian and pagan slaves into Naples from Gaul by Jewish merchants. Gregory wanted to stop the trade, but when a Jewish delegation informed him that they were authorized to engage in it by imperial government officials he simply imposed regulations. Slaves who were either Christian or intending to convert and ran away from Jewish masters seeking help from the church were to be given help and assistance in obtaining freedom by the church.[15]

But Gregory was also very anxious to convert the Jews, and his method was persuasion rather than force. When he learned of forced baptisms of Jews in Provence, he wrote to the bishops of Arles and Marseilles denouncing the practice: 'I appeal to your fraternity to preach frequently to these persons and appeal to them in such a manner that the kindness of the teacher more than anything else may make them desire to change their former mode of life.'[16] He wrote to the anti-Semitic bishop Peter of Terracina, who had twice expelled the Jews from their synagogue: 'Those who differ from the Christian religion must be won to the unity of the faith by gentleness, by kindness, by admonition, by exhortation, lest we repel by threats and ill treatment those who might have been attracted to the faith by the charm of instruction and the anticipated fear of the coming judge. It is more desirable that they should assemble with kindly feelings to hear from you the word of God than that they should tremble at the immoderate exercise of your severity.'[17] Similarly to the bishop of Naples, urging him to permit the Jews to celebrate their services, festivals and rites unhindered, he wrote: 'Those who really desire to win to the true faith such as are strangers to the Christian religion should endeavour to effect their purpose by kindly words not by harsh action, lest ill treatment should repel those whom just reasoning might have attracted.'[18]

This spirit of reasonableness Gregory was prepared to back up with more practical incentives. These included a reduction of rent and labour services to would-be Jewish converts in Sicily, the offer of free baptismal robes to those who could not afford them, and under certain circumstances the award of pensions to Jewish converts.[19]

Gregory's campaign against Donatism in Africa has been noted elsewhere, but it should be noted here that he sought to check it by appealing to the lay authorities and seeking to rally the Catholic hierarchy against it, without much success. There was schism too in Italy, where the Istrian church continued to adhere tenaciously to the 'Three Chapters'. By the time he became pope, Gregory had lost patience with the continuing intransigence of the Istrians. He did not regard their support for the 'Three Chapters' as a matter of genuine religious belief but as a mask for insubordination: 'They are enveloped so far in the blindness of their ignorance for no other reason but to escape from ecclesiastical discipline and have licence to live perversely as they please, since they understand neither what they defend nor what they follow.'[20]

So Gregory took action. Having secured imperial permission, he sent a body of soldiers under the command of a tribune and an imperial guardsman (*excubitor*) to Grado to summon Archbishop Severus of Aquileia to attend a synod in Rome to resolve the schism.[21] Immediately, two Istrian synods were convened, one in imperial territory and the other in Lombard, and both of them drew up petitions to the emperor. The first of these, from the Istrian bishops under Lombard rule, has survived.[22] It asserts the bishops' orthodoxy and loyalty to the empire, despite their subjection to 'the grievous yoke of the barbarians'. They complained that they had been summoned to appear in Rome before Gregory, who was a biased judge, and that they had the full backing of their people in the defence of their stand, which they saw as a defence of Chalcedon. They asked for a truce and promised that later, when the Lombards were defeated, they would happily present themselves in Constantinople and plead their case before the emperor, since the emperors were always just arbiters and restorers of ecclesiastical peace. They warned that unless harassment of them was halted and the rights of the church of Aquileia respected, their successors might well transfer their ecclesiastical allegiance to the archbishop of Gaul, and where ecclesiastical obedience went, political obedience would follow. Maurice took the point and ordered Gregory not to disturb the schismatic bishops, on account of the troubled state of Italy.[23] When civil peace was established ecclesiastical union might be restored. Maurice added a postscript in his own hand: 'God keep you many years, most blessed and holy father.' Gregory was angry, telling John of Ravenna that he would keep pressing the emperor on the subject; but he submitted to the order.[24] However, his irritation is revealed in a letter he wrote to John of Ravenna in 592, when he heard that John was raising alms for the relief of Grado after a serious fire. Gregory observed acerbically that 'compassion should be shown first to the faithful and afterwards to the enemies of the church', reminding him that Severus had money enough to spend on bribes in Constantinople to advance his cause.[25]

Nevertheless, as time went by and the imperial enclave of Istria remained the only area of 'Three Chapters' support inside the Empire, there was a drift back to orthodoxy. But the schismatics persecuted anyone wanting to reconcile with Rome. In 595 the bishops Peter of Altinum and Providentius (see unknown) contacted the papal *apocrisiarios* Castorius in Ravenna, expressing the desire to discuss reunion with Gregory, and the pope wrote urging them to come to Rome and promising them his protection.[26] In 599 there was another approach to the pope when the bishop of the island of Caprea and his congregation contacted the exarch about reconciliation. The bishop eventually pulled out of the negotiations, probably because of persecution by schismatics. His congregation insisted on continuing the discussions, however, and the bishop retired to Sicily in despair. The Capreans sent a delegation to Rome announcing their return to the fold and asking for a new bishop. Gregory, scrupulous as ever, insisted that they send a deputation to their exiled bishop in Sicily. If he wished to return, Gregory would pay his expenses to Rome; if he wished to stay in Sicily but return to the Catholic faith, he would be provided for. If he would not return or wished to remain in schism, Gregory ordered the archbishop of Ravenna to appoint someone to administer the see of Caprea, subject to the metropolitan jurisdiction of Ravenna, until the end of the schism. He commended the returning schismatics to both the exarch and the archbishop.[27] In 602 Bishop Firminus of Tergeste and his clergy and congregation were received back into the Catholic communion and signed undertakings not to break with Rome on pain of eternal damnation.[28]

But Gregory's success in winning back reconciled Istrians was seriously handicapped. Firstly there was the attitude of the exarch, who in 599, as a result of the Caprean episode, wrote to Gregory sending a copy of the emperor's order on the Istrians and reminding him of the imperial instruction not to harass them.[29] Gregory replied that the order did not mean repulsing the legitimate desires of those who actively wished to be reconciled. He also expressed his concern that the exarch's *major domus* had leaked to the schismatics, probably for money, the contents of the Caprean bishop's petition for orthodoxy. It was almost certainly this which caused his flight to Sicily and is a revealing insight into the 'dirty tricks' at the exarch's court which hampered the work of reunion.

The second problem was the persecution of returning Istrians by the schismatics. The Caprean bishop's flight to Sicily has already been alluded to. In 596 a *religiosus*, John, returning to the fold from the Istrian schism, retired to Sicily with a papal pension.[30] In July 599 a group of reconciled Istrians travelled to Constantinople to complain to the emperor of the wickedness, presumably in the form of persecution, that they had suffered at the hands of the Istrian bishops.[31] In 593 the deacon Felix, having been reconciled to Rome, fled there from Istria and then retired to Sicily with a papal pension and a promise of protection.[32] In June 603 Gregory appealed to the exarch to come to the aid of the reconciled bishop Firminus, claiming that Archbishop Severus, having failed to persuade him to return to schism, was stirring up riots in Firminus' city.[33]

In the absence of any evidence of missionaries being sent to Istria from Rome, we must assume that the work of conversion was carried on by pious laymen and government officials. This is certainly suggested by letters of congratulation on their propagation of the true faith which were sent to Basilius *vir clarissimus*, Mastalo and Theodosius, who sound like imperial functionaries.[34] Gregory specifically congratulated Gulfaris *magister militum* on his work in winning back souls to Catholicism and urged him to extend his protection to reconciled schismatics who were being harassed and persecuted.[35]

Despite his clear impatience with it, Gregory loyally obeyed Maurice's order until the emperor's death. But as soon as Phocas was emperor and had sent as exarch Smaragdus, who had during his previous tenure of the office kidnapped Archbishop Severus and forced him to recant, Gregory wrote to Smaragdus urging a resumption of his former strong line:[36]

We hope that the fervour of zeal which you formerly showed in this matter will be kindled to greater heat than ever and that you will be the more ready to punish and restrain the enemies of God, as the defence of the soul in the sight of God is more precious than that of the body. Let the uprightness of the faith which is strong within you arm you against those who go astray. Let the body of the church now rent asunder in your dominions be restored during your rule to its former wholeness. You will be repaid for your exertions in the matter by Him who is the author of uprightness and unity. For we trust in God's mercy that our eternal enemies [i.e. the Lombards] will find you the stronger against them, in proportion as the enemies of the true faith find you terrible against themselves through your love of God.

Whether or not Smaragdus applied force, the natural momentum towards reconciliation gathered strength, and on Severus' death there was schism and the election of two patriarchs of Aquileia – a schismatic one in Aquileia under the protection of the Lombards, and an orthodox one in Grado under imperial rule.[37] Inevitably the schism had now divided on political boundaries, and within the Lombard kingdom the conversion of the royal family to Catholicism led ultimately in 698 to the formal extinction of the 'Three Chapters' schism within its borders too.

Although Christianity had been the official religion of the Empire for some two centuries, paganism and pagan practices remained deeply rooted in the West. Even in Rome astrology, which the church had consistently denounced, flourished. Gregory preached against it, seeking to discredit it by ridicule.[38] But he was much more concerned to eradicate overt paganism, which prevailed in some of the more remote areas of the imperial West. Uncivilized, mountainous and backward, Sardinia had clung to the old religion and the old gods with considerable tenacity. Perhaps the most famous Sardinian pagan was Symmachus, who, having received conversion to Catholicism, became pope at the end of the fifth century. At the end of the sixth, paganism was still rife on the island and the situation was exacerbated by the fact that the metropolitan of Sardinia was the foolish and ineffectual archbishop Januarius of Caralis.

In 594 Gregory decided that direct action would have to be taken, and he dispatched to the island two special commissioners, Abbot Cyriacus and Bishop Felix, probably of Portus. Their mission was twofold: to investigate, report on and try to correct the deficiencies in Januarius' pastoral administration, and to make an assault on the problem of paganism. It is the evangelizing nature of the mission which perhaps explains the presence of Abbot Cyriacus, a forerunner of Abbot Augustine of the English mission. The reports that the commissioners sent back prompted a sheaf of letters from Gregory, which give a revealing insight into his conversion strategy and involve the use of persuasion and force and the involvement of the lay authorities.

He summed up his general anti-pagan policy in a letter to Januarius in 599:[39]

> We vehemently exhort your fraternity to maintain your pastoral
> vigilance against idol-worshippers and soothsayers and
> magicians; to preach publicly among the people against the men
> who do such things, and recall them by persuasive exhortation
> from the pollution of such sacrilege and from the temptation of
> divine judgment and peril in the present life. If, however, you
> find them unwilling to change their ways, we desire you to
> arrest them with a fervent zeal. If they are slaves, chastise them
> with blows and torments to bring about their correction. But if
> they are free men, let them be led to penitence by strict
> confinement, as is suitable, so that they who scorn to listen to
> words of salvation which reclaim them from the peril of death,
> may at any rate by bodily torments be brought back to the
> desired sanity of mind.

On the basis of information supplied by Felix and Cyriacus, Gregory proposed a programme of specific corrective action. He ordered Januarius to revive the long-derelict see of Fausiana as a base of missionary activity: 'We are aware that, owing to the absence of priests, there are still pagans there, living like wild beasts and entirely ignorant of the worship of God.'[40] He ordered Januarius to ensure that there were no pagans on the estates of any of the Sardinian bishops: 'If I find a pagan peasant belonging to any bishop whatever in the island of Sardinia, I shall deal severely with that bishop.'[41] Rather subtler than the application of blows and torments, but perhaps no less painful, he suggested the imposition of financial sanctions on church tenants who remained pagan: 'If any peasant should be found so perfidious and obstinate as to refuse to come to the Lord God, he must be weighted down with such a great burden of rent as to be compelled by the very pain of the exaction to hasten to the right way.'[42]

Gregory did not confine his exhortations to the church. He encouraged the nobles and landowners to convert the pagans on their estates and to report their progress to the pope. He wrote:[43]

I have learned from the report of my brother and fellow bishop Felix and my son the servant of God Cyriacus that nearly all of you have peasants on your estates given to idolatry. And this has greatly saddened me because I know that the guilt of subjects weighs down the life of their superiors, and that, when sin in a subject is not corrected, the sentence rebounds on the master. Wherefore, my magnificent sons, I exhort that with all care and solicitude you be zealous for your souls and see what account you will render to Almighty God for your subjects. For indeed, they have been committed to you for this end, that they may serve for your advantage in earthly things and you, through your care for them, may provide for their souls in the things that are eternal. If, then, they pay what they owe you, why do you not pay them what you owe them. That is to say, your Greatness should assiduously admonish them, and restrain them from the error of idolatry, so that by their being drawn to the faith you may make Almighty God propitious to yourselves.

It is a perfect definition of the Christian paternalism which Gregory saw as the duty of the landlord.

A major obstacle to the implementation of Gregory's programme was the attitude of the imperial government's representatives on the island. In 595 Gregory indignantly informed the empress Constantina that the governor (the *praeses*) permitted the open practice of paganism on payment of a bribe. Indeed, he even forced those pagans who had been converted to Christianity to continue to pay the bribe. When Bishop Felix had confronted him with these facts, the governor had admitted them but explained that it was the only way he could recoup the money he had paid out to get the job in the first place.[44] Gregory's remonstrance seems to have had some effect, however, for whether the governor was removed or mended his ways Gregory was writing to *Praeses* Spesindeus in 600 urging him to assist Bishop Victor of Fausiana in his successful evangelizing of the pagans.[45]

Gregory's mission certainly achieved some success. He reported happily in 600: 'Many of the barbarians and provincials in Sardinia by God's grace are hastening to embrace the Christian faith with the utmost devotion.'[46] Perhaps his most spectacular success, however, was with the Barbaricini, a tribe of pagan bandits who had been expelled from Africa by the Vandals and had taken up residence in Sardinia and imposed a reign of terror.[47] Gregory described them as 'senseless animals [who] know not the true God but worship trees and stones'. Just as Felix and Cyriacus arrived in Sardinia, the imperial military commander, Duke Zabardas, had inflicted a heavy defeat on the Barbaricini, and in imposing peace terms insisted – perhaps at the suggestion of the papal commissioners – on including conversion to Christianity. Gregory praised Zabardas and promised to report favourably on him to the emperor.[48] He also wrote to Hospito, the Barbaricini chief, who unlike his men was already a Christian, urging him to bring about the baptism of his tribe and call on the help of Felix and Cyriacus to do so.[49]

Paganism was not confined to Sardinia, however; it existed also in Sicily, Corsica and Campania. In August 593 the bishop of Tyndaris, a remote Sicilian see, complained to Gregory about the number of idol-worshipping pagans in his diocese. Some, he explained, had been converted, but others remained, protected by 'the patronage of powerful people or by the nature of the place in which they lived'. Gregory commended the bishop's zeal in conversion and urged the praetor of Sicily to give him every assistance in eliminating paganism.[50] In June 601 Gregory wrote to the rector Adrian in Sicily praising his pursuit and punishment of soothsayers and magicians.[51] In 597 Gregory was writing to Bishop Peter of Aleria in Corsica, where there had been some backsliding to paganism among recent converts. He urged Peter to bring back the lapsed converts and impose a few days' penance on them, as a mild punishment; and as to those as yet unconverted, 'to make haste by admonishing, beseeching, by alarming them about the coming judgment and also by giving reasons why they should not worship trees and stones, gather them to Almighty God'. He sent him 50 *solidi* for the purchase of baptismal robes.[52] Even closer to home, there were pagans in Campania, for in April 598 Gregory was ordering Bishop Agnellus of Terracina to search out the tree-worshippers in his diocese and to administer such chastisement that others would be deterred from paganism. He also asked the local military commander, Count Maurus, to assist him in the process.[53]

It is likely that these were the major areas of concern in the campaign against paganism. John the Deacon, who had consulted the complete Papal Register in the archives, lists the Barbaricini, the Sardinians and the peasants of Campania as those Gregory won to the faith 'by the use of just force'.[54]

Gregory was equally keen to eliminate paganism outside imperial Italy. In Gaul he enlisted the aid of Queen Brunhild, pinning his hopes on a great reform council which would initiate the necessary action. But the major area of paganism remaining in what had once been the Roman Empire was the province of Britain, now divided between the beleaguered Romano-British kingdoms in the western parts of the island, practising their own very individual form of Celtic Christianity, and the pagan kingdoms of the Anglo-Saxon invaders in the rest of the island. It was to the English that Gregory dispatched his most celebrated and far-reaching mission.[55] I have deliberately left it until last because it is important to see it in the context of the missionary activities undertaken elsewhere, particularly within the Empire.

The principal sources for the English mission are Bede's *Ecclesiastical History* completed in 731, and Gregory's Register. Bede, the greatest of the Anglo-Saxon historians, included in his work a brief biography of Gregory, compiled from the *Liber Pontificalis*, the *Regula Pastoralis*, the *Magna Moralia*, the *Libellus Synodicus* of 595, and Gregory of Tours' *Historia Francorum*. His work also contained copies of papal letters brought back from Rome by the priest Nothhelm. But it seems not to have drawn on the earliest extant life of Gregory, by the Anonymous of Whitby, written between 704 and 714.[56]

Bede's account has long been accepted as authentic, but in recent years it has been subjected to detailed scrutiny following a major attack on it launched by Dom Suso Brechter.[57] The most celebrated story about Gregory is the one first reported in the *Whitby Life* and also recounted by Bede, both drawing on an oral tradition common in England.

The *Whitby Life* says:

There is a story told by the faitnful that, before he became pope, there came to Rome certain people of our nation, fair-skinned and light-haired. When he heard of their arrival he was eager to see them; being prompted by a fortunate intuition, being puzzled by their new and unusual appearance, and, above all, being inspired by God, he received them and asked what race they belonged to. (Now some say they were beautiful boys, while others say that they were curly-haired, handsome youths.) They answered, 'The people we belong to are called Angles.' 'Angels of God', he replied. Then he asked further, 'What is the name of the king of that people?' They said, 'Aelli,' whereupon he said: 'Alleluia, God's praise must be heard there.' Then he asked the name of their own tribe, to which they answered 'Deira' and he replied, 'They shall flee from the wrath of God to the faith.'

After this encounter, Gregory asked the pope's permission to go to England on an evangelizing mission. The pope was willing to allow it but the people of Rome were not, and so Gregory stayed; but he fulfilled his desire to convert the English when he himself became pope.[58] Bede tells much the same story, except that he makes the English boys slaves and says the meeting took place in the Forum.[59]

This charming story epitomizes many of the problems facing scholars when they examine the evidence on the English mission. Brechter dismisses it as a Northumbrian legend and says that Gregory's interest can only be traced as far back as his known purchase of Saxon slaves in 595. Bede in his version is careful to say that the authority of the story is a 'tradition of our ancestors which has come down to us'. He can adduce no written or Roman evidence for it, and the fact that he tacks it on to the end of his account suggests that it was popular, but unproved to his satisfaction. The Anonymous of Whitby, on the other hand, had access to sources not available to Bede, for he names Gregory's mother as Silvia and may be drawing on a separate Roman tradition. None of the elements in the story is inherently unlikely. There was a regular slave trade between Britain and Gaul, and between Gaul and Italy. Aelle was king of Northumbria in the period before Gregory's election, 560–88. The development of puns was popular among educated ancients. Gregory was certainly interested in the English, for in September 595 he asked the Gallic rector Candidus to buy English slave boys of seventeen or eighteen and send them to Rome to serve in the monasteries, and to ensure that, since they were pagans, they were accompanied by a Christian priest, who could baptize them if they died on the way.[60] It has been argued that he intended them to accompany Augustine's mission; but none of them went, because it is known that no one on the mission could speak English. Yet Gregory told the bishop of Autun in 599 that he had sent the mission to England after 'long thought'.[61] But how long is 'long'?

It seems inherently unlikely that Gregory would have been allowed to go on the English mission before his election. He makes no mention of it in any of his works. He was specifically withdrawn from his monastery for diaconal duty in Constantinople. Perhaps the solution lies in his letter of July 596 to Queen Brunhild:[62]

> It has come to our knowledge that the nation of the Angli is desirous of being converted to the Christian faith, but that the priests in their neighbourhood neglect them and are remiss in handling their desires by their own exhortations. On this account therefore we have taken thought to send them the servant of God Augustine whose zeal and earnestness are well known to us, with other servants of God. And we have also charged them to take with them some priests from the neighbouring parts with whom they may be able to ascertain the disposition of the Angli, and, as far as God may grant it to them, to aid their wishes by their admonition.

The whole tone of this letter suggests that the mission was an immediate response by Gregory on learning of a particular state of affairs, and not a long-cherished ambition. It surely cannot be coincidence that Gregory was sending for English slave boys in 595 and dispatching missionaries in early 596. It is more likely that both were part of one plan, and that this plan was inspired by something like the encounter with the English slaves in the Forum – but an encounter which took place during rather than before his pontificate. This would certainly explain why suddenly, out of the blue, the pope sent for English slaves, and, having sent for them, dispatched Roman missionaries. The 'long thought' he spoke of could be of the order of several months or a year therefore. The letter to Brunhild suggests that, having learned from somewhere that the English wanted conversion and that the neighbouring bishops – who from the context of the letter must be the Frankish bishops – were doing nothing about it, he sent for English boys to train, and in the meantime sent missionaries. But he did so in haste – so much so that he sent no interpreters with them and dispatched no commendatory letters to pave their way. He acted, in fact, just as he had when he learned of the state of affairs in Sardinia, and, as in Sardinia, he put a senior monk at the head of the mission. It is difficult to see how he could have got this information about England if not from slaves, for he had no links with the country and no knowledge of it. Although the story of his own intended mission is simply hagiographical embroidery, there may well be a kernel of truth in the story of the meeting with the slave boys.

England was a far-off country of which Gregory knew comparatively little. He knew it was a former province of the Roman Empire, largely overrun by Germanic tribes 150 years before. He knew they had built their tribal kingdoms on the ruins of Romano-British society. He knew that in the western parts of the island and in Ireland the natives retained their independence and their own distinctive and individual form of Christianity. But between Rome and the churches of Ireland and Wales, just as between Rome and the kingdoms of the Angles and Saxons, there was no contact.

The Anglo-Saxons were pagans, and their paganism, with its veneration of Woden, 'the promoter of strife', and Thor, the hammer-wielding thunder god, with its ritualized curses, its casting of the runes, its exaltation of prowess in battle and courage under arms, was the virile warrior religion of conquerors. But the days of conquest were done. Now was the period of consolidation, development, and emergence into the community of civilized nations. It can be seen that barbarian rulers progressed naturally from being conquerors who practised paganism or heretical forms of Christianity to adopting Catholicism, the religion of the Roman Empire and therefore pre-eminently of civilization and respectability. Clovis of the Franks and Reccared of the Visigoths had both been converted from Arianism to Catholicism as the age of conquest gave way to the age of consolidation.

The time was ripe for a similar development in England. Aethelbert, king of Kent, was the most powerful ruler among the English kings, acknowledged as overlord (*bretwalda*) by his fellow rulers. His kingdom faced the continental coast, and his contacts with the Franks resulted in his marriage to Bertha, the Christian daughter of King Charibert of Paris.[63] Part of the wedding agreement was that she should retain her faith and bring with her to Kent a Frankish bishop, Liudhard.[64] A later tradition has it that Liudhard sowed the seeds of Christianity, and this is given support by Gregory's claim that the English were desirous of getting Christianity.[65] Liudhard would be one obvious source of knowledge of the faith. Aethelbert's initial amenability to tolerating the missionaries might also suggest that

Liudhard had done some preliminary work in softening up the court. There was therefore a bridgehead, something for Augustine to build on.

Perhaps following the precedent of Abbot Cyriacus in Sardinia, Gregory sensibly chose as his missionaries to England forty monks, whose disciplined, corporate, simple life would be a recipe for survival in an alien and perhaps hostile land.[66] The head of the mission was Augustine, prior of St Andrew's, whose 'zeal and earnestness' Gregory reported to Queen Brunhild.[67] They set out in 596 with very little preparation. They had no knowledge of the country and took no interpreters, and Gregory apparently provided them with no commendatory letters to assure them of assistance along the way. When they reached Aix in Gaul their spirits failed them, because of the horror stories of English savagery that they heard and their ignorance of the language. They therefore sent Augustine back to Rome to beg for their recall.[68] Gregory sent Augustine back with a letter of encouragement and a sheaf of commendatory letters to ecclesiastical and secular worthies to aid their passage across Gaul.[69] His letter to the monks appointed Augustine as their abbot, instructing them to obey him and encouraging them to continue.[70] He also suggested that they take Frankish interpreters.[71]

By spring 597 the missionaries had reached the English Channel, and they crossed to the isle of Thanet where, according to tradition, the first Saxon invaders had landed 150 years before. They sent the king word that they had arrived with a joyful message, and Aethelbert provided them with necessaries and bade them wait for several days until he had decided what to do. Bede paints a vivid picture of what then transpired:[72]

> Some days afterwards the king came to the island and, sitting in the open air, commanded Augustine and his comrades to come thither to talk with him. He took care that they should not meet in any building, for he held the traditional superstition that, if they practised any magic art, they might deceive him, and get the better of him as soon as he entered. But they came endowed with divine not devilish power and bearing as their standard a silver cross and the image of our Lord and Saviour painted on a panel. They chanted litanies and uttered prayers to the Lord for their own eternal salvation and the salvation of those for whom and to whom they had come.

The king wisely declared that, although interested, he could not immediately abandon the age-old religion of his people, but he gave them permission to preach, and a residence in his capital city of Canterbury. The missionaries set themselves up as a monastic community, and began preaching and holding services in the church of St Martin, a renovated Roman building used by the queen. The king permitted but did not force the work of conversion. It proceeded rapidly, however, and on Christmas Day, 597, 10,000 persons were baptized, and Augustine in 598 sent the priest Laurentius and the monk Peter to Rome to acquaint Gregory with the progress of the mission and submit to him a list of specific questions which had arisen.[73] Gregory did not reply until 601, probably because of his illness, but now he sent a fresh supply of missionary monks under the Gallic abbot Mellitus, sacred plate and ornaments, relics, and holy books. He also sent a sheaf of letters. One of them formally granted Augustine the *pallium* as archbishop of the English and pre-scribed the organization of the English church.[74] There were to be two ecclesiastical provinces, based on London and York, each with twelve suffragan bishops. York was to be subject to Augustine during his lifetime, but thereafter each archiepiscopate was to be independent, each was to receive the *pallium*, and precedence would be determined by seniority of ordination. It is clear from this that Gregory was describing the Roman province of Britain and had no idea of the new arrangement in the English kingdoms, and the evidence indicates that Augustine remained at Canterbury and made little attempt to implement the plan. Gregory also dispatched his replies to Augustine's questions on such matters as division of ecclesiastical revenues, forms of service, consecration regulations, and baptismal and communion rules. There were also two very interesting letters to King Aethelbert and Queen Bertha respectively.

To Aethelbert he wrote:

> So, my most illustrious son, watch carefully over the grace you
> have received from God and hasten to extend the Christian faith
> among the people who are subject to you. Increase your
> righteous zeal for their conversion; suppress the worship of
> idols; overthrow their buildings and shrines; strengthen the
> morals of your subjects by outstanding purity of life, by
> exhorting them, terrifying, enticing and correcting them, and by
> showing them an example of good works; so that you may be

rewarded in heaven by the One whose name and knowledge you have spread on earth. For He whose honour you seek and maintain among the nations will also make your glorious name still more glorious even to posterity.

He went on to compare the king to Constantine and to urge him to listen to the advice of Augustine.[75] At the same time he wrote to Bertha, thanking her for her help, chiding her gently for not having converted her husband sooner, and urging her to keep him at the good work.[76]

With the backing of the king, Augustine started renovating derelict Roman churches, one of which became Canterbury cathedral. Gregory had in one of his *responsiones* informed Augustine that he, Augustine, had no authority over the bishops of Gaul but that he did have authority over the bishops of Britain. With Aethelbert's help Augustine arranged a meeting with the Welsh bishops, which took place in 602 or 603 in the border country. The Welsh church was monastic, clannish, non-Latin and fiercely independent. It had a different method of dating Easter, a different form of baptism and a different tonsure. At the first conference, Augustine urged the Welsh bishops to join him in preaching Christianity, but they refused to give up any of their particular practices. A second conference was held, but the Welsh bishops took umbrage at Augustine's remaining seated, in the Roman fashion, when they entered, and rejected out of hand his rather condescending proposal that if they gave up their dating of Easter and their form of baptism and joined in the work of preaching the gospel, their other outlandish ways could be tolerated. So Augustine and the Roman missionaries carried on alone. Mellitus and Justus were consecrated as bishops of London and Rochester respectively, and Laurentius was ordained by Augustine before his death to succeed him in Canterbury. Augustine died *circa* 605, and the English mission was to suffer many vicissitudes; but the breakthrough had been made and there was to be no turning back.[77]

Gregory's missionary strategy with regard to England is clear.[78] He wanted a programme of conversion by encouragement and conciliation, by working with and through the lay authorities and by eschewing force. He was willing to be adaptable in matters of ceremonial and practice. When Archbishop Leander of Seville had asked Gregory what the Catholic church in Spain should do about the ceremony of baptism, because the Roman church's triple immersion had been the custom of the Spanish Arians whereas the Catholics had practised single immersion, Gregory advised the continuation of single immersion. 'As long as there is unity in the faith, difference in custom is not prejudicial to the Holy Church', he said.[79] Similarly he wrote to Augustine:[80]

My brother, you know the customs of the Roman church in which, of course, you were brought up. But it is my wish that if you have found any customs in the Roman or Gaulish church or any other church which may be more pleasing to Almighty God, you should make careful selection of them and sedulously teach the Church of the English, which is still new in the faith, what you have been able to gather from other churches. For things are not to be loved for the sake of a place, but places are to be loved for the sake of their good things. Therefore choose from every individual church whatever things are devout, religious and right. And when you have collected these as it were into one hurdle, see that the minds of the English grow accustomed to it.

Gregory's desire to avoid the use of force is demonstrated by a letter to Mellitus. Gregory had urged Aethelbert to destroy idols and temples in the letter sent to encourage him. But he had second thoughts, and a month after the second batch of missionaries left he wrote to Mellitus countermanding the order for destruction of the temples:

Since the departure of our company and yourself I have felt much anxiety because we have not happened to hear how your journey has prospered. However, when Almighty God has brought you to our most reverend Bishop Augustine, tell him what I have decided after long deliberation about the English people, namely that the idol temples of that race should by no means be destroyed, but only the idols in them. Take holy water and sprinkle it on these shrines, build altars and place relics in them. For if the shrines are well built, it is essential that they should be changed from the worship of devils to the service of the true God. When this people see that their shrines are not destroyed they will be able to banish error from their hearts and be more ready to come to the places they are familiar with, but now recognizing and worshipping the true God.

He went on to suggest that their ceremonies of sacrificing animals should be turned into celebrations of saints and martyrs and their animal sacrifices eaten.[81]

What were Gregory's motives in sending the English mission? Several have been adduced. The idea that Gregory wanted to beat the Welsh and Irish churches to the conversion of the English is not borne out by the evidence.[82] Bede quotes Gildas as saying that the British bishops neglected the work of conversion.[83] Gregory knew nothing of either the Welsh or the Irish church or their activities. The idea that he wished to extend papal jurisdiction is similarly not borne out by the evidence.[84] His correspondence emphasized the moral rather than jurisdictional aspects of the mission. It has been pointed out that England became devoted to Gregory in particular rather than simply to Rome in general.[85] Gregory himself said that he was sending missionaries because the English needed converting and the Frankish bishops were neglecting the task.[86] The whole of Gregory's outlook and world-view leads inexorably to the conclusion that his interest in the English was purely pastoral, and there is no reason to doubt the paean of praise which appeared in the *Magna Moralia* and was quoted by Bede:[87]

> For the almighty Lord has covered with his lightning cloud the ends of the sea: because, by the brilliant miracles of preachers, he has brought even the ends of the world to the faith. For behold, he has now penetrated the hearts of almost all nations. Behold he has joined together in one faith the boundaries of the East and the West. Behold the tongue of Britain which only knew how to utter barbarous sounds has long since begun to sound the divine praises with the Hebrew Alleluia! Behold the once swelling ocean is calmed beneath and subject to the feet of the saints; and its barbarous motions, which earthly princes could not subdue with the sword, are now, through the fear of God, bound by the mouths of priests with words only; and he that when an unbeliever stood not in awe of fighting troops, now as a believer fears the tongues of the humble. For because the virtue of the Divine knowledge is poured into him by precepts, by heavenly words and by the brightness of miracles, he is so curbed by the dread of the same divinity that he fears to do wrong and longs with all his desire to attain eternal glory.

Dom Suso Brechter launched a comprehensive attack on Bede's account, even questioning his scholarly integrity. He based his account solely on Gregory's letters, and on the basis of them rejected the *'non Angli sed Angeli'* story, claimed that the famous *responsiones* of Gregory were eighth-century forgeries, that Aethelbert was not baptized in 597 but at some unspecified date before his death in 616, that Augustine was not consecrated at Arles in 597 but at Autun en route for England, and that London and not Canterbury was Augustine's see.

These points have been taken up and discussed in detail by many scholars and are clearly worth examining. The authenticity of the *responsiones* has been investigated and is being investigated. At the moment the best-informed judgment is that 'in a broad sense, and with the exception of an important interpolation, the collection may be held to be Gregorian.'[88] The idea that London and not Canterbury was Augustine's see is absurd. It depends solely on Gregory's letter setting out arrangements for the English church, and wilfully ignores both the testimony of Bede and the logic of the situation. Canterbury was politically and spiritually the centre of Augustine's activities. It was the capital of Aethelbert, on whose goodwill so much depended; it was the seat of the earliest churches, the centre of preaching and baptism. London was the capital of the kingdom of Essex, admittedly under Aethelbert's influence but so far from the mainstream of the conversion work as to be wholly inappropriate. Augustine was buried in Canterbury and ordained his successor Laurentius to that see. But it can be seen that he attempted to fulfil Gregory's wishes in part by ordaining as bishop of London Mellitus, leader of the second group of missionaries.

The remaining two problems are less straightforward. Bede says quite explicitly that Aethelbert, who died in 616, died twenty-one years after his conversion to Christianity. This would date the conversion to 595. But Bede also says that 616 was twenty-one years after the arrival of Augustine and his mission.[89] He is a little off-beam in his calculations, but the clear implication is that Aethelbert was converted in the first year of the mission. Bede also suggests that it was the king's conversion which stimulated large numbers of others to come over, and that would certainly explain the baptism of 10,000 at Christmas 597 and the apparent rapidity of conversion. It is entirely in keeping too with the mood of the letters to Aethelbert and Bertha. Brechter claims that these two letters, though implying that Aethelbert permitted conversion, indicate that he was himself not converted. He further argues that the letter to Bertha is an encouragement to her to convert her husband and for that reason Bede suppressed it, and that Gregory does not mention the king's conversion in his letter to Eulogius of Alexandria announcing the success of Augustine's mission. But this evidence is extremely flimsy. Although Gregory does not explicitly mention Aethelbert's conversion in the letters, the clear implication is that Aethelbert himself has been converted and Gregory now wants him to spread the conversion to his people. The letter to Bertha may be absent from Bede's account simply because he never received a copy of it or because he decided to leave it out for reasons of balance.[90] There is no reason to suggest that he suppressed it. The fact that the king is not mentioned in the Eulogius letter is neither here nor there. Both the course of the mission and the tone of the letters strongly suggest that Aethelbert was converted and baptized in 597. But he did not enforce conversion, because strong elements of paganism remained in his kingdom, including his own son Eadbald, who led a brief pagan reaction on his death.

On the question of Augustine's consecration, however, Bede and Gregory are in direct conflict, and it is necessary to make a choice between them. Bede says:[91]

> Meanwhile Augustine the man of God went to Arles and, in accordance with the command of the holy father Gregory, was consecrated archbishop of the English race by Aetherius, archbishop of that city. Then he returned to Britain and at once sent to Rome the priest Laurentius and the monk Peter to inform the blessed Pope Gregory that the English race had received the faith of Christ and that he himself had been made their bishop.

The period he is talking about is late 597 or early 598. But in July 598 Gregory wrote jubilantly to Eulogius of Alexandria about the news he had received from Britain via Laurentius and Peter:[92]

> While the nation of the English, situated at the ends of the earth, remained up to this time unbelievers worshipping trees and stones, I decided, with the aid of your prayers and the inspiration of God, to send a monk of my own monastery to them to preach. And with my leave, he was made a bishop by the bishops of Germany and with their encouragement, he reached that nation at the end of the world. And now letters have just arrived telling us of his safety and of his work.

Before these letters even arrived, Gregory wrote to Queen Brunhild in September 597 calling Augustine 'our brother and fellow bishop'.[93] This confirms the implication of the Eulogius letter that, although Augustine set out as a prior and was created abbot when the monks lost heart, it was intended that he be consecrated en route. It has been suggested that this was unlikely, on the analogy of the later missionaries Boniface and Willibrord, who began evangelizing first and were later made archbishops. But there is a difference in that each of them initiated his mission himself, whereas it was the pope who initiated Augustine's mission. There is, moreover, an exact parallel to it in the seventh century. When Pope Honorius I, who prided himself on his imitation of Gregory, sent Birinus to convert the West Saxons, he arranged for him to be consecrated en route by Archbishop Asterius of Milan in Genoa.[94] There would have been a good reason for Augustine to be consecrated by the bishops of Gaul – to enlist their aid and support and involve them in the mission, again something implied in the Eulogius letter. When Gregory refers to the bishops of Germany, he probably means Gallia Lugdunensis, which Sidonius Apollinaris called Germania Lugdunensis because of the German origins of the Burgundians who now ruled the area.[95] Its metropolitan see was Lyons, much further north than Arles and more appropriate for the ordination. There are no grounds for suggesting as Brechter does that Syragrius of Autun consecrated Augustine. It is, in fact, unlikely, for Gregory, in granting him the *pallium*, insisted that Syragrius remain subordinate in the hierarchy to his metropolitan Aetherius of Lyons. The likelihood is that it was Aetherius of Lyons who consecrated Augustine on his way to England.

Bede must have had some reason for saying that Augustine went to Gaul to get consecration from Aetherius of Arles. He was a careful historian and utilized the best evidence available. The *Whitby Life* had assumed that Augustine was consecrated in Rome before he set out. That would have been an obvious assumption for Bede to make in the absence of other evidence. The *Whitby Life* also mentioned only one set of missionaries, knowing nothing of Mellitus and the reinforcements.[96] In this the author followed the *Liber Pontificalis*, which mentioned only one set, a view also taken by Bede in an earlier work, *De Ratione Temporum*.[97] But when Bede received copies of the papal letters, he knew there were two sets of missionaries and amended his *Ecclesiastical History* accordingly. One mistake Bede did make was to confuse Aetherius of Lyons and Vergilius of Arles, who were contemporaries and not successive archbishops of Arles. He seems to have done this on the basis of a letter to Pelagius of Tours and Serenus of Marseilles attributed by scribal error, presumably Nothhelm's, to 'Aetherius of Arles', a composite of Aetherius and Vergilius.[98] In attributing Augustine's consecration to Aetherius of Arles, Bede had the right man, the wrong see and the wrong year. I believe that this was due to a faulty piece of deduction, made in good faith. The *Whitby Life* said Augustine was consecrated in Rome, and that was presumably a tradition current in England. When Bede received the copies of the Gregorian letters, in which Augustine was appointed abbot, he knew that this was not true. By the time of the next letter in the chronological sequence, to Vergilius of Arles, he was called 'Bishop Augustine'. But Bede knew there had been no communication with Gregory in the meantime, and that 'Aetherius of Arles', whom he assumed to be the papal vicar and Vergilius' predecessor, had been encouraged to meet and help Augustine, so he put two and two together – and got five. Augustine had to be bishop in time for his envoys to take the news to Gregory, so Bede invented a trip to Gaul for consecration in Arles, in order to fit the facts as he understood them.

When set in context, then, Gregory's English mission can be seen as part of an overall missionary policy which the pope conceived as one of his primary duties. There is no question here of sending missionaries to win the barbarian West to Rome as an alternative power base for the papacy. It was a matter of moral and pastoral duty.

Chapter Fifteen

Gregory and Monasticism

Gregory's monastic vocation was central to his being. It determined his life-style, influenced his policies and informed his entire outlook and attitude. He was the first monk to become pope, and although he was probably elected not because he was a monk but because he was a deacon and administrator, a former *apocrisiarios* with the ear of the emperor, and a holy, generous and revered Roman, his eminence and enthusiasm for the cause made him a powerful proponent of monastic life. Indeed, Gregory is the third of a trio of major monastic figures in the sixth century, following Benedict of Nursia and Cassiodorus of Vivarium. It used to be argued that these three were in a sense responsible for the 'great leap forward' in monasticism in the sixth century; but though this 'leap forward' certainly occurred, it is much more likely that it was a response to the wars, famines, plagues and invasions, which produced an understandable desire in many people to flee from the world. In the light of recent research it is necessary to modify our views of the contemporary influence exercised by both Cassiodorus and Benedict, and it is, in fact, almost certainly the case that of the three it was Gregory who exercised far more immediate influence on the structure and nature of monasticism.

Monasticism had originated in the deserts of Egypt in the early fourth century and had taken two different paths – the solitary ascetic life of the hermit, and the cenobitic life of the monastic community, devoted to life and work in common. From Egypt, both forms spread to Palestine, Syria and Asia Minor. It was the cenobitic aspect which gained momentum, helped by the appearance of St Basil's Rule, a widely admired and imitated set of regulations for monastic life. Monasticism came west in the mid-fourth century, and although it began slowly, by the mid-fifth century it was established. In Italy both cenobitic and eremitic monasticism existed, and various different rules – those, for instance, of Basil, Cassian, Macarius and Pachomius – were followed. Gregory's *Dialogues* show cenobitic monasticism flourishing, and the mountains full of hermits festering with sores, lashing themselves, rolling in beds of nettles to conquer carnal desire, casting out demons, and causing water to spring from rocks, jars to fill with oil, the dead to rise and the lame to walk.

Although Gregory's wonder-workers included bishops and priests as well as monks and hermits, there is no doubt that monks held a special place in popular affection because of the sanctity of their lives, their total devotion to spirituality, and their withdrawal from the world, in contrast to the secular clergy, who by the nature of their duties were necessarily out and about in the world. This sometimes led to difficulties between the two orders, as for instance when the priest Florentius, jealous of Benedict's fame, tried to poison him, and when bishops in Gregory's reign sought to subject the monasteries to their control. The monks in fact formed a potential rival power structure to the ordered clerical hierarchy – something which became apparent in the East during the Iconoclastic controversy of the eighth century and which Gregory himself precipitated in Rome in the seventh century.

The future history of monasticism was to be significantly affected by the work of the three great men already mentioned. Benedict of Nursia was the first. All that is certainly known of his life is contained in Book 2 of Gregory's *Dialogues*, a collection of stories gathered from Benedict's disciples and admirers. It contains no dates, but they have been approximately adduced from internal evidence and are generally accepted. Benedict was born in Nursia *circa* 480, the son of a well-to-do country gentleman. He was sent by his father to Rome to study the liberal arts, but was so appalled by the worldliness of his fellow students that he withdrew from the world *circa* 500 and became a hermit near Subiaco. There his reputation for holiness prompted a community of monks to invite him to become their abbot, but rebelling against the strict discipline he imposed they later tried to poison him. He retired again to a hermit's life, attracted disciples, and founded twelve monasteries, including one at Subiaco which he governed himself until, after Florentius tried to poison him, he migrated to Monte Cassino *circa* 525 and founded a new monastery, which he ruled until his death *circa* 545.

It was probably at and for Monte Cassino that Benedict wrote, in accessible, colloquial Latin, his Rule (*Regula Benedicti*) which he called 'a very little rule for beginners'.[1] Gregory dubbed it 'outstanding in good judgment and clearly expressed', and this was indeed its virtue – a clear systematization and codification of all aspects of monastic life.[2] It is, however, important to stress that Benedict was not the first to write a Rule, and his Rule was only one of many utilized in Italy. His Rule was not, as used to be thought, officially promulgated for the use of all Italian monasteries, nor was it intended for use by a 'Benedictine order', a concept alien to monasticism at this time.[3] It was, like that of Basil, for use in his own monastery and perhaps for adaptation in others; but because of its excellence it survived, and eventually, in the late seventh and early eighth centuries, it spread to northern Italy, Gaul, and finally to England, where it was widely adopted. It was not in general use in Italy in the sixth century, and the evidence suggests that it was not until the tenth century that it was exclusively used by the monasteries of Rome.[4] It is therefore quite unrealistic to think of Gregory's monastery of St Andrew or Augustine's mission as being in any meaningful sense 'Benedictine'.[5]

This is not the place to go into the controversy about the relationship between the *Regula Magistri* and the *Regula Benedicti* in detail, [6] but it can be summed up as follows. The discovery just before World War II of similarities between the Rule of Benedict and the so-called 'Rule of the Master' precipitated a controversy which has raged in the learned journals ever since. The debate about the precise relationship between the two Rules, which came first and who wrote which, even prompted the suggestion that Benedict did not write his Rule at all. It has now been conclusively demonstrated that Benedict's Rule is Italian and dates from the mid-sixth century, and there seems little reason to doubt that Benedict did write it.[7] There also seems little reason to doubt, much as this might offend pious Benedictines, that the 'Rule of the Master' is anterior to that of Benedict: the Master's Rule is almost certainly early-sixth-century and perhaps from southern France.[8] But the fact that Benedict used the Master's Rule does not detract from his own achievement. He used several other rules (Cassian, Augustine, the Egyptian Fathers). His importance lies not in the uniqueness but in the nature of his Rule – and this brings us back, after all the debates, to Gregory's verdict on it, which surely explains its durability and success.

Benedict's importance can be seen in retrospect to be twofold. In the long term, his importance is as creator of his Rule, which gained currency in sixth-century Italy because of the enthusiasm of his disciples, but much greater currency in Western Europe as a whole in the eighth century. He preached a simple life-style, a regime of work, prayer and study, and a commonsense organizational approach to the government of a monastery. His achievement was to distil from various sources a workable, sensible programme of monastic life, government and occupation, based on an underlying ethic and a profoundly felt ideal. His importance in the sixth and seventh centuries, however, derived not so much from his Rule as from his starring role in the popular and widely read *Dialogues* of Gregory. Benedict was the archetypal holy man, whose life-style, saintliness and self-discipline, humility, and virtue take up one of the four books of the *Dialogues*. He was the exemplar of the monastic life, to be emulated by all would-be monks and saints.

The contribution of Cassiodorus was rather different, and again it must be put into perspective. During the Middle Ages the monasteries became repositories of learning, where priceless manuscripts were collected and copied and where the familiar texts of the ancients were preserved for succeeding generations. This aspect of monastic life is often said to be the legacy of Cassiodorus, who decisively linked monasticism with learning; but this view needs qualification.

The scion of a family of administrators who had served with distinction in both the imperial East and Ostrogothic Italy, Cassiodorus successively occupied the posts of quaestor, master of the offices, and praetorian prefect. He actively propagated the Romano-Gothic alliance with a history of the Goths published between 526 and 533. Around 538 he retired from public life and went to Constantinople, whence he returned after the reconquest and turned his pleasant country house at Vivarium near Seyllacium into a monastery. Although not its abbot, he did direct its principal area of activity, its scholarship. He was proud of Rome's scholarly history and he aimed to foster it ('Let other people bear arms and let the Romans forever be armed only with eloquence'). He had concerted a plan with Pope Agapitus for a Christian university of Rome, and although this came to nothing, he set up at Vivarium a library and *scriptorium*, staffed by a small but dedicated group of translators and copyists.[9]

He set out his educational theories in his *Institutiones*, urging the study of the liberal arts ('the knowledge of these subjects is undoubtedly useful and not to be shunned and so it seemed to the Fathers of the Church') and the preservation of the great works of the past ('Of all the work that can be accomplished by manual labour, none pleases me so much as the work of the copyist').[10] He himself wrote a treatise on orthography to facilitate this work, and his *scriptorium* produced translations from the Greek of the histories of Socrates, Sozomen and Theodoret, the *Antiquities* of Josephus, Gaudentius' treatise on music, and exegetical works by Origen, Clement of Alexandria and Chrysostom. The works of Western writers like Boethius, Ambrose, Augustine, Cassian and Jerome were collected and copied. Commentaries on the Psalms and the Pauline Epistles were prepared under his direction.

Although Vivarium under Cassiodorus was a remarkable place, we must be careful not to overrate his achievement. The literary activities of Vivarium did not continue after Cassiodorus' death, and his library was broken up and dispersed, the bulk of it apparently going to the Lateran library in Rome.[11] Nor was Cassiodorus the first or the only monastic figure to associate monastic life with literary endeavour, exegetical work, copying and translation, for there had been a flourishing tradition of such activities in Ostrogothic Italy.[12] The monastery of Castrum Lucullanum near Naples, under the direction of Abbot Eugippius, was in the forefront of the movement and a very real precursor of Vivarium. In Rome, the prolific Dionysius Exiguus conducted his literary career from an as yet unidentified monastery. It has been suggested, indeed, that most monasteries had *scriptoria*, though Benedict's silence on this aspect of monasticism still perplexes scholars.[13] Both in the monasteries and in the church there was throughout the sixth century a growing interest in the preservation and interpretation of biblical manuscripts and the works of the Church Fathers. But if Cassiodorus' activities at Vivarium were not unique, his influence was nevertheless seminal, and that influence derived from his writings rather than his example.[14] His *Institutiones* were among the most important schoolbooks of the early Middle Ages, the Vivarium translations remained in use for centuries, and the treatise on orthography played a significant role in the copying work of medieval monasteries. So, like Benedict, Cassiodorus' influence was strong fundamentally in the long term rather than the short.

In the short term Gregory was unquestionably the most significant of the three. He was the legislator, the popularizer, and the champion of monasticism in all its forms, regarding it as the most perfect expression on earth of man's search for God. He made no major innovation in the scheme or ideal of monastic life, he composed no

Rule, set up no *scriptorium:* his great aim was to strengthen and propagate.[15]

First he encouraged the foundation and endowment of monasteries. He set the example himself, founding and endowing six monasteries on his Sicilian estates and turning the Roman family home into the monastery of St Andrew. He gave monasticism a further fillip by living a monastic life-style in the Lateran, surrounding himself with monkish confidants and promoting monks to high office, and by promoting the spiritual life of the cloister in his writings, notably the *Dialogues.*

He consistently encouraged wealthy laymen and pious noblewomen to found and endow monasteries and nunneries, and he took energetic steps to see that funerary foundation bequests were promptly carried out.[16] He united monasteries which had suffered from enemy depredation, and where monasteries had fallen on hard times subsidized them with land grants, rent rebates and cash handouts.[17]

A second consistent and characteristic theme was the maintenance of discipline. During this time, with monasteries in constant danger of attack, pillage and destruction, with many communities being dispersed, there was a grave danger of indiscipline, carnal lapses and the abandonment of vows. Gregory used rectors, abbots and bishops to correct this situation.[18] There were serious irregularities among the monastic communities on the Tyrrhenian islands, sometimes occasioned by the influx of large numbers of refugees, many of them women, from the mainland. So he sent special commissioners to reform the monasteries and root out abuses on Gorgona, Monte Cristo, Capri and Eumorphiana.[19] There were reports of widespread indiscipline among the monasteries of Campania, and the rector was ordered to activate the local bishops to check it.[20] There were two successive investigations of the monastery on the slopes of Mount Etna.[21]

Throughout his dealings with the monasteries Gregory stressed the necessity of preserving the fundamental conditions and principles of the monastic life: the permanence of the monastic vocation, poverty, chastity, and the preservation of the peace of the cloister. To this end, he consistently forbade monks to migrate from monastery to monastery or to wander about at will.[22] He ordered runaway monks and nuns to return to the cloister.[23] He forbade monks to own private property, and banned women from monasteries and their environs.[24] There is in the Gregorian Register one revealing exception to Gregory's usual sharp and peremptory order for the return of the renegade monks to their monastery. The Syracusan patrician Venantius, who had been a monk and seems to have been a friend of Gregory's, abandoned the cloister, married a beautiful and imperious woman, Italica, fathered two daughters, and became the centre of a dilettante literary circle hostile to the spirit of monasticism. Gregory did not order him back to the monastery, but he spent a good deal of time and effort in writing to Venantius and seeking to persuade him, by argument, reproach and remonstrance, to return of his own free will. Venantius died shortly before Gregory himself, still out in the world. The case of Venantius demonstrates once again that there was in Gregory's cosmology one law for the rich and another for the poor.[25]

To preserve monastic seclusion, Gregory ordered that officials be appointed to deal with the secular business of the monasteries in order to prevent crowds of people invading them, and banned the holding of public masses by bishops in monasteries.[26] In general, all these decisions were variations on the already established basic themes of monastic life; but he did make two disciplinary innovations, when he fixed a minimum age for abbesses, and prescribed a novitiate of two years where Benedict had recommended one and Justinian three.[27]

Just as papal authority was deployed to correct internal indiscipline, it was also used to protect the monasteries against oppression. Oppression by bishops, laymen, secular clergy, even Roman church functionaries, whether it took the form of seizure of property or invasion of privacy, was strenuously resisted by the pope. But perhaps his greatest success in his dealings with the lay authorities came when he persuaded the emperor to modify the law he had issued banning civil servants and soldiers from entering churches or monasteries until their period of service had expired.[28]

Gregory's most important contribution to the growth of monasticism was perhaps that he defined it in terms of its relations with the secular clergy and in particular the bishops. The canons of the church councils repeatedly confirmed the jurisdictional rights of bishops over monasteries, but they had rarely attempted to define these rights with any precision. This lack of definition permitted acts of oppression by bishops, and it was to remove the uncertainty that Gregory acted. Ideally the bishops would have liked complete freedom of jurisdiction over the monasteries, and the monasteries would have liked complete freedom from their jurisdiction. Gregory had to steer a path between the two. He maintained the bishops' right to jurisdiction but sought to confine it exclusively to spiritual matters: the consecration of monasteries, the installation of new abbots, the superintending of discipline, and the provision of mass. To safeguard the rights of the monks, on the other hand, he increasingly issued charters of privilege, in order to confirm rather than create what he saw as their rights. The charter issued in 598 to the monastery of SS. John and Stephen in Classis illustrated this process admirably.[29] To preserve its peace and check the oppression it had suffered from successive archbishops of Ravenna, Gregory defined its rights with great precision. Its revenues and property were to remain intact. Disputes between the monastery and the church of Ravenna were to be settled before mutually agreed arbitrators. The monastic congregation was to choose its own abbot without outside interference. The abbot's authority was not to be impaired. Monks were not to be removed from the monastery without the abbot's permission. The bishop was not to undertake too frequent visitations so that the monastery was not burdened unduly with entertainment expenses. It seems likely that all or most of these abuses had occurred, and this demonstrates the multifarious ways in which a bishop could presume on his jurisdiction.

In more general terms, Gregory drew a sharp distinction between monks and clergy. He did not forbid clerics from entering monasteries or monks from entering the clergy, but he was quite clear that the two careers could not be combined. He permitted the ordination of monks as priests within the monastery only so that they could serve as chaplains and say mass.

It can be seen, then, that Gregory translated his deep personal commitment to monasticism into a very practical policy of protecting, advancing and defining the rights of Italian monasteries. Their continued growth and expansion in succeeding centuries can to some extent be said to have been made possible by the passionate concern and juridical precision with which Gregory, backed by the full weight and prestige of papal authority, sought to clarify their role and their rights within the body of the faithful.

Chapter Sixteen

The Legacy of Gregory

By 604, Gregory's life had run its course. Racked with pain and unable to walk, he had striven with all his might to secure for Rome a firm and lasting peace with the Lombards. But his schemes had crumbled. The exarch had broken the peace, the Lombards had risen up in arms, and in 603 there had been a series of catastrophic reverses for the Empire. Although Smaragdus had concluded a truce, it was only a breathing space. Rome, for all Gregory's endeavours, was still in mortal danger, and the 'unspeakable' Lombards were poised to strike again, just as they had been when Gregory ascended the throne of St Peter. On top of this, the city was in the grip of a terrible famine, and the populace, seeking a scapegoat, turned on the pope. Assailed by anxiety for the future, worn down by the burdens of office, and execrated by the people he had striven so hard to succour and support, Gregory died on 12 March 604. According to tradition, the mob converged on the Lateran, purposing to burn Gregory's books, but were deflected from this intention by the intervention of his disciple Peter. Gregory was buried in St Peter's, along with his predecessors, and the clergy and people turned their attention to the election of a successor.

What memory and what legacy did Gregory leave behind? There is an interesting difference in emphasis here, and one which perhaps throws some light on his permanent legacy. In the East, where by the ninth century he was celebrated as a saint, his reputation was initially based on the *Dialogues*, translated into Greek by Pope Zacharias (741–52). It became an indispensable item in both monastic and secular libraries and earned him the surname *Dialogos* to distinguish him from other sainted Gregories. The *Regula Pastoralis*, translated into Greek by Anastasius of Antioch in Gregory's own lifetime, increased Gregory's éclat, and it is evident that his reputation in the East was as a writer and teacher. The accounts of his life in Greek martyrologies and synaxaries comprised in the main the miracles attributed to Gregory in John the Deacon's biography. It was not until the eleventh century that there was any mention of his conversion of the English.[1]

In Spain too Gregory was revered as a great writer, and in the mid-seventh century Taio, the future bishop of Saragossa, journeyed to Rome to examine his works in the Lateran archive and later made a collection of excerpts from them in his *Liber Sententiarum*. Gregory himself had sent copies of the *Regula Pastoralis* and the *Magna Moralia* to his correspondents in Spain.[2]

In England, Gregory was revered as the apostle of the island. It was the pope rather than Augustine of Canterbury whom they regarded as the source of their conversion. He was consistently referred to by English writers as 'the teacher of the English', 'our own St Gregory', 'this apostolic saint of ours', 'our apostle'. The *Dialogi* and the *Regula Pastoralis* were translated into English by King Alfred and his scholars. The earliest life of Gregory was composed in the early years of the eighth century by an anonymous monk of Whitby.[3] As J. M. Wallace-Hadrill has written: 'The English felt drawn to Rome; that much is clear; but they reserved their love for the Pope who first helped them. It was of Gregory the heir of St Peter, not of Rome impersonally, that the English liked first to think.'[4]

In Rome, however, there was an almost complete silence until the ninth century. Peter Llewellyn has found only four spontaneous references to Gregory in Roman sources between his death and the ninth century.[5] In 642 Taio of Saragossa found his works neglected in the Lateran.[6] The brief, clerically composed biography of Gregory in the *Liber Pontificalis*, dating probably from the reign of Honorius I, is scrappy and grudging. It was Pope John VIII (872–82) who first realized that there was a flourishing northern tradition celebrating Gregory, although he was almost forgotten in Rome. Besides the *Whitby Life*, there was a Lombard life by Paul Warnfrid, a monk of Monte Cassino who died in 797. So Pope John VIII commissioned the Roman deacon John to write a life of Gregory from Roman sources, restoring him to a Roman context and rescuing him, as it were, from the hands of the barbarians.

It is clear from this survey that in the Dark Ages Gregory's reputation rested on his writings and on his conversion of the English. His neglect in Rome can be attributed almost certainly to his elevation of the monks as a rival centre of power to the clerical establishment. By the mid-seventh century the clergy had won the battle, and the eclipse of the monastic power bid obscured with it the celebrity of its instigator.

Gregory was the last of the great Latin patristic writers, and his works were extremely varied and highly influential. Probably the most popular were the *Regula Pastoralis* and the *Dialogues*. The *Regula Pastoralis* had been planned when Gregory was in Constantinople, but it was not actually written until the early years of his pontificate.[7] It is generally agreed to have been dedicated to Archbishop John of Ravenna, and was probably written in response to John's letter reproving Gregory for his unwillingness to undertake the papal office.[8] It was disseminated widely in both the East and the West.[9]

In one of his sermons Gregory had lamented the worldliness of the bishops, censuring their abuse of power, desire for profit, hunger for praise and weakness for gossip.[10] So from his own experience and meditation on the role of the episcopate he drew up a picture of the ideal bishop, centring his description firmly on the role of the bishop as preacher and saver of souls. Wallace-Hadrill writes of the *Regula Pastoralis* that it 'would by itself constitute a claim to great originality: no westerner before him had looked as he looked at the work of a bishop, the art of arts, the art of the government of souls; or had traced a bishop's motives in accepting office, even to the roots of self-deception'.[11]

The *Dialogues* and the *Homilies* epitomize the new folk-preaching that was so influential in the Middle Ages and represent the new form of learning that Gregory and the Gregorians stood for. The new learning was simple, straightforward and accessible to ordinary people, a pastoral, allegorical, inspirational form of culture which laid great stress on the character, spirituality and endurance of the holy man. It constituted a clean break with the old high culture of the sixth century which had been centred on an intellectual elite, and deeply immersed in the theological complexity and philosophical traditions of the East. The new culture, strongly influenced by the monastic ideal and grounded in Gregory's concept of a pastoral episcopate, emphasized simple truths – suffering and spirituality and goodness – rather than the mastery of abstruse points of theological dogma.

The *Dialogues* were written in 593, in the form of conversations between Gregory and his disciple Peter the Deacon. A more appropriate title would perhaps have been 'The miracles of the Italian Fathers', which was its 'working title'.[12] It is a book devoted to miracles, visions and prophecies, designed to demonstrate the holiness of the holy man and to convert the unbeliever, which is why a copy was sent to Queen Theodelinda, a Catholic but schismatic.[13]

The stories are sometimes profound, sometimes droll, as when a priest casually calling to his servant 'Come on, you devil, take off my boots' found the actual Devil starting to remove them miraculously.[14] The stories spoke to people plainly and simply, through their own experience, and this accessibility was not unique to Gregory the Great. Gregory of Tours had already made collections of miracle stories, and Caesarius of Arles in the early sixth century made a classic *apologia* for adopting colloquial speech in his sermons: 'I humbly ask that the ears of the learned tolerate some rustic expressions without complaining so that the Lord's flock receive celestial nourishment in simple and down to earth language.'[15] That is a sentiment which Gregory would have endorsed, for the teaching of the poor and ignorant was one of Gregory's guiding priorities, and lies also behind his defence of religious paintings, which he called 'the books of the unlearned', criticizing Bishop Serenus of Marseilles for destroying some of these in an access of iconoclastic zeal.[16]

There is no doubt that Gregory's writings, coming as they did from the most exalted churchman in the West, gave a powerful fillip to this growing educational trend. The same idea lay behind his *Homilies*. Gregory's belief that a bishop's principal duty was preaching the faith led him, despite his ill-health, to deliver two series of sermons which were eventually published. The forty *Homilies on the Gospels*, delivered in 591–2 and published in 593, and the twenty-two *Homilies on Ezekiel*, delivered in 592–3 and published in 601–2, were the product of some of Rome's darkest hours, the children of plague and siege.[17] Simple and straightforward expositions of fundamental ideas, illuminated by anecdotes and allegories, they can be seen in retrospect as forerunners of the *Dialogues*.

But whereas the *Dialogues* and the *Homilies* looked forward to the popular preaching of the future, the *Magna Moralia* looked back to the old form of laborious allegorical exegesis of the Bible pioneered by Origen and directed specifically at the clergy. The *Magna Moralia* was in this tradition: thirty-five books of exposition on Job, an allegorical and mystical interpretation of the story plus a disputation on Christian ethics, not intended for the general public. The work was begun in Constantinople at the behest of Gregory's monkish companions and his friend, Archbishop Leander of Seville, to whom it was eventually dedicated. The first part of the work was expounded to his circle in the Placidia palace, the latter part dictated after his return to Rome, and the whole was then edited and integrated in 595. It is lengthy, exhaustive and exhausting – so much so that although greatly admired, it was excerpted by the papal notary Paterius to provide an accessible selection of extracts for study.[18] Gregory defended its lack of shape and rambling discursiveness on the unassailable grounds that it had been inspired directly by the Holy Ghost. But Erich Caspar has written of it: 'it completely lacks the spiritual force of Augustine, who in his commentary on the Psalms was able to raise such a play of thought into images of great lyrical beauty.'[19] The basic allegory of the whole piece saw Job as a prototype of Christ and the Christian church, suffering the assaults of heretics and unbelievers. But it is perhaps for the form rather than the content that Gregory's exegetical work is important. It played a vital role in the transmission of the art of exegesis from the ancient world to the medieval.[20] Proceeding from the basic assumption that 'sacred scripture far excels all knowledge and all lore without comparison', Gregory set out the fundamental scheme for exegesis in the preface to the *Magna Moralia*, outlining the twofold historico-allegorical and moral interpretative pattern which so strongly influenced the biblical scholars of the Middle Ages.[21]

Gregory employed the same scheme in the lectures he delivered on the Heptateuch, the Book of Kings, the Prophets, the Book of Proverbs and the Song of Solomon, which were taken down in note form by the monk Claudius and subsequently prepared for publication.[22] From this corpus of work, two homilies on the Song of Solomon and the commentary on the first sixteen chapters of Kings have survived.[23]

Gregory's contemporary reputation as writer and exegete is testified to by the many requests he received for copies of his works, by the accounts of public readings of them which Gregory so greatly deprecated, by requests for new interpretations of, for instance, the acts of Samson, and by the circulation of pirate editions of his homilies and even of Greek forgeries purporting to come from his pen.[24]

Matters theological lie outside the scope of this book, but it is important to note that Gregory's achievement as the last of the 'Big Four' Latin Fathers, following Tertullian, Ambrose and Augustine, was not to initiate a new theological departure or philosophical debate but to summarize what had gone before, to emphasize what seemed to him the cardinal points of Christian doctrine, and to make accessible the more complex and sophisticated doctrines articulated by his predecessors. It has been said of Gregory that he 'nowhere promulgated an original thought; he has rather preserved in everything the traditional doctrine'.[25] His influence on the theology of the Middle Ages was therefore immense. The medieval dominance of Augustine's ideas derived from their Gregorian manifestation and prevailed through the Gregorian transmission. Gregory was not a controversialist or a theoretician; he was not an original or speculative thinker. He was impatient of abstract thinking, committed to grounding Christian belief in recognizable personal experience. He was therefore pre-eminently a synthesizer and popularizer. His position was based on tradition and authority, hence the legalistic framework within which he cast the doctrines of merit, penance and retribution. For him, faith and not reason was the basis of Christianity, and the Bible and tradition were the sources of religious knowledge. His doctrines of Christ and God, the Trinity and the Incarnation, Penance and Purgatory, were distillations of the accepted orthodox thinking. He relied heavily on Augustine, in particular for his views on grace and predestination, the church and the sacraments.[26]

Gregory's second legacy is the English church, and it was the conversion of the Anglo-Saxons to Christianity and the consequent veneration of his memory in England that kept the flame of his reputation burning brightly in the West while he was being quietly forgotten in Rome. It was from England in the eighth century that the great missionary archbishops Boniface and Willibrord came to convert Germany and Flanders. Indeed, Boniface tried to obtain copies of Gregory's letters to the English mission as guidelines for his own evangelization programme.[27] Although after Gregory the papacy initiated few missionary offensives of its own, it was to Rome, because of Gregory, that the missionaries looked for legitimization and authoritative pronouncements on ritual, dogma, organization and discipline. Always there were Gregory's instructions to Augustine, 'referred to so often in succeeding ages that they assumed the force of canon law', as prime directives for all aspiring apostles of the heathen. By his actions and his example, then, Gregory can be seen to have played an important part in the christianization of Western Europe.[28]

For latter-day historians one of Gregory's most important legacies is the papal Register, 854 letters surviving from the fourteen volumes kept in the archive and consulted by John the Deacon for his biography.[29] They bear eloquent testimony to what is now seen to be one of Gregory's major achievements – the running of the complex and variegated papal administration in all its aspects. It is important to put this in perspective, however. The survival of the Gregorian letters only serves to point up the absence of any comparable collection. But what we know of, for instance, Gelasius I suggests that he may have been just as active in the fields of discipline and law, liturgical reform, central and patrimonial administration, and control of the episcopate.[30] It was, after all, Gelasius who first organized the papal patrimony and compiled the great account book still in use in the ninth century. John the Deacon describes Gregory as a careful follower of Gelasius.[31] There are hints too that Pelagius I mastered many of the same areas of government when undertaking the reconstruction after the Gothic Wars.[32] Pelagius II and Honorius I seem, from the tantalizing scraps of evidence that survive, to have been far from negligible performers in administration. If all the Registers had survived, a balanced picture would be much more likely. Since they are unlikely ever to surface, however, Gregory's reign provides the unique example of a close-up, impressively documented account of the early medieval papacy at work, and one which highlights Gregory's undeniable qualities as a ruler.

What, then, is the verdict of history on Gregory I? He was unquestionably a great man. He was on the one hand a man of profound *Christianitas*. Not an original thinker, he was nevertheless the last of the great Western patristic writers: popularizer and transmitter of Augustine, major link in handing on the exegetical tradition of the ancients, major force in the development of popular homiletic preaching. He powerfully promoted monasticism and propagated the Christian faith, through his missions to convert pagans and heretics, through his own teaching and writings. He was also a man of deep and abiding *Romanitas* – conservative and legalistic, devoted to the Christian Roman Empire and to the city of Rome, administrator and estate manager, paterfamilias and proconsul.

While his desire was to contemplate and to meditate in the privacy of his monastery, he subordinated his personal inclination to his duty. He returned to the hurly-burly of public life. He ascended the throne of St Peter at a time of encroaching darkness, in the certain knowledge that the end of the world was at hand. He did his duty as a Christian, a gentleman and a Roman. No one could have asked for more. Well did he deserve the title his epitaph bestowed – 'The Consul of God'.

> The tumult and the shouting dies,
> The captains and the kings depart,
> Still stands thine ancient sacrifice,
> An humble and a contrite heart.

Abbreviations

AB	*Analecta Bollandiana*
Acta SS.	*Acta Sanctorum*
AHR	*American Historical Review*
ASR	*Archivio della Reale Deputazione Romana di Storia Patria*
Bede, *HE*	Bede, *Historia Ecclesiastica*
BHL	*Bibliotheca Hagiographica Latina*
Cass., *Inst.*	Cassiodorus, *Institutiones*
Cass., *Var.*	Cassiodorus, *Variae*
Chron. Pat. Grad.	*Chronica Patriarcharum Gradensium*
CIL	*Corpus Inscriptionum Latinorum*
CJ	*Codex Justinianus*
CSEL	*Corpus Scriptorum Ecclesiasticorum Latinorum*
EL	*Ephemerides Liturgicae*
ep.	*epistulae*
ET	English translation
Greg., *Dial.*	Gregory I, *Dialogi*
Greg., *ep.*	Gregory I, *epistulae*
Greg., *Homil. in Evang.*	Gregory I, *Homiliae in Evangelia*
Greg., *Homil. in Ezech.*	Gregory I, *Homiliae in Ezechielem*
Greg., *MM*	Gregory I, *Magna Moralia*
Greg., *RP*	Gregory I, *Regula Pastoralis*
Greg. Tur., *HF*	Gregory of Tours, *Historia Francorum*
Greg. Tur., *Glor. Mart.*	Gregory of Tours, *Liber in Gloria Martyrum Beatorum*
Greg. Tur., *Vit. Pat.*	Gregory of Tours, *Liber Vitae Patrum*
HL	Paulus Diaconus, *Historia Langobardorum*
JEH	*Journal of Ecclesiastical History*
JL	P. Jaffe, ed., *Regesta Pontificum Romanorum*
JRS	*Journal of Roman Studies*
JTS	*Journal of Theological Studies*
LD	*Liber Diurnus*
Lib. Pont. Rav.	Agnellus Andreas, *Liber Pontificalis Ecclesiae Ravennatis*
LP	*Liber Pontificalis*

267

MAH	*Mélanges d'archéologie et d'histoire de l'école française de Rome*
Mansi	J. D. Mansi, *Sacrorum Conciliorum Nova et Amplissima Collectio*
MGH	*Monumenta Germaniae Historica*
MGH aa	*auctores antiquissimi*
MGH ep.	*epistulae*
MGH ep. Aust.	*epistulae Austrasicae, ep.* iii, pp. 110–53
MGH ep. Lang.	*epistulae Langobardicae, ep.* iii, pp. 691–715
MGH ep. Merov.	*epistulae Aevi Merovingici, ep.* iii, pp. 434–68
MGH Scr. Rer. Merov.	*Scriptores Rerum Merovingicarum*
MGH Scr. Rer. Lang.	*Scriptores Rerum Langobardicarum et Italicarum*
PG	J. P. Migne, *Patrologia Graeca*
PL	J. P. Migne, *Patrologia Latina*
Procopius, *BG*	Procopius, *De Bello Gothico*
Procopius, *BP*	Procopius, *De Bello Persico*
RB	*Revue Bénédictine*
Rer. It. Script.	L. A. Muratori, *Rerum Italicarum Scriptores*
Settimane	*Settimane di Studio del Centro Italiano di studi sull'Alto Medio Evo*
SMGBO	*Studien und Mitteilungen zur Geschichte des Benediktinorders und seiner Zweige* 57 (1939), pp. 209–24
Troya, *CDL*	Carlo Troya, ed., *Codice Diplomatico Longobardo*

Notes

1 The World of Gregory the Great

1 Pelagius I, *ep.* 85.
2 Procopius, *BG* vii. 30.
3 A. Chavasse, 'Les Messes du Pape Vigile dans le Sacramentaire Léonien', *EL* 64 (1950), pp. 161–213, *EL* 66 (1952), pp. 145–219.
4 Greg., *ep.* iv. 4.
5 Greg., *Dial.* ii. 5.
6 Greg., *Homil. in Evang.* i. 1. 5.
7 Paulus Diaconus, *HL* iv. 22.
8 It is first mentioned in *LP, Vita Johannis III*, p. 305. According to Duchesne this was composed under Pelagius II. But E. Griffe, 'Le *Liber Pontificalis* au temps du Pape St Grégoire', *Bulletin de Littérature Ecclésiastique* 57 (1956), pp. 65–70, argues persuasively that at the time of Gregory I the *Liber Pontificalis* only went up to the reign of Vigilius (537–55) and that subsequent lives were added in the early seventh century. The story is also retailed in Paulus Diaconus, *HL* ii. 6; Isidore of Seville, *Chronica* 402; Fredegar, *Chronica* iii. 65. If Griffe is correct, the Narses story can be dated no earlier than fifty years after the actual events.
9 Greg. Tur., *HF* iv. 41, cf. Paulus Diaconus, *HL* ii. 32.
10 Greg., *Dial.* i. 4, iii. 27, 28.
11 Paulus Diaconus, *HL* ii. 32.
12 G. Luzzatto, *An Economic History of Italy* (London, 1961), p. 20.
13 *LP, Vita Benedicti I*, p. 308.
14 Paulus Diaconus, *HL* iii. 19.
15 C. Troya, ed., *CDL* iv. i. 30.
16 Greg. *Dial.* iii. 8, *ep.* i. 66.
17 S. Brechter, 'Monte Cassino: erste Zerstörung', *SMGBO* 56 (1938), pp. 109–50.
18 *MGH ep. Merov.* 9.
19 Greg. Tur., *HF* vi. 42.
20 *MGH ep.* ii appendix 2.
21 The first holder of the post may have been the patrician Decius, mentioned in Pelagius II's letter to Gregory though not specifically as exarch. He was probably a Roman aristocrat and perhaps the son of one of the last Western consuls, Flavius Decius jr, who fled to Constantinople during the Gothic wars. There is no other reference to this patrician, and if this Decius was exarch it can only have been briefly.
22 Paulus Diaconus, *HL* iii. 18; *MGH ep.* ii appendix 3. i.
23 *MGH ep. Aust.* 40.
24 *MGH ep. Aust.* 41.
25 Greg. Tur., *HF* x. 3; *MGH ep. Aust.* 40.
26 Paulus Diaconus, *HL* iii. 35.
27 Procopius, *BP* ii. 22–3.
28 Greg., *Dial.* iv. 36.
29 Greg., *ep.* ix. 232.

30 Paulus Diaconus, *HL* ii. 26.
31 Greg., *Dial.* iii. 8.
32 Paulus Diaconus, *HL* ii. 4, iv. 4;
   Greg., *Dial.* iv. 26.
33 *LP, Vita Benedicti I,* p. 308.
34 Paulus Diaconus, *HL* iii. 23.
35 Greg. Tur., *HF* x. 1; Paulus
   Diaconus, *HL* iii. 24; *LP, Vita
   Pelagii II,* p. 309.
36 Paulus Diaconus, *HL* iv. 4;
   Greg., *ep.* ii. 4.
37 Paulus Diaconus, *HL* iv. 2.
38 Paulus Diaconus, *HL* iv. 14;
   Greg., *ep.* ix. 232.
39 J. B. Bury, *History of the Later
   Roman Empire* (London, 1923),
   ii. p. 62.
40 Gelasius I, *Tractate VI.*
41 Greg., *Dial.* i. 4; Cass., *Var.* iv.
   22, 23.
42 Greg., *ep.* x. 2.
43 P. Brown, 'The Rise and
   Function of the Holy Man in
   Late Antiquity', *JRS* 61 (1971),
   pp. 80–101; P. Brown, 'Sorcery,
   Demons and the Rise of
   Christianity: from Late
   Antiquity into the Middle
   Ages', *Religion and Society in the
   Age of St. Augustine* (London,
   1972), pp. 119–46.
44 Greg., *Dial.* iii. 7.
45 Greg., *Dial.* i. 4.
46 On the survival of paganism,
   see E. Vacandard, 'L'idolâtrie
   en Gaule au VIe et au VIIe
   siècle', *Revue des Questions
   Historiques* 65 (1899), pp.
   424–54; S. McKenna, *Paganism
   and Pagan Survivals in Spain*
   (Washington, DC, 1938). There
   is a selection of original sources
   on paganism in J. N. Hillgarth,
   ed., *The Conversion of Western
   Europe 350–750* (Englewood
   Cliffs, NJ, 1969). Cf. also St
   Caesarius of Arles, *Sermones*
   129, 130, 265, 278, 279, 277.
47 *PL* 87, p. 444.
48 Greg., *ep.* viii. 4.
49 Greg., *Dial.* iii. 27.
50 Cass., *Inst.* i. 32.
51 Greg., *Dial.* ii. 8.
52 Greg., *Dial.* ii. 19.
53 Greg., *Dial.* viii. 19.
54 Liutprand, *Leges* 84. i. (727),
   MGH Leges iv. p. 142.
55 Greg. Tur., *Vit. Pat.* vi. 2.
56 *Vita S. Radegundis* ii. 2.
57 Greg. Tur., *HF* viii. 15.
58 *MGH Scr. Rer. Merov.* iv. p.
   260.
59 H. Delehaye, *The Legends of the
   Saints* (London, 1962).
60 Paulus Diaconus, *HL* iv. 36.
   This process was not just
   confined to Rome. As already
   noted, the temple of Apollo on
   Monte Cassino became a chapel
   of St Martin, and the temple of
   Apollo where the demons
   gathered (Greg., *Dial.* iii. 7)
   became a chapel of St Andrew.
61 Greg. Tur., *Glor. Mart.,
   Praefatio.*
62 Greg., *Dial.* i. 10.
63 *Whitby Life* 22.
64 Greg., *ep.* iv. 30.
65 *LD* 12, 16, 17.
66 Greg., *Dial.* iii. 15, i. 2; Greg.
   Tur., *HF* iii. 29.
67 Greg., *ep.* ix. 45, 59, 181, xi. 19.
68 Cummian, *De Controversia
   Paschali,* pp. 977–8.
69 P. Llewellyn, *Rome in the Dark
   Ages* (London, 1971), p. 173–98.
70 *Collectio Avellana* 218; Greg., *ep.*
   iv. 30.
71 John McCulloch, 'The cult of
   relics in the letters and
   Dialogues of Pope Gregory the
   Great', *Traditio* 32 (1976), pp.
   145–84.
72 Greg., *ep.* iv. 30.
73 Greg., *ep.* i. 25 (Patriarch
   Anastasius of Antioch), i. 29
   (Andreas *vir illustris*), i. 30
   (*Quaestor* John), iii. 47 (Bishop
   Columbus of Numidia), vi. 6
   (King Childebert of Gaul), vii.
   23 (Princess Theoctista), vii. 25
   (imperial physician Theodore),
   viii. 33 (ex-consul Leontius), ix.
   228 (King Reccared of Spain),

xi. 43 (Governor Asclipiodotus
of Provence), xii. 2 (patricians
Savinella, Columba and Galla
in Africa), xiii. 45 (Patriarch
Eulogius of Alexandria).
74 Greg., *ep.* vi. 6.
75 Greg., *ep.* xiii. 45.
76 Greg., *Homil. in Ezech.* ii. 6. 22.

2 Gregory's Early Life

1 The evidence is examined in
detail in W. Stuhlfath, *Gregor
der Grosse* (Heidelberg, 1913),
appendix 1.
2 Greg. Tur., *HF* x. 1 calls it *de
senatoribus primis*.
3 *MGH ep.* ii appendix i; Greg.
Tur., *HF* x. 1.
4 Joannes Diaconus, *Vita Gregorii*
iv. 83.
5 Greg., *ep.* i. 39, 42, ii. 38
(Antoninus); i. 63, ix. 92
(Consentius).
6 Joannes Diaconus, *Vita Gregorii*
i. 9; her name is known from
the *Whitby Life* 1.
7 Greg., *Dial.* iv. 16; *Homil. in
Evang.* 38.
8 Greg., *ep.* i. 37.
9 For a detailed discussion, see J.
Richards, *The Popes and the
Papacy in the Early Middle Ages
476–752* (London, 1979), pp.
238–40.
10 Greg. Tur., *HF* x. 1.
11 Close textual exegesis of his
works has yielded the evidence
of his rhetorical training. See
H. M. Swank, *Gregor der Grosse
als Prediger* (Berlin, 1934);
Kathleen Brazzel, *The Clausulae
in the Works of St. Gregory the
Great* (Washington, DC., 1939).
12 Joannes Diaconus, *Vita Gregorii*
i. 1.
13 P. Courcelle, 'St Grégoire le
Grand à l'école de Juvenal',
*Studi e Materiali di storia delle
religioni* 38 (1967), pp. 120–4;
Th. Delforge, 'Le *Songe de*

Scipion et la vision de St
Benoît,' *RB* 69 (1959), pp.
351–4; L. Weber, *Hauptfragen
der Moraltheologie Gregors des
Grossen* (Freiburg, 1947), pp. 57,
66; P. Riché, *Education and
Culture in the Barbarian West*
(Columbia, SC, 1976), pp.
146–7.
14 Riché, *op. cit.*, pp. 148–51.
15 Dag Norberg, *In Registrum
Gregorii Magni Studia Critica*
(Uppsala, 1937–9), 2 vols; J. F.
O'Donnell, *The Vocabulary of the
Letters of St. Gregory the Great*
(Washington, DC, 1935); R. M.
Hauber, *The Late Latin
Vocabulary of the Moralia of St.
Gregory the Great* (Washington,
DC, 1938).
16 Greg., *ep.* vii. 29, iii. 63, xi. 55.
He had to have the trial records
of Adrian of Thebes read for
him because they were in
Greek (iii. 7).
17 Greg., *ep.* xi. 55.
18 Greg., *ep.* i. 28, viii. 27, x. 14,
21. On the knowledge of Greek
in the West in the sixth
century, see P. Courcelle, *Late
Latin Writers and their Greek
Sources* (Cambridge, Mass.,
1969). On Gregory's knowledge
of Greek, see Joan M. Petersen,
'Did Gregory the Great Know
Greek?', *Studies in Church
History* 13 (1976), pp. 121–34.
19 Greg., *ep.* vii. 31, viii. 29.
20 F. Halkin, 'La Juridiction
Suprême du Pape', *AB* 89
(1971), p. 310.
21 John of Salisbury, *Policraticus* ii.
26. On the development of the
medieval legend of Gregory's
enmity to profane culture, see
T. Buddenseig, 'Gregory the
Great, destroyer of pagan
idols', *Journal of the Warburg and
Courtauld Institutes* 38 (1965),
pp. 44–65.
22 Greg., *ep.* v. 53.
23 Greg., *ep.* xi. 34.

24 P. Riché, *op. cit.*, pp. 152–7; C. Dagens, *St Grégoire le Grand: culture et expérience chrétiennes* (Paris, 1977), pp. 31–54; H. de Lubac, *Exégèse Médiévale* (Paris, 1959–61), ii. I, pp. 53–77.

25 Greg., *In Librum Primum Regum Expositionum Libri* v. 30.

26 On the background to Gregory's view see G. L. Ellspermann, *The Attitude of Early Christian Latin Writers Towards Pagan Literature and Learning* (Washington, DC, 1949); M. L. W. Laistner, 'The Christian Attitude to Pagan Literature', *History* 20 (1935), pp. 49–54.

27 Greg., *MM* xviii. 74.

28 Greg., *ep.* iv. 2.

29 *Ibid.*, note h.

30 Joannes Diaconus, *Vita Gregorii*, i. 4.

31 Greg., *ep.* ii. 38.

32 Boethius, *De Philosophiae Consolatione* iii. 4.

33 Greg., *ep.* xi. 4. See also his advice to Praetor Justin of Sicily (i. 2).

34 Greg., *MM, Praefatio* = Greg., *ep.* v. 53a. On Gregory's conversion see C. Dagens, 'La conversion de St Grégoire le Grand', *Revue des Études Augustiniennes* 15 (1969), pp. 149–62.

35 Greg. Tur., *HF* x. 1.

36 *MGH ep.* ii appendix 1.

37 E. Caspar, *Geschichte des Papsttums* (Tübingen, 1933), ii, p. 342.

38 Joannes Diaconus, *Vita Gregorii* i. 6.

39 Greg., *Dial.* iv. 21, i. 4, iii. 22.

40 Greg., *Dial.* iv. 55.

41 Greg., *Dial.* iii. 36, iv. 22, iv. 33, 49; Greg., *ep.* viii. 29, ix. 222.

42 Greg., *ep.* xi. 26; Joannes Diaconus, *Vita Gregorii* i. 11–14.

43 Greg., *Dial.* iv. 21, iii. 22, i. 4. Indeed, several of Gregory's monks were Valerian refugees.

44 *MGH ep.* ii appendix 2; Joannes Diaconus, *Vita Gregorii* i. 33; Greg., *Dial.* iii. 36.

45 *MGH ep.* ii appendix 1; Greg., *ep.* i. 14a; Greg., *Dial.* iii. 36.

46 S. Brechter, 'War Gregor der Grosse Abt vor seiner Erhebung zum Papst?', *SMGBO* 57 (1939), pp. 209–24.

47 The argument against the Rule of Benedict being in use at St Andrew's is forcefully put by K. Hallinger, 'Papst Gregor der Grosse und der Hl. Benedikt', *Studia Anselmiana* 42 (1957), pp. 231–319. The use of the Rule is defended by O. Porcel, *La Doctrina Monastica de San Gregorio Magno* (Madrid, 1951).

48 Justinian, *Novellae* 5, 133.

49 A. de Vogüé, 'La Règle du Maître et les *Dialogues* de St Grégoire', *Revue d'Histoire Ecclésiastique* 61 (1966), i, pp. 44–76.

50 Hallinger, *op. cit.*, argues that Gregory did not even know the Rule, but this view is contradicted by Gregory's own testimony (*Dial.* ii. 36) and has not found general support.

51 St Benedict of Nursia, *Regula Monachorum*, ed. J. McCann (London, 1952).

52 Monks who tried to run away from St Andrew's were invariably caught out by miracles (Greg., *ep.* xi. 25).

53 Greg., *ep.* xii. 6.

54 Greg., *Dial.* iv. 47.

55 Greg., *Dial.* iv. 55.

56 Greg., *Dial.* i, *Praefatio.*

57 Greg., *ep.* v. 53a.

58 Joannes Diaconus, *Vita Gregorii* i. 25.

59 Greg., *ep.* v. 53a.

60 *MGH ep.* ii appendix 3.

61 Greg., *ep.* i. 75.

62 Greg., *ep.* xiii. 22.

63 Greg., *ep.* iv. 34.

64 *LP, Vita Pelagii II*, p. 309.

65 J. B. De Rossi, *Inscriptiones Christianae* ii, pp. 63, 106, 157.
66 Menander, *Fragmenta* 29.
67 Greg., *ep.* v. 53a.
68 Greg., *ep.* i. 41.
69 Greg., *ep.* v. 53a.
70 Greg., *MM* xiv. 72–4; Bede, *HE* ii. 1; Paulus Diaconus, *Vita Gregorii* 9; Joannes Diaconus, *Vita Gregorii* i. 28–30.
71 *MGH ep.* ii. appendix 2.
72 Greg. Tur., *HF* x. 1; Joannes Diaconus, *Vita Gregorii* i. 40.
73 *MGH ep.* ii appendix 3. i. Redemptus' see is not given but a likely identification would be the homonymous bishop of Ferentis of Greg., *Dial.* iii. 38.
74 *MGH ep.* ii appendix 3. ii.
75 Paulus Diaconus, *HL* iii. 20; *MGH ep.* ii appendix 3. iii.
76 Greg., *ep.* ii. 51.
77 Paulus Diaconus, *HL* iii. 26.
78 Greg. Tur., *HF* x. 1.
79 Joannes Diaconus, *Vita Gregorii* i. 39–40; Paulus Diaconus, *Vita Gregorii* 10; Greg. Tur., *HF* x. 1.
80 Paulus Diaconus, *HL* iii. 24; Greg. Tur., *HF* x. 1. The suggestion of O. Chadwick, 'Gregory of Tours and Gregory the Great', *JTS* 50 (1949), pp. 38–49, that the account of this is interpolated from the reign of Gregory II, in which Rome also experienced heavy floods, has not found support.
81 Greg. Tur., *HF* x. 1.
82 *Whitby Life* 7; Paulus Diaconus, *Vita Gregorii* 13; Joannes Diaconus, *Vita Gregorii* i. 44.
83 Greg., *ep.* i. 30 (*Quaestor* John); i. 26 (Archbishop Anastasius of Corinth); i. 29 (*vir illustris* Andreas); i. 31 (Philippicus, *comes excubitorum*); i. 3 (*scholasticus* Paul); i. 4 (Patriarch John of Constantinople); i. 5 (Princess Theoctista); i. 6 (Narses, patrician); i. 7 (ex-Patriarch Anastasius of Antioch).

84 Greg., *ep.* i. 20.

3 Character and Outlook

1 Joannes Diaconus, *Vita Gregorii* iv. 84. See G. B. Ladner, *I Ritratti dei Papi nell'antichità e nel medio evo* (Vatican, 1941), pp. 70–5.
2 Greg. Tur., *HF* x. 1.
3 Greg., *ep.* v. 53a.
4 Greg., *Dial.* iii. 33.
5 Joannes Diaconus, *Vita Gregorii* i. 7.
6 *Ibid.*, i. 9.
7 Greg., *ep.* xii. 6.
8 Greg., *Homil. in Evang.* ii. 21, 22.
9 Greg., *ep.* iii. 61.
10 Greg, *Homil. in Evang.* ii. 34. i.
11 Greg., *ep.* ix. 227.
12 He was ill in July 598 (Greg., *ep.* viii. 29), October 598 (ix. 13), May 599 (ix. 147), July 599 (ix. 173, 175), August 599 (ix. 227, 232), January 601 (xi. 18), February 601 (xi. 20, 26), August 602 (xii. 6), July 603 (xiii. 45).
13 Greg., *ep.* ix. 232.
14 Greg., *ep.* x. 14.
15 Greg., *ep.* xi. 20.
16 Greg., *ep.* xiii. 26.
17 Greg., *ep.* xiv. 12.
18 Greg., *RP* i. 11.
19 Greg., *Dial.* iii. 33, 35, iv. 16, xi. 56. The physician is mentioned in *ep.* xiii. 44.
20 Greg., *ep.* xi. 21.
21 Greg., *ep.* xiii. 45.
22 Greg., *ep.* xiv. 15.
23 *Whitby Life* 23.
24 Greg., *RP* iii. 12.
25 Paulus Diaconus, *Vita Gregorii* 15.
26 Greg., *ep.* x. 14, 15.
27 Greg., *ep.* ii. 52; Greg., *Homil. in Evang.* i. 7. 4.
28 Greg., *MM* iii. 43, 60.
29 *MGH ep.* ii appendix 1; Greg., *ep.* i. 14a, i. 39a, iv. 17a, v. 53a, vi. 50a, xii. 16a.

30 Bede, *HE* ii. 10, 11, 17.
31 Greg., *ep.* vii. 9.
32 Greg., *ep.* x. 16.
33 Greg., *ep.* xii. 16a.
34 Greg., *ep.* xii. 6.
35 *Ibid.*
36 Greg., *ep.* xii. 5 (Oportunus); ii. 38 (Pretiosus).
37 Greg., *ep.* v. 36.
38 Greg., *ep.* iii. 52.
39 Greg., *ep.* ii. 50.
40 Greg., *Homil. in Ezech.* i. 11. 5–6.
41 Greg., *ep.* viii. 25.
42 Greg., *ep.* i. 39a.
43 Greg., *ep.* ix. 26.
44 Greg., *ep.* ix. 107.
45 Greg., *Dial.* iv. 18.

4 Gregory's World-View

1 Greg., *ep.* xiii. 1.
2 Greg., *Homil. in Ezech.* ii. 6, 22, i. 7. 22, 23.
3 Greg., *ep.* viii. 22.
4 Greg., *ep.* iii. 63.
5 E. Caspar, *Geschichte des Papsttums* (Tübingen, 1933), p. 347.
6 Greg., *ep.* vi. 14.
7 Greg., *ep.* v. 37.
8 Greg., *ep.* v. 45.
9 Greg., *Homil. in Evang.* i. 1. 5.
10 Greg., *Homil. in Evang.* i. 1. 3, i. 4. 2; Greg., *ep.* iii. 29, 61, iv. 23, 44, ix. 232, xi. 37.
11 Greg., *ep.* xi. 37.
12 Greg., *ep.* iii. 29.
13 This feeling is put into context by S. Mazzarino, 'The judgements of God as an historical category', *The End of the Ancient World* (London, 1966), pp. 58–76.
14 C. Dagens, *St Grégoire le Grand* (Paris, 1977) p. 347.
15 Greg., *MM* xxxv. 35. See Dagens, *op. cit.*, pp. 312–19.
16 Greg., *Homil. in Ezech.* ii. 9. 6.
17 Greg., *Dial.* ii. 36.

18 Greg., *MM* xxiv. 28. Cf. *MM* xxxiii. 26.
19 Greg., *MM* xx. 19.
20 Greg., *MM* xxvii. 62; Greg., *Dial.* ii. 1.
21 Greg., *Homil. in Ezech.* ii. 2.
22 E. C. Butler, *Western Mysticism* (London, 1951), p. 67.
23 Greg., *MM* xxv. 3.
24 Paulus Diaconus, *HL* iv. 5.
25 Greg., *ep.* xi. 30.
26 Greg., *Homil. in Ezech.* i. 11. 6.
27 Greg., *Dial., Praefatio.*
28 Greg., *Homil. in Ezech.* ii. 2. 7–8.
29 Greg., *RP* iii. 5.
30 Greg., *MM* xxi. 22.
31 Greg., *ep.* vi. 12.
32 Greg., *ep.* ix. 123; *ep.* ix. 98 (to Bishop Felix of Portus), vii. 27 (to Narses *religiosus*), iii. 18 (to Theodore *consiliarius*).
33 Greg., *ep.* ix. 191, 200, 144.
34 Greg., *RP* iii. 4.
35 Greg., *MM* xxv. 34.
36 Greg., *MM* xxv. 37.
37 Greg., *ep.* i. 39a.
38 Greg., *ep.* ii. 38.
39 Greg., *ep.* v. 29.
40 On the development of papal ideology in the fourth and fifth centuries, see W. Ullmann, *A Short History of the Papacy in the Middle Ages* (London, 1972), pp. 4–27, and 'Leo I and the theme of Papal Primacy', *JTS* n.s. 11 (1960), pp. 25–51; E. Caspar, *op. cit.*, vol. i; F. Dvornik, *Byzantium and the Roman Primacy* (New York, 1966).
41 F. Susman, 'Il Culto di San Pietro a Roma dalla morte di Leone Magno a Vitaliano', *ASR* 84 (1961), pp. 1–192.
42 Greg., *ep.* v. 59.
43 *PL* 20. 552.
44 Greg. Tur., *HF* v. 20.
45 *MGH ep. Merov.* 9.
46 Greg., *ep.* viii. 10.
47 Greg., *ep.* ii. 52.
48 Gelasius I, *ep.* 4.
49 On appeals to Rome from the

East, see J. J. Taylor's 'Eastern Appeals to Rome in the Early Church: a little known witness', *Downside Review* 89 (1971), pp. 142–6; P. Bernadakis, 'Les appels au Pape dans l'église Grecque jusqu'à Photius', *Echos d'Orient* 6 (1903), pp. 30–42, 193–264.

50 Greg., *ep.* v. 37. Cf. Ullmann, *A Short History of the Papacy in the Middle Ages*, p. 57: 'While the idea of Papal *principatus* was in the foreground of Gregory's dealings with Western governments, not once did the term appear in all his official correspondence with the Imperial government.'

51 Greg., *ep.* iii. 30, ix. 26, ii. 50.

52 Ullmann, *A Short History of the Papacy in the Middle Ages*, pp. 54–7.

53 N. Sharkey, *St. Gregory the Great's Concept of Papal Primacy* (Washington, DC, 1950). He cites at least fifty-eight references to *Princeps Apostolorum*, p. 7 n. 35.

54 Greg., *Homil. in Ezech.* ii. 6. 9.

55 Greg., *ep.* xi. 24, ii. 50, viii. 29, ix. 27.

56 Greg., *ep.* ii. 52.

57 K. F. Morrison, *Tradition and Authority in the Western Church 300–1140* (Princeton, NJ, 1969), pp. 124–40.

58 Greg., *ep.* v. 42, vi. 58, vii. 37.

59 Greg., *ep.* vii. 37.

60 Greg., *ep.* v. 59.

61 For a full discussion of the theory, see F. Dvornik, *Early Christian and Byzantine Political Philosophy*, 2 vols (Dumbarton Oaks, 1966).

62 Gelasius I, *ep.* 12.

63 J. Richards, *The Popes and the Papacy in the Early Middle Ages 476–752* (London, 1979), pp. 9–28.

64 Greg., *RP* iii. 4.

65 Greg., *ep.* iii. 61.

66 Greg., *ep.* v. 37.

5 The Gregorian Court Circle

1 Joannes Diaconus, *Vita Gregorii* iv. 80.

2 Greg., *ep.* vii. 37.

3 Joannes Diaconus, *Vita Gregorii* ii. 12.

4 Greg., *ep.* v. 53a.

5 Greg., *ep.* v. 57a.

6 Greg., *ep.* xi. 56a. i.

7 Greg., *ep.* iii. 50.

8 Joannes Diaconus, *Vita Gregorii* ii. 11.

9 *Ibid.*, iii. 7.

10 *LP, Vita Gregorii I*, p. 312.

11 Greg., *ep.* xiii. 41.

12 Greg., *Dial., Praefatio*.

13 Greg., *ep.* vi. 24, iii. 54.

14 For example, F. H. Dudden, *Gregory the Great: His Place in History and Thought* (London, 1905), i, p. 305, and T. Hodgkin, *Italy and her Invaders* (Oxford, 1896), v, pp. 310–19.

15 Greg., *ep.* ii. 38.

16 Greg., *Dial. passim*.

17 Greg., *ep.* iii. 54.

18 Greg., *ep.* ix. 11.

19 Greg., *ep.* ix. 219.

20 Joannes Diaconus, *Vita Gregorii* iv. 69.

21 Greg., *ep.* i. 6.

22 *MGM ep.* ii appendix 2.

23 *MGH ep. Aust.* 32.

24 Greg., *ep.* ii. 1.

25 Greg., *ep.* v. 44.

26 Greg., *ep.* iii. 51, 52, 66, vii. 23, 25, 29.

27 Greg., *ep.* vii. 27, 28.

28 Greg., *ep.* i. 11.

29 Greg., *ep.* xi. 29.

30 Greg., *ep.* xii. 6.

31 Greg., *ep.* xiii. 41.

32 Greg., *ep.* i. 25, 26.

33 Greg., *ep.* viii. 16.

34 Greg., *ep.* v. 35.

35 Greg., *ep.* xiii. 45. The other letter (*ep.* xiv. 3) gives Bishop John of Palermo permission to

exchange with Epiphanius a derelict house in Rome belonging to the church of Palermo.

36 Greg., *ep.* ix. 8.
37 Greg., *ep.* iii. 5.
38 Greg., *Dial.* ii. 8.
39 Greg., *Dial.* iii. 20.
40 Greg., *ep.* ix. 72.
41 Greg., *ep.* i. 50.
42 Greg., *ep.* iv. 11.
43 Greg., *ep.* vi. 31.
44 Greg., *ep.* iii. 55, iv. 6, 15; v. 7, 20, 23, 28, 32, 33, vi. 4, 13, 20, 36, vii. 19, 38, 41 (Cyprian); i. 42, ix. 8, xiii. 22 (Servusdei).
45 Joannes Diaconus, *Vita Gregorii* ii. 11; Greg., *ep.* xi. 15.
46 Greg., *ep.* v. 26, vi. 12, ix. 97.
47 Joannes Diaconus, *Vita Gregorii* ii. 11.
48 Greg., *ep.* xi. 15.
49 Greg., *ep.* v. 6.
50 Greg., *ep.* vii. 29.
51 Greg., *Dial.* ii. 18.
52 Greg., *ep.* iii. 54.
53 Greg., *ep.* iii. 40, 41.
54 Greg., *ep.* viii. 26.
55 Greg., *ep.* ix. 19.
56 Greg., *ep.* xi. 6, 14.
57 Greg., *ep.* xiii. 47, 49, 50.
58 Greg., *ep.* vii. 13.
59 Greg., *ep.* iii. 18.
60 Greg., *ep.* vi. 24.
61 Greg., *Dial.* iv. 12, 17, 19, 38.
62 Greg., *Dial.* iv. 12.
63 Joannes Diaconus, *Vita Gregorii* ii. 11; Greg., *ep.* ix. 44, 67.
64 Greg., *ep.* vii. 36.
65 Greg., *ep.* iv. 17a, ix. 75, viii. 3, 30, v. 57, 62.
66 Greg., *ep.* v. 57.
.67 Greg., *ep.* v. 57a.
68 Greg., *Dial.* iv. 26, 51, 55; *ep.* ix. 98.
69 Greg., *ep.* iv. 23, 25, 26, 27, v. 2.
70 They include his predecessor Pope Pelagius II, Bishop Albinus of Reate, Bishop Redemptus of Ferentis, Abbot Valentio of St Andrew's, and

Julian, *secundicerius defensorum* (*Dial.* i. 4, iii. 38, iv. 30, iii. 22, iv. 22).
71 'An old pauper from Tuder', 'an old priest from Ocriculum', 'an old cleric from Ferentis', 'an old shoemaker of Rome', 'the old monk Laurio' (*Dial.* iv. 33, i. 10, i. 9, i. 7, iv. 31, iii. 12).
72 Tribune John, Vicar John, Antonius *vir illustris*, Stephanus *vir illustris*, Liberius *vir magnificus* (*Dial.* iii. 19, iii. 10, iii. 52, iv. 53, ii. 26, iv. 36).
73 Greg., *Dial.* i. 7, iv. 32, iii. 20, iv. 12, 17, 38.
74 Greg., *Homil. in Evang.* ii. 39. 10.
75 Greg., *Dial.* iii. 15, 9, 10, 11, iv. 53, i. 4, 11, 12.
76 Greg., *ep.* ii. 1.
77 J. B. De Rossi, *Inscriptiones Christianae Urbis Romae* (Rome, 1861–88), ii, p. 127.
78 *LP*, *Vita Sabiniani*, p. 315.
79 Joannes Diaconus, *Vita Gregorii* iv. 69.
80 *LP*, *Vita Sabiniani*, p. 315.
81 Paulus Diaconus, *Vita Gregorii* 29.
82 *LP*, *Vita Bonifacii III*, p. 316; *LP*, *Vita Bonifacii IV*, p. 317; Bede, *HE* ii. 4; De Rossi *Inscriptiones Christianae* ii, p. 128.
83 De Rossi, *Inscriptiones Christianae* ii, p. 127; *LP*, *Vita Deusdedit*, p. 319.
84 *LP*, *Vita Bonifacii V*, p. 321.
85 *LP*, *Vita Honorii I*, pp. 323–7. Cf. also J. Richards, *The Popes and the Papacy in the Early Middle Ages 476–752* (London, 1979), pp. 179–80.
86 *LP*, *Vita Adeodati*, pp. 346–7.

6 Central Administration: (1) War, Finance and Supply

1 Greg., *ep.* i. 7.
2 Greg., *ep.* v. 40. Cf. also v. 42, viii. 2.

3 Greg., *ep.* ix. 162, ix. 207.
4 Greg., *ep.* vii. 3, viii. 19, ix. 11.
5 Greg., *ep.* viii. 22.
6 Greg., *Homil. in Ezech.* i. 2. 26, i. 11. 6.
7 Greg., *ep.* v. 39.
8 Greg., *ep.* v. 36.
9 Greg., *ep.* i. 2.
10 Greg., *ep.* ix. 106.
11 Greg., *ep.* x. 8.
12 Greg., *ep.* ix. 115. Cf. ix. 31.
13 Greg., *ep.* i. 70.
14 *LP, Vita Sabiniani*, p. 315; Paulus Diaconus, *HL* iv. 24.
15 O. Bertolini, 'Per la storia della diaconie Romane nell'alto medio evo alla fine del secolo VIII', *ASR* 70 (1947), pp. 1–145; J. Lestocquoy, 'L'administration de Rome et des Diaconies du VIIe au IXe siècle', *Rivista di Archeologia Cristiana* 7 (1930), pp. 261–98.
16 Greg., *ep.* xii. 6.
17 Greg., *ep.* ix. 239.
18 Greg., *ep.* ii. 38.
19 Greg., *ep.* i. 39a; iii. 5.
20 Greg., *ep.* i. 2.
21 Greg., *ep.* i. 70, vii. 19.
22 Greg., *ep.* i. 47, 59.
23 Greg., *ep.* v. 38. When Gregory refers to 'sovereigns', he is including Maurice's son, Theodosius, who had been made co-emperor.
24 Greg., *ep.* xiv. 2.
25 Greg., *ep.* ix. 113.
26 Greg., *ep.* ix. 53.
27 Greg., *ep.* ix. 79.
28 Greg., *ep.* ix. 6.
29 Greg., *ep.* ii. 36.
30 Greg., *ep.* xi. 4.
31 Greg., *ep.* ix. 103.
32 Greg., *ep.* i. 35.
33 Greg., *ep.* ix. 4.
34 Greg., *ep.* ix. 55, 56, 57.
35 Greg., *ep.* ix. 182.
36 Greg., *ep.* ix. 63, 130.
37 Greg., *ep.* ix. 130.
38 Greg., *ep.* ix. 4.
39 Greg. *ep.* viii. 16. On the growth of the papal administration in the sixth and seventh centuries, see J. Richards, *The Popes and the Papacy in the Early Middle Ages 476–752* (London, 1979), pp. 289–306.
40 Joannes Diaconus, *Vita Gregorii* ii. 54.
41 Greg., *ep.* v. 57a.
42 Greg., *ep.* i. 11.
43 Greg., *ep.* v. 30, vii. 23, viii. 22, vii. 25.
44 Greg., *ep.* vii. 9.
45 On the *quadripartitum* see A. H. M. Jones, 'Church Finance in the 5th and 6th centuries', *JTS* n.s. 11 (1960), pp. 84–94.
46 *Continuatio Prosperi Havniensis* 17.
47 Joannes Diaconus, *Vita Gregorii* ii. 24. Cf. *ep.* viii. 7.
48 Joannes Diaconus, *Vita Gregorii* ii. 51, Greg., *ep.* xiii. 23.
49 Joannes Diaconus, *Vita Gregorii* ii. 30.
50 Greg., *ep.* i. 23, ii. 3, v. 35, ii. 38, xi. 2.
51 Joannes Diaconus, *Vita Gregorii* ii. 27, Greg., *ep.* vii. 23.
52 Greg., *ep.* i. 44, 65, iv. 28.
53 Greg., *ep.* ix. 109, ix. 136, ii. 38.
54 Greg., *ep.* i. 37, x. 12.
55 Greg., *ep.* i. 37, 57.
56 Greg., *ep.* iii. 21.
57 Greg., *ep.* iii. 55, iv. 43.
58 Greg., *ep.* vi. 4.
59 Greg., *ep.* vi. 45, 36, iv. 31.
60 Joannes Diaconus, *Vita Gregorii* ii. 26, 28.
61 Paulus Diaconus, *Vita Gregorii* 16.
62 *LP, Vita Gregorii*, p. 313.
63 Greg., *ep.* ix. 124–7.
64 *LP, Vita Gregorii*, p. 312; Greg., *Dial.* iii. 30, Greg., *ep.* iv. 19, iii. 19, Joannes Diaconus, *Vita Gregorii* ii. 31, 32.
65 Greg., *ep.* i. 42, iv. 42, v. 28, ix. 209, i. 39, v. 9, ii. 38, x. 1.
66 Greg., *Dial.* iii. 29, 14, 21, 33.
67 Greg., *ep.* iii. 17, ii. 10, vi. 42.
68 Greg., *ep.* v. 30, Joannes

Diaconus, *Vita Gregorii* ji. 27.
69 Greg., *ep.* iv. 6, 42.
70 Greg., *ep.* i. 48.
71 Greg., *ep.* i. 66.
72 Greg., *ep.* ix. 93, 94.
73 Greg., *ep.* iv. 15.
74 Greg., *ep.* viii. 26, ix. 19.
75 Greg., *ep.* ii. 42, iii. 41.
76 Greg., *ep.* vii. 13.
77 Greg., *ep.* vii. 35.
78 Greg., *ep.* iii. 40, 41, 42, iv. 17, ix. 52.
79 Greg., *ep.* vii. 23.
80 Greg., *ep.* iii. 16.
81 Greg., *ep.* vi. 32.
82 Greg., *ep.* ii. 42.
83 Greg., *ep.* i. 51.
84 Greg., *ep.* iii. 41.
85 Greg., *ep.* ix. 142.
86 *Ibid.*
87 Greg., *ep.* xi. 3.
88 Greg., *ep.* ii. 17, vi. 27, x. 13.
89 *LD* 9.
90 Greg., *ep.* i. 8, ii. 42, iii. 13, ii. 44, 48, iii. 20, ix. 60.
91 Greg., *ep.* ix. 102, 143.
92 Greg., *ep.* ix. 199.
93 Greg., *ep.* ix. 51.
94 Greg., *ep.* ix. 52.
95 Greg., *ep.* ix. 58, 59, 71, xiii. 18.
96 Greg., *ep.* xii. 4.
97 Greg., *ep.* xiii. 38. Uvintarit was probably a Lombard mercenary.
98 Greg., *ep.* xiii. 39.
99 Greg., *Dial.* iii. 37.
100 Greg., *Dial.* iii. 29.
101 *Vita S. Cethei, Acta SS.,* June ii, pp. 688–93.
102 Greg., *ep.* ix. 49, xiii. 39, ix. 59, ix. 166, ix. 107.
103 Greg., *ep.* i. 78.
104 *MGH ep. Lang.* 4.
105 Greg., *ep.* ix. 87.
106 Greg., *Dial.* iii. 14, 21, 33.

7 Central Administration: (2) Law, Discipline and Liturgy

1 Greg., *ep.* viii. 27.
2 Greg., *ep.* xiii. 50.
3 Greg., *ep.* ii. 38.
4 Greg., *ep.* viii. 3.
5 Greg., *ep.* ix. 48.
6 G. Damizia, 'Il *Registrum Epistolarum* di San Gregorio Magno ed il *Corpus Iuris Civilis',* *Benedictina* 2 (1948), iii–iv, pp. 195–226.
7 Greg., *ep.* vi. 62, ix. 104, i. 6, ix. 4, 121.
8 Greg., *ep.* ix. 128, i. 42.
9 Greg., *ep.* i. 53, ix. 52, iii. 40, iv. 17, vii. 13, 35.
10 Greg., *ep.* i. 64.
11 Greg., *ep.* ix. 2.
12 Greg., *ep.* v. 57a.
13 Gelasius I, *ep.* 14; Greg., *ep.* viii. 3, 35, iv. 23, v. 62.
14 Greg., *ep.* iv. 34, i. 42.
15 Greg., *ep.* i. 42.
16 Greg., *ep.* iv. 5.
17 Greg., *ep.* v. 18, iv. 26.
18 Greg., *ep.* i. 18, vii. 39, ix. 25, xii. 10, 11 (bishops); v. 5, 17, 18, viii. 24, ix. 25 (priests); iv. 26, v. 17, 18, xii. 3 (deacons); v. 17 (subdeacons).
19 Greg., *ep.* v. 5.
20 Greg., *ep.* v. 17, 18, v. 4, xiv. 2.
21 Gelasius I, *ep.* 14, 15, 16, 17; Greg., *ep.* xi. 56a, v. 48, i. 64, viii. 7.
22 Greg., *ep.* viii. 7, v. 27, xiii. 46, iv. 11.
23 Greg., *ep.* xiii. 22. Cf. ix. 122, 129, xiv. 4.
24 Greg., *ep.* ix. 110.
25 Greg., *ep.* xiii. 31.
26 Greg., *ep.* i. 81.
27 Greg., *ep.* viii. 27.
28 Gregory conceded the *pallium* to the archbishops of Ravenna, Milan, Salona, Corinth, Prima Justiniana, Arles, and Canterbury, and to the bishops of Messina, Syracuse, Palermo, Autun, and Nicopolis.
29 *PL* 80, p. 482.
30 *JL* 912 (Pope Vigilius to Auxanius of Arles); Greg., *ep.* viii. 4 (to Queen Brunhild on Syragrius of Autun's *pallium*).

31 Greg., *ep.* iii. 52.
32 Greg., *ep.* iii. 66.
33 Greg., *ep.* v.11.
34 Greg., *ep.* v. 15.
35 Greg., *ep.* v. 61.
36 Greg., *ep.* vi. 31.
37 Greg., *ep.* ix. 167.
38 Chalcedon 9, 19; Justinian, *Novellae* 123.
39 Greg., *ep.* ii. 5, iii. 53, 49, ix. 125, ix. 163, vii. 39. They are discussed in detail in Chapter 9.
40 Greg., *ep.* vi. 38.
41 Greg., *ep.* iii. 45.
42 Greg., *ep.* xiii. 29, x. 4, vi. 23, iii. 40, 42.
43 Greg., *ep.* i. 47.
44 Greg., *ep.* ii. 47.
45 Greg., *ep.* iii. 36.
46 Greg., *ep.* iv. 9. Cf. iv. 10.
47 Greg., *ep.* iv. 26.
48 Greg., *ep.* iv. 24, 26.
49 Greg., *ep.* viii. 35.
50 Greg., *ep.* ix. 11.
51 *Ibid.*
52 Greg., *ep.* ix. 198, 203, 204, x. 17.
53 Greg., *ep.* xiv. 2.
54 Greg., *ep.* iv. 26, xiii. 38, x. 2, ix. 69; x. 19; xii. 39; iv. 5; v. 32.
55 Greg., *ep.* iv. 22.
56 Greg., *ep.* iii. 54.
57 Greg., *ep.* v. 19.
58 Greg., *ep.* i. 39a. Cf. ix. 79.
59 Greg., *ep.* i. 35, ix. 4, 182, xi. 4, 16.
60 Greg., *ep.* iii. 1.
61 Greg., *ep.* x. 17.
62 F. H. Dudden, *Gregory the Great: His Place in History and Thought* (London, 1905), p. 391. He discusses the question at length and with great clarity and insight.
63 The best introductions to the subject are Th. Klauser, *A Short History of the Western Liturgy* (London and New York, 1969), and J. A. Jungmann, *Missarum Sollemnia: Eine genetische Erklärung der römischen Messe* (5th edn, Vienna, 1962), 2 vols.
64 Joannes Diaconus, *Vita Gregorii* ii. 17.
65 Walafrid Strabo, *De Rerum Ecclesiasticarum* 22; *Codex Carolinus, ep.* 89; Egbert of York, *Dialogus per interrogationes et responsiones de institutione ecclesiastica* xvi. 1, 2.
66 A Stuiber, *Libelli Sacramentorum Romani* (Bonn, 1950).
67 A. P. Lang, *Leo der Grosse und die Texte des Altgelasianums mit Berücksichtigung des Sacramentum Gregorianums* (Steyl, 1957); B. Capelle, 'Messes du Pape St Gélase dans le Sacramentaire Léonien', *RB* 36 (1945–6), pp. 12–41, and 'Retouches Gélasiennes dans le Sacramentaire Léonien', *RB* 61 (1951), pp. 1–14; C. Coebergh, 'Le Pape St Gélase, auteur de plusieurs messes et préfaces du soi-disant Sacramentaire Léonien', *Sacris Erudiri* 4 (1952), pp. 46–102; A. Chavasse, 'Les Messes du Pape Vigile dans le Sacramentaire Léonien', *EL* 64 (1950), pp. 161–213, *EL* 66 (1952), pp. 145–219; H. Ashworth, 'The influence of the Lombard invasions on the Gregorian Sacramentary', *Bulletin of the John Rylands Library* 36 (1953–4), pp. 305–27, and 'Gregorian Elements in the Gelasian Sacramentary', *EL* 67 (1953), pp. 9–23.
68 A. Chavasse, *Le Sacramentaire Gélasien* (Paris, 1957).
69 Greg., *ep.* ix. 26.
70 S. P. Van Dijk, 'The Urban and Papal Rites in the 7th and 8th centuries', *Sacris Erudiri* 12 (1961), pp. 411–87.
71 Th. Klauser, *Capitulare Evangeliorum* (Münster, 1935).
72 M. Andrieu, ed., *Les Ordines Romani du Haut Moyen Age* (Louvain, 1951).

73 H. Ashworth, 'The Liturgical
Prayers of St. Gregory the
Great', *Traditio* 15 (1959), pp.
107–61, and 'Did St. Gregory
the Great compose a
Sacramentary?', *Studia Patristica*
ii (Berlin, 1957), pp. 3–16; B.
Capelle, 'La main de St
Grégoire dans le Sacramentaire
Grégorien', *RB* 49 (1937), pp.
13–28; C. Coebergh, 'Le *Libelli
Sacramentorum* de St Grégoire le
Grand et le Sacramentaire
publié sous son nom', *Studia
Patristica* 8 (1966), pp. 176–88.
74 This view is supported by K.
Gamber, 'Das
Sonntagsmessbuch von Jena
und die Neufassung der
Sonntagsmessen durch Gregor
den Grossen', *Traditio* 15 (1959),
pp. 107–61, and C. Coebergh,
'Le *Libelli Sacramentorum* de St
Grégoire le Grand'.
75 J. Deshusses, 'Le Sacramentaire
Grégorien pré-Hadrianique', *RB*
80 (1970), pp. 213–37.
76 Greg., *ep.* ix. 26.
77 H. Ashworth, 'Did St.
Augustine bring the
Gregorianum to England?', *EL* 72
(1958), pp. 39–43.
78 Joannes Diaconus, *Vita Gregorii*
ii. 6; Walafrid Strabo, *De Rerum
Ecclesiasticarum* 22; Egbert of
York, *Dialogus* xvi. 1, 2.
79 S. P. Van Dijk, *op. cit.*
80 S. P. Van Dijk, 'Gregory the
Great – Founder of the Urban
Schola Cantorum', *EL* 77 (1963),
pp. 345–56.
81 On Gregorian chant, see W.
Appel, *Gregorian Chant*
(Bloomington, Ind., 1958), and
J. Smits van Waesberghe,
Gregorian Chant (London, 1949).

8   Patrimonial Administration

1 On the papal patrimony see M.
Moresco, *Il Patrimonio di San
Pietro* (Turin, 1916); E.
Spearing, *The Patrimony of the
Roman Church in the time of
Gregory the Great* (Cambridge,
1918); P. Partner, *The Lands of
St. Peter* (London, 1972); H.
Grisar, 'Ein Rundgang durch
die Patrimonien des heiligen
Stuhles um das Jahr 600',
Zeitschrift für katholische Theologie
i (1877), pp. 321–61, and
'Verwaltung und Haushalt der
päpstlichen Patrimonien um
das Jahr 600', *ibid.*, pp. 526–63;
J. Richards, *The Popes and the
Papacy in the Early Middle Ages
476–752* (London, 1979), pp.
307–22.
2 Greg., *Dial.* iii. 30; *ep.* iii. 19, iv.
19.
3 Greg., *ep.* iii. 17, ix. 74, ii. 10.
4 Theophanes, *Chronographia* a.m.
6224.
5 Agnellus, *Lib. Pont. Rav.* III.
6 F. H. Dudden, *Gregory the
Great: His Place in History and
Thought* (London, 1905), i, p.
296.
7 *JL* 633, Pelagius I, *ep.* 83.
8 Greg., *ep.* ix. 205, 206.
9 Greg., *ep.* i. 73.
10 Greg., *ep.* vi. 6, 51, iii. 33.
11 Greg., *ep.* vi. 10. Cf. also P.
Grierson, 'The *Patrimonium
Petri in Illis Partibus* and the
Pseudo-Imperial coinage in
Frankish Gaul', *Revue Belge de
Numismatique* 105 (1959), pp.
95–III.
12 Joannes Diaconus, *Vita Gregorii*
ii. 53 (North Africa), Greg., *ep.*
ii. 23 (Illyricum), *ep.* iii. 36
(Sardinia), i. 50 (Corsica).
13 Greg., *ep.* xi. 6. Cf. P. Fabre,
'Le Patrimoine de l'Église
Romaine dans les Alpes
Cottiennes', *MAH* 4 (1884), pp.
283–420.
14 *LD* 51–6.
15 Greg., *ep.* ix. 29.
16 These estates are discussed in
more detail in Richards, *op. cit.*,

pp. 311–14.

17 For a detailed discussion of leases and estate structure, see E. Spearing, *The Patrimony of the Roman Church in the time of Gregory the Great* (Cambridge, 1918).

18 Greg., *ep.* ii. 38.

19 Greg., *ep.* i. 70.

20 Greg., *ep.* ix. 78.

21 Greg., *ep.* xiii. 37, *LD* 52.

22 Greg., *ep.* ix. 33, 31, i. 2, *LD* 51–6.

23 Greg., *ep.* ix. 30.

24 Pelagius I, *ep.* 12, 88.

25 Greg., *ep.* ii. 38.

26 Greg., *ep.* i. 68, ix. 22.

27 Greg., *ep.* ii. 38.

28 Greg., *ep.* i. 9, 80, 71, 42, v. 33, ix. 40, 192.

29 Greg., *ep.* i. 42.

30 Greg., *ep.* i. 53.

31 Greg., *ep.* iii. 43.

32 Greg., *ep.* ii. 38, vii, 27, ix. 29, 30.

33 Greg., *ep.* xi. 24.

34 Joannes Diaconus, *Vita Gregorii* ii. 53, Greg., *ep.* ii. 38, ix. 199.

35 *JL* 633,

36 For details see Richards, *op. cit.*, pp. 314–15.

37 Joannes Diaconus, *Vita Gregorii* ii. 53.

38 Pelagius I, *ep.* 4, 9; Greg., *ep.* vi. 51.

39 Greg., *ep.* v. 31.

40 Greg., *ep.* vi. 5. Cf. vi. 6.

41 Greg., *ep.* vi. 51, 53.

42 Greg., *ep.* i. 73, 74, 75.

43 Greg., *ep.* i. 82, ii. 46, xii. 8, 9.

44 Greg., *ep.* i. 36.

45 Greg., *ep.* ii. 22, 45, iii. 22, v. 6.

46 Greg., *ep.* ii. 23.

47 Joannes Diaconus, *Vita Gregorii* iii. 53.

48 Greg., *ep.* ix. 203, 204. Cf. iii. 36, ix. 2, i. 50, ix. 110, xi. 58.

49 The known transfers of power took place in Lucania-Bruttium from the notary Peter to the subdeacon Sabinus (Greg., *ep.* ii. 3, v. 9, ix. 88, xiv. 9); in

Apulia, where the *defensor* Sergius was replaced by the notary Romanus (*ep.* viii. 8, 9, ix. 112, Joannes Diaconus, *Vita Gregorii* ii. 53); in Ravenna the notary Castorius was replaced by the subdeacon John (*ep.* iii. 54, ix. 234, xi. 16, xii. 13); in Tuscia where the *defensor* Candidus was replaced by the notary Eugenius (Joannes Diaconus, *Vita Gregorii* ii. 53, Greg., *ep.* ix. 96, 110).

50 Joannes Diaconus, *Vita Gregorii* ii. 53, Greg., *ep.* ix. 96, ix. 110.

51 Greg., *ep.* i. 23, 37, 53, 57, iii. 1, 39, iv. 31. Peter of Campania is not to be confused with Peter of Sicily, see Richards, *op. cit.*, pp. 319–20.

52 Joannes Diaconus, *Vita Gregorii* ii. 53, ix. 110, xiv. 14.

53 Greg., *ep.* iii. 26, 29, Joannes Diaconus, *Vita Gregorii* ii. 53.

54 Greg., *ep.* ix. 205, 206.

55 Greg., *ep.* i. 1, ii. 38.

56 Greg., *ep.* iii. 35.

57 Pelagius II's Sicilian rector was the deacon Servusdei, and Honorius I's was the deacon Cyriacus.

58 Greg., *ep.* iii. 27, iv. 43. Cf. i. 42.

59 Greg., *ep.* ix. 22.

60 Greg., *ep.* ii. 38, vii. 27, ix. 29, xi. 24.

61 Greg., *ep.* xiii. 24, xiv. 4, 5.

62 Greg., *ep.* i. 1.

63 Greg., *ep.* i. 39a.

64 Greg., *ep.* i. 42.

65 Greg., *ep.* ix. 108.

66 Greg., *ep.* v. 7.

67 Greg., *ep.* xiii. 37.

68 *Ibid.*

9 Gregory and the Episcopate: (1) Sicily

1 H. Hurten, 'Gregor der Grosse und der mittelalterliche Episkopat', *Zeitschrift für*

Kirchengeschichte 73 (1962), pp. 16–41.

2 Greg., *ep.* viii. 19, ix. 21, 195.

3 Greg., *ep.* vi. 23.

4 The subject of papal electoral policy is discussed in J. Richards, *The Popes and the Papacy in the Early Middle Ages 476–752* (London, 1979), pp. 323–31.

5 J. Eidenschink, *The Election of Bishops in the Letters of Gregory the Great* (Washington, DC, 1945).

6 Greg., *ep.* vii. 16.

7 Greg., *RP* i. 10.

8 Greg., *RP* i. 2.

9 Greg., *ep.* x. 19.

10 Joannes Diaconus, *Vita Gregorii* iii. 7.

11 There is a detailed discussion in Richards, *op. cit.*, pp. 342–62.

12 Greg., *ep.* i. 1.

13 Greg., *ep.* i. 18.

14 Joannes Diaconus, *Vita Gregorii* i. 6, iii. 7; *MGH ep.* ii appendix 2; Greg., *Dial.* iii. 36, i. 8, iv. 32.

15 Greg., *ep.* ii. 8.

16 Greg., *ep.* i. 70.

17 Greg., *ep.* iii. 27.

18 Greg., *ep.* ii. 30.

19 Greg., *ep.* iii. 12.

20 Leontius, *Vita S. Gregorii Agrigentini.*

21 Greg., *ep.* xiii. 22.

22 Greg., *ep.* iii. 53.

23 Greg., *ep.* ii. 19.

24 Greg., *ep.* i. 39.

25 Greg., *ep.* ii. 51.

26 Greg., *ep.* iii. 49.

27 Greg., *ep.* v. 12.

28 Greg., *ep.* iv. 12. Cf. i. 64.

29 Greg., *ep.* vi. 8.

30 Greg., *ep.* i. 71.

31 Greg., *ep.* v. 57a.

32 He sent him two books of his *Homilies* for correction and comment (Greg., *ep.* iv. 17a) and entrusted to him many investigations and arbitrations (*ep.* ix. 75, viii. 3, 30, v. 57, 62).

33 Greg., *ep.* iii. 49, 59, vi. 4 (see Richards, *op. cit.*, p. 397 n. 43); *ep.* ii. 43.

34 Greg., *ep.* ii. 43.

35 Greg., *ep.* ii. 51.

36 Greg., *ep.* iii. 49.

37 Greg., *ep.* v. 32.

38 Greg., *ep.* v. 20.

39 Greg., *ep.* v. 54.

40 Greg., *ep.* vi. 18, 40.

41 Greg., *ep.* vii. 18.

42 Greg., *ep.* xiii. 21.

43 Greg., *ep.* iv. 34, vi. 30, viii. 7.

44 Greg., *ep.* ix. 32. Cf. ix. 238.

45 Greg., *ep.* xiii. 16.

46 Greg., *ep.* xiii. 14.

47 F. H. Dudden, *Gregory the Great: His Place in History and Thought* (London, 1905), i, p. 387.

48 Greg., *ep.* ii. 38, v. 4, vi. 39, 47, ix. 20, 21, 38, xi. 30.

49 Greg., *ep.* ix. 38, xi. 19, ix. 119.

50 Greg., *ep.* xiii. 40.

51 Greg., *ep.* vi. 8, 18.

52 Greg., *ep.* xiii. 46.

53 Greg., *ep.* v. 23.

54 Greg., *ep.* vi. 13.

55 Greg., *ep.* ix. 25.

56 Greg., *ep.* x. 1.

57 Greg., *ep.* xiii. 22.

58 Greg., *ep.* xii. 15, xiii. 22, iii. 59, ix. 180.

59 Greg., *ep.* vi. 9.

60 Greg., *ep.* xiii. 16.

61 Greg., *ep.* vii. 19.

62 Greg., *ep.* xiv. 4.

63 Greg., *ep.* v. 40.

64 G. Rohlfs, *Scavi Linguistici nella Magna Graecia* (Rome, 1933). Of the 461 inscriptions preserved in the catacombs of Syracuse, only 44 are Latin, the rest Greek. See V. Strazzulla, 'Museum Epigraphicum', *Documenti per servire alla storia di Sicilia*, series 3, vol. 3 (Palermo, 1897).

65 G. Morosi, *Studi dei Dialetti Greci della terra d'Otranto* (Lecce, 1870).

66 L. White, Jr, 'The

Byzantinization of Sicily', *AHR* 42 (1936), pp. 1–21.

67 P. Charanis, 'On the question of the Hellenization of Sicily and Southern Italy in the Middle Ages', *AHR* 52 (1946), pp. 74–87; S. Borsari, *Il Monachesimo Bizantino nella Sicilia e nell'Italia Meridionale pre-Normanne* (Naples, 1963).

68 See P. B. Gams, *Series Episcoporum Catholicae Ecclesiae* (Ratisbon, 1873).

69 Fulgentius Ferrandus, *Vita S. Fulgentii Ruspensis* 12.

70 Pelagius I, *ep.* 44.

71 Greg., *ep.* iv. 36.

72 Leontius, *Vita S. Gregorii Agrigentini* 2, 17.

73 *Vita S. Zosimi* 1, 3.

74 *LP, Vita Hormisdae*, p. 269.

10   Gregory and the Episcopate: (2) Italy

1 Greg., *ep.* iii. 4.
2 Greg., *ep.* iii. 43.
3 Greg., *ep.* iv. 5.
4 Greg., *ep.* vii. 19.
5 Greg., *ep.* ix. 129, 134.
6 Greg., *ep.* iii. 45.
7 Greg., *ep.* vi. 21.
8 *Gesta Episcoporum Neapolitanorum* 25.
9 Greg., *ep.* i. 14.
10 Greg., *ep.* ii. 5.
11 Greg., *ep.* ii. 12.
12 Greg., *ep.* ii. 13.
13 Greg., *ep.* v..57a attests his seniority.
14 Greg., *ep.* ii. 18.
15 Greg., *ep.* ii. 26.
16 Greg., *ep.* iii. 1, 2.
17 Greg., *ep.* iii. 15.
18 Greg., *ep.* iii. 35.
19 Greg., *ep.* iii. 58.
20 Greg., *ep.* ix. 47.
21 Greg., *ep.* ix. 53.
22 Greg., *ep.* ix. 76.
23 Greg., *ep.* ix. 159.
24 *Gesta Episcoporum Neapolitanorum* 26.
25 Greg., *ep.* x. 19.
26 Greg., *ep.* xi. 19; *Gesta Episcoporum Neapolitanorum* 27.
27 Greg., *ep.* xi. 53.
28 Greg., *ep.* xiii. 29.
29 Greg., *ep.* iii. 34.
30 Greg., *ep.* v. 13.
31 Greg., *ep.* v. 14.
32 Greg., *ep.* v. 27.
33 Greg., *ep.* ix. 72.
34 Greg., *ep.* x. 4.
35 Greg., *ep.* xi. 15.
36 Greg., *ep.* xiii. 4.
37 *LP, Vita Vigilii*, p. 298.
38 Greg., *ep.* i. 55.
39 Greg., *ep.* i. 56.
40 Greg., *ep.* ii. 28.
41 Greg., *ep.* ii. 15.
42 Greg., *ep.* iii. 24.
43 Greg., *ep.* iii. 25.
44 Greg., *ep.* v. 48.
45 Greg., *ep.* ix. 139, 140.
46 Greg., *ep.* ix. 138.
47 Greg., *ep.* ix. 210.
48 Greg., *ep.* v. 57a.
49 *BHL* 3062.
50 Greg., *ep.* i. 58.
51 Greg., *ep.* ix. 45.
52 Agnellus, *Lib. Pont. Rav.* 98.
53 Greg., *ep.* i. 24a, ii. 28, 45.
54 Greg., *ep.* v. 21.
55 Greg., *ep.* v. 24.
56 Greg., *ep.* v. 51.
57 Agnellus, *Lib. Pont. Rav.* 99.
58 Greg., *ep.* vi. 2.
59 Greg., *ep.* vi. 63. Cf. vi. 28, vii. 39, 40. Secundinus is probably to be identified with Secundus, 'servant of God', who was involved in the peace negotiations with Agilulf. The papal scribes sometimes made errors with names like that, e.g. calling the same man Sabinus and Sabinian, Marcellus and Marcellinus.
60 Greg., *ep.* ix. 139, 149, 155, 177, 178, 234.
61 Greg., *ep.* xi. 21.
62 Agnellus, *Lib. Pont. Rav.* 103.
63 *Catalogus Episcoporum*

284 Notes to Pages 177–88

Mediolanensium, p. 99.

64 Greg., *ep.* iii. 26.
65 Greg., *ep.* iii. 26, 36.
66 Greg., *ep.* iv. 1.
67 Greg., *ep.* iv. 37.
68 Greg., *ep.* xi. 6.
69 Greg., *ep.* xi. 14.
70 *Catalogus Episcoporum Mediolanensium*, p. 99.
71 Greg., *ep.* vii. 38.
72 Greg., *ep.* ii. 24.
73 Greg., *ep.* x. 6, 7.
74 F. Ughelli, *Italia Sacra* (12 vols, Venice, 1717–33) vi, p. 599.
75 Greg., *ep.* x. 13.
76 Greg., *ep.* xiv. 11.
77 Greg., *ep.* ii. 37.
78 Greg., *ep.* ii. 39, 40.
79 Greg., *ep.* iii. 13, 14.
80 Greg., *ep.* i. 77.
81 Greg., *ep.* ix. 223, xi. 15.

11 **Gregory and the Lombards**

1 Greg., *ep.* v. 6.
2 Paulus Diaconus, *HL* iii. 35.
3 On Gregory's relations with the Lombards see in particular G. P. Bognetti, *L'Eta Longobarda*, 4 vols (Milan, 1966–8), and O. Bertolini, 'I papi e le relazioni politiche di Roma con i ducati Longobardi di Spoleto e di Benevento', *Rivista di Storia della Chiesa in Italia* 6 (1952), pp. 1–46.
4 Greg., *ep.* i. 30.
5 Greg., *ep.* i. 3.
6 Greg., *ep.* ii. 7.
7 E.g. Centumcellae (Greg., *ep.* i. 13, *Dial.* iv. 27), Nepe (*ep* ii.14), Naples (ii. 34), Terracina (viii. 19), Misenum (ix. 53, 65, 121), Sipontum (ix. 112, 174), Aprutium (ix. 71), Hortona (*Vita S. Cethei*), Squillace (*ep.* viii. 32), Hydruntum (ix. 200).
8 Greg., *ep.* ii. 4 (Nepe), ii. 34, 35 (Naples). The situation in Naples was eventually

remedied, and a succession of *magistri militum* appear later in the reign: Maurentius in 598 (ix. 17, 53, 69), Gudiscalcus (Gottschalk) in 599 (x. 5), and Guduin in 603 (xiv. 10). The last two sound like Germanic *condottieri.*

9 Greg., *ep.* ii. 32.
10 Greg., *ep.* ii. 33.
11 *LP, Vita Gregorii*, p. 312; Paulus Diaconus, *HL* iv. 8.
12 Greg., *ep.* ii. 45.
13 *Ibid.*
14 Paulus Diaconus, *HL* iv. 8.
15 Greg., *ep.* ii. 45.
16 Greg., *ep.* ii. 45.
17 Greg., *ep.* v. 36.
18 *Whitby Life* 23. Paulus Diaconus, *Vita Gregorii* 26, repeats it but leaves out the diet, simply saying that the ruler fell ill and besought Gregory's prayers for recovery.
19 Paulus Diaconus, *HL* iv. 16.
20 Paulus Diaconus, *HL* iv. 8, *LP, Vita Gregorii*, p. 312.
21 Paulus Diaconus, *HL* iv. 8, Greg., *ep.* v. 36.
22 Paulus Diaconus, *HL* iv. 8.
23 For discussion of the see of Capua, see above, pp. 169–70.
24 Greg., *Homil. in Ezech.* ii. 10, 22, 24, *Praefatio.*
25 Greg., *ep.* v. 36.
26 *MGH aa* ix. 339.
27 Greg., *ep.* iv. 2.
28 Greg., *ep.* v. 34.
29 Greg., *ep.* v. 30.
30 Greg., *ep.* v. 36.
31 Greg., *ep.* vi, 63. Some people have thought that this was Abbot Secundus of Trent, confidant of Queen Theodelinda. But he is probably to be identified with the Ravennate deacon Secundinus, through whom Gregory sought to influence Archbishop Marinianus (vi. 24). He was both a senior cleric and apparently a friend of Rome

and would be an appropriate envoy for the imperial side.

32 Greg., *ep.* vii. 42.
33 Greg., *ep.* vi. 32, vii. 23, 25.
34 Paulus Diaconus, *HL* iv. 12.
35 Greg., *ep.* vii. 19.
36 Greg., *ep.* vii. 26.
37 On the recovery of Picenum, see above, pp. 102–3.
38 Paulus Diaconus, *HL* iv. 16.
39 Greg., *ep.* ix. 11, 44, 67.
40 Greg., *ep.* ix. 11.
41 Greg., *ep.* ix. 44.
42 Greg., *ep.* ix. 66, 67.
43 Greg., *ep.* ix. 240.
44 Greg., *ep.* v. 39.
45 Greg., *ep.* ix. 102, 143.
46 Greg., *ep.* ix. 65.
47 Paulus Diaconus, *HL* iv. 20, 28.
48 Greg., *ep.* xi. 31.
49 Greg., *ep.* xiii. 45.
50 He first appears in the Register in June 603 (Greg., *ep.* xiii. 36).
51 Paulus Diaconus, *HL* v. 28.
52 *Ibid.*, iv. 27.
53 *Vita S. Barbati* 1.
54 Greg., *ep.* i. 17.
55 Greg., *ep.* i. 17, ii. 4.
56 Paulus Diaconus, *HL* iv. 6.
57 Columban, *ep.* 5.
58 Greg., *ep.* iv. 2.
59 Greg., *ep.* iv. 3.
60 Greg., *ep.* iv. 4.
61 Greg., *ep.* iv. 33, 37.
62 Greg., *ep.* iv. 37.
63 Greg., *ep.* vii. 14.
64 Greg., *ep.* ix. 186.
65 Greg., *ep.* xiv. 12.

12 Gregory and the West

1 See especially W. Ullmann, *A Short History of the Papacy in the Middle Ages* (London, 1972), pp. 54–6.
2 Greg., *ep.* i. 82, 75, ii. 46.
3 W. H. C. Frend, *The Donatist Church* (Oxford, 1952); C. Diehl, *L'Afrique Byzantine* (Paris, 1896).
4 R. A. Markus, 'Donatism: the last phase', *Studies in Church History* i (1964), pp. 118–26, and 'The Imperial administration and the church in Byzantine Africa', *Church History* 36 (March 1967), pp. 3–8.
5 Greg., *ep.* vi. 59.
6 Greg., *ep.* i. 72, iv. 32.
7 Greg., *ep.* vi. 61.
8 Greg., *ep.* i. 72.
9 Greg., *ep.* i. 82.
10 Frend, *op. cit.*, p. 309 n. 5.
11 Greg., *ep.* iii. 47.
12 Greg., *ep.* ii. 46, iv. 35.
13 Greg., *ep.* v. 3.
14 Greg., *ep.* iii. 47.
15 Greg., *ep.* iii. 46.
16 Greg., *ep.* iv. 7.
17 Greg., *ep.* iv, 32, 35, vi. 59, 61, vii. 2, viii. 13, 15.
18 Greg., *ep.* ix. 24, 27, xiii. 12.
19 Greg., *ep.* ii. 46, i. 82, iv. 13, 34, viii. 14, xii, 3, 8, 9.
20 Greg., *ep.* vii. 2.
21 Greg., *ep.* vii. 2.
22 Greg., *ep.* ix. 24, 27.
23 Greg., *ep.* i. 72.
24 Greg., *ep.* viii. 10.
25 Greg., *ep.* xii. 12.
26 Greg., *ep.* i. 82, xii. 8, 9.
27 D. Mandic, 'Dalmatia in the Exarchate of Ravenna from the middle of the 6th century to the middle of the 8th century', *Byzantion* 34 (1964), pp. 347–74.
28 Greg., *ep.* ii. 50.
29 Greg., *ep.* ii. 20, 21.
30 Greg., *ep.* i. 10.
31 Greg., *ep.* i. 19.
32 Greg., *ep.* ii. 20.
33 Greg., *ep.* ii. 21, 22.
34 Greg., *ep.* ii. 23.
35 Greg., *ep.* ii. 45.
36 Greg., *ep.* ii. 50.
37 Greg., *ep.* iii. 22, 32.
38 Greg., *ep.* iii. 46.
39 Greg., *ep.* vi. 26 (soldiers, officials and people), v. 29 (palace and people), iv. 16 (suffragan bishops).
40 Greg., *ep.* vi. 26.
41 Greg., *ep.* iv. 16.
42 Greg., *ep.* iv. 20.

43 *Ibid.*
44 Greg., *ep.* v. 6.
45 Greg., *ep.* iv. 38.
46 Greg., *ep.* ix. 158.
47 Greg., *ep.* v. 29.
48 Greg., *ep.* v. 39.
49 Greg., *ep.* v. 6.
50 Greg., *ep.* vi. 3.
51 Greg., *ep.* vi. 25.
52 Greg., *ep.* vi. 26, 46.
53 Greg., *ep.* vii. 17, viii. 11, 24.
54 Joannes Diaconus, *Vita Gregorii* iv. 11.
55 Greg., *ep.* viii. 11, 24.
56 Greg., *ep.* ix. 234.
57 Greg., *ep.* viii. 11. Cf. iii. 8.
58 Greg., *ep.* ix. 237.
59 Greg., *ep.* ix. 158.
60 Greg., *ep.* ix. 237, ix. 149, 155, 176.
61 Greg., *ep.* ix. 155, 178.
62 Greg., *ep.* ix. 177, 178.
63 Greg., *ep.* viii. 36.
64 Greg., *ep.* ix. 237.
65 There was one minor case. Gregory acquitted the priest Luke of Thessalonica of heresy after he had appealed to Rome claiming innocence (*ep.* xi. 55).
66 Greg., *ep.* iii. 6, 7.
67 Greg., *ep.* iii. 38.
68 Greg., *ep.* v. 57, 62, 63.
69 E. A. Thompson, *The Goths in Spain* (Oxford, 1969), pp. 94–101.
70 Greg., *ep.* i. 41.
71 Greg., *ep.* ix. 227a.
72 Greg., *ep.* ix. 228.
73 Greg., *ep.* i. 41a, i. 41, v. 53, 53a, ix. 227.
74 Greg., *ep.* xiii. 47, 49. 50.
75 Thompson, *op. cit.*, pp. 320–34.
76 W. Goffart, 'Byzantine Policy in the West under Tiberius II and Maurice', *Traditio* 13 (1957), pp. 73–118.
77 Greg., *ep.* ix. 229.
78 Greg., *ep.* ix. 227a.
79 P. D. King, *Law and Society in the Visigothic Kingdom* (Cambridge, 1972), pp. 123–4.
80 On the state of Gaul see Gregory of Tours, *Historia Francorum*, and S. Dill, *Roman Society in Merovingian Gaul* (London, 1926). On papal relations with Gaul, see E. Delaruelle, 'L'Église Romaine et ses relations avec l'Église Franque jusqu'en 800', *Settimane* 7. 1 (1960), pp. 143–84.
81 Greg., *ep.* v. 60.
82 Greg., *ep.* v. 58, 59, 60.
83 Greg., *ep.* v. 58.
84 Greg., *ep.* vi. 5. Cf. vi. 55, 57, viii. 4, ix. 212, 213, xi. 46, 48, 49, xiii. 7.
85 Greg., *ep.* xi. 49.
86 Greg., *ep.* viii. 4.
87 Greg., *ep.* xi. 40, ix. 220.
88 *Vita S. Desiderii*; Fredegar iv. 24, 32.
89 Greg., *ep.* ix. 222.
90 Greg., *ep.* ix. 218.
91 Greg., *ep.* ix. 219.
92 Greg., *ep.* ix. 213.
93 Greg., *ep.* ix. 215.
94 Greg., *ep.* xi. 10.
95 Greg., *ep.* xi. 46, 49, 47, 50, xi. 38, 40.
96 Greg., *ep.* xiii. 7.
97 Fredegar iv. 42.
98 Greg., *ep.* xiii. 7.

13 Gregory and the East

1 S. Vailhé, 'Le Titre de Patriarche Oecuménique avant St Grégoire le Grand', *Échos d'Orient* 11 (1908), pp. 65–70, 161–71.
2 Greg., *ep.* v. 41.
3 Greg., *ep.* i. 24.
4 Greg., *ep.* v. 39, 41, 44.
5 Greg., *ep.* iii. 52.
6 Greg., *ep.* iii. 63.
7 Greg., *ep.* v. 44.
8 Greg., *ep.* vi. 14, 15, 16, 17, 62.
9 Greg., *ep.* v. 45.
10 Greg., *ep.* v. 44.
11 Greg., *ep.* v. 37, 39.
12 Greg., *ep.* v. 41.

13 Greg., *ep.* vii. 24.
14 Greg., *ep.* viii. 29.
15 Greg., *ep.* vii. 30.
16 Greg., *ep.* vii. 7.
17 Greg., *ep.* vii. 4, 5, 6.
18 Greg., *ep.* vii. 31.
19 Greg., *ep.* vii. 28, 30.
20 Greg., *ep.* ix. 156.
21 Greg., *ep.* xiii. 43.
22 *LP, Vita Bonifacii III*, p. 316;
   Paulus Diaconus, *HL* iv. 36.
23 *LD* 73.
24 To Anastasius, Greg., *ep.* i. 7,
   24, 25, 27, v. 41, 42, vii. 24, 31,
   viii. 2; to Eulogius, i. 24, v. 41,
   vi. 58, vii. 31, 37, viii. 28, 29,
   ix. 175, x. 14, 21, xii. 16, xiii.
   44, 45; to Domitian, iii. 62, v.
   43, vii. 7, ix. 4.
25 Greg., *ep.* iii. 61.
26 Greg., *ep.* iii. 64.
27 Greg., *ep.* viii. 10.
28 Greg., *ep.* i. 43.
29 Greg., *ep.* xiv. 7, 8, 13.
30 Greg., *ep.* xi. 29.
31 Greg., *ep.* xiii. 34. Cf. xiii. 42.

14 Gregory's Missionary Activities

1 Greg., *MM* iii. 43.
2 Greg., *ep.* v. 7, ii. 37.
3 See S. Katz, 'Gregory the Great
   and the Jews', *Jewish Quarterly
   Review* 24 (1933–4), pp. 113–36;
   E. A. Synan, *The Popes and the
   Jews in the Middle Ages* (London
   and New York, 1965); B.
   Blumenkranz, *Juifs et Chrétiens
   dans le Monde Occidental
   430–1096* (Paris, 1960).
4 Greg., *ep.* 11. 6.
5 Greg., *ep.* ix. 38.
6 Greg., *ep.* ix. 195.
7 Greg., *ep.* i. 34, ii. 6.
8 Greg., *ep.* ix. 195.
9 Greg., *ep.* ix. 38.
10 Greg., *ep.* vii. 21, vi. 10, 30, ix.
   213, 215.
11 Greg., *ep.* iii. 37.
12 Greg., *ep.* xiii. 3.
13 Greg., *ep.* iv. 21.
14 Greg., *ep.* vi. 29, ix. 104.
15 Greg., *ep.* iv. 9.
16 Greg., *ep.* i. 45.
17 Greg., *ep.* i. 34.
18 Greg., *ep.* xiii. 15.
19 Greg., *ep.* ii. 38, ii. 7, viii. 23,
   iv. 31.
20 Greg., *ep.* viii. 4.
21 Greg., *ep.* i. 16.
22 Greg., *ep.* i. 16a.
23 Greg., *ep.* i. 16b.
24 Greg., *ep.* ii. 45.
25 Greg., *ep.* ii. 45.
26 Greg., *ep.* v. 56.
27 Greg., *ep.* ix. 141, 148, 150, 152,
   154, 155.
28 Greg., *ep.* xii. 13.
29 Greg., *ep.* ix. 154.
30 Greg., *ep.* vi. 36.
31 Greg., *ep.* ix. 201.
32 Greg., *ep.* iv. 14.
33 Greg., *ep.* xiii. 36.
34 Greg., *ep.* ix. 153, 161.
35 Greg., *ep.* ix. 160.
36 Greg., *ep.* xiii. 36.
37 Paulus Diaconus, *HL* iv. 33;
   Chron. Pat. Grad. 3.
38 See in particular Greg., *Homil.
   in Evang.* x. 4, M. L. W.
   Laistner, 'The Western Church
   and Astrology during the Early
   Middle Ages', *Harvard
   Theological Review* 34 (1941), pp.
   251–75, and J. Fontaine,
   'Isidore de Séville et
   l'astrologie', *Revue des Études
   Latines* 31 (1953), pp. 271–300.
39 Greg., *ep.* ix. 204.
40 Greg., *ep.* iv. 29.
41 Greg., *ep.* iv. 26.
42 Greg., *ep.* iv. 26.
43 Greg., *ep.* iv. 23.
44 Greg., *ep.* v. 38.
45 Greg., *ep.* xi 12.
46 Greg., *ep.* xi. 12.
47 Procopius, *De Bello Vandalico* i
   13.
48 Greg., *ep.* iv. 25.
49 Greg., *ep.* iv. 27.
50 Greg., *ep.* iii. 59.
51 Greg., *ep.* xi. 33.

52 Greg., *ep.* viii. 1.
53 Greg., *ep.* viii. 19.
54 Joannes Diaconus, *Vita Gregorii* iii. 1.
55 On Augustine's mission see H. Mayr-Harting, *The Coming of Christianity to Anglo-Saxon England* (London, 1972); S. Brechter, *Die Quellen zur Angelsachsenmission Gregors des Grossen* (Münster, 1941); R. A. Markus, 'The chronology of the Gregorian mission to England: Bede's narrative and Gregory's correspondence', *JEH* 14 (1963) pp. 16–30; P. Meyvaert, *Bede and Gregory the Great* (Jarrow Lecture 7, 1964).
56 On its dating see B. Colgrave, 'The earliest life of St Gregory the Great, written by a Whitby monk', *Celt and Saxon*, ed. N. K. Chadwick (Cambridge, 1964), pp. 109–37.
57 Brechter, *op. cit.*.
58 *Whitby Life* 9.
59 Bede, *HE* ii. 1.
60 Greg., *ep.* vi. 10.
61 Greg., *ep.* ix. 222.
62 Greg., *ep.* vi. 57.
63 Greg. Tur., *HF* iv. 26; Greg., *ep.* ix. 26.
64 Bede, *HE* i. 25.
65 Goscelin, *Vita S. Augustini* 20.
66 Bede, *HE* i. 25.
67 Nothing is known of Augustine before his dispatch to England. Goscelin's eleventh-century life adds virtually nothing to the earlier sources.
68 Bede, *HE* i. 23.
69 Greg., *ep.* vi. 49, 50, 51, 52, 53, 56, 57.
70 Greg., *ep.* vi. 50a.
71 Bede, *HE* i. 25.
72 *Ibid.*
73 Greg., *ep.* viii. 29; Bede, *HE* i. 27.
74 Greg., *ep.* xi. 39.
75 Greg., *ep.* xi. 37.
76 Greg., *ep.* xi. 35.
77 Bede, *HE* ii. 2–3.

78 See R. A. Markus, 'Gregory the Great and a Papal Missionary Strategy', *Studies in Church History* 6 (1970), pp. 29–38.
79 Greg., *ep.* i. 41.
80 Bede, *HE* i. 27. ii.
81 Greg., *ep.* xi. 56.
82 H. Mayr-Harting, *op. cit.*, p. 59.
83 Bede, *HE* i. 22.
84 W. Ullmann, *A Short History of the Papacy in the Middle Ages* (London, 1972), pp. 54–5.
85 J. M. Wallace-Hadrill, 'Rome and the Early English Church: some questions of transmission', *Settimane* 7 (1960), i, pp. 519–48.
86 Greg., *ep.* vi. 49, 51.
87 Greg., *MM* xxvii. 21. It has generally been assumed that this was added to *Magna Moralia* after completion and refers to the English mission. Brechter argues that it is a quotation from Tertullian and pre-dates the mission. Even if this is so, it is an indication of Gregory's outlook and confirms the primarily spiritual view of the English mission.
88 M. Deanesly and P. Grosjean, 'The Canterbury edition of the Answers of Pope Gregory I to St. Augustine', *JEH* 10 (1959), pp. 1–49.
89 Bede, *HE* ii. 5.
90 Balance (Meyvaert, *op. cit.*, p. 10); non-receipt (Markus, 'Chronology', p. 21).
91 Bede, *HE* i. 27.
92 Greg., *ep.* viii. 29.
93 Greg., *ep.* viii. 4.
94 Bede, *HE* iii. 7.
95 Sidonius Apollinaris, *ep.* v. 7.
96 *Whitby Life* 11.
97 *LP, Vita Gregorii*, p. 312, Bede, *De Ratione Temporum* 531.
98 Bede, *HE* i. 24.

15   Gregory and Monasticism

1 St Benedict of Nursia, *Regula*

Monachorum, ed. J. McCann (London, 1952). On the development of Benedictinism, see E. C. Butler, *Benedictine Monachism* (London, 1919).

2 Greg., *Dial.* ii. 36.

3 J. Chapman, *St. Benedict and the Sixth Century* (London, 1929), pp. 194–204, was the great proponent of the official promulgation theory.

4 G. Ferrari, *Early Roman Monasteries* (Rome, 1957), p. 386.

5 K. Hallinger, 'Papst Gregor der Grosse und der Hl. Benedikt', *Studia Anselmiana* 42 (1957), pp. 231–319, and S. Brechter, 'Monte Cassino: erste Zerstörung', *SMGBO* 56 (1938), pp. 109–150, and 'War Gregor der Grosse Abt vor seiner Erhebung zum Papst?' *SMGBO*, 57 (1939), pp. 209–24.

6 For discussion and bibliography, see D. Knowles, *Great Historical Enterprises* (London, 1963), pp. 135–95.

7 Dom Anscario Mundo, 'L'authenticité de la *Regula Sancti Benedicti*', *Studia Anselmiana* 42 (1957), pp. 105–58.

8 G. Penco, *Sancti Benedicti Regula* (Florence, 1958).

9 On Cassiodorus and his work, see A. van de Vyver, 'Cassiodore et son oeuvre', *Speculum* 6 (1931), pp. 244–92, and 'Les *Institutiones* de Cassiodore et sa fondation à Vivarium', *RB* 63 (1941), pp. 59–88; P. Riché, *Education and Culture in the Barbarian West* (Columbia, SC, 1976), pp. 129–35; P. Courcelle, *Late Latin Writers and their Greek Sources* (Cambridge, Mass., 1969), pp. 331–409, and 'Le Site du Monastère de Cassiodore', *MAH* 55 (1938), pp. 259–307.

10 Cassiodorus, *Inst.* 26. 30.

11 Courcelle, *Late Latin Writers*, pp. 361–409.

12 Riché, *op. cit.*, pp. 130–31, 158–61.

13 Riché, *op. cit.*, p. 119.

14 L. W. Jones, 'The influence of Cassiodorus on medieval culture', *Speculum* 20 (1945), pp. 433–42; 22 (1947), pp. 254–6.

15 F. H. Dudden, *Gregory the Great: His Place in History and Thought* (London, 1905) ii, pp. 173–200, discusses this in exhaustive detail, and I have little to add to his clear and coherent discussion.

16 Monasteries and nunneries were founded on the islands and the mainland by the patrician Rustica (Greg., *ep.* iii. 60), Theodosia (iv. 8), Bishop Venantius of Luna (viii. 5), *vir spectabilis* Romanus (ix. 10, 165), Alexandra *clarissima femina* (ix. 170), the lady Lavinia (i. 50), the deacon Proculus (xiii. 18), Themotea *illustris femina* (ii. 15), notary Valerian (ix. 58), Januaria *religiosa femina* (ix. 180), the priest John (iv. 42), the lady Pompeiana (ix. 164).

17 Unions (Greg., *ep.* x. 18, xi. 54, xiii. 4); subsidies (ii. 3, ix. 96, xiii. 23, i. 54).

18 Rectors (Greg., *ep.* i. 40, 50), abbots (i. 50, v. 55), and bishops (iv. 9, v. 4).

19 Greg., *ep.* i. 50 (Corsica), i. 45 (Monte Cristo), xiii. 48 (Capri), i. 48 (Eumorphiana).

20 Greg., *ep.* xiii. 31. Cf. i. 40.

21 Greg., *ep.* v. 55, xiv. 16.

22 Greg., *ep.* v. 4, vii. 32, i. 40, iii. 3, i. 38, 39, v. 33, vii. 32.

23 Greg., *ep.* ii. 29, viii. 8, 9, x. 9.

24 Private property banned (Greg., *ep.* i. 40, xii. 6); women banned (iv. 40, xiv. 16, i. 40, ii. 29).

25 The Venantius letters are discussed in detail by Dudden, *op. cit.*, ii, pp. 194–200.

26 Greg., *ep.* i. 67, iii. 3; v. 49, vi. 44.
27 Greg., *ep.* iv. 11; x. 9.
28 Greg., *ep.* iii. 61, viii. 10.
29 Greg., *ep.* viii. 17.

16   The Legacy of Gregory

1 F. Halkin, 'Le Pape St Grégoire dans l'hagiographie Byzantine', *Orientalia Periodica Christiana* 21 (1955), pp. 109–14, and H. Delehaye, 'St Grégoire le Grand dans l'Hagiographie Grecque', *AB* 23 (1904), pp. 449–54.
2 Ildefonsus of Toledo, *De Viris Illustribus* i; Taio of Saragossa, *Liber Sententiarum, PL* 80, pp. 727–990.
3 J. M. Wallace-Hadrill, 'Rome and the Early English Church: some questions of transmission', *Settimane* 7 (1960), i, pp. 519–48.
4 *Ibid.*, p. 520.
5 P. Llewellyn, 'The Roman Church in the 7th Century: the Legacy of Gregory I', *JEH* 25 (1974), p. 364.
6 *MGH aa* 14, pp. 287–90.
7 Greg., *MM* xxx. 13.
8 Greg., *ep.* i. 24a. The *Whitby Life* 31, Paulus Diaconus, *Vita Gregorii* 14, Joannes Diaconus, *Vita Gregorii* iv. 73, say John of Ravenna. Isidore of Seville, *De Viris Illustribus* 39, 40, says John of Constantinople.
9 Copies were sent to the priest Columbus and Bishop Venantius of Luna (Greg., *ep.* v. 17), Leander of Seville (v. 53), John of Ravenna (i. 24a). It was translated into Greek by Anastasius of Antioch (xii. 6).
10 Greg., *Homil. in Evang.* i. 17.
11 J. M. Wallace-Hadrill, *Early Medieval History* (Oxford, 1975), p. 10.
12 Greg., *ep.* iii. 50.
13 Paulus Diaconus, *HL* iv. 5.

14 Greg., *Dial.* iii. 20.
15 St Caesarius of Arles, *sermon* 86.
16 Greg., *ep.* ix. 208, xi. 10.
17 The *Homilies on the Gospels* are dated by *Homil. in Evang.* i. 38 and the *Homilies on Ezekiel* by Greg., *ep.* xii. 16a.
18 Joannes Diaconus, *Vita Gregorii* ii. 11.
19 E. Caspar, *Geschichte des Papsttums* (Tübingen, 1933), p. 338.
20 On Gregory's role in the history of exegesis, see H. de Lubac, *Exégèse Médiévale*, 3 vols (Paris, 1959–61), and B. Smalley, *The Study of the Bible in the Middle Ages* (New York, 1952).
21 Greg., *ep.* v. 53a.
22 Greg., *ep.* xii. 6.
23 P. Verbraken, 'Le Commentaire de St Grégoire sur le Premier Livre des Rois', *RB* 66 (1956), 159–217, and B. Capelle, 'Les Homélies de St Grégoire sur le Ier Cantique', *RB* 41 (1929), pp. 204–17.
24 Greg., *ep.* ix. 13, xi. 55, iv. 17a.
25 A. von Harnack, *Lehrbuch der Dogmengeschichte* iii (Leipzig, 1890), pp. 233–44.
26 His thought is discussed in detail by F. H. Dudden, *Gregory the Great: His Place in History and Thought* (London, 1905), ii, pp. 285–443.
27 St Boniface, *ep.* 33, 54, 75.
28 See R. E. Sullivan, 'The Papacy and Missionary Activity in the Early Middle Ages', *Medieval Studies* 17 (1955), pp. 46–106; J. N. Hillgarth, ed., *The Conversion of Western Europe 350–750* (Englewood Cliffs, NJ, 1969); O. Bertolini, 'I Papi e le missioni fino alla meta del secolo VIII', *Settimane* 14 (1967), pp. 327–63.
29 Joannes Diaconus, *Vita Gregorii* iv. 71.

30 J. J. Taylor, 'The Early Papacy at Work: Gelasius I', *Journal of Religious History* 8 (1974–5), pp. 317–32.

31 Joannes Diaconus, *Vita Gregorii* ii. 24.

32 Pelagius I, *Epistulae*, ed. P. M. Gasso and C. M. Batlle. See also J. Richards, *The Popes and the Papacy in the Early Middle Ages 476–752* (London, 1979), pp. 159–61.

Bibliography

Primary Sources

Collections

Acta Sanctorum, collecta a socii s. Bollandianus (Antwerp, 1643–).
Corpus Inscriptionum Latinorum (Berlin 1863–).
Codex Justinianus, ed. P. Krueger (Berlin, 1877).
Regesta Pontificum Romanorum, ed. Ph. Jaffe (2nd edn. by W. Wattenbach, S. Loewenfeld, F. Kaltenbrunner, and P. Ewald, Leipzig, 1885).
J. D. Mansi, *Sacrorum Conciliorum Nova et Amplissima Collectio* (Venice, 1759–98).
J. P. Migne, *Patrologia Graeca*, 161 vols (Paris, 1857–66).
J. P. Migne, *Patrologia Latina*, 217 vols (Paris, 1841–64).
Monumenta Germaniae Historica, ed. G. H. Pertz etc. (Berlin/Hanover, 1826–).
Rerum Italicarum Scriptores, ed. L. A. Muratori, 25 vols (Milan, 1723–51).
J. B. De Rossi, *Inscriptiones Christianae Urbis Romae* (Rome, 1861–88).
A. Thiel, ed., *Epistulae Romanorum Pontificum Genuinae* (Braunsberg, 1868).
C. Troya, ed., *Codice Diplomatico Longobardo* (Naples, 1852).

Individual Works

Agnellus Andreas, *Liber Pontificalis Ecclesiae Ravennatis*, MGH Scr. Rer. Lang., pp. 265–391.
Anonymus Valesianus, MGH aa ix, pp. 306–28.
Arator, *De Actibus Apostolorum*, CSEL 72.
Bede, *Historia Ecclesiastica*, ed. B. Colgrave and R. A. B. Mynors (Oxford, 1969).
Bede, *De Ratione Temporum*, MGH aa xiii, pp. 247–327.
St Benedict of Nursia, *Regula Monachorum*, ed. J. McCann (London, 1952).
Boethius, *De Philosophiae Consolatione*, CSEL 87.
St Boniface, *epistulae*, MGH ep. iii, pp. 215–433.
St Caesarius of Arles, *sermones*, in *Sancti Caesarii opera omnia*, ed. Germain Morin, vol. i (Maredsous, 1937–42).
Cassiodorus, *Institutiones*, ed. R. A. B. Mynors (Oxford, 1937).
Cassiodorus, *Variae*, MGH aa xii, pp. 3–385.
Catalogus Episcoporum Mediolanensium, Rer. It. Script. i. 2, pp. 96–103.
Chronica Patriarcharum Gradensium, MGH Scr. Rer. Lang., pp. 329–97.

Codex Carolinus, MGH ep. iii, 2, pp. 469–657.

Collectio Avellana, CSEL 35.

Columban, *Epistulae, MGH ep.* iii, pp. 154–90.

Continuatio Prosperi Havniensis, MGH aa ix, pp. 337–9.

Council of Chalcedon Canons, in W. Bright, ed., *The Canons of the First Four General Councils* (Oxford, 1892).

Cummian, *De Controversia Paschali, PL* 87, pp. 969–78.

Egbert of York, *Dialogus per interrogationes et responsiones de Institutione Ecclesiastica,* Mansi, 12, pp. 482–7.

Fredegar, *Chronica, MGH Scr. Rer. Merov.* ii, pp. 18–168.

Fredegar, *Chronicon IV cum continuationibus,* ed. J. M. Wallace-Hadrill (London, 1960).

Fulgentius Ferrandus, *Vita S. Fulgentii Ruspensis, Acta SS.* Jan. i, pp. 32–45.

Gelasius I, *Epistulae,* Thiel ed., pp. 287–483.

Gelasius I, *Tractates,* Thiel ed., pp. 510–607.

Gesta Episcoporum Neapolitanorum, MGH Scr. Rer. Lang., pp. 398–424.

Goscelin, *Vita S. Augustini, PL* 80, pp. 43–95.

Gregory I, *Dialogi,* ed. U. Moricca (Instituto Storico Italiano, Rome, 1924).

Gregory I, *Epistulae, MGH ep.* i, ii.

Gregory I, *Homiliae in Evangelia, PL* 76, pp. 1075–1312.

Gregory I, *Homiliae in Ezechielem, PL* 76, pp. 785–1072.

Gregory I, *Magna Moralia, PL* 75, p. 515 – *PL* 76, p. 782.

Gregory I, *In Librum Regum Expositionum Libri* vi, *PL* 79.

Gregory I, *Liber Regulae Pastoralis, PL* 77, pp. 13–128.

Gregory of Tours, *Historia Francorum, MGH Scr. Rer. Merov.* 1. i.

Gregory of Tours, *Liber in Gloria Martyrum, MGH Scr. Rer. Merov.* 1. 2.

Gregory of Tours, *Liber Vitae Patrum, MGH, Scr. Rer. Merov.* 1. 2.

Ildefonsus of Toledo, *De Viris Illustribus, PL* 96, pp. 195–206.

Isidore of Seville, *chronica, MGH aa* xi, pp. 423–81.

Isidore of Seville, *De Viris Illustribus, PL* 83, pp. 1081–1106.

Joannes Diaconus, *Vita Gregorii Magni, PL* 75, pp. 59–242.

John of Salisbury, *Policraticus,* ed. C. J. Webb (Oxford, 1909).

Jonas, *Vita S. Columbani, MGH Scr. Rer. Merov.* iv, pp. 61–108.

Justinian, *Novellae,* ed. R. Schoell and W. Kroll (Berlin, 1963).

Leges Langobardorum, MGH Leges iv.

Leontius, *Vita S. Gregorii Agrigentini, PG* 98, pp. 550–715.

Liber Diurnus Romanorum Pontificum, ed. T. Sickel (Vienna, 1889).

Liber Pontificalis, ed. L. Duchesne, 3 vols (Paris, 1955–7).

Marius of Aventicum, *Chronicon, MGH aa* xi, pp. 37–105.

Menander Protector, *Fragments, Fragmenta Historicorum Graecorum,* ed. C. Mueller (Paris, 1851), iv, pp. 201–69.

Die nichtliterarischen lateinischen Papyri Italiens aus der Zeit 445–700, ed. J. O. Tjader (Lund, 1955).

Les Ordines Romani du Haut Moyen Age, ed. M. Andrieu (Louvain, 1951).

Paulus Diaconus, *Historia Langobardorum, MGH Scr. Rer. Lang.,* pp. 45–187.

Paulus Diaconus, *Vita Gregorii Magni, PL* 75, pp. 42–60.

Pelagius I, *Epistulae quae supersunt,* ed. P. M. Gasso and C. M. Batlle

(Monserrat, 1956).
Procopius, *Wars* and *Anecdota*, ed. H. B. Dewing (London, 1914–40), 7 vols.
Sidonius Apollinaris, *Epistulae, MGH aa* viii.
Taio of Saragossa, *Liber Sententiarum, PL* 80, pp. 727–990.
Theophanes, *Chronographia, PG* 108, pp. 63–1164.
Vita S. Barbati episcopi Beneventani, MGH Scr. Rer. Lang., pp. 556–63.
Vita S. Cethei, Acta SS. June ii, pp. 688–93.
Vita S. Desiderii, MGH Scr. Rer. Merov. iii, pp. 620–48.
Vita S. Radegundis, MGH Scr. Rer. Merov. ii, pp. 358–95.
Vita S. Zosimi, Acta SS. March iii, pp. 835–9.
Walafrid Strabo, *De Rerum Ecclesiasticarum, PL* 114, pp. 919–66.
Whitby Life of Gregory the Great, ed. B. Colgrave (Lawrence, Kansas, 1968).

Secondary Sources

Appel, W., *Gregorian Chant* (Bloomington, Ind. 1958).
Ashworth, H., 'Did St. Augustine bring the *Gregorianum* to England?', *EL* 72 (1958), pp. 39–43.
Ashworth, H., 'Did St. Gregory the Great compose a Sacramentary?', *Studia Patristica* ii (Berlin, 1957), pp. 3–16.
Ashworth, H., 'Gregorian Elements in the Gelasian Sacramentary', *EL* 67 (1953), pp. 9–23.
Ashworth, H., 'The influence of the Lombard invasions on the Gregorian Sacramentary', *Bulletin of the John Rylands Library* 36 (1953–4), pp. 305–27.
Ashworth, H., 'The liturgical prayers of St. Gregory the Great', *Traditio* 15 (1959), pp. 107–61.
Batiffol, P., *St. Gregory the Great* (ET, London, 1929).
Bernadakis, P., 'Les Appels au Pape dans l'Église Grecque jusqu'à Photius', *Echos d'Orient* 6 (1903), pp. 30–42, 193–264.
Bertolini, O., 'I Papi e le missioni fino alla meta del secolo VIII', *Settimane* 14 (1967), pp. 327–63.
Bertolini, O., 'I papi e le relazioni politiche di Roma con i ducati Longobardi di Spoleto e di Benevento', *Rivista di Storia della Chiesa in Italia* 6 (1952), pp. 1–46.
Bertolini, O., 'Per la storia della diaconie Romane nell'alto medio evo alla fine del secolo VIII', *ASR* 70 (1947), pp. 1–145.
Blumenkranz, B., *Juifs et Chrétiens dans le Monde Occidental 430–1096* (Paris, 1960).
Bognetti, G. P., *L'Eta Longobarda,* 4 vols (Milan, 1966–8).
Bolton, W. F., 'The supra-historical sense in the *Dialogues* of Gregory I', *Aevum* 33 (1959), pp. 206–13.
Borsari, S., *Il Monachesimo Bizantino nella Sicilia e nell'Italia Meridionale pre-Normanne* (Naples, 1963).
Bourque, E., *Études sur les Sacramentaires Romains,* 2 vols (Rome, 1958).
Brazzel, K., *The Clausulae in the Works of St. Gregory the Great* (Washington, DC, 1939).

Brechter, S., 'Monte Cassino: erste Zerstörung', *SMGBO* 56 (1938), pp. 109–50.

Brechter, S., *Die Quellen zur Angelsachsenmission Gregors des Grossen* (Münster, 1941).

Brechter, S., 'War Gregor der Grosse Abt vor seiner Erhebung zum Papst?', *SMGBO* 57 (1939), pp. 209–24.

Bresslau, H., *Handbuch der Urkundenlehre* (Leipzig, 1889).

Brown, P., 'Relics and Social Status in the age of Gregory of Tours', 1976 Stenton Lecture (Reading University, 1977).

Brown, P., 'The Rise and Function of the Holy Man in Late Antiquity', *JRS* 61 (1971), pp. 80–101.

Brown, P., 'Sorcery, Demons and the Rise of Christianity: from Late Antiquity into the Middle Ages', *Religion and Society in the age of St. Augustine* (London, 1972), pp. 119–46.

Buddenseig, T., 'Gregory the Great, destroyer of pagan idols', *Journal of the Warburg and Courtauld Institute* 38 (1965), pp. 44–65.

Bury, J. B., *History of the Later Roman Empire*, 2 vols (London, 1923).

Butler, E. C., *Benedictine Monachism* (London, 1919).

Butler, E. C., *Western Mysticism* (London, 1951).

Capelle, B., 'Les Homélies de St Grégoire sur le Ier Cantique', *RB* 41 (1929), pp. 204–17.

Capelle, B., 'La main de St Grégoire dans le Sacramentaire Grégorien', *RB* 49 (1937), pp. 13–28.

Capelle, B., 'Messes du Pape St Gélase dans le Sacramentaire Léonien', *RB* 56 (1945–6), pp. 12–41.

Capelle, B., 'Retouches Gélasiennes dans le Sacramentaire Léonien', *RB* 61 (1951), pp. 1–14.

Capelle, B., 'Le Sacramentaire Romain avant St Grégoire', *RB* 64 (1954), pp. 157–67.

Caspar, E., *Geschichte des Papsttums*, 2 vols (Tübingen, 1933).

Chadwick, O., 'Gregory of Tours and Gregory the Great', *JTS* 50 (1949), pp. 38–49.

Chapman, J., *St Benedict and the Sixth Century* (London, 1929).

Charanis, P., 'On the question of the Hellenization of Sicily and Southern Italy in the Middle Ages', *AHR* 52 (1946), pp. 74–87.

Chavasse, A., 'Les Messes du Pape Vigile dans le Sacramentaire Léonien', *EL* 64 (1950), pp. 161–213; *EL* 66 (1952), pp. 145–219.

Chavasse, A., *Le Sacramentaire Gélasien* (Paris, 1957).

Coebergh, C., 'Le *Libelli Sacramentorum* de St Grégoire le Grand et le Sacramentaire publié sous son nom', *Studia Patristica* 8 (1966), pp. 176–88.

Coebergh, C., 'Le Pape St Gélase, auteur de plusieurs messes et préfaces du soi-disant Sacramentaire Léonien', *Sacris Erudiri* 4 (1952), pp. 46–102.

Colgrave, B., 'The earliest life of St. Gregory the Great, written by a Whitby monk', *Celt and Saxon*, ed. N. K. Chadwick (Cambridge, 1964), pp. 109–37.

Cooper-Marsdin, A., *Caesarius, Bishop of Arles* (Rochester, 1903).

Courcelle, P., *Late Latin Writers and their Greek Sources* (ET, Cambridge, Mass., 1969).

Courcelle, P., 'St Grégoire le Grand à l'école de Juvénal', *Studi e Materiali di storia della religioni* 38 (1967), pp. 120–24.

Courcelle, P., 'Le Site du Monastère de Cassiodore', *MAH* 55 (1938), pp. 259–307.

Crivellucci, A., 'Le Chiese Cattoliche e i Longobardi Ariani', *Studi Storici* 4 (1895), pp. 385–423; 5 (1896), pp. 154–77; 6 (1897), pp. 93–115, 345–69.

Cross, F. L., 'Early Western Liturgical Manuscripts', *JTS* 116 (1965), pp. 61–7.

Dagens, C., 'La conversion de St Grégoire le Grand', *Revue des Études Augustiniennes* 15 (1969), pp. 149–62.

Dagens, C., *St Grégoire le Grand: culture et expérience chrétiennes* (Paris, 1977).

Daly, L. J., *Benedictine Monasticism: its formation and development through the 12th century* (New York, 1965).

Damizia, G., 'Il *Registrum Epistolarum* di San Gregorio Magno ed il *Corpus Iuris Civilis*', *Benedictina* 2 (1948), iii–iv, pp. 195–226.

Deanesly, M., *St. Augustine of Canterbury* (London, 1964).

Deanesly, M., and Grosjean, P., 'The Canterbury edition of the Answers of Pope Gregory I to St. Augustine', *JEH* 10 (1959), pp. 1–49.

Delaruelle, E., 'L'Église Romaine et ses relations avec l'Église Franque jusqu'en 800', *Settimane* 7. 1 (1960), pp. 143–84.

Delehaye, H., 'St Grégoire le Grand dans l'Hagiographie Grecque', *AB* 23 (1904), pp. 449–54.

Delehaye, H., *The Legends of the Saints* (ET, London, 1962).

Delforge, Th., 'Le *Songe de Scipion* et la vision de St Benoît', *RB* 69 (1959), pp. 351–4.

Deshusses, J., 'Le Sacramentaire Grégorien pré-Hadrianique', *RB* 80 (1970), pp. 213–37.

Diehl, C., *L'Afrique Byzantine* (Paris, 1896).

Diehl, C., *Études sur l'administration Byzantine dans l'Exarchat de Ravenne* (Paris, 1888).

Dill, S., *Roman Society in Merovingian Gaul* (London, 1926).

Doizé, J., 'Le Rôle Politique et Social de St Grégoire le Grand pendant les guerres Lombardes', *Études* 99 (1904), pp. 182–208.

Duchesne, L., *L'Église au Sixième Siècle* (Paris, 1925).

Duchesne, L., 'Les Évêchés de Calabrie', *Mélanges Paul Fabre* (Paris, 1902), pp. 1–16.

Duchesne, L., 'Les Évêchés d'Italie et l'invasion Lombarde', *MAH* 23 (1903), pp. 83–116; 25 (1905), pp. 365–99.

Duchesne, L., 'Le Sedi Episcopali nell'antico Ducato di Roma', *ASR* 15 (1892), pp. 478–503.

Dudden, F. H., *Gregory the Great: His Place in History and Thought*, 2 vols (London, 1905).

Dvornik, F., *Byzantium and the Roman Primacy* (ET, New York, 1966).

Dvornik, F., *Early Christian and Byzantine Political Philosophy*, 2 vols (Dumbarton Oaks, 1966).

Eidenschink, J., *The Election of Bishops in the Letters of Gregory the Great* (Washington, DC, 1945).

Ellspermann, G. L., *The Attitude of Early Christian Latin Writers Towards Pagan Literature and Learning* (Washington, DC, 1949).

Fabre, P., 'Le Patrimoine de l'Église Romaine dans les Alpes Cottiennes', *MAH* 4 (1884), pp. 283–420.

Fedele, P., 'Il Fratello di Gregorio Magno', *ASR* 42 (1919), pp. 607–13.

Ferrari, G., *Early Roman Monasteries* (Rome, 1957).

Ferrua, A., 'Gli Antenati di San Gregorio Magno', *La Civilta Cattolica* 115 (1964), iv, pp. 238–46.

Ferrua, A., 'Nuove Iscrizioni della Via Ostiense', *Epigraphica* 21 (1959), pp. 97–116.

Fischer, E. H., 'Gregor der Grosse und Byzanz', *Zeitschrift der Savigny-Stiftung für Rechtsgeschichte* 67 (1950), pp. 15–144.

Fontaine, J., 'Isidore de Séville et l'astrologie', *Revue des Études Latines* 31 (1953), pp. 271–300.

Frend, W. H. C., *The Donatist Church* (Oxford, 1952).

Gamber, K., 'Das Sonntagsmessbuch von Jena und die Neufassung der Sonntagsmessen durch Gregor den Grossen', *Traditio* 15 (1959), pp. 107–61.

Goffart, W., 'Byzantine Policy in the West under Tiberius II and Maurice', *Traditio* 13 (1957), pp. 73–118.

Goubert, P., *Byzance Avant l'Islam*, 2 vols (Paris, 1965).

Goubert, P., 'Notes Prosopographiques sur la Sicile Byzantine à l'époque de l'empereur Maurice et du Pape St Grégoire le Grand', *Studi Bizantini* 7 (1953), pp. 365–73.

Gregorovius, F., *Rome in the Middle Ages* (London, 1894).

Grierson, P., 'The *Patrimonium Petri in Illis Partibus* and the Pseudo-Imperial coinage in Frankish Gaul', *Revue Belge de Numismatique* 105 (1959), pp. 95–111.

Griffe, E., 'Le *Liber Pontificalis* au temps du Pape St Grégoire', *Bulletin de Littérature Ecclésiastique* 57 (1956), pp. 65–70.

Grisar, H., 'Ein Rundgang durch die Patrimonien des heiligen Stuhles um das Jahr 600', *Zeitschrift für katholische Theologie* i (1877), pp. 321–61.

Grisar, H., 'Verwaltung und Haushalt der Päpstlichen Patrimonien um das Jahr 600', *Zeitschrift für katholische Theologie* i (1877), pp. 526–63.

Guillou, A., *Studies on Byzantine Italy* (London, 1970).

Halkin, F., 'La Juridiction Suprême du Pape', *AB* 89 (1971), p. 310.

Halkin, F., 'Le Pape St Grégoire dans l'hagiographie Byzantine', *Orientalia Periodica Christiana* 21 (1955), pp. 109–14.

Hallinger, K., 'Papst Gregor der Grosse und der Hl. Benedikt', *Studia Anselmiana* 42 (1957), pp. 231–319.

Harnack, A. von, *Lehrbuch der Dogmengeschichte* iii (Leipzig, 1890).

Hartmann, L. M., *Geschichte Italiens im Mittelalter* (Stuttgart, 1923), 2 vols.

Hartmann, L. M., *Untersuchungen zur Geschichte der Byzantinischen Verwaltung in Italien 540–750* (Leipzig, 1889).

Hauber, R. M., *The Late Latin Vocabulary of the Moralia of St. Gregory the*

Great (Washington, DC, 1938).

Hillgarth, J. N., ed., *The Conversion of Western Europe 350–750* (Englewood Cliffs, NJ, 1969).

Hodgkin, T., *Italy and her Invaders* (Oxford, 1896), vols 3, 4, 5, 6.

Howorth, H. H., *St. Gregory the Great* (London, 1912).

Hurten, H., 'Gregor der Grosse und der mittelalterliche Episkopat', *Zeitschrift für Kirchengeschichte* 73 (1962), pp. 16–41.

Jones, A. H. M., 'Church Finance in the 5th and 6th centuries', *JTS* n.s. 11 (1960), pp. 84–94.

Jones, A. H. M., *The Later Roman Empire*, 3 vols (Oxford, 1964).

Jones, L. W., 'The influence of Cassiodorus on medieval culture', *Speculum* 20 (1945), pp. 433–42; 22 (1947), pp. 254–6.

Jungmann, J. A., *Missarum Sollemnia: eine genetische Erklärung der römischen Messe*, 2 vols (5th edition, Vienna, 1962).

Katz, S., 'Gregory the Great and the Jews', *Jewish Quarterly Review* 24 (1933–4), pp. 113–36.

Kellett, F. W., *Pope Gregory the Great and his Relations with Gaul* (Cambridge, 1889).

King, P. D., *Law and Society in the Visigothic Kingdom* (Cambridge, 1972).

Klauser, Th., *Capitulare Evangeliorum* (Münster, 1935).

Klauser, Th., *A Short History of the Western Liturgy* (ET, London and New York, 1969).

Knowles, D., *Great Historical Enterprises* (London, 1963).

Ladner, G. B., *I Ritratti dei Papi nell'antichità e nel medio evo* (Vatican, 1941).

Laistner, M. L. W., 'The Christian Attitude to Pagan Literature', *History* 20 (1935), pp. 49–54.

Laistner, M. L. W., *Thought and Letters in Western Europe 500–900* (London, 1957).

Laistner, M. L. W., 'The Western Church and Astrology during the Early Middle Ages', *Harvard Theological Review* 34 (1941), pp. 251–75.

Lancia di Brolo, D. G., *Storia della Chiesa in Sicilia nei dieci primi secoli del Christianesimo*, 2 vols (Palermo, 1880–4).

Lang, A. P., *Leo der Grosse und die Texte des Altgelasianums mit Berücksichtigung des Sacramentum Gregorianums* (Steyl, 1957).

Lanzoni, F., *Le Diocesi d'Italia dalle origini al principe del secolo VII* (Faenza, 1923).

Lecrivain, C., *Le Sénat Romain depuis Dioclétien* (Paris, 1888).

Lestocquoy, J., 'L'administration de Rome et des Diaconies du VIIᵉ au IXᵉ siècle', *Rivista di Archeologia Christiana* 7 (1930), pp. 261–98.

Llewellyn, P., 'The Roman Church in the 7th Century: the Legacy of Gregory I', *JEH* 25 (1974), pp. 363–80.

Llewellyn, P., *Rome in the Dark Ages* (London, 1971).

Lubac, H. de, *Exégèse Médiévale*, 3 vols (Paris, 1959–61).

Luzzatto, G., *An Economic History of Italy* (ET, London, 1961).

McCulloch, J., 'The cult of relics in the letters and *Dialogues* of Pope Gregory the Great', *Traditio* 32 (1976), pp. 145–84.

McKenna, S., *Paganism and Pagan Survivals in Spain* (Washington, DC,

1938).

Magoulias, H. J., *Byzantine Christianity: Emperor, Church and the West* (Chicago, 1970).

Malnory, A., *St Césaire, Évêque d'Arles* (Paris, 1894).

Mandic, D., 'Dalmatia in the Exarchate of Ravenna from the middle of the 6th century to the middle of the 8th century', *Byzantion* 34 (1964), pp. 347–74.

Mann, H. K., *Lives of the Popes in the Middle Ages* (London, 1906–32), vols i, ii.

Markus, R. A. 'The chronology of the Gregorian mission to England: Bede's narrative and Gregory's correspondence', *JEH* 14 (1963), pp. 16–30.

Markus, R. A., 'Donatism: the last phase', *Studies in Church History* i (1964), pp. 118–26.

Markus, R. A., 'Gregory the Great and a Papal Missionary Strategy', *Studies in Church History* 6 (1970), pp. 29–38.

Markus, R. A., 'The Imperial administration and the church in Byzantine Africa', *Church History* 36 (March 1967), pp. 3–8.

Marrou, H.-I., *A History of Education in Antiquity* (ET, London and New York, 1956).

Martroye, F., *L'Occident à l'époque Byzantine* (Paris, 1904).

Mayr-Harting, H., *The Coming of Christianity to Anglo-Saxon England* (London, 1972).

Mazzarino, S., *The End of the Ancient World* (ET, London, 1966).

Meyvaert, P., *Bede and Gregory the Great* (Jarrow Lecture 7, 1964).

Meyvaert, P., *Gregory, Benedict, Bede and Others* (London, 1977).

Minasi, G., *Le Chiese di Calabria* (Naples, 1896).

Moresco, M., *Il Patrimonio di San Pietro* (Turin, 1916).

Morosi, G., *Studi dei Dialetti Greci della terra d'Otranto* (Lecce, 1870).

Morrison, K. F., *Tradition and Authority in the Western Church 300–1140* (Princeton, NJ, 1969).

Mundo, A., 'L'authenticité de la *Regula Sancti Benedicti*', *Studia Anselmiana* 42 (1957), pp. 105–58.

Norberg, D., *In Registrum Gregorii Magni Studia Critica*, 2 vols (Uppsala, 1937–9).

O'Donnell, J. F., *The Vocabulary of the letters of St. Gregory the Great* (Washington, DC, 1935).

Partner, P., *The Lands of St. Peter* (London, 1972).

Penco, G., *Sancti Benedicti Regula* (Florence, 1958).

Petersen, J., 'Did Gregory the Great know Greek?', *Studies in Church History* 13 (1976), pp. 121–34.

Petersen, J., 'The identification of the *Titulus Fasciolae* and its connection with Pope Gregory the Great', *Vigiliae Christianae* 30 (1976), pp. 151–8.

Picard, J. C., 'Étude sur l'emplacement des tombes des Papes du IIIe au Xe siècle', *MAH* 81 (1969), pp. 725–82.

Pingaud, L., *La Politique de St Grégoire le Grand* (Paris, 1872).

Poole, R. L., *The Papal Chancery* (Cambridge, 1915).

Porcel, O., *La Doctrina Monastica de San Gregorio Magno y la Regula Monachorum* (Madrid, 1951).

Recchia, V., 'La visione di San Benedetto e la *compositio* del secondo libro dei *Dialoghi* di Gregorio Magno', *RB* (1972), pp. 140–55.

Richards, J., *The Popes and the Papacy in the Early Middle Ages 476–752* (London, 1979).

Riché, P., *Education and Culture in the Barbarian West* (ET, Columbia, SC, 1976).

Rohlfs, G., *Scavi Linguistici nella Magna Graecia* (Rome, 1933).

Romano, G., and Solmi, A., *Le Dominazioni Barbariche* (Milan, 1940).

Rusch, W. G., *The Later Latin Fathers* (London, 1977).

Schuster, I., 'Les ancêtres de St Grégoire et leur sépulture de famille à St Paul de Rome', *RB* 21 (1904), pp. 112–23.

Schuster, I., *St. Benedict and his Times* (ET, London, 1953).

Sharkey, N., *St. Gregory the Great's Concept of Papal Primacy* (Washington, DC, 1950).

Smalley, B., *The Study of the Bible in the Middle Ages* (New York, 1952).

Smits van Waesberghe, J., *Gregorian Chant* (London, 1949).

Spearing, E., *The Patrimony of the Roman Church in the time of Gregory the Great* (Cambridge, 1918).

Stein, E., 'La disparition du Sénat de Rome à la fin du VIe siècle', *Bulletin de la classe de lettres de L'Académie Royale de Belgique*, series 5, vol. 25 (1939), pp. 308–22.

Stein, E., 'La Période Byzantine de la Papauté', *Catholic Historical Review* 21 (1935–6), pp. 129–63.

Strazzulla, V., 'Museum Epigraphicum', *Documenti per servire alla storia di Sicilia*, series 3, vol. 3 (Palermo, 1897).

Stuhlfath, W., *Gregor der Grosse* (Heidelberg, 1913).

Stuiber, A., *Libelli Sacramentorum Romani* (Bonn, 1950).

Sullivan, R. E., 'The Papacy and Missionary Activity in the Early Middle Ages', *Medieval Studies* 17 (1955), pp. 46–106.

Susman, F., 'Il Culto di San Pietro a Roma dalla morte di Leone Magno a Vitaliano', *ASR* 84 (1961), pp. 1–192.

Swank, H. M., *Gregor der Grosse als Prediger* (Berlin, 1934).

Synan, E. A., *The Popes and the Jews in the Middle Ages* (London and New York, 1965).

Tarducci, F., 'San Gregorio Magno e la vita monacale del suo tempo', *Rivista Storica Benedettina* 4 (1909), pp. 169–80.

Taylor, J. J., 'The Early Papacy at Work: Gelasius I', *Journal of Religious History* 8 (1974–5), pp. 317–32.

Taylor, J. J., 'Eastern Appeals to Rome in the Early Church: a little known witness', *Downside Review* 89 (1971), pp. 142–6.

Testa, O. M., 'Le chiese di Napoli nei suoi rapporti con Papa Gregorio I', *Rivista Storica Italiana* 7 (1890), pp. 457–88.

Thompson, E. A., *The Goths in Spain* (Oxford, 1969).

Ughelli, F., *Italia Sacra* (Venice, 1717–33), 12 vols.

Ullmann, W., 'Leo I and the theme of Papal Primacy', *JTS* n.s. 11 (1960), pp. 25–51.

Ullmann, W., *A Short History of the Papacy in the Middle Ages* (London, 1972).

Vacandard, E., 'L'idolâtrie en Gaule au VIᵉ et au VIIᵉ siècle', *Revue des Questions Historiques* 65 (1899), pp. 424–54.

Vailhé, S., 'Le Titre de Patriarche Oecuménique avant St Grégoire le Grand', *Échos d'Orient* 11 (1908), pp. 65–70, 161–71.

Van Dijk, S. P., 'Gregory the Great – Founder of the Urban *Schola Cantorum*', *EL* 77 (1963), pp. 345–56.

Van Dijk, S. P., 'Recent Developments in the study of the Old Roman Rite', *Studia Patristica* 8 (1966), ii, pp. 299–300.

Van Dijk, S. P., 'The Urban and Papal Rites in the 7th and 8th Centuries', *Sacris Erudiri* 12 (1961), pp. 411–87.

Verbraken, P., 'Le Commentaire de St Grégoire sur le Premier Livre des Rois', *RB* 66 (1956), pp. 159–217.

Verbraken, P., 'La tradition manuscrite du Commentaire de St Grégoire sur le Cantique des Cantiques', *RB* 73 (1963), pp. 277–88.

Vogüé, A. de, 'La Règle du Maître et les *Dialogues* de St Grégoire', *Revue d'Histoire Ecclésiastique* 61 (1966), pp. 44–76.

Vyver, A. van de, 'Cassiodore et son oeuvre', *Speculum* 6 (1931), pp. 244–92.

Vyver, A. van de, 'Les *Institutiones* de Cassiodore et sa fondation à Vivarium', *RB* 63 (1941), pp. 59–88.

Wallace-Hadrill, J. M., *Early Medieval History* (Oxford, 1975).

Wallace-Hadrill, J. M., 'Rome and the Early English Church: some questions of transmission', *Settimane* 7 (1960), i, pp. 519–48.

Weber, L., *Hauptfragen der Moraltheologie Gregors des Grossen* (Freiburg, 1947).

White, L., Jr, 'The Byzantinization of Sicily', *AHR* 42 (1936), pp. 1–21.

Whitney, J. P., 'The Growth of Papal Jurisdiction before Nicholas I', *Reformation Essays* (London, 1939), pp. 130–68.

Index

Note: all clergy listed are from the Roman clergy
unless otherwise stated